POST-HOLOCAUST POLITICS

POST-HOLOCAUST POLITICS

BRITAIN, THE UNITED STATES,

& JEWISH REFUGEES, 1945–1948

ARIEH J. KOCHAVI

THE UNIVERSITY OF NORTH CAROLINA PRESS

CHAPEL HILL AND LONDON

© 2001

The University of North Carolina Press

All rights reserved

Designed by Richard Hendel

Set in Minion and Mantinia types

by Tseng Information Systems, Inc.

Manufactured in the United States of America

The paper in this book meets the guidelines for
permanence and durability of the Committee on
Production Guidelines for Book Longevity of the
Council on Library Resources.

Library of Congress Cataloging-in-Publication Data

Kochavi, Arieh J.

Post-Holocaust politics : Britain, the United States,
and Jewish refugees, 1945–1948 / by Arieh J. Kochavi.

p. cm.

Includes bibliographical references (p.) and index.

ISBN 0-8078-2620-0 (cloth : alk. paper)

1. Refugees, Jewish — Government policy — Great
Britain.   2. Refugees, Jewish — Government policy —
United States.   3. Holocaust survivors — Europe.
4. Great Britain — Emigration and immigration —
Government policy.   5. United States — Emigration
and immigration — Government policy.   6. Jews —
Europe — Migrations.   7. Palestine — Emigration and
immigration.   I. Title.

HV640.5.J4 K63   2001

362.87′089′924041 — dc21   2001023404

05 04 03 02 01   5 4 3 2 1

CONTENTS

ILLUSTRATIONS AND MAPS

PREFACE

Between 1945 and 1948 more than a quarter of a million Jews fled from countries in Eastern Europe and the Balkans to the West, where they were given temporary shelter in the Displaced Persons (DP) camps hastily erected by the Allies in Germany and Austria. Sailing clandestinely from both sides of the Iron Curtain, the Zionists tried to bring as many Jewish refugees as they could to the shores of Palestine. These efforts helped establish the State of Israel, not so much because of the numbers involved as because of the dramatic way in which they publicized the plight of the Jewish refugees and enabled the Jewish community in the United States to influence White House policy by linking its vote to a solution to the DP problem.

Britain was not only one of the four powers that occupied Germany and Austria after the war, it also held the Mandate in Palestine. Hence the question of what to do with the vast majority of Jewish DPs who refused repatriation became paramount for London. The Middle East was pivotal to Britain both economically—because of its huge oil resources—and strategically—because it helped to secure the land route to India and also formed a buffer against the expansionist ambitions of the Soviet Union. As the cooperation of the Arab countries was essential to safeguarding these interests, Britain quickly moved to frustrate Zionist attempts to transfer Jews from Europe to Palestine. Insistence on strictly separating the Palestine question from the DP problem became a mainstay of British policy.

With the end of World War II, relations between Arabs and Jews in Mandatory Palestine deteriorated rapidly. As Whitehall saw it, Jewish immigration was a crucial problem for the Arab countries and the indigenous Arabs in Palestine. Because Britain's interests in the Arab world carried more weight than helping the Zionists build their homeland, the government decided not to allow Jewish influx into the country to increase. Thus after having significantly contributed to defeating the Axis powers and thereby helping save the lives of many Jews, Britain became the main barrier for Jewish refugees wanting to reach the haven the Zionists were setting up in Palestine. This policy also resulted in increased resistance against Britain on the part of the Zionists, both the moderate majority of the Yishuv (Hebrew: settlement; the prestate Jewish community in Palestine) and the more militant factions. A memo submitted to Foreign Minister Ernest Bevin in late 1946 succinctly diagnosed Britain's difficulties: "So a vicious circle is set up. The more refugees arrive in the west, the greater the activity of Zionists in organizing illegal immigration; the greater the number of illegal immigrants making their way to the coast of Palestine, the greater the need for His Majesty's Government to take measures to prevent such influx from destroying the chance of an agreed solution to the problem. The stricter these measures, the larger the number of Jewish refugees piling up in camps in Europe."[1]

This book deals with Britain's policy toward the survivors of the Holocaust and attempts to explain why Britain proved unable to prevent the Jewish DP problem from becoming the most effective political weapon for the Zionists in their struggle against the British in Palestine. This is a history neither of the Palestine problem nor of the Jewish-Arab conflict, nor, for that matter, of the suffering of the Jewish refugees. Rather, my focus is the diplomatic and operative campaign on which Britain embarked to prevent the Jews from leaving Europe and reaching Palestine. Waged on both sides of the Iron Curtain, this battle should be seen against the background of the struggle over the formation of world power relations after World War II in which Britain had such an important stake. The countries Britain confronted fall into three categories, each of which called for discrete tactics and diplomatic methods: the United States, the Soviet Union and its satellites, and Italy and France.

Of these, the United States was the most important. U.S. policy toward the Jewish DPs played a crucial role in Britain's failure to separate the Palestine question from the Jewish DP problem. Differences over how Jewish DPs ought to be treated and where they should be resettled caused continuing confrontations between Whitehall and the White House and, on a personal level, created tension between President Harry S. Truman and Prime Minister Clement Attlee and Foreign Secretary Ernest Bevin. The American occupation zones in Germany and Austria served as the main temporary haven for Jewish refugees fleeing Eastern Europe. Although the United States was not without its own internal differences, U.S. policy on the issue manifested a close interaction between domestic politics and foreign policy. Because of the pervasive political influence the British ascribed to American Jewry, they saw it as the main reason why the White House would not support a British solution for the Jewish DP problem.

Washington's policy also influenced the attitudes of governments on both sides of the Iron Curtain toward British efforts to halt illegal Jewish migration. The overwhelming majority of the Jewish refugees who were gathering in the DP camps in Germany, Austria, and Italy and joining the illegal sailings to Palestine had been citizens of East European countries. Britain exerted pressure on the governments of Poland, Czechoslovakia, Hungary, Rumania, Yugoslavia, and Bulgaria to stop this Jewish exodus, whether by land or by sea, but was largely unsuccessful. The reasons for this failure, of course, have to be analyzed against the backdrop of the escalating Cold War. As Moscow played an indirect, and at times overtly direct, role in enabling the Jews to flee, I examine Soviet motives — as understood by the British — together with the situation the Jews encountered in these countries during the Communist takeovers. Important aspects here are the attitudes of the local regimes and populations and the role played by anti-Semitism.

Since both Italy and France served as temporary refuges for tens of thousands of clandestine Jewish refugees and as important embarkation points for the illegal sailings to Palestine, Britain also came into conflict with their governments. Admittedly, Italy was a former enemy country subject to certain restrictions imposed by the Allies, but Paris and Rome reacted similarly to Britain's approaches. The British learned to their dismay that even though Italy and France were on the western side of the Iron Curtain, they were not necessarily more responsive to London's entreaties, as disputes over geopolitical issues spilled over into the negotiations over the Jewish DPs.

At the same time, the British had to find a solution for the Jewish DP problem in their own occupation zones in Germany and Austria. Here Whitehall geared its efforts to turning its political principles into an operative policy that hinged on the denial that the Jews formed a "nation" and that Jewish DPs were any different from other DPs. In addition to the DPs themselves, British Jewry and Zionist organizations in both Britain and the United States were quick to reject this policy. Moreover, together with measures to halt illegal Jewish immigration into Palestine, London started a propaganda campaign intended to minimize the humane aspect of the Jewish DP problem.

Non-Jewish DPs formed the great majority of the people who had been displaced by World War II. From the moment during the later stages of the war when the Allies began formulating guidelines on how to handle the problem until the end of the 1940s, their policies toward the DPs underwent several changes. Here the main focus is on the policy toward Polish DPs, who not only — after the repatriation of Soviet citizens — constituted the largest national group among the DPs in both the British and American occupation zones but also enjoyed the political support of the large Polish community in the United States and had been given a moral commitment by Britain. The analysis of the policy the British and the Americans evolved toward the non-Jewish DPs helps bring to the fore the differences in the policies they adopted toward the Jewish DPs.

Until the summer of 1946, the Jewish DPs constituted only a minor proportion of the total DP population and even at their peak, toward the end of 1947, formed only about 25 percent of all DPs in Germany. In view of these figures, the amount of time the two Western leaderships devoted to the Jewish DP problem appears disproportionally high, especially when one considers the domestic and international challenges they were facing after the war. The intensive contacts on the subject between London and Washington and, in particular, the disputes that arose over the policy to be adopted, offer a unique perspective on what was clearly a complicated relationship. Similarly, Whitehall's negotiations with governments on either side of the Iron Curtain over the Jewish refugees serve as a case study for an analysis of the international arena after the war, especially the way Britain's relations with different countries grew more difficult as its status declined in the postwar world. In this respect, too, the reports relayed by British diplomats throw significant new light on the situation of the Jews in the United States and countries within the Soviet sphere of influence.

The main thesis of this book is that it was Whitehall's efforts to secure Britain's interests in the Middle East that largely dictated British policy toward the Jewish DPs. The development of the Jewish DP problem into an effective political weapon for the Zionists in their battle over Palestine stemmed from the transformation of this problem into an electoral issue in the American political arena together with the attempts on the part of the Soviets to undermine Britain's influence in the Middle East. In other words, when governments on both sides of the Atlantic and the Iron Curtain were preoccupied with the reconstruction of their countries and the future shape of postwar power relations, the determination of the Zionists to establish a Jewish state in Palestine, the refusal of East European Jews to rehabilitate their lives in their home countries, and the illegal sailings intended to bring them to Palestine prevented the tragedy of the Holocaust from sinking into oblivion. In the policies the Great Powers evolved in response, considerations of a political, not a humane, nature played a decisive role. Unfortunately for Britain, both the White House and the Kremlin supported the goals of the Zionists, albeit for entirely different reasons.

For the research and writing of this book I received generous assistance from the Council for the Exchange of Foreign Scholars, the United States–Israel Educational Foundation (the Fulbright Program), and the Inter-University Project on the Ha'apala Study, Tel Aviv. In the course of my research I visited archives and libraries on both sides of the Atlantic, among them the National Archives,

College Park, Maryland; the Franklin D. Roosevelt Library, Hyde Park, New York; the Harry S. Truman Library, Independence, Missouri; the Public Record Office, Kew, England; the Middle East Center, St. Antony's College, and Rhodes House, Oxford; and the main archives in Israel. The generous and kind help I invariably could count on did much to make these visits not only efficient but also enjoyable. I owe a special debt of gratitude to Professor Anita Shapira for discussions on my thesis during the early stages of my research. I am grateful, too, to my friend and editor, Dick Bruggeman, who as always proved a delightful interlocutor, and to Galit Bitan, ever helpful as my research assistant. Last but, of course, not least, I am grateful to my wife, Orna, and my kids, Talia, Uri, and Doron, who learned to live with me spending part of my time in the past.

ABBREVIATIONS AND ACRONYMS

AAC	Anglo-American Committee of Inquiry Regarding the Problems of European Jewry and Palestine
BDBJ	Board of Deputies of British Jews
CFM	Council of Foreign Ministers
DP(s)	Displaced Person(s)
IGCR	Intergovernmental Committee on Refugees
Irgun	National Military Organization
IRO	International Refugee Organization
JDC	American Jewish Joint Distribution Committee
JRU	Jewish Relief Unit
LHI	Israeli Freedom Fighters
MP	Member of Parliament
MRP	Mouvement Républicain Populaire
NKVD	People's Commissariat of Internal Affairs
PAC	Polish-American Congress
SHAEF	Supreme Headquarters Allied Expeditionary Force
UN	United Nations
UNRRA	United Nations Relief and Rehabilitation Administration
UNSCOP	United Nations Special Committee on Palestine
USSR	Union of Soviet Socialist Republics
WJC	World Jewish Congress

POST-
HOLOCAUST
POLITICS

INTRODUCTION

Ostensibly Britain came out of World War II with its empire and its political prominence in the international arena intact. But the war had exacted a heavy toll from the country's population and left its economy much weakened. More than 265,000 British soldiers had fallen in battle and about 90,000 civilians had been killed, two-thirds in German air raids. The war had cost Britain about one-quarter of its national wealth, and one-third of its merchant fleet had gone down. From £476 million in August 1939 London's foreign debt increased sevenfold to £3,300 million in June 1945. When the Conservative Party lost the general elections in July, the task of coping with this difficult economic situation fell to Labour.[1] For the next three years, until the implementation of the Marshall Plan in mid-1948, government policies were dictated to a large extent by the harsh reality the war had bequeathed to the country. That is, while London remained determined to play a significant role in shaping the postwar world, Whitehall gradually came to recognize that Great Power pretensions were a thing of the past, and the government began seeking ways of reducing overseas spending by, among other things, withdrawing British troops from abroad. Still, during the fiscal year 1946–47 Britain spent 18.8 percent of its national income on defense — overseas defense commitments more or less equaled the budgetary deficit for that year, as 457 million people in different parts of the globe were under British rule in 1945.[2]

In the postwar years, Britain also bore the brunt of checking Soviet expansionist ambitions. Not only had Russia taken over Rumania, Bulgaria, Poland, Hungary, Czechoslovakia, and parts of Germany and Austria, but it was also striving to dominate events in Greece and Turkey, and Soviet soldiers were stationed in northern Iran. Assessing the new international situation this created, Foreign Secretary Ernest Bevin concluded that Moscow sought the decline of the British Empire and was bent on replacing Britain in the areas it might evacuate. American cooperation was crucial for the British; without the support of the Americans, Britain's impact on the foundation of the postwar world would be critically reduced. But already a chill lay over its relations with Washington, which made disagreements during the first few months after the war over a policy toward the Soviet Union inevitable.[3]

For the Americans, this attitude stemmed to a large extent from their long-standing misgivings vis-à-vis Britain's imperialist ambitions and their aversion to the Labour Party's socialist tendencies. The British ambassador to the United States, Lord Halifax, highlighted the warnings U.S. financial and business circles were sounding to the effect that "America should beware of countenancing any proposal to grant extensive credits to Britain, which would be likely to employ them to underwrite state Socialism," and added:

> Whenever they find reason to complain of our actions, Americans do not fail to apply to us a number of ugly catchwords that owe much of their origin to the traditional mistrust of British policies and to the above-mentioned sense of rivalry, e.g., *balance of power, sphere of influence, reactionary imperialist trends, colonial oppression, old-world guile, diplomatic double-talk, Uncle Sam the Santa Claus* and *sucker,* and the like. Anti-British outbursts are as a rule the result of the propensity of Americans to oversimplify vexatious issues which lie beyond their immediate ken.[4]

Washington's priorities and objectives right after the war differed greatly from those of London. The Americans regarded the Pacific Ocean and East Asia, especially China, Japan, and Korea, as their sphere of influence, while they wanted to cut back their involvement in Europe as quickly as possible. Already at the Yalta Conference (4–11 February 1945), President Franklin D. Roosevelt had declared that Congress would not support the stationing of American forces in Europe for more than another two years. The Americans placed great hopes in the new United Nations Organization (UNO), set up especially to help resolve international disputes, and, to ensure its participation in the new body, were ready to accommodate the Soviet Union on a variety of points, including giving the USSR three votes instead of one.

President Harry S. Truman at first continued the policies of his predecessor. Thus in mid-June 1945 he refused, as Prime Minister Winston S. Churchill was urging, to keep Anglo-American forces about one hundred miles inside the Russian zone in Germany so long as Joseph Stalin had not acceded to various Western requests. Neither did Truman consult with Churchill before he informed Moscow that the United States had no territorial ambitions or ulterior motives in countries in East Europe, the Baltic republics, and the Balkans. Washington, furthermore, allowed the Soviets a free hand in Poland in exchange for their acceptance of a plan the Americans had introduced for voting procedures in the UN Security Council. Truman was aware of Stalin's fears that Anglo-American cooperation could be directed against the Soviets and wanted to dispel Russian suspicions. For example, only a few weeks after the war, the president dismantled the Supreme Headquarters Allied Expeditionary

Force (SHAEF) and declined an invitation from Churchill to stop over in London on the way to the Potsdam Conference. In many respects, the Americans played the role of mediator between Britain and the Soviet Union, a position first adopted by Roosevelt when he met with Stalin in Teheran (28 November–1 December 1943).

America continued to play down the import of London's views at the Potsdam Conference (17 July–2 August 1945). Here Truman's main objective was to get Stalin to reconfirm Soviet agreement to join the war against Japan. Wanting to terminate their military and economic obligations in Europe, the Americans did not regard territorial disagreements there as impinging on U.S. security, let alone justifying the repercussions of a rift with the Russians. This explains Washington's flexibility and readiness to comply with Russian demands and why Truman did not adopt Churchill's firm stand against Soviet intentions vis-à-vis East Europe.[5]

Nothing, however, could have prepared the British for Truman's abrupt announcement, on 21 August, of the immediate termination of the Lend-Lease Agreement. This effectively ended American economic assistance and was a severe blow for Britain. For three months (13 September–6 December 1945), the British and the Americans engaged in a series of tough negotiations about the terms of a new loan. London's hopes of receiving an interest-free loan of $5 billion quickly evaporated — Britain was to receive $3.75 billion at 2 percent annual interest, to be repaid over fifty years, beginning on 31 December 1951. The loan was made conditional on Britain meeting a variety of demands, which included a comprehensive agreement on protective and commercial tariffs, disbanding the sterling bloc, and allowing the free exchange of the pound sterling vis-à-vis the U.S. dollar within one year following approval of the agreement. After a fierce debate in Parliament that brought to the surface much bitterness toward the United States, the agreement was approved by a vote of 345 to 98 with 169 abstentions. Most Conservative members, including Churchill, abstained. On 10 May 1946, the Senate approved the agreement by 46 to 34; the House voted 219 in favor and 155 against on 13 July. Britain came in for sharp criticism in both the U.S. House of Representatives and the Senate. The main argument in favor of the agreement was the need to stand by Britain in view of the escalating tension with the USSR. Almost a year, however, passed between Washington's sudden scuttling of the Lend-Lease Agreement and Truman's signing of the law approving the loan to Britain on 15 July 1946.[6]

Another snub at Britain's international standing came with the initiative of U.S. secretary of state James F. Byrnes to convene the Council of Foreign Ministers (CFM) in Moscow (12–31 December 1945). Byrnes first approached the

Soviet commissar for foreign affairs, Vyacheslav Molotov, and only afterward asked Bevin for his opinion. When Bevin appeared to hedge, Byrnes made it clear that he intended to go to Moscow even if the British foreign secretary decided not to participate.[7]

One of the issues the Allies failed to resolve at the CFM meeting was Iran. When crisis erupted there a short time later, it served as a catalyst for Anglo-American rapprochement on a policy toward the Soviet Union. The Americans adopted an unyielding stance toward the Soviets during the months of March–May 1946, and close cooperation between Washington and London compelled the Soviets to withdraw their troops from Iran. Cooperation between the two Western powers continued through discussions of the CFM in Paris in the spring of 1946, when Byrnes and Bevin rejected out of hand Russian demands concerning the peace agreement with Italy. This time it was the Americans who stood firm against Soviet expansionist aims. The result was a one-month interruption in the CFM discussions; during the second stage (15 June–12 July 1946), East-West disagreements were resolved, each side accepting the idea that it would not interfere in regions falling within the other's sphere of influence.[8]

Another sign of Washington's renewed commitment to Europe was the anti-Soviet speech Byrnes gave in Stuttgart on 6 September in which he emphasized that American soldiers would remain in Germany as long as the other powers kept their armies there. When, on 12 March 1947, in a joint session of the two houses of Congress President Truman introduced what was to become known as the Truman Doctrine, it signaled a turning point in relations between the United States and Britain. The president highlighted the need to "support free peoples who are resisting attempted subjugation by armed minorities or by outside pressures" and asked Congress to authorize economic assistance to Greece and Turkey as well as to send military and civilian personnel there.[9] This came after the Foreign Office had informed the State Department that, as of 31 March 1947, Britain would have to halt all aid to both these countries because of its own economic difficulties. Significantly, the Truman Doctrine owed much to Bevin's efforts from the moment he became foreign secretary.

The failure of the second CFM meeting in Moscow (10 March–25 April 1947) further deepened Anglo-American cooperation. On 5 June, Secretary of State George C. Marshall, who had replaced Byrnes in January, gave his famous speech at Harvard University giving his vision of the rehabilitation of all of Europe through American financial assistance. The initiative for a joint plan, he said, needed to come from Europe, and it was Britain, under Bevin's leadership, that organized the European response to the American challenge that eventually brought about the Marshall Plan. Cooperation between Britain and

America, which expanded as tension increased between East and West, could not, however, obscure the fact that relations were unequal. Whenever Washington's interests and priorities contradicted those of London, the Americans took unilateral action. As we will see, this became evident in the way the White House dealt with the Jewish DP problem and the Palestine question. When in the course of 1947 Britain's economic situation worsened, partly because of U.S. conditions for repayment of the loan, London became even more dependent on Washington, which further limited its ability to influence U.S. policies.[10]

Washington's interest in the Middle East increased after World War II because of the region's significant oil reserves. This was, however, very much "British territory." Britain viewed the Mediterranean, the Red Sea, the Persian Gulf, and the adjacent regions as its "natural dominion," for Egypt, Cyprus, and the Sudan had been under British rule ever since the end of the nineteenth century. When the Ottoman Empire was dismembered following World War I, Britain obtained a mandate over Iraq, Transjordan, and Palestine. During World War II, London accorded top priority to the defense of Egypt and the Suez Canal. By the end of the war, the Middle East was still vital for Britain's strategic interests, while its rich oil reserves would prove essential for Britain's economic rehabilitation. There were British soldiers in almost every Middle Eastern country, from Iran in the east to Libya in the west and Eritrea and Ethiopia in the south. British military installations could be found throughout the area, while the largest of Britain's overseas bases was the one near the Suez Canal, where about two hundred thousand soldiers were stationed.

Consequently, Bevin and the chiefs of staff were eager to bolster Britain's hold over the Middle East. One way of doing so was by creating new military alliances between Britain and the Arab countries, particularly Egypt, Transjordan, and Iraq, and by directing regional economic and social development. For example, on 22 March 1946, Britain recognized the official independence of Transjordan but immediately concluded a "Treaty of Alliance" with it that gave Britain certain military prerogatives. Egypt proved less amenable. The Anglo-Egyptian agreement of 1936 had allowed Britain to station troops in the region of the Suez Canal and in the Sinai and to reoccupy Egypt in case of war, but the Egyptians now wanted Britain to evacuate all its forces from the country.[11]

Whitehall's Middle Eastern policy had its detractors at home, too. In the winter of 1946, Prime Minister Clement Attlee and Chancellor of the Exchequer Hugh Dalton began to express doubts about the advantages of keeping military control of the Middle East. In late March, Attlee suggested disengaging from areas where there was a risk of confrontation with the Soviets. For Attlee, the growing nationalist movements in the Arab world signaled that Britain would not be able to maintain land, sea, and air bases in the region forever. Britain could withdraw from the Middle East and establish a line of defense that would cross Africa from Lagos to Kenya, where a large proportion of the British forces could be stationed. With Commonwealth defense concentrated in Australia, Kenya would constitute Britain's hub in the eastern half of the planet. The Arab countries and the Arabian desert were useful as a buffer zone between Britain and the Soviet Union. But the Cabinet Committee on Defence, led by Bevin, rejected Attlee's plan in early April 1946.[12]

In October 1946, Bevin and Egypt's prime minister Sidqi Pasha reached agreement on a draft treaty according to which the British agreed to depart from Cairo, Alexandria, and the Nile Delta by 31 March 1947 and from the rest of Egypt by 1 September 1949. For their part, the Egyptians agreed that in case of aggression by any of the country's neighbors, the British could be allowed back to their former bases in Suez and the Egyptians would cooperate with them as they had done in the course of World War II. The Egyptian Parliament, however, rejected the draft agreement reached in London, and at the end of January 1947, Sidqi's successor, Nokrashi Pasha, broke off talks with Britain and announced that Egypt would bring the matter before the United Nations.[13]

These developments prompted Attlee to repeat his argument in favor of Britain evacuating the Middle East. The chiefs of staff, however, remained adamant that the empire's overall strategic considerations required continued British rule over the Middle East while Bevin thought that the prime minister exaggerated the price Britain would be paying for insisting on retaining its status in the region. Nor did Bevin believe in the chances of an agreement with the Russians to convert the Middle East into a neutral zone. If a vacuum were created in the area, he maintained, the Russians would be quick to fill it, which meant that any British withdrawal would have serious consequences for its position worldwide. Once more Attlee came around to the position taken up by Bevin and the chiefs of staff. In general, the prime minister left his foreign secretary to steer Britain's foreign policy and usually backed his decisions in the cabinet.

London's decision to maintain dominance over the region, however, was beset by difficulties.[14] Not only had the talks with the Egyptians reached an impasse, but efforts to set up bases in Cyrenaica also proved unsuccessful. Unable to win Arab support for its solution to the Palestine question, Britain announced in February 1947 that it would transfer the issue to the UN. That same month the cabinet made two further momentous decisions. On 20 February, Attlee announced in Parliament his government's intention to transfer authority in India by June 1948, and the following day Britain informed the United States that budgetary constraints forced it to halt all economic and military support to Greece and Turkey. In the summer the UN Security Council failed to reach a decision on Egypt's protest against the British occupation, leaving Britain for the time being in control of its bases near the Suez Canal.[15]

In Palestine Britain was less successful. Britain's policy in the late 1930s had revolved around safeguarding its interests in the Arab world. Jewish immigration to Palestine was considered a highly sensitive issue. During the first three years after Hitler had come to power in Germany, more than 130,000 Jews had arrived in Palestine, resulting in an 80 percent increase of the Jewish community there. (In 1935 alone 62,000 Jews entered Palestine.) In April 1936, alarmed by the scope and nature of the immigration, the indigenous Arab population called a general strike directed against the Mandatory government, which intensified into a revolt that lasted until 1939. In mid-1937, the Peel Commission, set up by Whitehall to look into the causes of the revolt, recommended partitioning Palestine into two independent states, one Jewish and one Arab, and limiting the scope of Jewish immigration for the next five years to twelve thousand persons annually. Though these recommendations were not adopted, the British did restrict Jewish immigration to Palestine. Thus during 1937 and 1938, just as the situation of the Jews in Central Europe worsened, fewer than twenty-four thousand Jewish immigrants were able to make it into Palestine.[16]

The need to secure the goodwill of the Arab states also dictated London's position at the Evian Conference in July 1938, which had been convened at the invitation of President Roosevelt to find a solution for the increasing number of Jewish refugees from Germany and Austria. Lord Winterton, the British representative at the conference, ignored Palestine as a possible haven for part of the Jewish refugees. Before the conference, the Americans and the British had already reached an understanding, which would hold until the end of the war, to the effect that Britain would not ask the United States to change its immigration laws and the United States would refrain from insisting that the British allow Jewish immigration into Palestine. Wishing to forestall the clamor the Jewish community in Palestine was sure to make, as well as pacify American public opinion on the latter issue, the British were relatively generous in the Jewish immigration they allowed into Britain until the outbreak of the war. As a result, from Hitler's rise to power until London declared war on Germany, Britain absorbed approximately fifty thousand Jewish refugees, while during this same period, the United States took in fifty-seven thousand Jewish refugees.[17]

The White Paper of May 1939, which was intended to help enlist the support of the Arabs on the eve of the looming conflict in Europe to the side of Britain, envisioned the establishment, within ten years, of an independent Palestinian state with an Arab majority. It provided for the immigration of seventy-five thousand Jews for a period of five years (any further immigration would be conditional on Arab consent), and it limited the sale of land by Arabs to Jews.[18] The White Paper policy was largely ignored soon after the outbreak of World War II. Although the limitations on immigration and the sale of land were implemented, no steps were taken toward creating a Palestinian state. Churchill was outspoken in his opposition to the White Paper from the moment he joined the government as first lord of the admiralty, in September 1939, and also later, when he became prime minister (May 1940), which proved critical in eroding its validity. Churchill opposed the efforts of cabinet ministers and of the army high command to gain Arab support at what seemed almost any price.[19] For the Yishuv, these restrictions on immigration were of course a spur to intensify its illegal immigration activities (Hebrew: *Ha'apala*).

The *Patria* incident is a tangible illustration of Britain's change of policy toward illegal Jewish immigration. In early November 1940, two *Ha'apala* ships, the *Pacific* and the *Milos,* which had sailed from Rumania with 1,771 refugees aboard, were intercepted off the coast of Palestine. A third vessel, the *Atlantic,* which also had sailed from Rumania and had 1,783 refugees on board, was intercepted and brought into the port of Haifa on 24 November. The British Mandatory authorities transferred the illegal immigrants (*ma'apilim*) from the first two vessels to another ship, the *Patria,* on which all of them would be deported to Mauritius. Not only was this the first time since the outbreak of the war that the British decided to deport illegal immigrants instead of deducting their numbers from the legal immigration quota, but the British high commissioner in Palestine added that none of them would be allowed into Palestine even after the war had been concluded. In response, the Haganah (the Jewish underground defense organization directed by the Jewish Agency for Palestine) decided to sabotage the ship's engines so as to prevent the deportations. On 25 November, while the transfer of the passengers from the *Atlantic* was still in progress, there was an explosion on board the *Patria*. Clearly miscalculated, the charge proved too powerful for the body of the ship, which went down drowning 267 *ma'apilim*.

During discussions of the incident in the War Cabinet, Lord Lloyd, the colonial secretary, suggested that since most of the illegal immigrants had come from Central Europe, "it was reasonable to assume that the enemy had taken steps to ensure the presence among them of enemy agents." Still, the cabinet decided to allow those who had survived the *Patria* incident to remain in Palestine and to deport to Mauritius only those refugees who at the time of the explosion had still been on the *Atlantic*. This angered Lieutenant General Archibald Wavell, the British commander in chief in the Middle East, who immediately warned of several dangerous consequences: widespread disturbances by Arab Palestinians, increased influence of the Mufti, undermined confidence in the British in Syria and in Egypt, and intensified anti-British activity in Iraq that would force the cancellation of the opening of the Basra-Baghdad road. Churchill was unimpressed by the general's dramatic assessment and maintained that Arab loyalty would depend on British military success.[20] Incidents such as the *Patria* and, later, the *Struma* aroused much anger in the Yishuv. The *Struma* sank in February 1942 off the Turkish coast with only one survivor out of the total of 769 people on board, after British authorities had refused to admit the refugees into Palestine.[21]

Bitterness in the Yishuv toward Britain increased as the war progressed because of London's policy toward the rescue of European Jews. Even though U.S. policy was not much different, most of the rancor was directed at the British because, even though they refused to allow their own country to serve as a haven, they might have lifted restrictions on the entry of Jews into Palestine. Again, apprehension over Arab reaction in case large numbers of Jewish refugees made it to Palestine influenced Whitehall's attitude regarding several rescue proposals. More than ten thousand immigration certificates of the seventy-five thousand allocated by the White Paper would remain unused at the end of the war. Had it not been for the limitations on immigration, more Jewish refugees could have reached Palestine. While naturally London's and Washington's priorities were directed toward securing victory in the war, some more goodwill might have saved more Jews.[22]

No change regarding a political settlement of the Palestine problem occurred until mid-1943, when cabinet discussions began to focus on the future of the Holy Land. These deliberations led in July 1943 to the setting up of a cabinet committee, headed by the home secretary and a member of the Labour Party, Herbert S. Morrison, which was asked to come up with a long-term policy for the region. On 25 January 1944, the cabinet approved the committee's proposals for the partition of Palestine into a Jewish and an Arab state, but the cabinet decided to keep its decision secret until after Germany's defeat. In the course of 1944, the Foreign Office, led by Anthony Eden, opposed the partition plan, to the point of trying to undermine it. The chiefs of staff, for their part, emphasized the strategic importance of the Middle East for Britain and warned that adoption of the proposals would provoke the Arabs not just in Palestine but throughout the Middle East, threatening the outbreak of another revolt. This in turn would significantly harm the British war effort in Europe and the Middle East because it required the movement of British troops out of Italy and northern Europe to Palestine. The opponents of partition were strengthened by personnel changes in the Middle East when two supporters of the plan (not necessarily for reasons of Zionist sympathy) were replaced by persons who opposed it. Edward Grigg was appointed British minister resident in the Middle East in place of Lord Moyne, who had been assassinated in November 1944 by members of LHI (Hebrew acronym for Israeli Freedom Fighters, called by the British the "Stern Gang" after the name of its founder); and the high commissioner, Harold A. MacMichael, was replaced in September by Lord Gort. At the end of 1944, because of differences of opinion in his party and the cabinet and the assassination of Lord Moyne, who had been a close friend, Churchill ordered a suspension of cabinet discussions of the partition plan until after the general elections in Britain.[23]

Within a few months after the war it was clear that many of the Jews who had survived the Holocaust could not or did not want to return to the countries that had been their homelands in Eastern Europe or to rehabilitate themselves there and instead wished to go to Palestine. In their utter distress, the Jewish DPs formed the embodiment of the unspeakable tragedy that had been inflicted upon the Jewish people during the Nazi years and were a constant reminder of the horrors World War II had unleashed. Decision makers in London, however, continued to adhere to the principle that had guided them since the late 1930s, that is, enforcing a strict separation between the problem of the Jews in Europe and the Palestine question. On this issue there was no significant difference between the Conservatives and the (ostensibly pro-Zionist) Labour Party, which won the first postwar election. But by the mid-1940s, there was a different domestic political constellation in the United States, the Cold War had set in, and international power relations were shifting accordingly, with Britain seeing a noticeable decline in influence—all factors that were in favor of the Zionists when Britain set about confronting the problem of the Jewish DPs in Europe.

I

CONFRONTING THE JEWISH DISPLACED PERSONS

I · NONREPATRIABLE DISPLACED PERSONS IN GERMANY

Repatriation of the millions of displaced persons in the area that fell under the Supreme Headquarters Allied Expeditionary Force in Germany and Austria was high on the list of priorities of the Western powers in the immediate postwar period. Although eager for the DPs to return to their homelands, both the U.S. and British governments objected to forced repatriation, except in the case of Soviet citizens. The policy led to the creation of large DP communities in Germany and brought about an increase in tension between the Soviet bloc and the Western powers. Moscow refused to recognize the existence of a DP problem and insisted on the return of all DPs—most of whom had come from Eastern Europe—to their countries of origin. When it became clear that many DPs, given the options available, preferred to remain in the camps, the British and the Americans tried to induce them to return through a carrot-and-stick policy. By the winter of 1947–48, however, London and Washington had come to realize that repatriation was no longer a viable solution, mainly because of the escalating Cold War, and that resettlement overseas was the only way out for nonrepatriable DPs.

Tangible preparations for dealing with the DP problem had already been set in motion during the war. In November 1943, representatives of forty-four countries met at the White House at President Roosevelt's invitation and established the United Nations Relief and Rehabilitation Administration (UNRRA). Herbert H. Lehman, formerly governor of the state of New York and at the time head of the U.S. Office of Foreign Relief and Rehabilitation Operations, was appointed its director general. The objective of the organization was to provide food, clothing, medical supplies, and other forms of assistance to those awaiting repatriation. In May 1944, the organization accepted administrative responsibility for the refugee camps in the Middle East, which at the time held thirty-seven thousand Yugoslavian, Greek, Albanian, and Italian DPs. Following the Normandy invasion in June 1944, as the Allied forces advanced toward Germany, the number of DPs increased constantly and soon overwhelmed the poorly staffed and inadequately funded UNRRA. Responsibility for the millions of DPs and refugees fell for the most part on SHAEF. According to a SHAEF-UNRRA agreement of 25 November 1944, UNRRA agreed to work under the direct command of SHAEF while SHAEF acknowledged UNRRA's postwar responsibilities.[1]

SHAEF guidelines on the care of DPs and refugees in Germany were published on 28 December 1944 as "Administrative Memorandum No. 39." Army commanders were asked to undertake the quick and orderly repatriation of DPs from Allied countries. The military government was to set up camps and assembly points where Allied DPs would stay until they could be returned to their own countries. Ideally, DPs were to be assigned to separate camps on the basis of nationality. Nonrepatriable DPs were to be assembled in special centers suitable for a longer stay. The DPs would not be housed among the German population. The memorandum also set criteria for classifying the refugee population. A "displaced person" was any civilian who because of the war was living outside the borders of his or her country and who wanted to but could not return home or find a new home without assistance. These DPs were divided by origin into those from enemy, or former enemy, countries and those from Allied countries. An additional category dealt with persons who "have been denationalized, whose country of nationality cannot, after investigation, be determined, who cannot establish their right to the nationality claimed, or who lack the protection of any government." These were called "stateless persons" and were to receive the same treatment as DPs coming from Allied nations. Another category also entitled to the same treatment was that of "enemy and ex-enemy nationals persecuted because of their race, religion, or activities in favor of the United Nations."[2]

When SHAEF ceased functioning in mid-July 1945, responsibility for the care of the DPs was transferred to the victorious nations in the occupation zones the three major powers agreed on at the Yalta Conference (4–11 February 1945). The British zone was in the northwest, the country's industrial center now in ruins, and included the provinces of North Rhineland–Westphalia, Lower Saxony, Schleswig-Holstein, and Hamburg; the southwest parts of Germany were entrusted to American supervision; and the eastern part of the country, about 40 percent of German territory before the *Anschluss,* was assigned to Soviet control. Berlin, located in the Russian zone, fell under the joint supervision of the Allied powers. The Soviets and the Americans acceded, albeit unenthusiastically, to a British demand that the French also be allocated a zone of occupation in Germany and in Berlin. After Germany's unconditional surrender, the Allied forces had paramount authority in the country. The Potsdam Conference (16 July–2 August 1945) set up the Allied Control Council, charged with administering the country as a whole. The council was made up of the chief commanders of the four powers; decisions were to be made unanimously. Each Allied power, however, was accorded full authority to act independently in its own occupation zone through its chief commander.[3]

A Temporary Problem?

By July 1945, when the various armies withdrew to their occupation zones in Germany, about 3,869,000 refugees had been repatriated. Almost without exception, citizens of Western European countries — France, Holland, Luxembourg, and Belgium — chose to return home. Following the agreement reached at Yalta, Soviet citizens had been returned irrespective of their personal wishes. In contrast, the number of returning Poles — the second largest national group after the Russians — was negligible. From this point onward, each occupying power was left to deal with the DP problem in its own zone as it saw fit. The number of displaced persons in the British occupied zone was estimated at that time to be about 1,270,000. Of these, about 500,000 were Poles, 430,000 Soviet citizens, and 212,000 Italians. In the American zone the number of DPs was estimated at about 804,000, of whom approximately 320,000 were Poles, 84,000 Hungarians, 52,000 Soviet citizens, 50,000 Italians, and about 40,000 Yugoslavs.[4]

Rapid repatriation continued during the summer of 1945 so that when winter arrived, altogether approximately 1,238,000 DPs were left in the British, American, and French occupied zones. In the British occupied zone the number of DPs was now estimated at 639,000, of whom 510,000 were Poles and about 48,000 nationals of the former Baltic countries. Of the 533,000 DPs in the American zone, 255,000 were Poles, 84,000 from Baltic countries, and about 83,000 were Hungarians. The total number of DPs in the French zone was small, estimated at no more than 66,000; here too the Poles made up the largest group by far (about 51,000).[5]

Polish DPs constituted the main problem for the American and British occupation authorities, and not only because of their large numbers. Unlike Soviet DPs, Polish DPs could decide whether they wanted to return to Poland. At first

Germany—Zones of Occupation (Courtesy Public Record Office, Kew)

Koslin

Danzig

Königsberg

EAST PRUSSIA

Allenstein

POMERANIA

MERANIA

LOWER
SILESIA

Breslau

UPPER
SILESIA

Oppeln

—— International frontiers, 1937

– – Boundaries of occupation zones

▨ To be administered by the United States under agreement
with the United Kingdom

- - - - Western boundary claimed by Polish government; area
east of this line to be administered by Poland provisionally

▥ Area of East Prussia to be administered by the Soviet Union

0   50   100
                miles

the tendency was to return home, but, as time passed, aversion to repatriation grew. Many of the DPs had become disturbed by the dominant position Polish Communists had been able to achieve with the help of the Red Army forces garrisoned in their country. Others were dissuaded by the difficult living conditions at home, the result of the destruction and devastation of the long war. Some feared mobilization into the Polish army, while others were afraid they would be accused of treason for having cooperated with the Germans. Those from the eastern part of Poland now annexed to the Soviet Union refused to return, fearing an uncertain future. A group of about 150 Polish repatriation officers appointed by the Polish government in exile in London played a central role in reinforcing the DPs' reluctance. Lacking all sympathy with the new Communist regime in Poland, these officers intentionally painted a very bleak picture of the situation there. As it happened, even after the establishment of the Polish Provisional Government of National Unity (most of whose members were Communists) and the appointment of new repatriation officers, the former officers were allowed to continue their activities in the camps. As late as February 1946, 148 out of the 169 Polish officers working in the British zone in Germany were affiliated with the Polish government in exile.[6]

With characteristic optimism, the American army authorities planned for rapid repatriation of the Polish DPs. At the beginning of April 1945, General Dwight D. Eisenhower, then supreme commander of the Allied expeditionary forces, ordered that "all Poles found in the theatre of operations should be concentrated east of the Rhine" so that it would be possible to return them directly to their land of origin.[7] But as the Soviets were pushing for the repatriation of their own citizens, it was logistically difficult to repatriate the Polish DPs at the same time. At the end of August, in an attempt to facilitate DP repatriation to Poland, Brigadier General Eric Fischer Wood, deputy director of the Prisoners of War and Displaced Persons Division of the U.S. Group Control Council, signed an agreement with the Polish military authorities on repatriating Polish DPs. The American plan spoke of transferring ten thousand Polish DPs daily, with the Polish government agreeing to take responsibility for their care the moment they arrived in Poland. In retrospect, this plan proved overly ambitious.[8]

Though eager to solve the DP problem as quickly as possible, both the British and the Americans remained opposed to forced repatriation. Accordingly, the policy was to grant the DPs time and opportunity to decide their own futures. This policy was not accepted by Moscow and its satellites, who feared the camps would offer anti-Communist groups a ready chance to coalesce. The Soviets, who refused to acknowledge that there existed a DP problem, argued that the

Prisoners in Dachau, Germany, raise American flag on liberation, 30 April 1945
(Courtesy United States Holocaust Memorial Museum)

assistance they received through UNRRA was encouraging the DPs not to return to their homelands. Moscow demanded that UNRRA stop helping the DPs,
but the Americans and the British refused, arguing that this would turn UNRRA
into a political instrument.[9] Disagreement also arose between Moscow and the
United States about the attitude toward DPs from those countries and regions
which, following the war, had been annexed by the Soviet Union and whom
the Soviets now regarded as citizens of the USSR. On this issue, however, the
two Western powers differed. While the U.S. government was against repatriating to the Soviet Union against their will Soviet citizens who were not traitors,
deserters, renegades, or quislings, the British maintained that the Yalta Agreement meant that all Soviet citizens ought to be repatriated, by force if necessary.
Still, by the time Washington established this policy in December 1945, more
than 2,034,000 Soviet citizens had already been repatriated from Western Germany.[10] As tension between the two Western powers and the Communist bloc
escalated, the likelihood of the DPs returning to their home countries significantly diminished.

When they tried to translate these political-humanitarian principles into
action, however, both the British and American military authorities found that

doing so created difficulties. In the winter of 1945–46 the British came to realize that the DPs preferred to remain in the camps rather than return to the hardship that inevitably awaited them in their homelands. As it already had the responsibility for the twenty million Germans living in its occupation zone, the Control Commission for Germany (British Element), which administered the British zone, began looking for ways to encourage the DPs to return home. In mid-December 1945, Field Marshal Bernard L. Montgomery, the commander in chief of the British zone in Germany and the military governor, recommended that 1 April 1946 be set as a cutoff date after which "any displaced person who, without reasonable cause, refuses to return to his country would be taken out of his camp and set to work as a civilian in Germany living on German rations and under conditions parallel to Germans." [11] The Foreign Office rejected the suggestion, which it saw effectively as forced repatriation and therefore contrary to British policy, though the struggle then going on in Poland between the Communists and their opponents, who enjoyed the support of the British, may also have played a part in its attitude. [12]

Nevertheless, Whitehall tried to influence members of the Polish armed forces under British command to return to Poland of their own free will. Following negotiations with the Polish Provisional Government of National Unity, an understanding was reached in March 1946, according to which, in the words of Foreign Secretary Bevin, the British government "consider it to be the duty of all members of those Forces who possibly can do so to return to their home country without further delay." While promising to execute the policy announced by Churchill to help those who nevertheless felt compelled to remain abroad to start a new life outside Poland with their dependents, Bevin insisted that the support would be limited and that the British government intended to disband the Polish army, navy, and air force at present under British command as soon as this proved practicable. Moreover, London could not guarantee that all these people would be able to settle in "British territory at home or overseas." Bevin was confident that the overwhelming majority would decide to avail themselves of the chance they were given and warned that he could not guarantee "that there will be a further opportunity for them to return to Poland." [13]

British military authorities in Germany believed that the foreign secretary's statement would have little influence, if any. The majority of Polish troops, they maintained, would look on any announcement coming from the Warsaw government with suspicion, and most officers were sure the Polish government wanted only a select number of them to return, not the bulk. Polish soldiers who had served in the German army would normally have been the most likely to volunteer, but many of them had been put off by the threats of the Polish government against some among them. At most, 15 percent would volunteer to be repatriated.[14]

Washington, too, was concerned with the problem of those hard-core DPs who refused to return home. At the end of November 1945, Robert P. Patterson, the American secretary of war, told Secretary of State James F. Byrnes that as yet no plan of action was in place to help resettle the nonrepatriable stateless and displaced persons; according to conservative estimates, 350,000 of the 750,000 DPs in the American occupied zones in Germany and Austria had to be considered as stateless or nonrepatriable. The urgency to find a permanent, or at least a temporary, solution for these DPs outside Germany and Austria stemmed from the enormous problems created by the mass influx of ethnic Germans (*Volksdeutsche*) who had been deported from Eastern Europe (under the terms of the Potsdam Agreement) and by the scarcity of food, fuel, and adequate housing in Germany and Austria.[15] Byrnes shared Patterson's concern, but he hoped that when communications between Germany and other countries improved, "many of the non-repatriables will be able within a few months, assuming also the availability of shipping, to find places of residence for themselves in other countries."[16] As a prognosis, this was more wishful thinking than a realistic evaluation of the situation.

Like his British counterpart, the commander of the American zone in Germany, General Joseph T. McNarney, believed that accelerating the pace of the repatriation — which had dwindled greatly in the winter of 1945–46 — should be actively encouraged. McNarney wanted to have an announcement made public on 1 March 1946 to the effect that "not later than 1 June 1946 further care and maintenance to those who do not desire to be repatriated will be discontinued by the United States Government and that those persons affected by this termination of responsibility will be absorbed into the German population with rations and other allowances as provided German inhabitants." But McNarney, cognizant of the sensitivity President Truman was showing to the plight of the Jewish DPs, noted that DPs who had been persecuted because of religion, race, or political beliefs (that is, Jews) would remain the responsibility of the military government. The American commander even asked for authorization to forcibly repatriate unwilling DPs if their governments were interested in receiving them back. The secretaries of war and state supported McNarney's recommendation to close the camps.[17]

Toward the end of February 1946, Byrnes instructed John G. Winant, the American ambassador in London, to inform the British of the American intent to close the DP camps in the American occupied zone of Germany as of 1 July 1946 and asked him to inquire about British plans to do the same in their occupation zone.[18] The Americans thought that advance announcement would accelerate further repatriation. The War Office in London was opposed to the plan and pointed out some of the worrisome consequences to be expected from such a step: a shortage of housing for those deciding to remain; the dangers inherent in the absence of control over the movement of masses of people; and finally, renewed acts of violence by displaced persons who would be left without housing or a means of livelihood.[19] The British command in Germany, however, supported the closure of the camps and warned that if the Americans closed down their camps, the DPs would start flooding into the British camps.[20]

Though aware of the possible consequences, London rejected the position of its Control Commission in Germany. The British Foreign Office asked the Americans not to make any decision before the two nations had a chance to coordinate policies there because closing the camps at this point would entail "so many disquieting implications that a decision on the point of substance and on the consequential announcement to inmates cannot be reached without further examination." [21] Doubts now also came from Ernest F. Penrose, special assistant to the U.S. ambassador in London, who had made a thorough study of the problem of the DPs in Germany and Austria. Apprehensive of what would happen if the DPs were scattered among the German population, Penrose said it was a mistake to assume that most DPs would return to their homelands before the camps were closed or that the plans for resettlement of the DPs who refused repatriation would be completed by then.[22]

The State Department was not impressed by London's and Penrose's arguments and decided to make its new policy public at the UNRRA Council, due to convene in Atlantic City in mid-March 1946. Before that, at a press conference on 14 March, Byrnes announced the American intention to close the DP camps in August 1946, though this did not indicate any change in Washington's position rejecting forced repatriation.[23] Byrnes subsequently told the British that the United States would bring the plan to the UNRRA Council only for consideration and tried to mollify them by noting that the closing of the camps had been delayed from the end of June to August to allow in-depth reexamination of the subject, as the British had requested.[24] This was a rather flimsy argument since the public announcement he had already made had left the British with little room for maneuver. Aware of Whitehall's contrary position, Byrnes not for the first time preferred to confront the British with a fait accompli rather than to open the decision to debate.

By mid-April, Byrnes informed President Truman that the Departments of State and War had decided to close down the DP camps. Stressing the high cost of operating the camps, the secretary of state asserted that "there is no reason to believe they can be closed with less difficulty next year than now." By closing the camps in summer, he added, the Allies would be giving the DPs several months to make their arrangements before the onset of the winter. Byrnes held to this proposal in spite of strong criticism he knew existed among Catholic quarters, including the Federal Council of Churches and the National Catholic Welfare Conference.[25]

Unlike his cabinet secretaries and army officers, however, Truman could not ignore the opinions of interest groups among the American public. The fact that he was not an elected president made him even more sensitive to the weight of electoral calculations. Truman feared a strong reaction on the part of American Catholics, especially the roughly six million Poles, if the camps were closed before suitable arrangements had been made for those who had not yet managed or did not wish to return to their countries of origin. Since the end of the war, the Polish-American Congress (PAC), which represented the various American-Polish organizations in the United States, had demanded that the military government cease its pressure on the Polish DPs to return to "Russian-dominated Poland, where slavery instead of freedom awaits them."[26] Polish Americans traditionally voted Democrat, and Truman needed to retain their loyalty as much as Roosevelt had in the 1944 presidential election campaign, in which Truman ran as the vice-presidential candidate. It was generally accepted that the Polish Congress could influence the Polish American vote, and Truman needed that vote in the forthcoming midterm elections.[27] Thus, not surprisingly, the president froze the plan of his secretaries of state and war. In a statement to the press on 22 April 1946, Byrnes announced that following consultation with the president it had been decided to delay the closure of the DP camps beyond the August 1946 deadline.[28]

Washington's decision greatly upset General McNarney, who remained convinced that it would seriously harm the chances for mass repatriation. The commander of the American zone in Germany warned of a severe deterioration in the behavior of the DPs, who were already much demoralized by the state of uncertainty in which they were kept. In an unsuccessful attempt to influence the government to reconsider its decision, McNarney claimed that it effectively meant "the postponement of the inactivation of the Third Army in October [1946] and the retention of perhaps a full division beyond the planned date of redeployment because of the need for military police in large numbers." He also cited the expected aggravation of the housing shortage for soldiers and their families as well as for the DPs, whose number had grown following the influx of refugees from Eastern Europe. Moreover, if the DP camps were to be maintained indefinitely, the housing conditions there would have to be improved because in many cases the camps were not suitable for extended stays, especially during the winter months. The inevitable result would be an increase in the burden, which would fall on the German economy.[29]

The War Department, too, was disturbed by the president's decision. Howard C. Petersen, assistant secretary of war, argued that each day that passed without closing the camps down "makes the departure from the camps harder to initiate and the home-coming less inviting." He believed there was very little incentive for the DPs to return to their homelands "since most of them are unwilling to exchange the high standard of shelter and rations afforded in the camps for the hard labor and lower standards of living in their native countries." The assistant secretary of war went so far as to accuse the DPs of selfishness and lack of patriotism for preferring to remain in the camps rather than helping rebuild their countries.[30] In an evaluation of the situation presented to Truman in mid-June 1946, Secretary of War Patterson predicted that the president's decision not to close the DP camps would force the American military authorities in Germany to provide for at least three to four hundred thousand DPs. As he saw it, removal of the DPs from Germany was a *conditio sine qua non* for the successful administration of the occupied zone. Patterson was very concerned by the scarcity of food, which had forced the military government to significantly decrease ration allocations to the German population. (In May 1946, the ration was a mere 1,180 calories per day.) The need to feed hundreds of thousands of DPs only exacerbated the difficulties already encountered in supplying the minimal needs of the local population.[31] An additional problem would be the continued financing of the DP camps; in the summer of 1946 it cost about $6 million per month to operate the camps, not including those that housed Jewish DPs.[32]

Polish Displaced Persons Pressure the Western Powers

The administration looked for other ways to encourage the DPs, especially the Poles, to return home. Thus Washington decided to put an end to the DP camp activities of Polish officers who had supported the former Polish government in exile and had managed to retain a considerable amount of influence among the DPs even though they no longer had any official status. In mid-August 1946, the War Department required the military authorities immediately "to remove all London Poles from positions of influence in DP camps or camps assigned exclusively for hard core non-repatriables; to refrain from using them on any military staffs; and to deprive them of any official status and privileges whatsoever." [33]

London, too, was very concerned over the emergence of a large hard core of nonrepatriable DPs, particularly because of the economic costs of supporting them. Between 1 June 1945 and 30 June 1946 the British government had been forced to import 1,245,900 tons of food products into the British zone and to pay for them in dollars. At that time Britain itself was undergoing an economic crisis so severe that the Labour government had been forced to ration bread in Britain, an extreme step that had never been necessary during the war but now resulted in part from the need to supply wheat to Germany.[34]

The British Foreign Office did not expect international initiatives to provide any relief of the burden on the British Exchequer. It even doubted whether an efficient international organization that could support and resettle the DPs would ever be set up. Skepticism in London stemmed from the sharp disagreements that had become apparent in winter and spring of 1946 between the Western countries and those of the Communist bloc over the establishment of the International Refugee Organization (IRO). The bone of contention was the demand by Moscow and its satellites for forced repatriation. While the Soviets agreed to resettlement only in case of stateless persons, the West regarded this alternative as a solution for all DPs who refused repatriation. The problem was especially severe since UNRRA, which at that time was operating 98 camps in the British zone of Germany and 154 in the American zone, was to complete its assignment by the end of 1946.[35]

As hundreds of thousands of DPs continued to live in the British zones, voices in government circles during the summer of 1946 increasingly called for a reassessment of Britain's DP policy. The assumption was that it was still possible to convince many DPs to return to their homelands and that in the short run there was little chance of settling DPs overseas. In analyzing how to reduce the large number of DPs, the point of departure was that many DPs, especially Poles, "have become institutionalized and are unwilling to exchange a life of comparative ease at someone else's expense for the toil and poverty which would await them at home," thus echoing a point the Americans had made earlier that summer. To sway the DPs who refrained from returning out of inertia, it was suggested that their standard of living be lowered to that of the German population and that they be forced to go to work to earn their daily bread, though such measures were unlikely to change the position of those DPs who refused to return for political reasons. Since the British command could not provide employment for all the DPs, it was suggested that they be integrated into the German economy, while at the same time keeping track of their movements to prevent acts of vandalism and black market activities. Measures might also be necessary to protect the DPs from persecution and discrimination by the German population. The assumption was that making these plans public would persuade at least some of the DPs to return home.[36] As we saw, when a similar suggestion had been made by Montgomery several months earlier, London had still been hopeful that a large number of the DPs would voluntarily opt for repatriation.

Integrating the DPs into the German economy was an impractical idea if only because of the already difficult economic situation and the high rate of unemployment then prevailing. In the winter of 1946, industrial production in the British zone was still only 15 percent of what it had been in the region before the war.[37] The DPs were obliged to compete for places of work with hundreds of thousands of Germans who had been deported from Eastern Europe. According to a census conducted at the end of October 1946, there were 3.6 million German deportees and refugees in the British occupied zone; in the month of August alone about 156,000 had entered the British zone. Altogether, during the two years since the end of the war, about twelve million *Volksdeutsche* had entered Germany.[38] Moreover, with the transfer of civil administration to the Germans and a policy of interfering as little as possible in its activities, it became difficult for the military authorities to defend the DPs from exploitation at the hands of German employers.[39] Of the 60,000 DPs who were working in the British zone in the summer of 1946, 50,000 were employed by the army, a situation that changed little during the following year. Of the 130,000 DPs who were able to work in summer 1947, only 76,000 were employed. Of these, only 13,000 worked for German employers. The situation in the American zone was no different.[40]

The principles formulated in summer 1946 in London for a new policy toward the DPs were approved in mid-September by the Cabinet Overseas Reconstruction Committee with the participation of Bevin, Chancellor of the Exchequer Hugh Dalton, and John B. Hynd, Labour MP for Sheffield and chancellor of the duchy of Lancaster, who was in charge of the Control Office for Germany and Austria, though for the time being the new policy was not put into effect.[41] Meanwhile, efforts were being made to persuade DPs to repatriate. Polish DPs, apprehensive over the severe economic distress in Poland, were offered by UNRRA an allocation of sixty days of rations in advance if they agreed to return home. This initiative of UNRRA's secretary general Fiorello La Guardia was implemented between October and December 1946 and renewed during April and May 1947. For its part, the Polish government announced that with these rations people remained eligible for all normal rations and that all necessary facilities would be more available to returning Polish citizens. Edward Osóbka-Morawski, the Polish prime minister, declared that Poland greatly needed those citizens who were still outside Poland and "there exists no reason for further delay in returning."[42] The offer of extra food rations brought about a significant increase in October, when approximately 46,000 persons returned to Poland, but the number of returnees soon decreased again. In November and December approximately 45,000 DPs repatriated while in January and February 1947 only about 3,000 returned.[43] In mid-February 1947, after it became clear that the incentives were not yielding the desired results, Hynd told Parliament of the government's new policy.[44] At that time the number of DPs in the British zone was about 264,000, approximately 135,000 of them Poles and about 80,000 Balts.[45] The hopes London placed on the new policy never materialized: not only was there no substantial increase in the number of DPs accepting repatriation, but new refugees from Eastern Europe continued to enter the British and American zones. A query in the House of Commons elicited the response that as of 1 June 1947 there were 246,000 DPs in the British occupied zone, 113,000 of whom were Poles and about 71,000 citizens of the former Baltic countries.[46]

The British Foreign Office meanwhile also became concerned about the political fallout if the problem of the DPs remained unsolved. According to Bevin, Soviet foreign minister Vyacheslav Molotov was exploiting the problem of the DPs in Austria to reject any discussion of peace arrangements with that country during CFM meetings in Paris in the summer and autumn of 1946. Bevin expressed his frustration in a memorandum to Attlee, arguing that there was no reason "why, after so long, His Majesty's Government should continue to maintain either people who could reasonably be expected to go home or known Quislings and ex-enemies."[47]

The situation in the American zone was similar to that in the British zone. During the winter of 1947 about 367,000 DPs were still located there, and the administration could no longer avoid the pressure exerted by various ethnic groups, particularly the Polish Americans. The Polish-American Congress, well aware of the attempts of the military authorities in Germany to induce the Polish DPs to return to Poland, complained to the president about the discrepancy between the official policy, which prohibited forced repatriation, and the one that was being followed in practice. Hinting at the electoral potential of the six million American citizens of Polish extraction, Charles Rozmarek, president of the PAC, demanded that Polish DPs be treated like the Jewish DPs, namely as nonrepatriable. The U.S. president was also asked to appoint a special adviser on the affairs of the Polish DPs, who would work alongside the American zone commander in Germany, again similar to the arrangements for the Jewish DPs. Rozmarek pointed out that the adviser for Jewish DPs affairs had succeeded in considerably improving his people's situation and, implying that the administration was discriminating against Christian DPs when allocating entrance permits to the United States, asked whether the president's suggestion to admit one hundred thousand refugees to the United States "applies only to one group, or do you intend equal consideration for all nationalistic groups in proportion to their numbers?" In an attempt to exploit the painful defeat which the Democratic Party had suffered in the midterm elections in November 1946, Rozmarek stressed that "the unfair discrimination causes tremendous anxiety among millions of Americans of Polish descent, many of whom have relatives in the American Zone of Occupation in Europe," reminding the president that not only Jewish Americans possessed electoral clout.[48]

Washington vigorously rejected the argument that the military authorities in Germany were forcibly repatriating Polish DPs to Poland and refused to appoint an adviser for Polish DP affairs, explaining that the military authorities in Germany needed to reduce their personnel roster "in a field where they soon expect to be relieved of much of their present responsibility by reason of the transfer of certain functions to the International Refugee Organization."[49] (On 16 December 1946 the General Assembly approved the IRO constitution along with its first annual budget.) Considering that only one position was at issue, this was most certainly a dubious argument. More likely, the real reason was the administration's fear that a Polish adviser would only impede efforts to repatriate the Polish DPs.

Increasing tension between Britain and the United States on the one hand and the Soviet Union on the other during the winter of 1946–47 also intensified their disagreement over treatment of the DP problem. Inability to bridge the gap in positions was manifest at the meeting of the CFM in Moscow from 10 March to 25 April 1947. The Soviets adamantly rejected any attempt to resettle the DPs and insisted that the only solution was repatriation regardless of the desires of the DPs themselves. The Soviets accused the West of exploiting the DP issue in its political struggle against Moscow and its satellites, and they claimed that if DPs refused to return home, this was owing to Western pressure and propaganda. Attempts to formulate resolutions on the treatment of the DPs reflected the depth of the chasm that existed between the two sides. Generally speaking, the Soviets tried, unsuccessfully, to breach the exclusive responsibility which the Western powers exercised over the DPs in their respective occupation zones. For example, the Americans, British, and French rejected the Soviet proposal that administration of the DP camps "shall consist primarily of the representatives of states whose citizens are among the displaced persons." Another Soviet proposal that was rejected called for the establishment of a quadripartite committee to investigate the situation in DP camps located in the American, British, and French zones of occupation "in order to ascertain the desire and intention of these persons to return to their homeland." The three Western powers also disapproved a proposal prohibiting charging any expenses incurred for the maintenance of DPs and refugees to the account of the Germans. For their part, the Soviets rejected an American suggestion to transfer deliberations on the DP problem to the IRO. The Soviets, who had refused to join that organization, argued that the IRO had been authorized to deal with humanitarian not political matters. As they saw it, resettlement of the DPs was a political issue. Among the very few Soviet recommendations that were accepted were the proscription on antirepatriation propaganda in the DP camps and allowing representatives of the countries whose citizens were living in the camps to visit them. So as to prevent such visitors from exerting pressure on the DPs, it was decided that the visits would take place in the presence of occupation forces officers.[50]

Resettlement Options

In the end it was the growing Communist control in East European countries during the course of 1947 as well as the hatred and fear which the Soviet regime occasioned among the DPs that led London and Washington to the conclusion that repatriation was no longer a realistic solution to the DP problem. Resettlement was now regarded as the most practical alternative. Between November 1945 and the end of June 1947, when UNRRA ceased functioning, approximately 742,000 DPs were repatriated from Germany and about 202,000 from Austria under its auspices. (At the end of 1946 UNRRA's mandate had been extended until 30 June 1947.) In the spring of 1947 the organization was operating 762 DP centers in Germany, 416 of which were in the American and 272 in the British zones. When IRO took over from UNRRA on 1 July 1947, the new organization had the responsibility for the care of 712,000 refugees and DPs, of whom 643,000 had previously been the responsibility of UNRRA.[51]

The British Foreign Office suggested that one way of solving the DP problem was for the British government to pressure UN member states to open their doors to the DPs. This was part of a British decision to act energetically to have the DPs resettled in the face of Soviet opposition. Expected Soviet criticism was countered with the claim that the DPs were free to return home, and those who so desired had done so during the intervening months. Furthermore, even after resettlement, those who wished could return to their countries of origin.[52] During the CFM meeting in Moscow Bevin challenged the Russians by saying he was unable to comprehend why "110,000 Poles in the British Zone, in spite of all legitimate pressure, refuse to return to Poland and assist in rehabilitation of their country."[53]

At the same time, the British delegation at the UN was asked to point out that since the end of the war Britain had absorbed about three hundred thousand persons "who would otherwise have been in DP camps on the Continent." (Most of those absorbed in Britain were Polish soldiers who had served in the armed forces under British command and members of their families.) Britain further intended to admit a total of four hundred thousand persons, constituting 1 percent of the British population and about 50 percent of all the DPs remaining in Europe. Hence Britain's contribution compared favorably with that of other countries, especially the United States. When in April 1947 Congress shelved a bill introduced by William G. Stratton, Republican congressman from Illinois, that would have permitted an annual immigration of one hundred thousand refugees into the United States for four years, the British Foreign Office complained that "[if] the United States were to absorb refugees at half that [of the British] proportion, there would be no refugees left. It seems paradoxical that it is the most densely populated countries, such as Belgium and the United Kingdom, which are doing most in resettlement, while countries with ample resources for large-scale resettlement are timidly dallying with small-scale projects or are not taking in any DPs at all."[54]

The hopes the British placed on the Americans began to materialize in June 1948, when a bill was approved permitting 200,000 DPs to enter the United States over the course of two years. The legislation was worded in such a way as to give preference to DPs from the former Baltic states.[55] Between passage of the bill and the end of the IRO's mandate on 30 December 1951, the United States took in 312,000 DPs, constituting about 37 percent of the total 830,000 DPs who were resettled during that period. Britain's contribution during the same period was minimal, only about 17,000 persons. During the year ending 30 June 1948, however, 70,000 DPs were admitted by Britain compared with only 17,000 by the United States. Between June 1948 and December 1951 Australia accepted 176,000 persons (about 21 percent of all the DPs resettled during that period); Canada, 98,000 (12 percent); and Central and South American nations together only 68,000 DPs. During the four and one-half years of its operation, IRO resettled more than one million DPs (including about 357,000 Poles) and repatriated about 72,000 DPs (approximately 38,000 to Poland).[56]

In sum, British and American policy toward DPs in their occupied zones in Germany was influenced by political, economic, and humanitarian considerations.

Both governments favored repatriating the DPs, but they did not want to be seen as forcing DPs, most of them anti-Communists, to return to their homeland against their will. Public criticism of the forced repatriation of Soviet citizens also had an effect. Both powers recognized the political and propaganda significance of the refusal of the DPs to be repatriated, especially in light of the escalating Cold War. Moreover, Britain felt a certain obligation toward the Polish DPs, who were affiliated to London's Poles; the latter had fought under British command during the war and were encouraging the DPs not to return to Poland. For its part, the White House could not ignore the great concern American Catholics, especially those of Polish origin, were showing in policy decisions toward the Polish DPs.

During the first months after the war, London and Washington entertained hopes that the DPs would prefer repatriation to a life without purpose in the camps. When it became clear that this was not the case, British authorities, and to some extent also the Americans, pursued a policy of carrot and stick: economic incentives were offered to returnees, while at the same time the standard of living was lowered for those who chose to remain. For the most part, these steps were taken too late. By the end of 1947, the entrenchment of the DPs in the camps, escalation of the Cold War, and consolidation of Communist control in the Eastern European countries made the British and Americans realize that resettlement overseas was the only possible solution for the DP problem.

Among the hard-core DPs, those who could not or did not want to be repatriated, were the Jewish DPs. At the end of 1945 Jews constituted about 5 percent of all DPs in Germany, but as time passed, their percentage increased because of the repatriation of non-Jewish DPs and the arrival of tens of thousands of Jews who were fleeing Eastern Europe. By the end of 1947, Jewish DPs constituted about 25 percent of the total in the three occupation zones of West Germany.[57] Most of them were located in the American zone. In the British zone, the number of Jewish DPs remained almost constant between 1945 and 1948 because East European Jews for the most part avoided that region because of British policy. If the British had wanted to treat Jewish DPs just like all other DPs, they were soon to realize that a special policy was necessary.

JEWISH DISPLACED PERSONS IN BRITISH OCCUPATION ZONES

It fell to British forces to liberate the concentration camp at Bergen-Belsen. When British soldiers first entered the camp, they faced a horrendous reality. Inside, amid heaps of dead bodies, they found about sixty thousand people, most of them barely alive—thirty-five thousand people had died from starvation or disease during the previous four months; for fourteen thousand of those who had survived, liberation came too late and they succumbed within a few weeks. One of the first things the British did was to set up a hospital and mobilize medical students from London and from Belgium who, among other things, began feeding intravenously the many who were close to starvation. On the day of liberation half of the inmates were Jews. Close to ten thousand of these died soon after, but about four thousand were somehow fit enough to return to their home countries in Western Europe. Another four thousand, who claimed they were stateless, were moved to Lingen and Celle. Because of the relatively large number of Jews among the survivors in Bergen-Belsen, other Jewish refugees in the British zone began moving to the camp to be in Jewish surroundings.[1]

"Like All Others"

The Allies' displaced persons policy contained no special guidelines for Jewish survivors, except that Jewish nationals of all former enemy countries could claim the same treatment accorded to DPs from the Allied nations. The attitude was that Jews, like all other DPs, ought to return to their countries of origin and pick up their lives there as soon as possible. Very quickly, however, and against its will, London found itself facing the question of a separate policy toward the Jewish DPs.

Jewish organizations began to ask the British government for permission to send delegations to visit the liberated camps so as to provide medical, spiritual, and material assistance to the Jewish survivors. Leaders of the British section of the World Jewish Congress (WJC), for example, pointed out that many of the survivors were either stateless or citizens of former enemy countries and thus had no government or liaison officers who could intercede on their behalf. The WJC asked that a mission of Jewish representatives be allowed to visit the camps and that an additional group of volunteers be allowed to work there for a period of two or three months. For the Board of Deputies of British Jews (BDBJ), the recognized representative body of British Jewish community vis-à-vis the British government, it was almost incomprehensible that after their liberation displaced Jews of German and non-German origin were kept in the very camps in which they had been incarcerated by the Nazis and where they received food rations lower than those allocated to the Germans. Emphasis was placed on the need to take steps to improve the situation before winter set in and to move them out of the camps and into the towns. Another proposal called for attaching Jewish officers to the military government units in Germany and Jewish liaison officers in the various camps in which there were Jewish refugees.[2]

British military authorities in Germany did not much like the idea of Jewish organizations visiting the camps, stating that "we definitely cannot take care of persons who just wish to visit and then go home and make interesting report." Even when pressure from Jewish organizations made them agree to accept a delegation of a maximum of three persons representing all Jewish organizations, the military authorities insisted that "no one wants a visit from these people."[3] The War Office, at first in favor of a small group of visitors, changed its mind, telling a delegation of Jewish organizations in Britain that under present conditions such visits were a liability because of the transport and accommodation involved. Anyway, the DP problem was of such enormous proportions that no visitor would be able to get a true picture from what would necessarily be a very hurried inspection.[4]

At the same time, in late July, the military authorities also refused requests of Jewish organizations to segregate all Jewish DPs irrespective of their different nationalities and to provide them with preferential treatment. In a letter to the Marquess of Reading, the president of the British Section of the WJC, Lieutenant General Ronald Weeks, Montgomery's deputy military governor of the British occupied zone in Germany, maintained that segregation would result in a large body of Jews of many nationalities "who would probably refuse repatria-

Rabbi Leslie H. Hardman, chaplain in the British Army, reciting Kaddish at a mass grave in Bergen-Belsen (Courtesy Israel Ministry of Defense, Museums Unit)

tion and constitute a continuous embarrassment." He thought that "the policy should continue to be to emphasise a Jew's political nationality rather than his race and religious persuasion." Preferential treatment of Jews, Weeks argued, would be "unfair to the many non-Jews who have suffered on account of their clandestine and other activities in the Allied cause." He warned that possible irritation among non-Jewish DPs "might well have far-reaching results and give rise to persecution at a later date." While admitting that the Jews in Germany had been subjected to cruelties and hardship, he quickly pointed out that "there have been many other sufferers." The only suggestion Weeks viewed favorably was the appointment of Jewish liaison officers as "it might serve to canalise representations and complaints concerning the Jews and provide a safeguard against the results of ill-considered communications from Jews in the British

Survivors of the Holocaust in Bergen-Belsen after liberation
(Courtesy Israel Ministry of Defense, Museums Unit)

Zone to prominent members of the Jewish community in other countries" and thus prove advantageous to the military government.[5]

Considerations of a purely political, and not of an administrative, let alone humane, nature, however, took over very quickly. In mid-August 1945, the British military authorities rejected the proposal that Jewish liaison officers be appointed, arguing that this was too reminiscent of the Nazi theory that saw the Jews as a separate race. Jews wishing to return home would be taken care of by the regular liaison officers from their homelands, and the Intergovernmental Committee on Refugees (IGCR), established in July 1938 in Evian, would be on hand to take care of those Jews who were stateless or refused repatriation. The military authorities insisted that the Jews should be domiciled according to their country of origin—that is, nationality—since to do so according to race or religion might increase anti-Jewish feelings, resulting in potentially far-reaching repercussions. A corroborating factor was the fear that the appointment of Jewish liaison officers would set a precedent for other religious sects.[6]

This change of heart, and the disingenuous reasons used to back it up, may well have had to do with the information that had reached London at the beginning of August concerning the mission of Earl G. Harrison. Harrison's assignment, which had been approved by President Truman, had been to investigate the situation of those DPs who could not be repatriated, especially the Jewish DPs, and his preliminary recommendations—to separate Jewish DPs from the others and to allow one hundred thousand of them to enter Palestine—were very worrisome to London. Ian L. Henderson, the Foreign Office expert on refugees, thought that the Zionists were behind Harrison's recommendations: not recognizing the Jews as a separate category was of direct concern to the Zionists, "who like to pronounce as many Jews as possible to be 'stateless' so that they eventually be ripe for acquisition of a separate Jewish nationality and citizenship in a Jewish national state." Henderson doubted that a large percentage of the Jewish DPs, especially those coming from Poland, would ever want to leave Germany for Palestine.[7] Because Harrison's report was likely to reach highly placed figures in the U.S. administration and perhaps also Congress, Foreign Office officials looked for ways to neutralize the effect of possible American criticism. Since Britain's refusal to recognize the Jews as a separate nationality was a cornerstone of its policy and concentration of Jewish DPs in separate camps was out of the question, the Foreign Office suggested that Jewish welfare workers and liaison officers be allowed free access to their coreligionists.[8]

When Harrison's report came out, British military authorities in Germany rejected the criticism it contained of the British policy toward the Jewish DPs by claiming that they were being treated exactly like all other DPs. Jewish DPs who refused repatriation were placed together either with other citizens of their country of origin or with the stateless.[9] In a letter to Truman in mid-September 1945, Prime Minister Attlee argued that the Jews had not suffered more than other DPs and that if his officers were to classify the Jews as a separate race at the "head of the queue," other groups of DPs would react violently against them.[10] The British reiterated that separating the Jews would be tantamount to adopting the racist policies of Hitler, a moral contention that, at first glance, appears to make sense. But how moral was it, indeed, if one considers that those who asked for this separation were the very victims of Hitler's racism? As we will see, the reason for Whitehall's refusal to separate the Jewish DPs had more to do with Britain's policy vis-à-vis Palestine. London felt that the willingness of many Jewish DPs to give up their present citizenship was inspired by the hope that this would be the first step on their way to Palestine.[11]

After British Jewish leaders approached several high-level government officials, however, a change in attitude began to emerge. The same Henderson from the Refugee Department who had earlier believed the Zionists were exploiting the DP problem for their own purposes now suggested reassessing the matter. Considering that the Jews were living together with non-Jewish DPs, many of whom were anti-Semitic, and given the high probability that these Jews would have to remain for several more months in Germany, Henderson pointed to the inordinate suffering that had been the lot of the Jews during the past few years: they should not now be left to the mercy of anti-Semitic citizens of their countries of origin. Paul Mason, head of the department, did not concur. Acknowledging the existence of anti-Semitism, Mason stressed that it was Britain's task to eradicate it in the DP camps and wherever else it was found. Apart from that, some operative action might be necessary, but he did not want to go beyond appointing a Jewish liaison officer. The proposed candidate was Lord Reading, who, it was believed, enjoyed much respect in the Jewish world. In contrast to his wife, Eva, Reading was not a Zionist and thus could be expected to endorse the policy of separation on a national rather than a racial basis.[12]

So as to ensure their control over the Jewish DP problem, the British tried to limit, as much as possible, any ties that might develop between the Jewish DPs and Jewish organizations in Britain or representatives of the Jewish Agency. For example, many obstacles were placed in the way of representatives of organizations who wanted to send delegates to the Jewish DP congress in Bergen-Belsen, which, after several postponements, came together on 25 September 1945. Requests of the Jewish Agency and the British section of the WJC to send delegates were refused. A specific promise to allow a representative of the WJC to participate in the convention was not honored.[13] Not without reason, the occupation authorities and the War Office were afraid that visits of Jewish representatives from Britain would lead to increased pressure on Whitehall to change its policy toward the Jewish DPs and that visits of Zionist leaders from Palestine would strengthen Zionist tendencies among the DPs. Already there was a constant stream of complaints about the continuing plight of Jewish DPs in the British zone. A few days before the DP congress in Bergen-Belsen, for example, Eva Reading had complained to Montgomery that all representations on the most distressing situation of the Jews in the former concentration camps "have been bogged down in the War Office files with no action taken," as had the request to appoint a Jewish liaison officer.[14]

As London had foreseen, the resolutions adopted at the Bergen-Belsen conference reflected the emergence of strong Zionist convictions among the DP leadership. The conference, as its main objective, called upon Britain and the other Allied governments "to designate Palestine as a Jewish State" and immediately to admit one million Jews to Palestine, adding that no obstacle would prevent the Jews from reaching Palestine. Demands were made in connection with the DPs: recognition of the Jewish DPs as Jews and not as nationals of states to which they had no intention of returning; transfer of the administration of the camps and centers to Jews; appointment of Jewish liaison officers to the military government in Germany; recognition of a central Jewish committee as the official representative of the Jewish DPs in the British and American occupation zones; provision of vocational training in preparation for immigration to Palestine; and transfer of properties of Jewish communities that had been annihilated and of individuals who were left without heirs to a representative body of the Jewish people that would use them to develop Palestine.[15]

The participation of Jewish organizations in the Bergen-Belsen conference led to further pressure on the British government. The BDBJ, for example, requested a meeting with the prime minister to discuss the aspirations of the Jewish DPs to settle in Palestine, which they regarded as their national home.[16] Sidney Silverman, chairman of the British section of the WJC and also a Labour Party MP, and A. L. Easterman, political secretary of the WJC, who had managed to be present at the conference, submitted to the Foreign Office several demands, including removal of the guards and barbed wire fences around the camps and treatment of the Jewish DPs as free persons; concentration of the Jewish DPs in separate camps under the supervision of a Jewish administrator and appointment of Jewish liaison officers; assignment of a Jewish adviser to the military government; prohibition of forced repatriation and granting Jewish DPs the right to choose their own immigration destinations; and assistance to those DPs who wished to go to Palestine. Additional demands dealt with an improvement in the conditions of daily life.[17]

Silverman's demands received a willing ear from Brigadier A. C. Kenchington, chief of the Prisoners of War and Displaced Persons Division, Control Commission for Germany (British Element), who thought that some modification of British policy toward Jewish DPs was required if only because of the change of the U.S. policy, which "was no longer in line with ours." As he anticipated that considerable pressure would continue for the segregation of Jewish DPs who were not immediately repatriable, there should be no adverse and ill-considered reports on the situation of Jews in the British zone. He therefore suggested that Jewish DPs who were ready to be repatriated to their countries of origin should remain in the same camps as gentiles of the same nationality who were also going to be repatriated but that Jewish DPs who were not repatriable should be moved to special camps. Kenchington also supported the appointment of a suitable British Jewish army officer as adviser on all Jewish matters and allowing all Jewish welfare teams who wanted to come and work in the British zone to do so with the coordination of UNRRA. Moreover, a representative of the Jewish Agency should be attached forthwith to whatever organization was going to deal with the question of resettling those DPs who were not to be repatriated to their countries of origin.[18]

Kenchington was not alone in believing that some change of policy was needed. Major General Brian Robertson, the deputy military governor in the British zone in Germany, informed Professor Selig Brodetsky, president of the BDBJ and member of the Zionist Executive, that for reasons of administrative convenience he was ready to recommend concentrating the Jewish DPs in a separate camp. Robertson stressed, though, that if accepted, this step was not to be seen as recognition of any special status for Jewish DPs or as entailing any obligation toward their ultimate disposition. In a memorandum to the War Office, Robertson argued that a reassessment of the situation had brought him to the conclusion that if the Jews were not separated as a result of Britain's initiative, it would be forced on Whitehall. According to him, after completing repatriation of the Poles, two groups of Poles would remain, those who could not return home for political reasons, and the Jews, who would then be the larger group. Robertson believed that since these two groups had nothing in common, it was desirable to separate them. He also agreed to the assignment of a Jewish officer to his staff who could advise him on Jewish matters. If the policy of separation were adopted, he added, there would be no need for liaison officers in the camps.[19]

The War Office shifted the decision to the Foreign Office. Sir Orme Sargent, deputy under secretary of state, Foreign Office, resolutely rejected Robertson's central recommendation to separate the Jewish DPs, stressing the probable far-reaching political repercussions if such a step were taken. As a compromise, he agreed to permit the Jewish DPs to "live in self-contained groups" within the camps, which were set up on a national basis. He supported Robertson's recommendation to attach a liaison officer to his staff and suggested selecting someone prestigious, as Eisenhower had done in the American occupation zone.[20] Accordingly, on 19 November 1945, the chief of the Prisoners of War and Displaced Persons Division, Control Commission for Germany (British Element), notified the military commanders that the policy of segregating all DPs in accordance with their nationality, irrespective of their racial or religious group, was now modified in respect of Jews. In all camps containing Jews separate blocs or houses should be allotted for their use. Jews would be given the option of living in accommodations set aside for them. "Special camps exclusively for Jews," the instruction ended, "will not be established." [21]

The British hoped that this compromise would satisfy British Jewish organizations and at the same time not deviate from their principal policy of not recognizing all Jewish DPs as a separate category. The Foreign Office was by now very well aware that the issue of the Jewish DPs was being used by the Zionists as an anti-British weapon that could prove highly effective. They were concerned over Truman's extensive intervention in the matter of the Jewish DPs, especially when he adopted Harrison's recommendation that one hundred thousand Jews be allowed to enter Palestine. Under those circumstances, the opposition to separating Jewish DPs only strengthened. [22]

The importance for the British of continuing to deny that the Jewish DPs formed a separate category was also demonstrated by their refusal to recognize the Central Jewish Committee in Bergen-Belsen as the representative of the German Jews and the Jewish DPs in their occupied zone. In fact, the British refused to recognize the committee as representative even of the Jewish DPs in Bergen-Belsen. The first Central Jewish Committee of Bergen-Belsen, headed by Josef (Yossel) Rosensaft, was elected on 17 April 1945, two days after the camp was liberated. [23] Rosensaft was born in Bendin in 1911. In May 1943, he had been captured with his family in the ghetto of his hometown. He escaped while he was being transported to Auschwitz. In April 1944 he was caught and sent to a work camp near Auschwitz. Later he was sent to Camp Dora, where he stayed until he was transferred to Bergen-Belsen, a week before the camp was liberated. Relations between the British military authorities and Rosensaft were antagonistic from the start. As early as June 1945, Rosensaft succeeded in having the British military authorities cancel their plan to transfer Jewish survivors from Belsen to Lingen camp. Of strong character and clearly endowed with political talent, he skillfully maneuvered between the Control Office for Germany and Austria and the military authorities in Germany while enlisting support of Jewish organizations in both Britain and the United States as well as the American press. [24]

Thus it comes as no surprise that after a while the British military government in Germany wanted Rosensaft out of the way, not in the least because of his Zionist militancy. When, in December 1945, he asked them to let him travel to the United States to take part in a conference of the United Jewish Appeal, they agreed on the condition that he would not return to the British zone. Rosensaft rejected this proposal and decided to travel without permission. When the military government realized that he had disappeared, the Foreign Office quickly warned the British embassy in Washington of the damage he might cause to Britain in American public opinion. Foreign Office officials described him as a Zionist extremist who would do anything to malign the British military government and its policy toward Jewish DPs. The embassy was asked to report regularly on his political activity.[25] It was the hostility British military authorities in Germany felt toward Rosensaft and his people that partly prompted them to oppose granting the Central Jewish Committee official recognition as the representative of Germany's Jews and of the Jewish DPs in the British zone. But the main reason was their fear that recognition of the committee would be regarded as recognition by Britain of the Jews as constituting a separate nationality.[26]

A significant outcome of Rosensaft's visit to the United States was the attention he attracted to the plight of Jewish DPs in the British zone. For example, in an article published in the *New York Times,* a journalist quoted Rosensaft as claiming that in the Belsen camp there was no equipment to heat the buildings; that camp occupants had been forbidden to fell trees for firewood; and that there was a severe shortage of clothing, shoes, blankets, and medicines. Although most of the DPs in the camp were Jews, Rosensaft complained, Bergen-Belsen was not considered a Jewish camp. The DPs were forbidden to organize Zionist activities, and their internal camp newspapers were censored.[27] Local newspapers also reported on incidents between DPs and British soldiers provoked by a statement Bevin had made on 13 November 1945 which introduced an adverse change in British policy vis-à-vis Palestine.

Parliament was chosen as the appropriate arena to counter these attacks as well as complaints of Jewish organizations in Britain.[28] The chancellor of the duchy of Lancaster described in detail the policy toward the Jewish DPs in the British zone in Germany and especially in the "Höne camp," where about ninety-five hundred DPs were living at the time. Höne was the name of the village next to Bergen-Belsen where the British had turned former SS barracks into a refugee camp after they had evacuated and then burned down the concentration camp in June 1945. British officials thereafter always spoke of the Höne camp while, for obvious reasons, the DPs and Jewish organizations continued to use the name Bergen-Belsen. The minister also stressed that the Jewish DPs managed their own affairs; they had freedom of movement outside the camp; no limitations were placed on Zionist activities; and there was no censorship of the press. Food amounting to close to three thousand calories per day was allocated for pregnant women and the sick and for working people, a little over two thousand calories for DPs who were not working and for children. In response to a question about the appointment of Jewish advisers, he replied that the subject was being studied, but he rejected the demand that separate camps be set up for the Jewish DPs.[29]

When leaders and emissaries of the Jewish community in Palestine visited Bergen-Belsen, the picture they painted predictably differed from that given by Hynd. David Ben-Gurion, chair of the Jewish Agency and the prominent leader of the Yishuv, who visited Bergen-Belsen without London's knowledge, criticized the British harshly: "The treatment at Belsen is the closest thing one can imagine to Nazi methods. All the Jews are officially under Polish authority, even though, actually, very few Poles remain. Jewish children are forced to go to Polish schools and study in Polish. Jews have been compelled to live in the same rooms as Poles who reviled them and treated them rudely. The authorities are aware of this but claim that they are unable to do anything about it, since they are all Poles."[30] More balanced though no less bleak pictures were given by different Jewish functionaries. Judge Simon Rifkind, who had been chosen to become adviser on Jewish affairs to General Joseph McNarney, visited Bergen-Belsen in December 1945. From Dr. Hadassa Bimko of the Jewish Committee he learned that some of the living quarters were overcrowded because of a lack of heating and that there was a shortage of clothes. Dr. Bimko also expressed her opinion that Jews who had survived the concentration camps ought to be entitled to special treatment at the expense of German population and that Bergen-Belsen should become an entirely Jewish camp. Still, she expressed moderate optimism for the future following the replacement of the former commander of the camp, whom she felt had done everything possible to make the lives of the inmates thoroughly unpleasant. Since the arrival of the new commander, she concluded, there had been a great improvement in the conditions of the camp.[31]

Charles Zarback of the Jewish Relief Unit (JRU) noted in a report he submitted in mid-February 1946 that the Jewish DPs had begun to feel better once they were allowed to live in a separate Jewish section at Bergen-Belsen. Still, even under the new arrangement there had been cases of physical violence against individual Jews and a synagogue had been desecrated and religious books destroyed. "It is for this reason," Zarback explained, "that the Jewish DPs feel strongly against the camp being guarded by Polish soldiers and have requested that the Jewish Brigade be used for these duties." Zarback's report systematically examined the various aspects of life in Bergen-Belsen, and the result makes bleak reading. He talks of severe overcrowding, of cold rooms, of inadequate bedding for winter, and of the shortage of clothing and shoes. Contrary to Hynd, Zarback states that the official ration of two thousand calories per day could not make up for years of privation. He also pointed out that although a search bureau was established in the camp to locate relatives and friends, there were no facilities for sending or receiving letters to and from relatives outside Germany. On the more positive side, Zarback noticed the degree of personal freedom, the good relations between the inhabitants and the surrounding population, and the participation of the DPs in camp management.[32]

"Infiltrators" from the East

At the end of 1945, London began to receive reports about thousands of Jews from Poland and Hungary who, it was said, were "infiltrating" into the British occupation zones in Germany and Austria. No government policy had yet been formulated on how to deal with such refugees. The British Control Commission in Austria, which was responsible for administering the British zone in that country, estimated at the end of November that as of August about seven thousand Jews had entered the area, of whom three thousand had again already left, mainly for the American zone in Austria, some for Italy. The remaining four thousand were centered in two camps, Trofaiach and Judenburg. The commission believed that these people should not be regarded as displaced persons because they had not been driven from their homes either as a result of the war or because of persecution by the Germans or their allies. Still, even though these Jews made it clear that they would cause problems unless they were allowed to immigrate to Palestine, the Control Commission in Austria allowed them to take up residence in the camps and to receive the same treatment as DPs from the Allied countries.[33]

The military authorities in the British sector of Berlin, however, refused to provide food and shelter for these Jewish "infiltrators," as they too called them, or to allow them to continue on to the British occupation zone in Germany. Estimates spoke of about 250 Jews arriving from Poland each day. Among the British Control Commission in Germany there were those who thought that this movement was a deliberate attempt to increase the number of Jews in Germany as part of a propaganda campaign to generate world sympathy.[34] Accordingly, in December the British representative in the Directorate of Prisoners of War and Displaced Persons of the Allied Control Council rejected an American request for Britain to absorb these Jewish refugees because his government considered them Polish nationals who ought to be returned to their country of origin. Still, in view of the fact that the American, French, and Soviet occupation authorities were all granting these people asylum, and because of the criticism that a policy of this kind was likely to inspire in the world press, par-

Inside one of the barracks in Bergen-Belsen camp
(Courtesy Israel Ministry of Defense, Museums Unit)

ticularly in the United States, the British military authorities in Germany asked London to reconsider its attitude toward them.[35]

At the Refugee Department of the Foreign Office this influx of Jews from Poland was explained as part of a Zionist plot to embarrass British military authorities in Germany and to make it clear to the world that it was no longer possible for Jews to live in Europe and that their only option was immigration to Palestine. The department saw a connection between Jewish infiltration and the announcement Bevin had made on 13 November 1945 of his decision to set up the "Anglo-American Committee of Inquiry Regarding the Problems of European Jewry and Palestine," which, among other things, was to investigate the situation of the Jewish DPs and assess how many of them wished to immigrate to Palestine.[36] Differences of opinion prevailed at the department, however, over what steps ought to be taken. Ian Henderson believed that Britain could not be seen as the only Allied power refusing admittance to these Jews.[37] George Rendel, during the 1930s head of the Middle East Department in the Foreign Office and now responsible for liaison with international refugee organizations, thought otherwise. He maintained that every effort should be made to prevent these Jews from entering the British zone. Otherwise, he argued, "We may be playing the Jewish game and facilitating a maneuver which is not only likely to cause us great political inconvenience and expense but is

Taking a bath in a DP camp (Courtesy Yad Vashem, Jerusalem)

also likely to cause great suffering and hardship to the Jews themselves. If they are freely admitted into the British zone the effect will be to encourage other parties to come and our efforts to check the exodus will be defeated." [38]

Rendel opposed granting DP status, with all it entailed, to the Jewish infiltrators. He also thought they should not be gathered into a separate camp because this would imply recognition of the Jews as a nation and thus of their right to immigrate to Palestine. He was quite aware that Jews would greatly resent being housed together with German refugees or Germans expelled from Poland and Czechoslovakia "on the ground that they are being put together with people who have persecuted them in the past and also given treatment no more favourable than that accorded to the defeated enemy." But such treatment would be the most effective deterrent. [39] Rendel, who was to play a key role in formulating Foreign Office policy toward Jewish DPs, was a consistent and ardent supporter of adopting firm measures against them. It was almost axiomatic with him that the Jewish refugees were mere pawns in the hands of the Zionists.

These same views held sway in the Cabinet Overseas Reconstruction Committee, which adopted Rendel's position and, at the end of January 1946, decided to treat Jewish infiltrators on the same basis as German refugees and to allocate them the same reduced food ration. Bevin, who served as chairman of the committee, maintained that most of the Jews who were leaving Poland were doing so for political, namely Zionist, motives.[40] Obsessed with the Palestine problem, the foreign secretary refused to recognize that the exodus of Polish Jews at this time might not be inspired by Zionist agitation. He never bothered to delve deeper into the situation of the Jewish survivors in Poland and never paid much attention to the analysis of his diplomats in Poland on this issue.[41]

Continued pressure from Jewish organizations in Britain and criticism of British policies in the American press led Hynd to announce in Parliament, on 23 January 1946, that he had decided to appoint a Jewish adviser who would assist the British authorities. (In the American occupied zone an adviser for Jewish affairs had already been appointed in August 1945.) [42] But he continued to reject the idea of setting up separate camps, arguing again that the government had no intention of continuing Nazi policy by encouraging the view that the Jews were stateless.[43] In mid-April 1946, the position of adviser for Jewish affairs in Germany went to Colonel Robert Solomon, attorney and past chairman of the Jewish National Fund in Britain. Solomon was to advise on "all matters affecting Jewish persons in Germany" whether or not they were of German origin, and it was part of his responsibility to visit all centers where the Jews were located. He was given the rank of a head of branch in the Prisoners of War and Displaced Persons Division, and he had direct access to the deputy military governor and to Hynd. At his own request, Solomon did not receive a salary for his services.[44]

One could say that with the appointment of Solomon as adviser for Jewish affairs, Britain in effect recognized that there was a common denominator that bound all the Jewish DPs together, including the German Jews, and more or less admitted that the situation of the Jews was unique. If so, it meant a retreat of sorts from its previous position, which demanded that the Jews act through the liaison officers of their countries of origin. Not all British officials were happy with Solomon's appointment. Christopher Steel, the political adviser to Britain's commander in chief in Germany, expressed regret several months later "that a Jew was ever appointed as 'Jewish Adviser.'" Steel was certain that no Jew could be objective about Jewish affairs, and anyone who was not objective could not be expected to advise Whitehall reliably. The political adviser further thought that few Jews would be able to resist pressure from their coreligionists.[45] London, however, hoped that this concession would make it possible to avoid a more substantial capitulation, namely concentrating the Jews in separate camps.

Almost three weeks after his appointment, Solomon submitted a comprehensive plan for resettlement of the relatively small number of sixteen thousand Jews who at this time resided in the British zone in Germany. In his assessment,

Brichah: *Father and his child (Courtesy Israel Ministry of Defense, Museums Unit)*

Brichah: *Resting place (Courtesy Israel Ministry of Defense, Museums Unit)*

most of those whose country of origin was Germany, about five thousand in number, would agree to be resettled there. Of the remaining eleven thousand DPs, one thousand would need to be placed in retirement homes or in welfare institutions. Another thousand could be given immigrant visas to various places, and some of them were ready to leave Germany immediately. Ninety percent of the remaining nine thousand wanted to go to Palestine; of these more than half (65 percent) would not agree to a compromise, while the others, if offered the opportunity to go elsewhere, would do so. Thus the problem of the Jewish DPs in the British zone could be solved by issuing eight thousand immigration certificates to Palestine. Implementation of his program would make it possible to shut down all camps in which Jewish DPs were located, particularly Bergen-Belsen, which Solomon, too, realized was a magnet for Jews arriving from Eastern Europe.[46]

Among other things, Solomon's plan was intended as a response to British apprehensions of a new large-scale influx of Jewish refugees. In the spring of 1946 several hundred Jews from Hungary had made their way into the British zone in Austria. The British Commission in Austria was doubtful that these Jews could be returned to Hungary without the use of force. There was also uncertainty about the reaction of the Soviet authorities through whose zone in Austria the deportees would need to pass. But nondeportation presented the British command with a dilemma: admitting the new arrivals into the camps would encourage further Jewish infiltration, yet refusal to let them into the camps would cause the Jews to become a burden on the Austrian state and a potential menace to security. Of these two alternatives the British command in Austria preferred the risks entailed by barring entry.[47] But the British Control Office for Germany and Austria rejected their position for fear that refusing entry would be interpreted as favoring German refugees over Jewish refugees in Austrian camps under British military administration. The Control Office also opposed forced repatriation of the infiltrators to the countries from which they had fled.[48]

Solomon's plan was enthusiastically received by Hynd. Already under considerable pressure from Jewish organizations and Jewish public figures in Britain, the chancellor was eager to find a quick solution to the problem of Jewish DPs because they were causing difficulties out of all proportion to their relatively small numbers. The problem was that Solomon's plan was dependent on Colonial Office agreement to issue eight thousand immigration certificates to Palestine. At that time, spring and summer of 1946, talks were taking place with the Americans about a solution to the Palestine question and the Colonial Office objected to taking any action that might be interpreted as a change in the Palestine immigration policy. Britain was then allocating a monthly quota of fifteen hundred immigration certificates to Palestine. Moreover, in the summer of 1946 the number of illegal sailings of Jews from Europe to Palestine increased, and the Mandatory government was allocating the entire certificate quota to illegal immigrants who had been arrested on the shores of Palestine.[49]

Under the circumstances, Solomon's plan made no progress, which for the British military authorities meant they were back at square one. Faced with the continuing frictions between Jewish and Polish DPs in Bergen-Belsen, British authorities decided to remove the Polish DPs, with the result that the camp in effect became an exclusively Jewish DP camp.[50] London continued to deny, however, that this meant that Jewish DPs formed a separate category. The Refugee Department in the Foreign Office instructed the Control Office in London to continue classifying the Jews in the official statistical data according to their countries of origin and never to define them as Jews; significantly, in internal statistics the office did ask to classify all Jewish DPs as Jews.[51]

While giving in on the policy of no separate camps, London took vigorous action against Jewish infiltrators. Better weather was bound to bring a renewed influx of Jews from Eastern Europe—the number of Jews who left Poland during June and July 1946 reached about thirty thousand.[52] Most of them headed for the American occupation zones in Germany and Austria, where they were given the status and rights of DPs. According to reports London received at the beginning of August, two thousand Jews had made it into the Bergen-Belsen camp. Anxious to prevent incidents that "would be given great publicity and would be regarded as anti-Jewish policy," the British Control Commission in Germany decided to make no attempt to expel the newcomers by force. It was thought that only arrest or internment of the Jews in German prisons would stop them from returning to the camps.[53] To dissuade would-be infiltrators, it was decided not to allow refugees who had arrived after 1 July 1946 to remain in the DP camps and to allocate food to each camp according to the register of refugees who had been living there before that date.[54]

To the Control Office in London these steps were too moderate to halt the influx of more Jews. The office did not think withholding rations would be much of a deterrent because the Jews would overcome the problem with the help of UNRRA and the Jewish welfare organizations. The British Control Commission in Germany was told to prevent the further entry of Jews into Bergen-Belsen and to consider the possibility of removing those who had already entered the camp illegally and dispersing them throughout Germany.[55] This firm stand fell in line with London's decision at the time to step up its efforts to halt illegal immigration to Palestine. Accordingly, the Mandate government in Palestine began to deport to Cyprus illegal immigrants who had been detained on the coast of Palestine. Previous practice had been to intern such immigrants in Palestine and then to release them against the immigration quota. Part of the context for Whitehall's change of policy was Truman's rejection of the Morrison-Grady Plan, which envisioned provincial autonomy for Palestine, on the one hand, and an intensification of Jewish illegal sailings to Palestine in the summer of 1946, on the other.[56]

For their part, the British military authorities in both Germany and Austria were doubtful that they would be able to cope with a mass influx of Jews. British headquarters in Germany noted that infiltrators had no trouble in moving from the American and Russian zones to the British occupation zone. British headquarters in Austria pointed out that the Soviets were allowing Jews coming from the east to enter Austria without any hindrance and that the Americans were assisting the movement. Both Control Commissions were keenly aware of the obstacles that lay in the way of expelling the refugees back to the countries from which they had come. Headquarters in Germany cited two in particular: first, overland deportees would, at the first opportunity, abandon the train on which they were being transported and infiltrate back again on foot; and second, authorities in the various occupation zones or in neighboring countries would refuse to accept these people on the grounds that they did not originate there. Headquarters in Austria expressed doubts about the possibility of stopping a mass movement by force; employing arms for the purpose was not thought feasible "because of the effect on our troops who would be required to use them and from a political point of view."[57] But British apprehensions proved exaggerated. When winter arrived, it became clear that most Jews were avoiding the British zones, and the Control Office in London realized that arrest and deportation would be unnecessary. But they did endorse the suggestion of the military authorities in Germany to confiscate illegal food surpluses brought into the DP camps and to check which camps were now housing additional Jews.[58]

Withholding Food Rations

The new policy of withholding food rations from the infiltrators did cause severe distress at Bergen-Belsen. The camp's Jewish administration was forced to sustain these refugees from its own limited resources and from the assistance it received from Jewish welfare organizations.[59] On 23 August, Josef Rosensaft appealed to La Guardia, secretary general of UNRRA, to intervene. Rosensaft complained about the attitude not only the British military authorities but also UNRRA were adopting toward the Jewish refugees who had just arrived from

Poland, protesting that these Jews, who had been made to suffer simply because they were Jews, were now being treated as German refugees.[60] A few days earlier, in response to a British statement that Jews arriving from Poland were ineligible for UNRRA assistance, La Guardia had confirmed that UNRRA would continue to assist the Jews unless the UNRRA Central Committee expressly ordered otherwise. According to conservative estimates, he added, between sixty and seventy thousand Jews would flee Poland and as a humanitarian organization UNRRA could not ignore the problem.[61]

La Guardia went further and tried to influence Prime Minister Attlee to alter London's policy toward Jews arriving from Eastern Europe but failed. Attlee rejected La Guardia's request that the refugees be allowed to enter the British occupation zones and be given the same treatment as that extended to the displaced persons. The prime minister did not accept the argument that it was no longer possible for Jews to live in Poland and stressed that any improvement of living conditions in the camps would only swell the flow of refugees. Typically, he added that the exodus of the Jews from Poland was artificial and "engineered largely with a view to forcing our hands over Palestine." [62] Attlee was adamant in his stand, even though he knew that barely two months earlier there had been a pogrom in the Polish town of Kielce during which 41 of the 250 Jews who had settled in the city after the war were murdered; he rejected the analysis of British diplomats in Warsaw that conditions in Poland were intolerable for the Jews and that the pogrom had persuaded even those Jews to flee the country who until then were hesitant about leaving.[63] Like Bevin, Attlee viewed the Jewish DP problem only from the angle of the conflict over Palestine. Both British leaders ignored the human aspect of the issue and refused to acknowledge the difficulties the survivors of the Holocaust would face in their home countries in Eastern Europe.

About this time (August 1946), a press report citing an "Allied military source" claimed that UNRRA was serving as "an umbrella covering Russian secret agents and criminal elements engaging in wholesale dope peddling and smuggling." When an investigation initiated by La Guardia revealed that the "Allied military source" was General Frederick A. Morgan, UNRRA head in Germany, he demanded his resignation. The British general, who had been chief planner of the Allied invasion of Normandy, did not deny that he had spoken with journalists but insisted that his words had been misrepresented.[64] In fact, La Guardia had long wanted an excuse to have Morgan dismissed, among other reasons because of the latter's view that UNRRA was superfluous and that the military could better fulfill the organization's objectives. As Morgan's temporary replacement La Guardia appointed Myer Cohen, chief of the repatriates division in Washington. Publicly it was announced that Morgan's replacement was connected with plans for the reorganization of UNRRA.[65]

Morgan himself ascribed the reasons for his dismissal to the storm that had ensued from a press conference in the beginning of 1946 in which he had argued that European Jews had an organized plan to transfer Jewish immigrants to Palestine.[66] In a report to the British Foreign Office on his actions as head of UNRRA in Germany, Morgan claimed that La Guardia had been anxious to replace him with Cohen, whom he described as "a New York Jew whose qualifications to fill the post even temporarily are, otherwise than from the religious point of view, negligible." Morgan had no doubt that La Guardia was motivated by political ambition. He called the attention of the Foreign Office to "the ambition of the present Director General, himself half Jewish, and his desire to compete for Jewish favour at home in opposition to an opponent who is a pure Jew."[67] In the United States it was being reported at the same time that the Democratic Party was considering nominating La Guardia, who for twelve years had been mayor of New York City, as candidate for the United States Senate in place of Lehman, who had been La Guardia's predecessor in the UNRRA post.[68]

Morgan's dismissal troubled the British Foreign Office because it feared that Jewish circles in New York might persuade La Guardia to replace Morgan with "a prominent New York Jew" who would encourage Jewish immigration to Palestine.[69] A British delegation led by George Rendel was told by Colonel Taylor Wood of the State Department that Washington did not want a British citizen to succeed Morgan because the American public might interpret this as capitulation to British pressure and adoption of an anti-Jewish policy. In response, Rendel countered that American public opinion would be satisfied only if the person appointed by UNRRA did his job along lines acceptable to the Zionists and their supporters in the United States. He asserted that the problem of refugees and displaced persons was not a specifically Jewish problem and that the Jewish question was "extraneous" and had been "injected into this problem artificially." The British government, Rendel emphasized, had no intention of doing anything that would encourage Jews to leave Poland because their departure from that country was being engineered to compel Britain to change its policy in Palestine.[70] The disagreement between Rendel and Wood continued during the meeting of the UNRRA Central Committee in New York. Wood brought up the refusal of the British authorities in Germany to grant DP status to Jewish infiltrators, despite UNRRA decisions to the contrary. From the standpoint of the British government, Rendel explained, these infiltrators did not fall under the aegis of UNRRA, and the British government did not accept their categorization as persons fleeing persecution.[71]

Meanwhile, word spread that there was intense hunger in Bergen-Belsen because the authorities were withholding food from the infiltrators who had taken refuge in the camp. In December 1946 the Control Commission in Germany denied these rumors and estimated the number of Jews illegally living in the camp at three thousand, asserting that "they are not starving to death but they may be short of food. No official rations are drawn for them, but they are fed by other DPs' ration cards and from various other sources, including [the] black market." The Control Commission pointed out that the infiltrators in the camp had been informed by printed notices and loudspeakers that only if they were to leave the camp and went to live among the local German population would they receive food rations equal to those provided to German citizens. None of the infiltrators, the commission stressed, had chosen to take advantage of the transport vehicles put at their disposal to move their possessions.[72] The Control Commission in fact believed that while the Jewish Central Committee reported the population of the camp at a little over eleven thousand, there were at the most eight thousand people living in Bergen-Belsen, implying that Rosensaft was drawing DP rations for three thousand more people than were in the camp.[73]

Attempts by Jewish organizations to convince the British authorities to change their policies toward the Jewish infiltrators remained unsuccessful. Hynd explained that a change in policy would encourage many new refugees (not only Jews) to flood the camps and would prevent Britain from more quickly resolving the problem of the DPs by repatriation or resettlement. It would also prevent the British authorities from continuing to maintain the current standard of living in the camps.[74] In an effort to break the impasse, Rosensaft suggested, in January 1947, that the 1,868 infiltrators who, he claimed, still remained in Bergen-Belsen be given the same food rations as those allotted to the Germans without requiring them to leave the camp. Rosensaft argued that most of the infiltrators were old and sick; in the case of younger families, the women were pregnant or parents who wanted their children to attend the camp schools. As chairman of the committee, he assured the British that he would continue his efforts to convince the unauthorized residents to move to the areas to which they had been assigned and that he would work to prevent an increase in the number of infiltrators. Solomon, who supported Rosensaft's proposal, maintained that Rosensaft was doing his best to prevent more infiltrators from arriving at Bergen-Belsen and that anyway these people were very unpopular in the camp because they took up part of the rations provided for the genuine DP population.[75]

The Control Office in London was receptive to Rosensaft's suggestion. Hynd explained to Deputy Military Governor General Robertson that he wished to solve this problem as it threatened to strain relations with the Jewish community in Britain. The chancellor also wished to put an end to the frictions that had arisen with UNRRA following the organization's insistence that it should be allowed to supply food to the infiltrators.[76] In a memorandum to the Cabinet Overseas Reconstruction Committee, which had the final decision in the matter, Hynd wrote, "This is not an agreeable policy to administer because many of the 'infiltrees' can undoubtedly show that they suffered from persecution, and rightly or wrongly, they fear discrimination if injected into the German community. Few of them speak German, and in Höne they can find friends, synagogues and all the advantages of a Jewish community."[77] The committee, meeting on 23 April 1947 in the presence of the prime minister, did not take long to endorse Rosensaft's proposal, on condition that the camp leaders commit themselves to preventing the infiltration of new refugees.[78] But by that time there was already hardly any infiltration of Jews into the British zone.

Operative steps were agreed upon between Rosensaft and representatives of the Prisoners of War and Displaced Persons Division of the Control Commission.[79] Contacts between them were made possible following the Cabinet Overseas Reconstruction Committee's April decision, which also accorded recognition to the Jewish Committee of Bergen-Belsen and to Rosensaft as its spokesman. The initiative to do so had come from Hynd, who hoped to relieve the tension between the DP leadership in the British zone and the Control Commission. The chancellor agreed to recognize the Jewish committee in Bergen-Belsen as representing the entire camp and to accord similar recognition to all the committees in the various camps in the British zone as well as to a committee that would represent German Jews as a whole. But he continued to oppose recognizing the Bergen-Belsen committee as representing all Jews in the British zone.[80] Two years had elapsed between the time the Jewish committee had begun operating in Bergen-Belsen and its official recognition by the British authorities.

Though satisfied with this achievement, Rosensaft continued his efforts for recognition of the Central Jewish Committee as the representative of all Jewish DPs, including the German Jews.[81] In this he was aided by Member of Parliament Silverman, who broached the issue with Lord Francis A. Pakenham, who had succeeded Hynd in mid-April 1947. The new lord chancellor did not think the time ripe, especially as it was government policy to encourage the German

Jews to resettle in Germany—for London, reintegration of the German Jews in Germany worked to discredit the Zionist claim that the Jews could not rehabilitate their lives in Europe. Neither could he ignore the vigorous opposition of the military authorities in Germany to any change in the status of the Jewish committee or of Rosensaft. Army personnel in the British zone of Germany were scrupulous in avoiding the impression that the authority of the Bergen-Belsen committee extended beyond the boundaries of the camp.[82] Lord Pakenham's refusal to recognize the Central Jewish Committee of Bergen-Belsen as representing all Jewish DPs in the British zone in Germany by this time was more symbolic than practical: according to data from April 1947, of the 12,232 DPs in the British zone, 10,346 lived in Bergen-Belsen; the remainder were scattered among nine smaller camps.[83] In other words, it was merely one more expression of Britain's policy to deny the separate national existence of the Jewish DPs.

Separating German Jews from Jewish Displaced Persons

From the outset, the guidelines of the Supreme Command of the Western Allies entitled the German Jews to the same treatment as DPs from Allied countries because they were included in the category of nationals of enemy or former enemy nations who had been persecuted for reasons of race or religion or for activities in support of the Allies.[84] This principle, along with the Allies' suspension of all German legislation that discriminated against the Jews, was intended to help the German Jews resettle in Germany; British military authorities in Germany believed that no preferential treatment should be given to German Jews. Following complaints of Eva Reading that the Jews were treated by the British authorities along the same lines as the general German population, Lieutenant General Ronald Weeks, then deputy military governor of the British occupied zone in Germany, defended this policy, stating that "if we had attempted to exclude the Jews on the score of their sufferings, it would be equally logical to exclude all other Germans who had suffered at the hands of the Nazis." Except for those who had been found in concentration camps, German Jews, Weeks insisted, were treated like all other Germans. The former category were cared for by the military government in the same way as other inmates of these camps. When their health was sufficiently restored, they were allowed to return to their homes in Germany.[85]

Henderson, of the Foreign Office, disagreed with this policy. He maintained in mid-September 1945 that German Jews still living in the camps, as well as those living among the civilian population who could prove that they had been persecuted by the Nazis, should be given the same ration as that allotted to

Allied DPs. He rejected the argument that bestowing such treatment on Jews in the British zone would increase anti-Semitism among the Germans. As he put it, "The great majority of Germans will always be bitter anti-semites, and it would be salutary for them to see that our victory had brought an obvious improvement in the lot of victims of the late German government." [86]

Henderson's position, however, could not carry the day. London's desire to induce the German Jews to resettle in Germany clashed at times with policies of the military authorities, who wanted to encourage the Germans to take responsibility for their own lives and their own affairs. Thus, for example, General Robertson refused to allow German Jews who were being discriminated against by German officials with a Nazi background to complain to British military officers. Robertson felt that frequent intervention on the part of the military authorities in such cases was liable to defeat military government policy.[87] Similarly, the Control Office for Germany and Austria would not exempt German Jews from payment of taxes on the grounds that uniform treatment without discrimination was the cardinal principle of tax collection policy and that according preference on a racial basis "is really the converse of the Nazi policy and would scarcely assist the restoration of good relations between Jewish and non-Jewish inhabitants of Germany." [88] Furthermore, although the military authorities agreed that it would be desirable to return both private and community property to German Jews, they argued that there were too many practical difficulties for this to happen in the near future.[89]

At the end of December 1946, in the wake of increasing complaints by Jewish representatives about the attitude of the military authorities toward German Jews in the British zone, whom he called "highly sensitive" to the point of being in a "hysterical state," Hynd appealed to Robertson to respond sympathetically. Robertson was asked to treat them with great tact and to do his best to create an atmosphere of mutual understanding instead of the existing suspicion and mistrust. In particular, Hynd stressed the importance of dispelling the sense prevalent among German Jews that whatever they requested would automatically be rejected.[90] In a comprehensive report to the Cabinet Overseas Reconstruction Committee at the end of his assignment in April 1947, Hynd outlined the efforts that were being made to help German Jews resettle in their country. He noted the abrogation of discriminatory anti-Jewish legislation and also that German Jews who had been in concentration camps were accorded certain preferences in acquiring housing, employment, and food allocations. As to his efforts to work out a plan for returning Jewish property, he emphasized that everything possible had been done to minimize the difficulties in resettling the German Jews. Hynd recommended continuing to treat the German Jews as a separate community from the Jewish DPs and according official recognition to the committee that had been established by German Jews in the British zone.[91]

As it turned out, sensitivity on the part of the military authorities to avoid antagonizing the German population and the determination to separate the Jewish DPs from the German Jews only harmed the latter, who were dependent on the German authorities. The Control Commission for Germany, viewing the Jews as a cultural community and not a separate nationality, agreed to common operation between the two communities only in the field of spiritual welfare. Such an arrangement, it was maintained, would be in harmony with the principles of "treating Jews as a religious sect and not as a nationality."[92]

The number of German Jews in the British zone remained virtually unchanged and at the end of 1947 was put at five thousand. Altogether, noted Solomon in a detailed memorandum he submitted in November, there were thirty-seven communities, most of which were very small: only by restoring the foundations of Jewish community life would it be possible to convince Jews to remain in Germany and to induce other German Jews to return. The German Jews, he said, had not recovered from the shock of persecution and were understandably very apprehensive over what the German economy held in store for them. Many might indeed be persuaded to remain in Germany, but "as things stand at present, they are easily influenced by vigorous leaders of the foreign Jews who are absolutely determined that Germany is not a safe or proper place within which a Jew can be advised to begin his life anew." As a result, the situation of the Jewish DPs was much better than that of German Jews. Solomon concluded his report by stressing that the latter would agree to remain in the country if they felt that "their recent history is being taken into accord."[93]

British military authorities in Germany thought differently. They believed that it was in the best interests of the German Jews themselves to be treated as Germans. "If we were to grant them extra privileges by reason of their faith persecution would inevitably commence as soon as our protection was withdrawn." They must therefore "be treated in exactly the same way as other Germans who have suffered persecution at the hands of the Nazis."[94] While refusing to give German Jews preferential treatment or to protect them in case of discrimination by German officials, the military authorities demonstrated great sensitivity regarding the suggested representative and spokesman of the Union of Jewish Communities in the British zone of Germany. They considered Norbert Wollheim, vice-chair of the Central Jewish Committee at Bergen-Belsen, and regarded by the Jews and Solomon as the natural candidate, as not suitable for the post because he was a confirmed Zionist and an advocate of immigration. "So long as he holds these views," Major General V. J. E. Westropp, deputy of chief of staff (policy) maintained in mid-January 1948, "he could not properly represent German Jews, whom it is hoped will take up their rightful place in the community again."[95] Only when he understood that "Wollheim is not such a rabid Zionist as he appears to be" and, although anxious to leave Germany eventually, did not seem to care "whether he goes ultimately to Palestine or elsewhere," did Westropp agree to accept Wollheim as the representative of the German Jews.[96]

From the British point of view, resettlement of the German Jews in Germany had a significance that went beyond the confines of the immediate problem. It fell in line with the Labour government's insistence on dissociating the problem of the Jews in Europe from the question of Palestine. Ignoring the Jewish DPs' demand for recognition as part of a single, distinct nation was an integral part of the British government's anti-Zionist policy, which can be traced back to 1938, when the British Conservative government withdrew its support from partitioning Palestine into a Jewish and an Arab state and from the Balfour Declaration. Opposition of the Jewish DPs in Bergen-Belsen, led by Rosensaft with the aid of the Jewish organizations in Britain, and the sensitivity demonstrated by the White House and the American press to the plight of Jewish refugees in the British zones of occupation may have induced the British authorities to compromise in implementing their policies—but when it came to principle, they remained steadfast. Only thus can we explain why as late as October 1947, the Foreign Office could still instruct the British UN delegation "to separate the Jewish refugee problem from the Palestine question and to submerge it in the general refugee problem."[97]

COUNTERING ILLEGAL IMMIGRATION

Debating a Policy

Jewish illegal immigration to Palestine had begun already before World War II. Between 1938 and the outbreak of the war more than 17,000 *ma'apilim* (Hebrew term for Jewish immigrants) had arrived in Palestine. The last *ma'apilim* ships to reach Palestine for the entire war period were the *Pacific*, the *Milos*, and the *Atlantic* that had sailed from Rumania in November 1940.[1] Only after the Russian victories in southeastern Europe in the autumn of 1944 and Rumania's switch to the Allied side could illegal immigration from the Balkans resume. Reports from British diplomats in Rumania at the end of 1944 and the beginning of 1945 spoke of 150,000 impoverished and homeless Jews gathered there and of more than 100,000 Jews who were registered with the Jewish Agency for immigration to Palestine. The year before, the Colonial Office had given its commitment to the Jewish Agency that it would allow Jews who had somehow made it to Turkey to continue their journey to Palestine. This was canceled in October 1944, and in December, Britain also withdrew a guarantee it had given the Turkish government to ensure shelter for Jewish refugees reaching Turkey.[2]

At the end of the war, the Mandatory government still retained 10,938 immigration certificates of the 75,000 that had been allotted by the White Paper of May 1939. A British offer to give out of 1,500 visas per month to be charged against the remaining White Paper certificates was rejected by the Jewish Agency, which demanded that 100,000 Jews be allowed to enter Palestine.[3] This demand, in turn, was firmly opposed by London. The Cabinet Committee on

Palestine recommended continuing the immigration policy of the White Paper for the interim period, that is, between the end of the quota and publication of the long-term policy then under preparation, while trying to bring the Arab governments to agree to continued Jewish immigration at the rate of 1,500 persons per month.[4] The latter was important because British representatives in Arab countries were warning London that a continuing Jewish immigration without Arab consent was likely "to result in a wave of hostility throughout the Arab countries, spreading to the Moslems of India and threatening Great Britain's whole position in the Middle East."[5] Lawrence B. Grafftey-Smith, the British minister in Jedda, for example, warned Bevin that asking King Ibn Saud to acquiesce in further immigration would immediately prompt a meeting of the Arab League (founded in March 1945 and consisting of most Arab heads of state) "with the risk of taking mass temperature and some patriotic out-bidding of one country by another."[6] Reports from India, too, told the Foreign Office of the great interest there in the future of Palestine and that lead articles in both Muslim and Hindu papers opposed Zionism and supported the Arab cause.[7] Abd al-Rahman Azzam, secretary general of the Arab League, suggested during his visit to London in October 1945 that the Arab countries might be willing to admit Jewish refugees if Britain and the United States followed a similar course.[8] Azzam, of course, wanted to prevent Jewish refugees from reaching Palestine.

Meanwhile, the commanders in chief in the Middle East and the Mandatory government in Palestine were deliberating what countermeasures they ought to take against the expected renewal of illegal sailings. They envisaged moving on two levels: one, operative actions dependent on the capabilities of Britain itself; and the other, diplomatic efforts to enlist the cooperation and assistance of other governments.[9] Naturally there were differences of opinion. The commanders in chief in the Middle East were in favor of taking preventive measures in the ports of embarkation because once illegal immigrant boats had set sail it would be much more difficult to stop them and prevent them from landing on the shores of Palestine.[10] For his part, the commander of the British fleet, Admiral Andrew Cunningham, believed that this was impossible and that it was better to let the boats go but then to subtract the number of illegal immigrants from the monthly quota of certificates.[11] Each side, not surprisingly, tried to place the burden on the other. In early October, the commander in chief of the British forces in the Middle East, General Bernard C. Paget, suggested allowing small boats that had managed to evade the navy and had reached the shores of Palestine to unload their passengers under British supervision at one of the Palestinian ports while deducting the number of immigrants from the certificate quota but, at the same time, deporting passengers of large ships that had been intercepted to Cyprus (where he thought it would be possible to detain up to twelve hundred people).[12] Cyprus at the time was under British rule.

At the Foreign Office it was again George Rendel who came up with the bleak forecast that illegal immigrant sailings would "increase the risk of trouble and bloodshed in Palestine" and would throw the "whole system of regular immigration out of gear." He did not think it was a good idea to rely on the governments of the countries from which the illegal immigrants would be coming. From his experience in Bulgaria, where he had served at the beginning of the war, he argued that few European governments were capable of preventing the embarkation of people from inside their borders. Forcing the boats back to their ports of embarkation was more effective. The way Rendel saw it, if two or three were sent back, this would serve as a deterrent for the movement's organizers. As Jewish DPs were mere pawns in the hands of the Zionists in their struggle against Britain in Palestine, there was little reason to hesitate in taking extreme measures since, in any case, Britain would be severely criticized by the Zionists, who were encouraging immigration to Palestine of European Jews by all possible means.[13]

At first the Colonial Office also favored taking extreme measures against the illegal sailings. Well aware of the negative significance the Arabs attached to Jewish immigration, senior officials were disturbed by the possibility that the illegal immigration could develop into a mass movement, with the Zionists taunting the Mandatory government by publicizing their successes. General Alan Gordon Cunningham, then British high commissioner in Palestine, did not share the fears of the Colonial Office. He thought the measures proposed for combating the immigration were exaggerated because the number of persons involved was small and could easily be deducted from the certificate quota. In effect, until that time—mid-November 1945—all told only 569 *ma'apilim* in six sailings had reached Palestinian shores. Nor did British officials in Palestine think much of the Colonial Office's plan to stop all "suspicious" boats in open sea and force them to sail to Cyprus if they had illegal immigrants on board who would then be deported back to their point of embarkation. The reaction of the Yishuv to the deportation of Jews from Cyprus, they argued, would be no less extreme than if they had been deported from Palestine. Moreover, there was always the fear of more calamities, as in the case of the *Patria* and the *Struma*. It would be better to confiscate the vessels and punish the captains and owners.[14]

The Mandatory government's opposition to taking severe steps against illegal immigrants stemmed largely from fears of reprisals by the Yishuv. The Palestine government had already more than once felt the sting of operations carried out by the Haganah, the Irgun (Hebrew: Irgun Zvai Leumi, "National Military Organization," headed by Menahem Begin), and LHI, which between October 1945 and July 1946 cooperated under a common command, the Hebrew Resistance Movement. During the "Night of the Trains" at the end of October 1945, for example, railroad tracks throughout the country as well as the central railroad station in Lod had been sabotaged together with three boats of the Coast Guard in the ports of Haifa and Jaffa. British officials in Palestine wanted to prevent the situation from escalating, especially since until that time illegal immigration had been very limited.[15] That they had a point is shown by the attack on two British police stations in Givat Olga and Sidna-'Ali by Palmach units in reprisal for the detention on 22 November 1945 of twenty *ma'apilim*.[16]

When the Colonial Office ultimately adopted the position of the Palestine government, that is, to deduct illegal immigrants from the immigration quota, this policy presupposed the existence of such an immigration quota. Toward the end of 1945, only four hundred certificates remained in the White Paper quota, but no decision was in sight on policy regarding further Jewish immigration to Palestine.[17] Whitehall had asked the Arab countries to agree to continued Jewish immigration into Palestine until the report of the Anglo-American Committee (AAC) was published.[18] Since none of the Arab countries had responded with explicit agreement, the cabinet decided to approach them once again, now pointing out that immigration would be limited to first-degree relatives of Jews already in Palestine.[19] Meanwhile, nine hundred illegal immigrants who had sailed from Italy on the *Enzio Sereni* had been intercepted and were being held in the detention camp in Atlit because of the certificate quota problem. Because the Jewish underground might try to free the illegal immigrants by force (there had been one such successful attempt in October 1945), Arthur Creech Jones, then under secretary at the Colonial Office and not unsympathetic to the Zionist cause, urged Bevin not to wait for a reply from the Arab countries but to implement Whitehall's decision of 1 January 1946 to grant a monthly quota of fifteen hundred certificates. In summarizing the Arab stand, Creech Jones maintained that although no state individually nor the Arab League collectively had officially rejected the immigration proposal, no one was prepared to take responsibility for giving a definite reply. If the League was approached again, he warned, it was likely "that an evasive reply will again be received." Knowing that Bevin had set his hopes on the AAC, Creech Jones warned him that a Zionist attack on the detention camp in Atlit could result in casualties, in which case the committee might cancel its plans to visit Palestine. As a way out of the impasse, Whitehall decided to continue a monthly quota of fifteen hundred certificates for three months beginning on 15 December 1945, the day the White Paper quota allocation had come to an end. Meanwhile, the AAC was to complete its inquiry and submit its recommendations.[20]

The Arab press in Palestine increasingly mocked the British for their inability to prevent Jewish immigration. Editorials argued that "ships could not approach Palestine through the screen of aircraft and naval vessels without the consent of the British, and that there is a deep-laid plot to give the Jews their head, while all the outward appearances of opposing them are maintained."[21] According to Lord Killearn, British ambassador to Egypt, the Egyptian prime minister had the clear impression that illegal Jewish immigration was proceeding on a considerable scale, as shown by his estimation by the end of January 1946 that a total of six thousand Jewish immigrants had arrived illegally.[22] Actually, fewer than two thousand illegal immigrants had by then arrived in Palestine.[23]

By this time it was clear that Italy and Greece would provide little assistance in the struggle against illegal embarkation. Together with Arab complaints of British impotence, this led the British commanders in chief in the Middle East at the end of February 1946 to recommend reassessing the tactics against illegal immigration. They argued that current measures were not sufficient deterrent: every illegal immigrant knew that from the moment he or she boarded a boat for Palestine, eventual entry into the country was assured, either illegally or as part of the certificate quota; moreover, because of the financial inducements they were offered, ship captains and owners were ready to ignore the risks involved. The commanders suggested a two-pronged policy: first, as much as possible to act in concert with the Italian, Greek, and Turkish governments to cut off embarkation at the source; and second, to deport back to their ports of departure all illegal immigrants, who would be apprehended. The latter action, it was hoped, would encourage countries from which illegal immigrants had been sailing to increase their vigilance against the unlawful movements of people within their jurisdiction. The recommendation called for deportation of the illegal immigrants first to detention camps outside Palestine, for example Cyprus, and from there to the ports of embarkation.[24]

The Colonial Office, well aware of how the Yishuv would react, vigorously opposed this proposal. Moreover, acting decisively against organizers of the illegal immigration to Palestine required a policy decision in principle vis-à-vis the Jewish Agency and directed at disarming the Jews. Colonial Office official Trafford Smith suggested that as long as the report of the AAC had not been published and assessed, it was best to avoid a serious crisis in Palestine that was likely to bring riots and bloodshed. If in the future it were decided to take vigorous action against the Jewish Agency and the illegal Jewish organizations affiliated with it, that would be the right time to weigh taking steps against the illegal Jewish activity in Europe. In most cases, the Colonial Office official added, the sea voyage was the last stage in a long and arduous process that for most had begun somewhere in Central Europe and involved illegal border crossings from one country into another. The countries from which the illegal immigrants sailed would object to taking them back because these were not their own citizens but people who had illegally crossed their borders. Similarly, the suggestion to return the illegal immigrants to their countries of origin was dismissed as impractical: no one knew where these Jews, who had wandered across more than half of Europe before managing to set sail for Palestine, had originally came from. Neither would the situation in Cyprus allow moving the illegal immigrants to the island as an intermediate step before deporting them to their port of embarkation.[25]

To a large extent, as long as negotiations with the Americans on a comprehensive solution of the Palestine question were in progress, London preferred not to take extreme action against the illegal immigration. But doing so required that the number of illegal immigrants detained by the Palestinian government not surpass the monthly quota of certificates. In May, however, the number of *ma'apilim* already exceeded the quota following the arrival of two ships that had sailed from Italy (the *Eliahu Golumb* and the *Dov Hoz*) and one from Rumania (the *Max Nordau*).[26] The Colonial Office advised detaining the illegal immigrants in camps in Palestine and releasing them against the quotas allotted in the following months. Cunningham remained apprehensive of the possible reaction of the Yishuv and of attempts to free the illegal immigrants by force. Still, the Colonial Office insisted that because of the temporary uncertainty regarding future policy, every effort should be made to persist in the present policy.[27] At the same time, the British and the Americans were trying to overcome their differences about the AAC's recommendations.[28]

The chiefs of staff, concerned about the extra burden the military would have to carry as a result of the escalation of the illegal immigration and the need to hold the illegal immigrants in detention camps (at a time when the Palestine police force was understaffed by about 50 percent), urged the Colonial Office to reconsider its opposition to deportation of the illegal immigrants to a British occupation zone.[29] The Colonial Office, supported by the high commissioner, opposed the idea because of the reaction it was expected to provoke in the Yishuv. It was argued, furthermore, that the burden that would fall on the army if the illegal immigrants were deported would much extend beyond the task of guarding the detention camps. George Gater, permanent under secretary in the Colonial Office, warned of the probable political consequences in the United States if the illegal immigrants were deported to Tobruk, for example. Britain, he stressed, would be accused of transferring the Jews from one concentration camp, in Europe, to another, in North Africa. Gater mentioned Tobruk as a deportation site since Cyprus, on the advice of the governor of the island, would probably have to be ruled out as an option.[30]

Deportations to Cyprus

In the course of the summer of 1946 the British were confronted with a complicated situation. The pace of *Ha'apala* arrivals significantly increased while the security situation in Palestine was deteriorating, and on the diplomatic front discussions with the Americans on a solution to the Palestine question reached a critical stage. As it attached great importance to the formulation of a joint American-British policy for a solution of the Palestine question, the cabinet preferred to avoid taking more severe measures against the illegal immigrants so as not to jeopardize the discussions with the Americans. Military elements, however, warned of the dangers Britain could expect in Palestine, possibly in the entire Middle East, if no vigorous action was taken against the illegal immigration. For its part, the Mandatory government was having serious difficulties coping with the waves of illegal immigrants that were now arriving. The Atlit solution was no longer effective because the significant increase in the number of illegal immigrants forced the authorities to fill quotas several months ahead. In early July, the high commissioner called the attention of the Colonial Office to the severe lack of certificates as a result of the detention of three vessels within less than a month (the *Haviva Reik,* the *Josiah Wedgewood,* and the *Biriya*). Moreover, in the course of the sweeping arrests the British had made on "Black Saturday" (29 June 1946), approximately twenty-seven hundred Jews had been detained.[31]

On 11 July 1946, on the recommendation of Colonial Secretary George Hall, who mentioned the difficulties likely to arise on the island and his fears of another incident like the *Patria,* the cabinet decided not to deport illegal immigrants to Cyprus.[32] Almost certainly the arrival of Henry F. Grady at the head of an American delegation for discussions on the AAC's report also influenced the decision. Meanwhile, tension in Palestine further increased following the bombing of the King David Hotel (22 July 1946) for which Irgun claimed responsibility and in which, among others, forty-one Arabs had been killed.[33] Fearing Arab reaction, High Commissioner Cunningham advised stopping the immigration to Palestine altogether, proposing that vessels carrying illegal im-

*Ma'apilim at Haifa port following capture by the British, June 1946
(Courtesy Yad Vashem, Jerusalem)*

migrants that had set out from areas under Western control be returned to their points of embarkation and that ships arriving from Balkan ports, under Russian control, be sent to Tripoli or to Cyprus. As he saw it, confrontation with the Yishuv following deportation of illegal immigrants was inevitable, and the clash might as well occur sooner rather than later. Cunningham pointed out that subsequent to their arrival a large portion of the illegal immigrants joined underground organizations, especially Irgun and LHI, and added that there was good reason to believe that when allotting places on illegal immigrant vessels preference went to past "guerrilla fighters." [34]

At its meeting on 25 July, Sir Norman Brook, head of the British delegation negotiating with the Americans on the report of the AAC, was able to tell the cabinet that the American delegation had agreed to adopt the provincial autonomy plan for Palestine (the so-called Morrison-Grady Plan), which the British favored. The ministers did not wish to jeopardize this important achievement by taking anti-immigration measures that might irritate Washington and arouse American public opinion. Moreover, the problem of illegal immigration was expected to come to an end with the implementation of the Morrison-Grady Plan, which provided for the entry of one hundred thousand Jewish displaced persons. Thus cabinet members rejected the high commissioner's advice to halt immigration to Palestine and did not even discuss the idea of deporting the illegal immigrants.[35]

Within days, however, the cabinet was forced to review its position when the *Haganah,* which had sailed from Yugoslavia with almost twenty-seven hundred illegal immigrants on board, was detained. There were also reports that five hundred illegal immigrants were scheduled to arrive on another ship soon afterward. The cabinet was inclined to accept the advice of Attlee, then at the Peace Conference in Paris, to let the women and children go free and detain the men for an unlimited period of time, provided he was first told of the warning the chiefs of staff were sounding of the dangers Britain could expect if it became involved in incidents with Arabs and Jews simultaneously. The military stressed that confrontation with both sides would require reinforcing troops in Palestine, which ran counter to the plan to demobilize military personnel.[36] But Attlee persisted in his position even after being informed of Cunningham's warning that it would be impossible to hold additional illegal immigrants in Palestine and that, if more ships arrived, the situation would become intolerable.[37] The prime minister preferred to avoid taking any drastic action before Truman had made up his mind about the Morrison-Grady Plan.

Attlee was absent at the next cabinet meeting, on 30 July, when heavy pressure by both the military and civilian authorities in Palestine tipped the scales in favor of a decision to deport illegal immigrants to Cyprus before they landed in Palestine. Ministers heard a report by Sir John Shaw, first secretary of the Palestine government, on expected Arab reactions if illegal immigration continued. The chiefs of staff vigorously supported the deportation of all illegal immigrants to Cyprus, and the colonial secretary indicated that it would be possible to hold them there. Only because the prime minister was not present did the cabinet postpone a final decision.[38] At a cabinet meeting two days later, Attlee explained that deportation of illegal immigrants might cause further incidents that could only embarrass the British government. Still, he did not categorically rule out deportation, probably because on 30 July the American cabinet had put off its decision about the Morrison-Grady Plan.[39] The colonial secretary told the cabinet of the arrival of yet another vessel (the *Hehayal Ha'ivri*, "The Hebrew Soldier") with five hundred illegal immigrants on board and that another two thousand illegal immigrants were estimated to be en route to Palestine. He also mentioned that it would be possible to detain some eight to nine thousand Jews on Cyprus. Though, again, it did not come to a definite decision, the cabinet this time instructed the commander in chief in the Middle East to prepare plans for the deportation of illegal immigrants to Cyprus and the colonial secretary to complete preparations for their reception there.[40]

The formal decision to deport illegal immigrants to Cyprus was taken on 7 August, under pressure from military elements and government authorities in Palestine. The ministers were told that the only way to prevent an Arab uprising and a war with both Arabs and Jews was to deport all illegal immigrants. Furthermore, British military authorities in Palestine were ready to implement the deportation and prepared for the expected adverse reaction of the Yishuv. Foreign Office officials put forth another argument. To obtain Arab approval of the Morrison-Grady Plan, it was necessary to convince them that Britain was willing and able to carry out its obligations. "How can they have any faith in us," they asked rhetorically, "if we show that we are unable to control illegal immigration?"[41] The cabinet, still hoping that Truman would decide to implement the Morrison-Grady Plan, delayed announcing and implementing the deportation policy until the president had made a final decision. By that time, there were 2,252 illegal immigrant detainees in the camp at Atlit, another 2,232 were being held on the deck of a boat in the port of Haifa, and yet another 2,500 were already on their way to Palestine.[42]

Whitehall's hopes quickly vanished. On 12 August, Truman explained that "in view of opposition in this country" to the Morrison-Grady Plan, he was unable to support it.[43] The following day, London published its new policy of deporting illegal immigrants to Cyprus. The announcement sharply criticized the illegal immigration, stating that it was not a spontaneous manifestation on the part of Jews who saw Palestine as their only hope but a highly organized movement financed largely by Zionist sources and led by "unscrupulous people" who were disobeying the laws of many countries and exploiting the distress of Jewish refugees to further their own political aims in Palestine. Because some illegal immigrants were joining terrorist organizations in Palestine, the statement also blamed them for exacerbating the tension between Jews and Arabs in the country. The announcement clearly specified that the illegal immigrants would be held in detention camps in Cyprus while their future was being decided.[44] The very next day, 754 illegal immigrants who had arrived from France on the *Yagur* and another 536 who had arrived from Greece on the *Henrietta Szold* were deported to Cyprus.[45]

On the same day that Whitehall decided on deportation, Abd al-Rahman Azzam told the British ambassador in Cairo, Ronald I. Campbell, of the concern of the Arab League at the growing traffic of Jewish illegal immigrants. The majority of the illegal immigrants on these ships, he contended, "are not aged and helpless refugees but picked young men obviously chosen to provide recruits for the Jewish armed forces." There was no doubt in his mind that the British government could stop this traffic or at least reduce it to insignificant proportions. Although it might be difficult to prevent illegal immigrants from departing Europe for Palestine, Azzam maintained, "it is neither necessary nor just to allow ships intercepted en route to Palestine to complete their journey into Palestinian territorial waters and land their passengers." It was the British government's responsibility "to take all steps in their power to prevent the illegal immigrants from landing in Palestine and to arrange that such immigrants be given asylum elsewhere."[46] Britain's pronouncement on deportations to Cyprus was received with satisfaction, albeit cautiously, in the Arab countries. Palestinian Arabs, however, were more suspicious: if the British government was sincere in its intentions, it should have decided to deport the Jews somewhere much farther than Cyprus, particularly back to the countries from which they had embarked. Cyprus, as Palestinian Arabs correctly saw it, was but another springboard for Jewish immigration to Palestine.[47]

In many respects Britain's decision on deportation to Cyprus marked a watershed. Had it not been for the government's concern, before Truman's decision on the Morrison-Grady Plan, to keep Anglo-American contacts focused on a common solution to the Palestine question, the decision to deport the Jews to Cyprus would have been taken even sooner. There had also been the dramatic increase during the summer of 1946 of *Ha'apala* activities and Whitehall's apprehension of the Arab reaction these would provoke. "Black Saturday" may also have been a factor for it revealed the weakness of the Jewish community and for the British broke down a psychological barrier that stopped them from adopting severe measures against the Yishuv and its leadership. By the end of summer 1946, the two main factors that help explain British restraint vis-à-vis illegal Jewish immigration — apprehension of the reaction of Truman and of American public opinion and fear of possible reprisal on the part of the Yishuv — had lost their deterrent effect. The bombing of the King David Hotel in

July had also made it easier for the military to convince the cabinet that harsher measures against the illegal immigration were necessary if Britain did not want the situation to become more dangerous.

Deportation of the illegal immigrants to Cyprus did nothing, however, to limit the scope of the illegal immigration, while the shortage of internment facilities quickly became a troublesome burden. In its discussions on deportation to Cyprus, the cabinet never actually dwelled on the question of how to cope with detaining tens of thousands of illegal immigrants outside Palestine.[48] Perhaps the explanation of why this increasingly vexatious problem was initially ignored can partly be found in Cunningham's statement, several months later, that when the decision was taken, no one expected that deportation would continue for more than six months.[49]

Soon it became clear that the original plan, which foresaw the detention of ten thousand persons, was inadequate. Asked to look into the possibility of enlarging the capacity of the detention camps to twenty thousand, Sir Charles Wooly, the governor of Cyprus, warned of the negative reaction that could be expected from the local population and added that he did not want to see the island transformed into a detention camp for unlimited numbers of illegal immigrants. He set the maximum number of detainees who could be kept on the island at fifteen thousand.[50] Cyrenaica and Tripoli were suggested as alternative locations. The main disadvantage, of course, was that the distance between Haifa and Benghazi (in Cyrenaica) was five times that between Haifa and Cyprus and the distance to Tripoli was seven times greater. Royal Navy vessels were needed to accompany the deportations to Benghazi, so fewer ships would be patrolling the shores of Palestine, enabling many more illegal immigrants to land in Palestine, which in turn would increase Arab anxieties.[51] After a detailed survey, the chiefs of staff concluded that for both administrative and safety purposes it would be preferable to increase the capacity of the camps in Cyprus to twenty thousand rather than diverting illegal immigrants to other destinations.[52]

Detaining Jewish immigrants in Libya was firmly opposed by the Foreign Office. Recalling the anti-Jewish eruption that had occurred in November 1945 in Tripoli, Charles W. Baxter, head of the Eastern Department, Foreign Office, argued that sending illegal immigrants there would sabotage the attempts of the British military authorities in Libya (previously an Italian colony and at the time under British administration) to persuade the Arabs to agree to continued British control. Baxter believed that since British rule in Libya was temporary and the future of the country was to be decided in international negotiations, a concentration of Jewish illegal immigrants there might provoke criticism of the British on the part of various governments, especially the USSR, which was increasingly interested in weakening the British position in the region and in gaining favor in the Arab countries.[53] Cunningham also rejected the idea, maintaining that the reaction of the Jews to deportation of the illegal immigrants to Arab Tripoli would be more extreme than if they were deported to a British colony. He advocated deportation to a colony in Kenya, even though he was aware of the expected opposition to this site because of its distance from Palestine (it took a month to sail to Kenya and back as compared with one day and a half for Cyprus).[54]

One month after deportations to Cyprus had begun, no alternative internment location had been agreed on, and the governor of Cyprus was forced to agree to increase the capacity of the camps on the island to twenty thousand. Wooly made his agreement conditional on a commitment that when immigration to Palestine was renewed, illegal immigrants detained in Cyprus would receive top priority.[55] At the beginning of October 1946, Philip Mitchell, governor of Kenya, was asked by the Colonial Office to arrange for illegal immigrants to be held in Kenya as soon as the camps in Cyprus were full. Mitchell strongly opposed the idea, arguing that Kenya's economic situation precluded such activity while also maintaining a large military base in the country. In view of Britain's strategic plans in Africa, he continued, the introduction of a Jewish problem into East Africa would be an act lacking in political wisdom. Furthermore, it might well cause a confrontation between Britain and the powerful and influential Jewish community in South Africa. Mitchell, however, also injected a racial element into the argument by saying that in light of the difficult social and agrarian problems existing between the races, it would be unjustified and immoral to bring to the area many thousands of "the dregs of the European population." The solution, the governor of Kenya suggested, was to remove the illegal immigrants to islands somewhere in the Pacific, like the Fijis.[56]

While deportation of illegal immigrants to Cyprus could only exacerbate relations with the Yishuv, contacts with representatives of Arab countries made the British even more keenly aware of the extent of Arab opposition to Jewish immigration into Palestine. Between 9 September and 2 October 1946, British officials met with Arab delegates in London to discuss the Palestine problem. Both the Zionists and the Palestinian Arabs were conspicuously absent; they refused to discuss the provincial autonomy plan and boycotted the conference. The Arab delegation not only rejected the Morrison-Grady Plan but also demanded the termination of the Mandate, the establishment of a unitary state in Palestine with an assured Arab majority, and the immediate end of Jewish immigration. The Egyptian representative, Abdel Razzak Ahmad Sanhuri Pasha,

Ma'apilim *detention camp in Cyprus*
(Courtesy Israel Ministry of Defense, Museums Unit)

for example, clearly stated the Arab countries' opposition to further Jewish immigration into Palestine, "which was already saturated with Jews." Instead, he suggested transferring to Palestine some two hundred thousand Muslim DPs from the Balkans, the Crimea, and other parts of Russia. The Arabs, the Egyptian stressed, could not be asked to sacrifice their country because the Jews were being persecuted. A similar stand was taken by Dr. Fadhel Jamali of Iraq. The objective of the Jews in Palestine was political, and every Jew who entered the country was a potential terrorist or usurper. Playing down the tragedy of the Jews during World War II, Jamali demanded that the refugee problem be divorced from the question of Palestine. He accused Zionist propaganda of magnifying the extent of Jewish suffering. The Transjordan representative, Samir

Pasha Rifai, emphasized the damage the Jewish immigration issue was causing to relations between the Arab countries and Britain, and Azzam suggested moving the Jewish DPs to eastern Siberia, where the Soviet Union had created an autonomous Jewish republic, because the Jews were not anti-Russian and the Soviet government was opposed to the Zionist policy in Palestine.[57]

The London conference illustrated once again the importance the Arabs ascribed to the problem of Jewish immigration into Palestine. All Zionist efforts to influence the British to alter or at least moderate their immigration policy came to nothing. Zionist leaders made it clear that a change in the immigration policy would help reduce tension in Palestine and advance negotiations on the participation of a Zionist delegation at another conference on Palestine, which the British wanted to convene. Creech Jones, now colonial secretary, explained to the Zionists that immigration to Palestine would be one of the main topics at the proposed conference and that it was not possible to introduce a change at this stage because of the probable firm reaction by the Arabs.[58] The only compromise that the Colonial Office was willing to make was to allocate half of the monthly quota of immigration certificates to illegal immigrants detained in Cyprus.[59] Doing so did not constitute a departure from the existing immigration policy, but it could ease the shortage of internment space. This gesture by the Colonial Office was received with indifference by most of the Jewish public in Palestine because the deportations to Cyprus continued.[60] London remained adamant, even though it was aware that the cessation of the deportations and transfer of the detained illegal immigrants from Cyprus to detention camps in Palestine would improve relations with the Yishuv and was likely to help Britain's struggle against the terrorist operations of the Irgun and the LHI (between 1 October and 18 November 1946, ninety-nine British soldiers and policemen had been killed).[61]

The Arabs continued to apply pressure on London not to make any concessions on Jewish immigration. The Council of the Arab League decided on 28 November 1946 that continuation of Jewish immigration to Palestine constituted a violation of the commitment the British government had made in 1939 and therefore endangered the peace in the Middle East. "In fact," the Arab League statement read, "the Arabs see in all kinds of Jewish immigration into Palestine an illegal action. They do not approve of what the British Government calls legal immigration quotas. Consequently, they consider all Jews entering Palestine as illegal immigrants who should be sent back to where they came from."[62] The high commissioner reported to the Colonial Office that even forcing the illegal vessels to Cyprus did not satisfy the Palestinian Arabs, who accused the Mandatory government of aiding the illegal embarkations and threatened to put an end to the prevailing calm in the region.[63]

Britain's last major effort to reach a compromise between the conflicting aims of the Jews and the Arabs took place at a second conference held in London (27 January–13 February 1947). The British conducted parallel negotiations with delegations from Arab countries and the Zionists. The gap between the parties proved unbridgeable, the controversy over Jewish immigration forming one of the main obstacles. In a final endeavor to break the impasse, the British suggested what became known as the Bevin Plan. It called for a five-year trusteeship at the end of which an independent state would be established with an assured Arab majority. The Bevin Plan was an attempt more or less to combine the idea of provincial autonomy, preferred by the British, with the Arab demand for an unitary state. To placate the Jews and, more important, Truman, the plan spoke of the immigration of ninety-six thousand Jews to Palestine over a two-year period. Until the end of the trusteeship, the high commissioner, together with an advisory council, would continue to determine the extent of immigration in keeping with the economic absorption capacity of the country.[64]

Both the Arabs and the Zionists rejected the plan. The Arabs rejected it because they feared it would lead to partition and the establishment of a Jewish state in a part of Palestine. They were also firmly set against bringing ninety-six thousand Jewish immigrants to Palestine. The Zionists rejected the plan because it would perpetuate the Jews as a minority in an Arab country, and they wanted a sovereign Jewish state of their own. As a way out of the impasse, the cabinet meeting on 14 February accepted the recommendations of the foreign and colonial secretaries to transfer the Palestine question to the United Nations.[65] By taking this far-reaching decision, they did not, however, mean to imply that Britain was relinquishing its mandate. Apparently, Bevin regarded it as a merely tactical move, designed to instill fear in the opposing sides, and he told the ministers that he did not think the Jews and the Arabs wanted the matter transferred to the United Nations, adding that the Palestine question could always again be removed from the agenda of the General Assembly session due to convene in September. He also wanted to see whether he could resolve the problem by appealing directly to the leaders of the Arab countries. But that step entailed a considerable risk, and one may assume that Bevin would not have taken this course if he was still convinced, as were the chiefs of staff, that it was essential for Britain to continue maintaining a presence in Palestine. At this time, Attlee already believed that a British withdrawal was inevitable.

Protocols from the cabinet meetings leave little doubt that the *Ha'apala* activities and the actions of the Irgun and the LHI, which so bothered the British, played no part in this decision. It seems that the cabinet at this stage lacked the willpower to deal with the impasse in Palestine. It should, of course, also be seen in the context of two other far-reaching decisions that were to have wide ramifications for Britain's status in the international arena. The first was the momentous decision to transfer authority in India by June 1948, and the second ended Britain's economic and military support to Greece and Turkey.

Bevin and Creech Jones had no illusions that the cabinet decision would lead to an intensification of Zionist activity. The period between mid-February and September 1947, when the Palestine question was scheduled to come up in the United Nations, would prove critical. Both the foreign and colonial secretaries realized that improved weather conditions would bring an increase in illegal immigration, and continued deportation to Cyprus would cause an intensification of incidents and terrorist activity on the part of the Zionists. Despite these fears, the cabinet was persuaded by Bevin and Attlee to reject the recommendations and appeals of the Americans, in particular those of the new secretary of state, George C. Marshall, to increase the monthly immigration quota.[66] Whitehall held to its position although the ministers recognized that the illegal immigration was the only subject on which the entire Jewish community in Palestine was united and that the deportation of the illegal immigrants made it more difficult for the Jewish Agency to act against Irgun and LHI terror. "Every time an illegal immigrant ship enters Haifa," the high commissioner told London, the "whole of [the] Yishuv is immediately plunged into an intense state of hysterical emotional tension."[67]

British representatives in Arab countries tried to counter Zionist pressure. They warned London of the dangers inherent in increasing the quota to four thousand a month. Any concession on immigration, British diplomats pointed out, would be interpreted that "we were being blackmailed by threats of increased terrorism" and would encourage terrorist attacks against British lives and property in several Arab countries.[68] The high commissioner in Palestine had his doubts about these assessments. He thought that there would be no firm reaction by the Palestinian Arabs to a modest increase and wondered "why it should be stronger among Arabs outside Palestine." Disturbed by the intensifying Jewish terrorist attacks, Cunningham maintained that "without an increase [of the quota], there is little prospect of stopping terrorism by any military or other action short of war with the Jews."[69] The Cabinet Defence Committee preferred not to provoke the Arabs. The minister of defense, Albert V. Alexander, warned that any increase in immigration would result in active resistance by the Arabs and that the present British force in Palestine, if not heavily reinforced, would be unable to deal with active opposition by both Jews and Arabs.[70]

Bevin and Creech Jones's assessment of the expected increase in illegal sailings was well founded. In February 1947, three vessels with close to twenty-eight hundred illegal immigrants were caught along the coast. The belief was that thousands of illegal immigrants would soon set sail for Palestine. As the attempts to find an alternative to Cyprus were unsuccessful, the cabinet decided to increase the capacity of the camps there to thirty thousand.[71] The intelligence estimated in mid-April that already thirty-five thousand Jews were strategically situated for ready embarkation throughout Europe and nineteen ships were immediately available with an estimated carrying capacity of over twenty thousand. In addition, a further fourteen ships were undergoing repairs or refitting, and these had an estimated eventual carrying capacity of over seventeen thousand.[72] The colonial secretary, already having difficulty finding other sites for the internment of an expected twenty thousand additional persons, suggested allocating the entire monthly quota to illegal immigrants on Cyprus and renovating the camp in Rafiah to house about four thousand people. The Defence Committee rejected these proposals, arguing that the first would mean that only illegal immigrants could enter Palestine, and the War Office expressed doubts about the feasibility of the second proposal. But even if the two proposals had been adopted, there still was a gap of eight thousand places between the estimated scope of the illegal immigration and the number of places of detention thus made available. As it appeared obvious that there was no way that the number of expected illegal immigrants could be held to a satisfactory level on territory that was under British control, the suggestion was made to see whether it might be possible to borrow an island from the Italians for the purpose.[73] Though perhaps more realistic than transferring illegal immigrants to the Fiji Islands, the proposal seems to reflect a growing feeling among the British that they were caught between a rock and a hard place: strict implementation of their deportation policy was sure to provoke increasing hostility from the Yishuv, while enlarging the legal immigration quota for Jews was guaranteed to run into strong opposition from the Arabs.

With no alternative sites for detention, the Cabinet Committee for Illegal Immigration turned once again to the governor of Cyprus, now Lord Winster, and asked him to increase the capacity of the camps on the island.[74] Lord Winster made it clear that there was no possibility whatsoever of expanding the two existing camps and that setting up a third camp would entail the relocation of Cypriot farmers and no doubt provoke bitterness and enmity on the part of the local population. He expressed his concern over the adverse economic and political consequences that could be expected, not to mention the harm the decision would cause to British interests on the island. Holding more immigrants under arrest, he added, would necessitate reinforcement of the military units on the island, with all that entailed.[75] Lord Winster eventually agreed to add four thousand places in the existing camps, bringing their total capacity to thirty-four thousand. Crowding beyond this number, he warned the Colonial Office, would evoke angry and justified complaints about camp living conditions.[76] This situation partly explains why the high commissioner and the colonial secretary accepted a Jewish Agency proposal to have two thousand children aged six to seventeen moved from Cyprus to Palestine outside the immigration quota.[77]

Deportations Back to Ports of Embarkation?

The failure of deportation to Cyprus to deter the organizers or the illegal immigrants themselves, the estimates of large numbers of illegal immigrants expected, difficulties in finding an alternative to Cyprus, and the desire to deter governments from allowing illegal immigration vessels to sail from their ports all led various officials in Britain to conclude that there was no choice but to deport the illegal immigrants back to their ports of embarkation. This idea had been mooted a number of times since the end of the war, but it had so far been rejected. At the beginning of March 1947, word reached the authorities in Palestine that an illegal ship organized by Peter Bergson's people in the United States (the *Ben Hecht*) had set sail from France. The Bergson group supported the Zionist Revisionist movement that favored militant anti-British propaganda. The British therefore assumed that among these immigrants there might be militant revisionists who would join and reinforce the Irgun. Fearing the havoc these illegal immigrants might create on Cyprus, the high commissioner suggested deporting them to their port of embarkation in France, but this proposal the Colonial Office had to reject, albeit reluctantly, because Britain had no legal authority to force countries from which the vessels had sailed to take back people who were not their citizens but only had passed through there.[78]

Nevertheless, the idea of deportations to ports of embarkation was never dropped. On instruction of the Foreign Office, on 1 April 1947, Sir Noel Charles, British ambassador to Italy, informed Carlo Sforza, the Italian foreign minister, that the British government would in the future demand that Italy take back illegal immigrants who had set sail from Italian ports.[79] A similar announcement was made to the French Foreign Ministry in mid-May. The French countered, as anticipated, that France was only a country of transit and that people should be returned to the country from which they had set out.[80] The British Foreign Office preferred to deport illegal immigrants back to Italy since that was the site of the most intensive illegal activity and Italy held the largest number of Jewish refugees of any country along the Mediterranean. Moreover, Rome's ability to stand up to British pressure was thought to be more limited than that of Paris.[81] Charles, however, argued that the lack of Italian reaction to British warnings did not signify a willingness to cooperate but stemmed from their hope that Britain would not carry out its threat. The ambassador warned that the relations between the two countries were liable to suffer if the Italians were forced to take in illegal immigrants deported from or intercepted on their way to Palestine.[82]

In the spring of 1947, the British began monitoring the movements of a ship called the *President Warfield*, which in mid-June 1947 had entered French territorial waters from an Italian anchorage. Bevin regarded this ship as a test case for Britain's determination to put a halt to illegal sailings.[83] On 11 July 1947, the *President Warfield*, soon renamed the *Exodus 1947*, set sail from Sète in France with 4,530 illegal immigrants aboard. This was a bitter setback for the British, who had invested great effort in attempting to prevent its departure. On the following day, Bevin vigorously complained to Georges Bidault, the French foreign minister, for allowing the *Exodus* to leave France, and, apparently without first consulting with London, Bevin informed Bidault of British intentions "to make an example of this ship by obliging it to return to a French port with all its passengers."[84] Toward the end of the incident, Bevin wrote to MP Maurice Edelman explaining the reasons for the decision to return the vessel to its port of embarkation: "In view of the exceptional size of the *President Warfield*'s contingent and of the illicit manner in which they left France, His Majesty's government had no alternative but to arrange for the return of the illegal immigrants to their country of embarkation, France. It had become evident that the policy of sending illegal immigrants to camps in Cyprus, where they qualify for inclusion in the legal immigration quotas to Palestine, had only served to encourage the stream of illegal immigrants which has for months been flowing from Eastern Europe via countries with a Mediterranean seaboard."[85]

Some two weeks after the *Exodus* passengers had been forced back to Germany and disembarked there, on 20 September 1947, the cabinet decided to evacuate Palestine. The proximity of these events raises the question of what role, if any, the illegal sailings in general and the *Exodus* in particular may have played in that far-reaching decision. During the weeks preceding the cabinet decision on withdrawal, there seemed to be no sense of powerlessness or doubt among British officials regarding Britain's ability to cope with the illegal sailings, however much they may have been disturbed by them. Neither was there any intention of giving up the policy of deporting illegal immigrants back to their ports of embarkation.

What primarily caused the cabinet to take this historic decision was the majority recommendation of the United Nations Special Committee on Palestine (UNSCOP, 31 August 1947) to partition Palestine between the Jews and the Arabs. The setting up of a UN committee to study the Palestine problem had been decided on in mid-May at a special session of the General Assembly. UNSCOP, consisting of delegates of eleven neutral states, in large measure had been Whitehall's last remaining hope to help extricate Britain from the stalemate in which it found itself after it had failed to find a solution for the Palestine question acceptable both to the Arab countries and the Americans and the Zionists. The UNSCOP recommendation to establish a Jewish state now put an end to those hopes.[86]

Leading up to the decision were the events of the winter of 1946–47, when it had become clear that Britain's American orientation for a solution to the Palestine question had failed. The breakdown in the negotiations with the Arab countries and the Zionists in January–February 1947, together with the severe economic crisis that hit Britain during the winter, further persuaded several cabinet members, with the prime minister at their head, that the time had come to terminate the Mandate. This decision fell in with their overall belief that Britain ought to adjust its geopolitical policies to the country's postwar economic reality. Foreign Secretary Bevin, however, was less easily convinced, and further setbacks were needed before he would arrive at the same conclusion. Among these the UNSCOP report was perhaps the most decisive. Furthermore, after India gained independence on 15 August 1947, the cabinet showed growing unwillingness to continue to bear the risks involved in ruling strife-torn Palestine, especially since Britain still had its military bases in Egypt following the latter's failure at the end of August to bring the Security Council to compel Britain to evacuate Egypt. Finally, when the financial crisis in the summer of 1947 (following the free exchange between the pound sterling and the U.S. dollar) grew into a political one, it further impaired the government's strength and capability to enforce unpopular policies. Members of Parliament, public opinion, and the press were increasingly disturbed by the economic and political price Britain was paying for staying in Palestine, not to mention the lost lives of young soldiers.[87]

The failure of the British in their first attempt to deport illegal immigrants to their port of embarkation and the serious damage it had caused London's image and prestige in world opinion necessitated a reevaluation of the methods being used in that struggle. At the end of September, the Committee for Illegal Immigration recommended that the policy of deportation to the country of embarkation be implemented only in the case of illegal immigrants sailing from Italy or from the two countries that now constituted the main danger, Rumania and Bulgaria. In view of the French position in the *Exodus* episode, returning illegal immigrants to that country was no longer a possibility. Based on the experience of the *Exodus* affair, the committee recommended that illegal immigrants not be deported from the coast of Palestine before ensuring the cooperation of the government of the country to which the deportees were to be returned and its agreement to the use of force by the British soldiers on the boats and the local authorities on shore. If the attempt to deport the illegal immigrants to the country of embarkation failed, it was suggested that they be removed to Cyprus and not to Germany. Germany was eliminated as a possible destination for deporting illegal immigrants, mainly because of the sharp criticism leveled against Britain from all parts of the world for callously having returned German Jewish concentration camp survivors to Germany.[88]

The Colonial Office entertained a certain degree of optimism concerning the willingness of the Rumanian and Bulgarian governments to cooperate in the returning of the illegal immigrants.[89] British representatives in Rumania and Bulgaria, however, thought differently. According to the former, no goodwill should be expected on the part of the Rumanian government in anything connected with illegal immigration, and "it would be most unwise and even dangerous to suggest the return to Rumania and disembarkation here by force of any illegal immigrants who may have embarked at Rumanian ports." Furthermore, the two ports of Constanta and Sulina, from which illegal vessels could embark, were main transit points for Soviet commerce. The Soviet high command would object to the entry of British warships into these ports and removal by force of the illegal immigrants by British and Rumanian soldiers. The British consulate in Rumania warned of severe incidents if this were attempted. The British legation in Bulgaria also made it clear that there was no chance that the Bulgarian government would agree to accept back illegal immigrants who had sailed from its ports.[90] Under the circumstances, on 2 October 1947, about four thousand Rumanian Jews who had sailed from Bulgaria aboard the *Geula* and *Medinat Hayehudim* were deported to Cyprus.[91]

Ending the Mandate

After the cabinet had decided to evacuate Palestine, there were increasing voices among government circles in favor of putting an end to fighting illegal immigration because the struggle proved futile. The events surrounding the *Exodus* affair had largely ended the government's hopes of ceasing or at least considerably reducing the illegal sailings from countries in the West. In addition, the failure to find alternatives to Cyprus, together with the renewal of sailings from Communist bloc countries, made it clear that the difficulties that beset the campaign against illegal immigrants could only increase in the future. The problem of where to house the illegal immigrants became acute when word reached London that two large vessels, the *Pan York* and the *Pan Crescent*, each with a capacity of eight thousand passengers, were anchored in Rumania.

About seventeen thousand illegal immigrants were being held in October in Cyprus while the maximum capacity of the detention camps in the island was put at thirty-four thousand. The Colonial Office insisted that it was not possible to prepare more detention places, even temporary ones, within a short time, either in Cyprus or elsewhere. Thus it proposed announcing to the United Nations or to the Arab countries that after the detention camps in Cyprus were full, Britain would no longer be able to halt the illegal immigration.[92] The Colonial Office, however, was not the only one that was skeptical about continuing the struggle against the illegal sailings. A memorandum prepared for Bevin in the Foreign Office in mid-October, as background for his discussion with the prime minister on the subject of the illegal immigration, stated that "the only alternative to the policy of interning illegal immigrants is to repel them by naval action such as the laying of mine fields or by shooting at and possibly sinking illegal immigrant ships. Apart from the expense and delay involved in laying mine fields, mining, in the same way as shooting by naval units, would almost inevitably, in view of the determined temper of the Jews, involve serious loss of life." The author of the memorandum was also doubtful of the effectiveness of such an act given the late stage of the Mandate. In his opinion, "the only practicable policy appears to be, therefore, to expedite arrangements for withdrawal in order to cut down as far as possible the period during which we continue to be responsible for interning illegal immigrants."[93]

Bevin, however, strongly objected to the Colonial Office proposal that the entire immigration quota be allocated to illegal immigrants in Cyprus and that Britain give up its struggle against the illegal immigration as soon as possible. As long as Britain was responsible for the administration of Palestine, Bevin insisted, this struggle ought to continue, and he expected the Colonial Office to make arrangements to absorb additional detainees in Cyprus, even if this meant crowding in the camps, or else to suggest alternative locations.[94] The Cabinet Defence Committee accepted Bevin's position at its meeting on 1 November. Still, the foreign secretary recognized that all those detained in Cyprus ought to be transferred to Palestine before Britain completed the evacuation of its forces. He, therefore, expressed a willingness to allot the entire immigration quota to the illegal immigrants detained on Cyprus during the final stages of the withdrawal and even to incur the consequences of increasing the quota.[95] For their part, the commanders in chief in the Middle East wanted to shed their responsibility for stopping illegal immigration as soon as possible in order to meet the evacuation schedule. They declared that they could not prevent illegal immigration after the Cyprus camps had been filled to their capacity of thirty-four thousand or after 1 February 1948. For the interim period, between 1 February and 1 August 1948 (the intended date of evacuation), they stated that they would direct the immigrant ships to Tel Aviv unless the conditions of the vessels or the weather made this impossible, also so as not to interfere with the planned evacuation through the port of Haifa.[96]

Whitehall, however, was divided as to the policy that should be pursued after 1 February 1948. The Colonial Office believed that ongoing preventive measures, including deportation of the illegal immigrants to Cyprus, would signal Britain's intention to ignore the recommendation of the United Nations to increase the scope of Jewish immigration; the result would be a significant increase in illegal immigration and an inundation of the camps in Cyprus within a very short time. Under such circumstances, the Colonial Office argued, it would be very difficult to move the detained illegal immigrants in Cyprus to Palestine before the evacuation of British. Furthermore, the detention of illegal immigrants in the Cyprus camps was costing the Mandatory government about £250,000 per month, an expense that threatened to empty its coffers. But if the Jewish Agency were permitted to transfer up to sixty-five hundred persons a month — as the UN had recommended — illegal immigration would probably come to an end, making the evacuation of the Cyprus camps possible. The high commissioner maintained that increasing the immigration quota to Palestine would be seen as compensation for Britain's failure to adopt the UN recommendation that, no later than 1 February 1948, the Jews be assigned a port through which they would be allowed unlimited immigration. The Foreign and War Offices feared that a change in policy "would lead to trouble with the Arabs which might have more serious consequences for our withdrawal than a continued application of the policy of controlling immigration."[97] Accordingly, the Foreign Office also rejected a suggestion by the State Department that the illegal immigrants held in Cyprus be allowed to enter Palestine before the end of the Mandate in exchange for a Zionist promise to stop the illegal sailings.[98] The Foreign Office had its doubts about the value of Jewish Agency promises after the latter's failure to prevent the sailing of the *Pan* boats.[99]

Nevertheless, because they did want to start evacuating the camps on Cyprus, the Defence Committee and the colonial secretary ordered the commanders in chief in the Middle East and the high commissioner to increase the quota of Jews allowed to enter Palestine each month by several hundred, all without any official announcement and without the knowledge of the Arabs.[100] After the arrival in Cyprus of the two *Pan* ships (1 January 1948) there were 31,117 illegal immigrants being detained on the island. From that time until the end of the Mandate, eight more boats, carrying a total of 5,530 persons, were diverted to Cyprus. As late as 11 May 1948, the colonial secretary reported that 24,000 illegal immigrants were still on Cyprus.[101] Ironically, quickening the pace of removing detainees from Cyprus to Palestine by making them part of the unofficially increased quotas was also necessary because, if only for the sake of appearances, Britain persisted in keeping up its efforts against illegal Jewish immigration into the country until the final days of the Mandate. Acceleration of the removal of the illegal immigrants from Cyprus was intended, among other things, to make room for additional detainees. Whitehall's diplomatic campaign against the countries from whose ports the illegal immigrants sailed and against the flag states of the transport vessels involved also continued unabated. During the half year that elapsed between the UN General Assembly's decision at the end of November 1947 to partition Palestine and the establishment of the State of Israel in May 1948, 22,384 illegal immigrants on twelve carriers were deported to Cyprus. As late as April 1948, another three ships' passengers (*Tirat Zvi, Mishmar Ha'emek,* and *Nahshon*) were diverted to Cyprus.

Although the illegal immigration caused Britain considerable difficulties, especially from the summer of 1946, the pressure generated by the *Ha'apala* could not match the pressure exerted by the Arabs, who succeeded in making the question of Jewish immigration, and that of the illegal immigrants in particular, a test case for Anglo-Arab relations. Britain's desire to win the Arabs' support for its plan for a solution to the Palestine question and the concern for British interests in the Arab countries overrode any possible benefits that could be derived from acceding to Zionist immigration demands. Fear of disturbances by Palestinian Arabs, which were likely to erupt and receive the support of various Arab countries, neutralized any possible countermeasures by the Zionists. Whitehall's refusal to increase immigration quotas or to halt deportations to Cyprus as well as the continued struggle against the illegal sailings even after the UN partition decision reflected the government's order of priorities. The only concession made by London concerning immigration was the allocation of half of the monthly quota to illegal immigrants from Cyprus.

Britain did indeed succeed in apprehending most of the illegal immigrants who embarked for Palestine. Approximately fifty-one thousand *ma'apilim* of the about seventy thousand who had sailed for Palestine were intercepted and deported to detention camps in Cyprus and, in the case of the *Exodus,* Germany.[102] Very quickly, however, London recognized that deportation to Cyprus was not in itself sufficient to end or even limit the scope of the illegal sailings; moreover, the shortage of places of detention became more and more critical as time passed. The decision to send the illegal immigrants back to the ports from which they had embarked was, to a great extent, an admission of the failure of the Cyprus deterrent. Still, the deportations almost certainly obviated harsher reaction by the Arabs. From the Zionist perspective, the *Ha'apala* constituted the concrete expression of the link between the problem of the Jewish DPs in Europe and the question of Palestine that the British refused to make. The fact that tens of thousands of refugees succeeded in setting sail for Palestine was in itself a considerable achievement, especially since all the detainees eventually reached Palestine/Israel. Moreover, the very possibility of getting closer to Palestine constituted a source of encouragement for the Jews in the DP camps and those remaining in countries under Soviet influence. British actions against the illegal immigrants at times received wide media coverage, thereby helping the Zionists prevent the Jewish DP problem from sinking into oblivion, especially when, as early as 1947, international interest in the subject showed signs of waning.

Both the British and the Zionists were out to try to win world public opinion to their side, particularly in the United States. Britain's propaganda campaign had to contend not only with the fact that the illegal immigrants were survivors of the Holocaust seeking to leave the DP camps and the countries that had become the graveyards of their families but also with newspaper photographs and newsreels showing armed British soldiers on board destroyers transferring helpless refugees, including children and women, from wrecked boats to deportation ships that looked like floating jails. The British tried to deflect attention away from the agony of the illegal immigrants and to portray the Zionist activists as shrewd, unscrupulous people who were willing to adopt any means, including the exploitation of the suffering DPs, to achieve their nationalist goals. British officials kept reiterating that the illegal Jewish immigration was not a spontaneous exodus of desperate refugees but a carefully organized Zionist campaign to force the hand of His Majesty's government and increase the proportion of the Jewish population of Palestine.

In the winter of 1947–48, the British were closer than ever to admitting failure in dealing with the illegal immigration, but even then, apprehension of Arab reactions shifted the balance in favor of continuing the struggle. Success against the *Ha'apala* was largely dependent not on the measures taken in the Mediterranean and in Palestine but rather on the success of the campaign against the countries that allowed the illegal immigrants to sail from their ports.[103]

II

AMERICAN
OPPOSITION

4

JEWISH DISPLACED PERSONS AND AMERICAN POLICY-MAKING

For the first few weeks after the war the United States and Britain followed the same principles and acted in tandem vis-à-vis the huge number of displaced people seeking refuge in their zones of occupation. DPs were brought together in hastily constructed camps and divided according to country of origin. Because this policy applied also to Jewish DPs, victims of persecution and torture could find themselves thrown together with some of those who, only shortly before, had been their persecutors and torturers.[1] It did not take long for stories about the desperate reality of Holocaust survivors to reach Jewish leaders in the United States. Among the American Jewish soldiers writing home was army chaplain Abraham Klausner, who described the plight of the Jewish DPs to Rabbi Philip Bernstein, then executive director of the committee on army-navy religious activities, as follows: "Six weeks ago they were liberated. They were taken to a series of camps in the uniform of the concentration camp and remained garbed in that infamous outfit. They are housed in dwellings that are unfit for human occupation and are fed in many cases less than they received at the concentration camps. I do not use words recklessly."[2]

Before long Jewish organizations were approaching members of Congress and administration officials in an urgent appeal for action. U.S. treasury secretary Henry Morgenthau Jr., whose intervention in early 1944 had led to the creation of the War Refugee Board, now pressured the State Department to investigate the situation, suggesting that Earl Harrison, dean of the Law School of the University of Pennsylvania and U.S. delegate to the IGCR, be sent to report on the conditions of refugees who could not be repatriated, particularly Jews in Germany and Austria. On 22 June 1945 the idea was approved by Truman.[3]

Harrison's main recommendations were eventually adopted by the president and became the cornerstone of American policy toward the Jewish DPs.

The Harrison Report

Harrison left for Europe at the beginning of July, accompanied by Dr. Joseph Schwartz, European director of the American Jewish Joint Distribution Committee (JDC), Patrick Mallin, vice-director of the IGCR, and Herbert Katzki, of the War Refugee Board. Before setting out, Harrison was briefed by Zionist supporters in the United States. Schwartz was included to ensure that Jewish interests would be looked after.[4] At the end of July, Harrison relayed his first impressions and recommendations. He was very critical of the policy the military was following toward the Jewish DPs and advised establishing separate camps for them. He also urged that buildings be taken from Germans to house Jews and that management of the DP camps be transferred from the army to UNRRA. In a letter to Morgenthau, Harrison wrote that "most military authorities refuse to recognize Jews as a separate category in spite of admitted greater suffering and equally refuse to recognize their statelessness."[5] Morgenthau was quick to convey Harrison's messages to Joseph G. Grew, acting secretary of state.[6]

Washington did not take long to react. Chief of Staff George Marshall and Secretary of War Henry L. Stimson each informed General Eisenhower, then European theater commander, of Harrison's first impressions and preliminary findings. Stimson asked him to act as best he could to improve the situation.[7] Stimson may have been motivated partially by his knowledge of Morgenthau's sensitivity toward the plight of European Jews.[8] Eisenhower lost no time and on 10 August told Stimson that he intended to appoint a Jewish adviser. Only the day before he had rejected a similar suggestion by Rabbi Stephen S. Wise, a prominent American Jewish leader and president of the American Jewish Congress, that he appoint a Jewish liaison officer, claiming that liaison officers attached to headquarters were selected on a national basis and it would not be advisable to appoint one especially for the Jews. Eisenhower did not believe that all Jews should be regarded as stateless and informed the secretary of war that those Jews who did not want to return to their homelands or who were stateless had already been gathered in separate centers and that progress had been made in erecting additional facilities for them. Officers were given instructions to provide adequate housing for Jewish DPs, if need be at the expense of the general German population. He added that he thought of transferring responsibility for operating the camps to UNRRA by 1 October 1945.[9]

Eisenhower's measures, however, came too late to have any impact on the final version of Harrison's report, which was submitted to Truman on 24 August 1945. In it Harrison accused the U.S. Army of inhumane conduct toward the Jewish DPs, going so far as to say that the only difference between the treatment they had received at the hands of the Nazis and that of the American army was "that we do not exterminate them"; the fact remained that Jewish DPs were still being kept in concentration camps with American soldiers taking the place of SS guards. Separate camps should be set up for the Jews and they should receive preferential treatment to make up for the terrible suffering they had endured for years. Separation was also necessary for administrative purposes so that they could receive compensatory treatment. He criticized the fact that DPs were kept behind barbed wire fences and under armed guard and needed permits if they wanted to go out of the camps. Harrison was particularly irked that the German population, particularly in the rural areas, enjoyed better living conditions than the DPs. As to their accommodation, he attacked military government officers for manifesting "the utmost reluctance" about "inconveniencing the German population." According to him, Jewish DPs should be recognized as a special group: "Refusing to recognize the Jews as such has the effect, in this situation, of closing one's eyes to their former and more barbaric persecution, which has already made them a separate group with greater needs."

At the heart of Harrison's recommendations was the proposal to transfer one hundred thousand displaced Jews to Palestine; as he put it, the Jews "want to be evacuated to Palestine now, just as other national groups are being repatriated to their homes." In other words, repatriation for the Jews meant immigration to Palestine, even if not one of these Jews had ever lived there. No Jews could be asked to return to their land of origin. Harrison argued that it should be possible to alter the White Paper immigration policy without provoking severe reactions, and he called upon the president to appeal to Britain to allow the persecuted Jews "to resettle in Palestine." He quoted remarks Hugh Dalton, then chancellor of the exchequer, had made at the Labour Party convention in May 1945 (before the general elections) advocating allowing the Jews to enter Palestine without setting obstacles in their path because of the horrors they had suffered. As Harrison saw it, the American government should express its support for the transfer of some of the persecuted Jews to Palestine. At the same time, however, keenly aware of American sensitivity on the subject, Harrison was careful to dismiss the possibility of solving the problem of the Jewish DPs by allowing them to immigrate to the United States.[10]

Not surprisingly, Harrison's stinging language aroused a great deal of animosity, even bitterness, among the military commanders.[11] And his comparison of American soldiers with Nazis was clearly out of place. But the fact remained that the situation of the Jewish DPs right after the war, and especially at the time Harrison made his visit, was one of extreme hardship. Not only was the U.S. Army poorly equipped to handle the problems of the DPs, it did not accord the matter high priority given the many other huge tasks it was confronting. Major Irving Heymont, the U.S. military commander of the Landsberg DP camp, has left descriptions of the situation as he found it when he arrived there that confirm Harrison's impressions. At that time there were six thousand men, women, and children in the camp, around five thousand of whom were Jews: "The camp is filthy beyond description. Sanitation is virtually unknown. Words fail me when I try to think of an adequate description. . . . The army units we relieved obviously did nothing more than insure that rations were delivered to the camp. With a few exceptions, the people of the camp themselves appear demoralized beyond hope of rehabilitation. They appear to be beaten both spiritually and physically, with no hopes or incentives for the future." [12] In another letter Heymont described his shock when he first arrived at the camp: "The iron fence around the *kaserne* had been increased in height by the liberal use of barbed wire. The outside perimeter is patrolled by armed soldiers from the battalion. A soldier and a member of the camp police are stationed at the entrance gate. I learned that the people of the camp are permitted to leave only when they have a written pass. . . . I saw large numbers of DPs lolling along the fence and watching the Germans walking freely along the opposite street." [13]

The speedy reaction of the military, including the War Department, to Harrison's recommendations even before the final report had reached the president suggests that the issue was extremely sensitive for Washington. Publication in the press at the end of September 1945 of Harrison's report along with a letter (31 August) reprimanding Eisenhower made clear to all concerned the importance that Truman attached to the distress of the Jewish DPs. The president's responsiveness was interpreted by army commanders as an expression of the political power of American Jewry. Truman's criticism of Eisenhower revolved around the general's failure to determine the extent to which his own orders regarding the refugees were being carried out. It was not policy but rather its implementation, the president charged, that was responsible for the lamentable situation described in the report. This was cutting criticism of Eisenhower's performance as a commander.[14]

Eisenhower Reacts

The presidential censure left Eisenhower little choice but to give priority to the problem of the Jewish DPs, even though their number was negligible compared with the scope of the DP problem as a whole in the American occupation zone. He paid quick visits to five DP camps, some of them housing Jews only, and reported his impressions and conclusions to the president. Eisenhower thought that most countries would refuse to take in large numbers of Jews, most of whom wanted to go to Palestine. The military authorities were encouraging the DPs to look for employment and were trying to organize small businesses and agricultural work for them in the hope that they would be able to set up small settlements. The Jews, however, refused to consider Germany as their permanent home and preferred to wait rather than forcing themselves on a population that would never make them feel welcome. While admitting that the situation in the camps was not wholly satisfactory, Eisenhower noted the efforts that were being made to expand the camp boundaries by evicting local people from their homes and emphasized that there had been a tremendous improvement in the condition of the DPs over the past three months. As it was possible that some of his subordinates were not carrying out his instructions, he again had sent out directives about the treatment of DPs.[15]

One of Eisenhower's first acts after receiving Stimson's 10 August letter had been to appoint Rabbi Judah Nadich as adviser for Jewish affairs. Nadich took up his job on 24 August, the same day that Harrison submitted his findings, and obviously timed to meet the storm expected to ensue from Harrison's report. Nadich had been serving in the U.S. Army in Europe since the summer of 1942 and at the time of his appointment was stationed in Paris.[16] Nadich's first report was submitted on 16 September 1945 to General Walter Bedell-Smith, head of Eisenhower's staff. The Jewish adviser noted the crowded housing conditions, the need for supplementing the food ration and improving its quality, the shortage of clothing and shoes, and the lack of employment. He further observed that in some cases the policies of General Headquarters were not known to field officer ranks and that in other instances the latter were disregarding the directives. Nadich recommended that the personnel working with the DPs be selected carefully, and he mentioned instances when those dealing with the DPs had expressed anti-Semitic views. Despite the flaws, Nadich stressed, the situation as a whole was slowly improving. Bedell-Smith immediately contacted senior officers at General Headquarters and throughout Germany and, in Eisenhower's name, ordered them to remedy the situation. The general also distributed the report to all commanding officers who had dealings with the DPs.[17] This vigorous action was the direct result of Truman's letter to Eisenhower. After three months Nadich was replaced by Judge Simon Rifkind, who had been appointed by Secretary of War Robert Patterson as Eisenhower's personal adviser for Jewish affairs.[18]

Eisenhower's interest in the situation of the Jewish DPs did bring about an improvement. Letters Heymont sent at the time clearly demonstrate the sensitivity of the military authorities to their situation. There were frequent visits of senior officers, and clear directives were given to improve the situation of the DPs, partly by appropriating German homes for them but also by removing non-Jewish DPs from camps where Jewish DPs resided. Exactly one month after Harrison had presented his report, Heymont wrote: "It seems that it is now the policy to set up camps exclusively on a nationality basis for those DPs considered to be nonrepatriable and that the Jews are being considered as a separate nationality."[19] Zionist leaders, too, were satisfied with Eisenhower's attitude.

The U.S. military command, unlike the British, not only allowed David Ben-Gurion, chair of the Jewish Agency, to visit the American zone of Germany but even had him meet Eisenhower and his chief of staff, Bedell-Smith. The timing of Ben-Gurion's visit, October 1945, was highly fortuitous for the Zionists, coming on the heels of the publication of Harrison's report and Truman's letter to Eisenhower. At the end of his tour, Ben-Gurion submitted suggestions to Bedell-Smith: to concentrate the Jews in a separate region, either urban or rural; to allow the Jewish DPs to govern themselves, subject to the ultimate authority of the U.S. Army; to provide agricultural training through instructors who would come from Palestine; to confiscate Nazi farms; to provide vocational and paramilitary training to the DPs; and to establish weekly flights between the camps and Palestine to bring in instructors and books.[20] The Americans tended to agree with Ben-Gurion's suggestions, except for concentrating the Jews in a separate region, because many Jewish DPs living in the camps would object to being set apart in a distinctly Jewish area. Such segregation, Bedell-Smith thought, might also increase tension between the Jews still in Germany and the local German population and saddle the American forces with an extra security problem.[21] Given the outcome of his trip to Germany, it is not surprising to find Ben-Gurion praising Eisenhower and Bedell-Smith at every opportunity for their sensitivity and their humane approach to the problem of the Jewish DPs.[22]

Shortly before he completed his assignment in Germany in November 1945, Eisenhower submitted a detailed reply to Harrison's report. He indicated the improvements that had been introduced in the area since Harrison's visit in July, emphasizing the obstacles the occupation authorities were facing in providing housing because the population in need of housing in winter 1945–46 was double the number normally domiciled in the area. Eisenhower rejected Harrison's accusation that Jewish DPs were housed in concentration camps—if at the time of the envoy's report about a thousand Jews still remained there, this was because they needed to regain their strength before they could be transferred to a regular DP camp. He explained that guards were posted around the camps in response to stealing committed by the DPs themselves, to the death of over two thousand DPs who had been poisoned by various toxic alcoholic beverages they had drunk, and because DPs had been injured or killed in acts of violence when they were outside the camps. Eisenhower noted that his new directives called for the DPs themselves to guard the camp on a volunteer basis and without arms. He also had increased the food allotment to DPs in the camps from two thousand calories per day (as set by the Supreme Command of the Western Allies) to twenty-three hundred and twenty-five hundred for victims of racial, religious, or political persecution. This same ration would be provided to Jewish and other DPs who had left the camps and returned to their communities in Germany and Austria. Eisenhower criticized Harrison sharply for having overlooked the many other tasks the army had been dealing with, including the rescue of thousands of Jews and other victims from the concentration camps, the repatriation of those who agreed to return home, and the improvement it had brought in the terrible situation of the survivors within the short space of two months. "Perfection never will be attained," Eisenhower concluded, "but real and honest efforts are being made to provide suitable living conditions for these persecuted people until they can be permanently resettled in other areas."[23]

As Truman's letter to him had been made public, Eisenhower asked that his letter, too, be published. This was done on 17 October. Offended, Harrison hurried to respond.[24] Their public confrontation did not end there. Eisenhower next asked Harvey Gibson, who until his resignation in April 1945 had been commissioner of the American Red Cross in Britain and Western Europe, to investigate the situation in the DP camps. Gibson's favorable impressions of the situation of the DPs and the actions of the army officers were then conveyed to the American press.[25] Eisenhower's energetic efforts to improve the situation of the Jewish DPs and the campaign to minimize the impact of Harrison's report he conducted in the press until the completion of his assignment clearly indicate that he was aware of the weight the report carried in Washington.

Still, discrepancies remained between the instructions of the Supreme Headquarters and the way they were implemented in the field. Along with administrative difficulties, there was a lack of sympathy toward the Jewish DPs, bordering on anti-Semitism on the part of some of the American soldiers. As time passed and officers and enlisted men were rotated, this problem became more severe. Army personnel who arrived after the end of the war lacked the firsthand impression of the suffering the Jews had endured, and very quickly their attitude toward the Jews was largely influenced by their daily confrontations with the misery of the DPs, while the Germans they met were well mannered, orderly, and disciplined. Some claimed that relationships between U.S. soldiers and German women were a factor, too. Heymont recorded how he heard one of the officers visiting the camp incessantly mumbling that these "animals" were treated better than the Germans while "they don't even work as the Germans do." In later testimony, Rabbi Philip Bernstein, who from May 1946 until August 1947 served as an adviser for Jewish affairs, mentions that the Jewish DPs were considered to be troublemakers and extremists, often accused of antagonizing the Germans and making problems for the American army.[26]

At the high command level there were officers who did not like Jews, the most notorious of them being George S. Patton Jr., commander of the U.S. Third Army in southern Germany, who was in charge of the eastern part of the American occupation zone in Germany. Patton objected to Eisenhower's directive to accord preferential treatment to the Jewish DPs and was especially angered by the instructions to evict Germans from their homes in order to house Jews, which he saw as being contrary to "Anglo-Saxon conscience" and even illegal. His positive opinion of the Germans can be found in a letter to his wife at the end of August 1945, where he writes that the Germans were the only decent people he had met and that he preferred them to the Russians. Patton regarded the Jewish DPs with a complete lack of sympathy. The aversion and contempt he felt for the way Jewish DPs were living are evident in the comments he entered in his diary about the Harrison report. He writes, for example, that the assumption that the DPs are human beings is mistaken and especially in regard to the Jews, whom he described as "lower than animals." He did not think that their present way of life had any connection with what had happened to them under the Nazi regime but rather was the result of their being an inferior race.[27] Even after Patton's dismissal (unrelated to his anti-Semitic views), the situation of the Jewish DPs in the area under control of the Third Army remained the most difficult of all. Those who believed that the local population should not be made to suffer for the sake of the DPs but that German economic, social, and political life should be brought back to normal as soon as possible found ideological justification for their attitude in the growing urgency of the West to gain the support of German people in the face of the escalating Cold War.

The Harrison report and the presidential reprimand of Eisenhower had both short- and long-range consequences for American policy on Jewish refugees. Harrison had called for recognition of the Jews as a distinct national group entitled to separate camps and preferential treatment; designating Palestine as the main destination of the Jewish DPs; separating the political issue of the future of Palestine from the humanitarian goal of rehabilitating Jewish refugees there; highlighting the number of one hundred thousand as symbolizing the dimensions of the problem of Jewish DPs; and accepting that the United States could not serve as a location for resolving the problem of the Jewish DPs, while encouraging American intervention with the British government on the DP issue. That these recommendations became the cornerstone of U.S. policy toward the Jewish DPs for the next two years had to do not only with moral considerations but, increasingly, also with political calculations on Truman's part. While it is probably true that, when the full horror of the Nazi Holocaust was gradually unveiled with the liberation of the concentration camps, Truman felt genuine compassion and sympathy toward the camp survivors, soon his official statements and actions began to betray the greater weight the White House attached to political factors: the electoral and financial significance of the American Jewish community, the campaign in November that year for the mayoralty of New York City, and the crucial midterm elections in 1946.

Meanwhile, Eisenhower's visit to the camps, the instructions he kept sending out on how the Jewish DPs ought to be treated, and the parallel press coverage that helped stir public opinion back home about their plight did much to accelerate the creation of separate camps for the Jewish DPs and to improve their circumstances. Since the military had been made aware of the president's personal concern—any untoward incident could reach the White House in the shortest time via the press and Jewish organizations—it adapted a more circumspect attitude and even extended Truman's instructions to include Jewish refugees from Eastern Europe who had fled to Germany and Austria after the war.[28]

Matters between London and Washington were complicated, however, because U.S. policy toward the Jewish DPs, and in particular the demand that one hundred thousand Jewish DPs be transferred to Palestine, created the linkage between the Jewish DP problem in Europe and the question of Palestine that British policy-makers so strenuously strove to avoid. It was to drag them into prolonged, sometimes acrimonious negotiations on how to solve these two problems in a way that would be acceptable to both main powers, if not to all parties involved.

CONFLICTING ATTITUDES

Truman Intervenes

Along with Harrison's proposals about the treatment of the Jewish DPs in the American zone, Truman also adopted his recommendation that he appeal to Britain to allow one hundred thousand Jewish DPs to enter Palestine. On the same day that he censured Eisenhower, 31 August 1945, Truman informed Prime Minister Clement Attlee of Harrison's mission. Attaching a copy of his report, Truman called Attlee's attention to Harrison's suggestion that the problem could be solved by a quick transfer to Palestine of as many nonrepatriable Jews as possible and added that already at the Potsdam Conference he had noted that persecuted European Jews ought to be allowed into Palestine.[1] At the time Truman had appealed to Churchill, then prime minister, to remove the 1939 White Paper limitations on Jewish immigration to Palestine and during a press conference after his return from the Potsdam Conference had stated: "The American view on Palestine is that we want to let as many of the Jews into Palestine as it is possible to let into that country. Then the matter will have to be worked out diplomatically with the British and the Arabs, so that if a state can be set up there, they may be able to set it up on a peaceful basis. I have no desire to send 500,000 American soldiers there to make peace in Palestine."[2]

Truman's intention to announce his support for some of Harrison's proposals publicly did not sit well with London. In an attempt to influence Truman not to take this step, Foreign Secretary Bevin warned that if Truman applied pressure to allow one hundred thousand DPs to enter Palestine, he would announce in Parliament that he expected the Americans to send four divisions to keep order.[3] Obviously, Truman's remarks at the press conference had revealed the Americans' Achilles' heel.[4] Attlee informed Truman of the consequences he feared could be expected in the Middle East and among the ninety million Muslims in India if one hundred thousand Jewish DPs were moved to Palestine. He also mentioned that the Jews refused to accept the quota of fifteen hundred certificates per month. The British prime minister saw no reason to accord preferential treatment to the Jewish DPs and praised the policy of the British military authorities in Germany and Austria, which was to treat the Jewish DPs exactly the same as all others.[5]

The president's appeal to Britain to allow Jewish refugees to enter Palestine ended the tacit understanding that had emerged during the preparations for the Evian Conference in the spring of 1938 and had lasted throughout the war. Simply put, it meant that America would not demand that Britain allow Jewish refugees into Palestine as long as the British did not ask the United States to change its immigration legislation. The president's initiative may have stemmed from his own deep shock at the terrible tragedy that had befallen the Jewish people at the hands of the Germans, but it was also influenced by pressure put on him by Jewish organizations in the United States. In addition, sympathy for the survivors prevailed among members of Congress. For example, before leaving for Potsdam, Truman had been given a memorandum signed by 54 Senators and 250 members of the House of Representatives urging him to use his influence with the British government "to open forthwith the doors of Palestine to unrestricted Jewish immigration and colonization" and to work toward "establishing Palestine as a free and democratic Jewish Commonwealth at the earliest possible time." It seems that when he presented the British with his demand, Truman refused to see, or ignored, the possible implications of letting thousands of Jews move into Palestine. For him the transfer of Holocaust survivors to Palestine was a humanitarian act intended to make up for the appalling events of World War II.[6]

Lord Halifax, Britain's ambassador in Washington, more pragmatically attributed the president's position on the question of Jewish DPs to competition between the Democratic and Republican Parties for the "Jewish vote" in the key state of New York.[7] This Jewish vote was a relatively new factor in the American political arena. It first received expression in the presidential election campaign in 1944, when both candidates, Roosevelt and Thomas Dewey, supported "re-constitution of Palestine as a free and democratic Jewish commonwealth as well as unrestricted immigration to Palestine." Until then, the American Jewish community had had little political leverage, as shown during the war when it failed to persuade the administration to come to the aid of European Jews, including opening the gates to Jewish immigration. Fear of anti-Semitism during the 1930s and the early 1940s, the traditional support of the American Jews for the Democratic Party (approximately 90 percent of the Jews voted for Roosevelt in 1944), and the absence of a united Jewish front to a large extent neutralized any influence the Jewish community might have had on the administration.[8]

Soon after the end of the war, Halifax analyzed how the Jewish community had begun increasing its political power. The ambassador first called attention to the five million Jewish American citizens, many of whom held influential positions that gave them access to the White House, the government, and the press. He noted how the tremendous importance of the Jewish vote in the key state of New York enabled the Jews to apply considerable pressure on the administration, Congress, and public opinion. (New York had 47 electoral votes out of 266 the presidential candidate needed while the number of Jewish residents was about 14 percent.) Still, their influence depended primarily on their ability to enlist the support of non-Jewish leaders in the administration and in Congress. Non-Jewish public opinion was not much interested in solutions to the Palestine problem unless they involved immigration to the United States. Yet the horrors the Jews had suffered during the war affected certain circles in the United States. Influential liberals felt that more should have been done during the war to take Jews out of Europe and bring them to Palestine. It was argued that if the British had permitted more Jews to enter Palestine before the war, one million Jews could have been saved.[9] These same circles believed that Palestine was the natural refuge for Jews who wanted to leave Europe. According to Halifax, the average U.S. citizen "does not want them [Jews] in the United States and salves his conscience by advocating their admission to Palestine." In this way, the Jews enjoyed the support of the liberals, moved by humanitarian sentiments, as well as that of many anti-Semites. Non-Jewish public opinion, the ambassador added, tended to regard Palestine as the place where Britain was pursuing colonial policies and, because of imperialist considerations, encouraged the Arabs to act against the Jews with the aim of retaining its status in the Middle East. Halifax warned that any solution to the Palestine question that could be interpreted as the closing of doors to the immigration of Jewish Holocaust survivors would be represented by "liberal-minded critics" as an inhumane act, dictated by egotistical motives. He was particularly concerned by the possibility that British soldiers might kill Jews. If that happened, he warned, public opinion in the United States "might become violently inflamed against His Majesty's Government." Still, Halifax was not entirely pessimistic, drawing encouragement from the fact that the State Department was more favorably inclined toward the Arabs than to the Zionist cause.[10]

Halifax's assessment of State Department priorities was well founded. Several days after Truman took office, Secretary of State Edward R. Stettinius warned him not to yield to pressure Jewish leaders were expected to exert on him to support unlimited immigration of Jews to Palestine and the establishment of a Jewish state. Fearing that Zionist pressure and the tragedy the Jews had undergone in the course of the war would combine to sway the president, Stettinius emphasized that "the question of Palestine is . . . a highly complex one and involves questions which go far beyond the plight of the Jews of Europe." In other words, in view of the vital American interests in the region, "we feel that this whole subject is one that should be handled with the greatest care and with a view of the long-range interests of this country."[11]

When he drafted his plan for a solution to the problem of Palestine, Bevin did not ignore the electoral importance which the American administration attached to American Jews. In consultation with British representatives in Arab countries in mid-September 1945, Bevin singled out the Jewish vote in the United States as one of the central considerations that had led him to postpone a decision on long-term policy for Palestine.[12] Still, the foreign secretary recognized the need to counter the intensive campaign the Zionist organizations were waging in the United States against British policy in Palestine. Bevin learned from Halifax that the Zionists were exploiting the approaching 1946 midterm elections to mobilize support for their position and that both large parties were eager to capture the Jewish vote, especially in New York. Halifax was particularly bothered by the consensus among Democrats and Republicans in Congress in regard to the Zionist cause. He pointed to the debate in the Senate on 2 October 1945 in which representatives of both parties had called for the provision of quick and efficient assistance to those who had been the prime victims of Hitler and had denounced the limitations Britain imposed on large-scale immigration of Jews to Palestine. Republican senators, headed by Robert A. Taft of Ohio, Truman's major political rival, expressed strong support for Truman's proposal for the immediate granting of one hundred thousand immigration certificates to Jewish DPs. Taft, furthermore, wanted to see Britain's Palestine policy brought into current negotiations with Britain on a request it was then making for an urgently needed loan.

This hostility toward Britain in Congress greatly worried Halifax, and he urged Whitehall to try to solve "at least the problem of immigration." He thought there were two alternative courses of action his government could take. The first was to invite the Americans to share the responsibility for the implementation of their recommendations. Though this would rescue the British from the unpleasant situation that now allowed the Americans to criticize them all the time, it was not a very desirable move as far as the Americans were concerned. The second alternative, which Halifax believed to be the more practical, was to transfer the question of immigration to the United Nations.[13]

Anglo-American Negotiations

Halifax was clearly feeding into the deliberations of the British cabinet as it was trying to come to grips with the issue. In the cabinet session of 4 October 1945, Attlee stressed the need to reach a decision in light of American pressure (the White House had published Harrison's report just a few days earlier) — an announcement on British policy concerning Palestine should not be delayed beyond the third week in October. The cabinet should make public its fears that it expected an explosion in the Middle East if Britain allowed one hundred thousand Jews into Palestine. It was also argued that such a step alone could not solve the problem of European Jewry and that not all the Jews in Europe were living in intolerable conditions. Still, it could not be denied that Jews were living in difficult circumstances in Europe and in certain places were even subject to persecution. Conditions in the British zone, the cabinet stressed, were better than in the American one.

In line with the strategy he favored of cooperation with the Americans, Bevin suggested adopting a new approach to the problem. His idea was to involve the Americans in a joint policy on Palestine, if only to put an end to the pressure Washington was exerting on London regarding the admittance of one hundred thousand Jewish DPs. The foreign secretary told his cabinet colleagues that American agitation over the Palestine issue "was poisoning British relations with the United States Government in other fields."[14] Bevin was not unaware of the risk he was taking by involving the Americans in the Palestine problem, as shown, for example, by his private correspondence with Halifax. Zionist propaganda in New York, he wrote, had diminished the possibility of bringing Jews and Arabs to the negotiating table. Bevin sharply condemned the electoral tactics the White House was applying in the New York mayoralty campaign of November 1945: "I feel that the United States has been thoroughly dishonest in handling this problem. To play on racial feelings for the purpose of winning an election is to make a farce of their insistence on free elections in other countries."[15] Bevin thought the White House was cynically exploiting the plight of Jewish DPs in the local elections (approximately 20 percent of the population of New York City was Jewish).

Nevertheless, Halifax was instructed to convey to American secretary of state Byrnes Britain's suggestion to set up an Anglo-American inquiry committee.

He did so on 19 October. After rejecting reports that the conditions of the Jewish DPs were worse than those of the other Nazi victims and briefly reporting on the steps that had been taken to improve their situation, Halifax restated that integrating the Jews in the rehabilitation of living conditions in the countries from which they had come remained an important part of Britain's policy. Accordingly, the proposed Anglo-American committee was to examine the position of the Jews in British and American occupied Europe; to estimate the number of Jews who could not be resettled in their countries of origin; to look into the possibility of relocating DPs in non-European countries; and to consider other ways of meeting the needs stemming from the situation. The idea was for the committee first to visit the American and British occupation zones in Europe so as to make an updated assessment of the nature and dimensions of the problem. The committee was to recommend plans of action to both governments for the interim period, until a permanent solution could be proposed to the United Nations, and it would consider the question of Jewish immigration into Palestine as one option among others. Halifax informed Byrnes of the situation in Palestine and told him the government was to make a declaration in Parliament on 25 October about its plans for Palestine's future. If the United States were to agree to take part in the inquiry committee, he added, there would also be an announcement to that effect.[16]

Byrnes tended to favor the idea of a joint inquiry committee but told Halifax that if they wanted the president to agree, the objectives of the committee ought to be modified. As Truman's position was "almost entirely coloured by the New York election," Byrnes was unhappy that the proposals placed only slight emphasis on Palestine, and he was afraid the Jews would regard them as "merely evasive and dilatory devices." The American counterrecommendation spoke of examining the political, economic, and social conditions in Palestine "as they bear upon the problem of Jewish immigration and settlement therein and the well-being of the peoples now living therein"; examining the situation of the Jews in European countries where they had been the victims of Nazi and fascist persecution and the steps that had been or would be taken in these countries to enable them to live there without discrimination or persecution; estimating the number of those of them who would wish or be obliged to migrate to Palestine or to other countries outside Europe; listening to the opinions of the sides involved in the matter, including representatives of the Arabs and the Jews, on the Palestine question and on ways to achieve a permanent solution to the problem; and recommending to the governments of the United States and Britain the steps that should be taken in European countries or the assistance that should be given in transferring and settlement in non-European countries.[17]

The differences between the two proposals reflected the different objectives of each of the two countries. The British suggestion emphasized a solution for the problem of the Jewish DPs in Europe whereby Palestine as the destination of the immigration was more or less hidden away in the general definition of "other countries outside Europe." Such wording could be interpreted as a retreat on the part of the president from his previous declarations on the matter and thus was unacceptable to the Americans. Moreover, "other countries outside Europe" might be interpreted as meaning that the United States was the main destination for Europe's Jewish DPs, especially as the experience of the last few years had shown that the various other non-European countries were not inclined to open their doors to Jewish refugees. Thus the American proposal put Palestine central in any solution for the problem of the Jewish DPs.

Even though it largely ran counter to Britain's objectives, Bevin accepted Byrnes's proposal about the goals of the joint committee in order to secure American participation. There were further compromises, one of which was the American demand that the committee be given 120 days in which to submit its report, while Bevin was not interested in limiting the time span of its activity.[18] Bevin even went so far as to concede to Byrnes's demand that any announcement in Parliament about setting up the committee be delayed until after the New York elections. According to Byrnes, any statement in Parliament to the effect that the American government had agreed to take part in a joint inquiry committee was liable to be interpreted as an attempt on the part of the United States to postpone large-scale immigration to Palestine, which in turn "would inflame the million or so Jewish voters as also their sympathies and altogether destroy the prospects of the Democratic candidate whose Republican rival for Mayor was . . . a Jew."[19]

Byrnes further warned Bevin that if the request to postpone the announcement of the establishment of the committee was not heeded, the president would for electoral reasons find himself obliged to come out with a clear statement on the question of the migration of Jews from Europe to Palestine. Such a declaration, the secretary of state stressed, not only would endanger the suggested cooperation between the two governments in finding a solution to the Palestine problem but would also inevitably have an adverse effect on Anglo-American relations. Once the elections were out of the way, Byrnes promised, "everything would be plain sailing for us both."[20] The secretary of state did not have to back up his warning by explicitly mentioning the negotiations for the American loan, which Halifax knew was already running into serious difficulties in Congress.[21]

Timing was a delicate issue for London, too. The annual pilgrimage to Mecca that year took place in November, culminating on 14 November. For a considerable period before and after that date, there would be the traditional gathering of millions of Muslims from all parts of the world, including a large contingent from India. British representatives in the Middle East strongly urged that no announcement be made during this period. In their view, there was a strong possibility that pressure would be brought to bear at Mecca on the various Arab governments to harden their attitude toward Jewish immigration. If the announcement was regarded as unfavorable to the Arabs, the result might be a serious antiforeign demonstration, which in this setting would have widespread consequences. Furthermore, if King Ibn Saud felt that he had been let down by both Britain and America, he might no longer be so willing to restrain antiforeign elements during the pilgrimage.[22] A frustrated Bevin was forced to give in: "I recognize the difficulties they are faced with," he wrote to Halifax, "but I really do not think that this is sufficient to determine foreign policy."[23] To his ambassadors in the Arab countries he wrote that the excited feelings over Palestine that were making themselves felt in New York's electoral campaign apparently precluded further progress toward an understanding with the Americans until after November.[24]

Several motives led Bevin to yield to Washington's demands vis-à-vis a joint Anglo-American committee. First, he assumed that involving the Americans would defuse the quarrel between the two countries over both the Palestine question and the Jewish DP problem and thereby put an end to pressure from Washington on the question of the Jewish DPs. He also thought that once the New York elections were over, the White House would return to setting U.S. foreign policy detached from considerations of internal politics and that it would then come around to adopting the British course. Last, getting the United States involved in the Palestine problem fitted in with Bevin's general aim of preventing the Americans from returning to isolationism as they had done after World War I. Bevin knew that Britain could not on its own block Moscow's attempts to expand the Soviet sphere of influence. Two days before he suggested setting up an Anglo-American committee to the cabinet, the first meeting of the Council of Foreign Ministers in London (September 11–October 2, 1945) had ended in total failure, leading Bevin to the conclusion that efforts to reach an understanding with the Soviets were useless.[25]

The difference in approach also comes through clearly in the communiqués that were issued in Washington and London announcing the establishment of the joint inquiry committee. In his speech in Parliament, Bevin set out his views on the problem of the Jewish DPs, the Palestine question, and the degree to which they were related, none of which was to be found in the official version of the committee's objectives. While he identified with the anguish of the Jews following the catastrophe that had befallen them, Bevin reviewed the efforts Britain was making to improve their situation, adding that the Jews should not be driven out of Europe and that Palestine alone could not be the solution for the Jewish problem.[26] During the press conference after his parliamentary statement, Bevin said, "I am very anxious that the Jews in Europe shall not overemphasize their racial position. The keynote of the statement I made in the House is that I want the suppression of racial warfare, and therefore, if the Jews, with all their sufferings, want to get too much at the head of the queue, you have the danger of another antisemitic reaction through it all."[27]

This was not the only time Bevin would make a controversial statement at a critical moment. On this occasion it raised a storm among both Zionist and non-Zionist Jews and did much to label Bevin as anti-Semitic.[28] Such language as he had used was not uncommon among certain government officials in London, as shown, for example, by a letter Attlee sent to Truman on 16 September.[29] What made the difference, of course, was the forum and the timing. Rather than reflecting anti-Semitic sentiments, Bevin's admittedly insensitive remarks signaled a clear sense of frustration. Throughout his long political career Bevin until then had never expressed anti-Semitic views.[30] Covert prejudice can probably be found in most human beings and more easily comes to the surface in moments of stress and anger, and Bevin was known for having difficulty controlling his temper. In the communiqué put out by Washington Truman simply reiterated that his policies had remained unchanged since his 31 August letter to Attlee, and this included the proposed distribution of one hundred thousand certificates to the Jewish DPs.[31]

The negotiations on setting up the AAC committee strengthened London's concern about what it saw as the undue influence of American Jewry on White House decisions concerning Palestine, and British diplomats began devoting more attention to the outlook of American Jews and to their general standing within overall American society. In a comprehensive report sent to the Foreign Office early in 1946, the British embassy in Washington reported the results of polls conducted by Elmo Roper for *Fortune* magazine which showed that 80 percent of the American Jews who had an opinion about Palestine defined themselves as pro-Zionist. Normally, the embassy commented, most American Jews paid very little attention to Zionism, "but at times like the present when its emotional tides are running high, and in a country where the most moderate championship of the Arab cause produces immediate and violent accusations of antisemitism (the Arabs are not counted as Semites), few can afford to stay off the Zionist bandwagon." Anti-Semitism in the United States, according to Roper, was in direct proportion to the concentration of Jewish population: strongest in the Northeast and Midwest and in large cities; weakest in the Far West, the South, and in small towns where the percentage of Jews was negligible.[32]

In early January 1946, the AAC began hearing testimony in Washington. Members then flew to London, and on 5 February it divided into working groups, each of which visited different areas of Europe. The Soviets prevented the committee from touring their occupation zones in Germany and Austria, as well as Bulgaria, Rumania, and Hungary, claiming there was no need because the Soviet government did not allow any racial discrimination.[33] The true reason behind Moscow's refusal to cooperate had more to do with the fact that the Soviets had not been asked to participate in the negotiations that preceded the committee's establishment or in the committee itself.

In Europe visits of the AAC concentrated on the DP camps. The British were well aware that the Zionists had sent special delegations from Palestine to Europe to "prepare" the DPs for the visit of the committee to the camps.[34] But in the words of AAC member Richard Crossman, a Labour MP and a firm political opponent of Bevin, "Even if there had not been a single foreign Zionist or a trace of Zionist propaganda in the camps these people would have opted for Palestine."[35] Crossman describes the meeting with the DPs as follows:

> They [the committee members] had smelled the unique and unforgettable smell of huddled, homeless humanity. They had seen and heard for themselves what it means to be the isolated survivor of a family deported to [a] German concentration camp or slave labour. The abstract arguments about Zionism and the Jewish state seemed curiously remote after this experience of human degradation. . . . For the first time we could appreciate the patient impatience of the witnesses in Washington and London who had tried to shove into our uncomprehending minds even a shadow of an idea of what was happening in Austria and Germany.[36]

In the final report of the AAC, which was submitted on 20 April 1946, there are several sections describing the situation of the DPs. The AAC was "deeply impressed by the tragedy of the situation of these Jewish survivors in the centers and by the tragedy of their purposeless existence. Many months have passed since they were freed from Nazi oppression and brutality, but they themselves feel that they are as far as ever from restoration to normal life."[37]

Of the AAC's ten recommendations, the second directly stemmed from its visits to the DP camps. It proposed "that 100,000 certificates be authorized immediately for the admission into Palestine of Jews who have been the victims of

Nazi and Fascist persecution" and that preference be given to those DPs in the camps and to Jews in liberated Germany and Austria who were no longer in the camps. Here the committee had adopted one of Harrison's recommendations that had Truman's support. While the committee estimated the number of Jewish refugees and DPs in various European countries to be 391,000, it suggested an immediate solution only for the estimated 98,000 DPs then in Germany, Austria, and Italy. In the end, however, the committee failed to find the exact wording that could bridge the gap between Washington and London, if such a formula existed at all, given the disparity in their objectives. Within only a few days after the report had been submitted, disagreement between the two sides again came to the surface.

Although he was fully aware of the problematics involved, within the British Cabinet Defence Committee, which discussed the report on 24 April, Bevin was the only one in favor of accepting it, not the least since the report's recommendations had been made unanimously (at the beginning of their investigation, Bevin had assured AAC members that if the report were submitted unanimously, he would adopt it). Bevin hoped that this would lead the U.S. government to cooperate in solving the Palestine problem. While not concealing his apprehension of how the Arabs would react to proposals that asked for one hundred thousand certificates to be distributed and the 1939 White Paper restrictions on the sale of land to Jews to be lifted, Bevin believed that with American participation the recommendations could be put into practice. Attlee, however, was highly critical of the report, arguing that in effect no country except for Palestine would contribute to the absorption of the remnants of European Jewry. He anticipated that implementation of the recommendations would arouse the anger of both the Arabs and the Jews against Britain, and he felt certain that the Americans would press to allow the DPs into Palestine. George Hall, the colonial secretary, thought that adoption of the proposals should be conditional on American readiness to share responsibility for their implementation, and he did not rule out the possibility of transferring responsibility for Palestine to other countries. The chief of the imperial general staff, Viscount Alanbrooke, had reservations about this possibility, stressing the strategic importance of Palestine as the last remaining British foothold in the eastern Mediterranean in light of the unsettled situation in Egypt. He also mentioned the importance of the sources of oil in the Middle East.[38]

British diplomats in the Arab countries were seriously disturbed by the AAC report. Grafftey-Smith, British consul in Jedda, maintained that from the point of view of the British government's relations with Middle East states and the Muslim world, "this is a disastrous report." He urged Whitehall to reject the recommendation of Jewish immigration out of hand because the Arabs considered the indefinite continuation of Jewish immigration "too high a price to pay for an increasing standard of living up to the level of Jewish civilization." He therefore suggested that with the publication of the committee's report, Whitehall should make it clear that it was not bound automatically and irrevocably by its recommendations.[39] H. Stonehewer Bird in Baghdad argued that the report reversed the principle that immigration should be continued only if the Arabs consented and "that no term or limit is proposed for schemes so that Arabs will foresee ultimate Jewish numerical equality or unqualified superiority." Granting one hundred thousand certificates, he maintained, "represents a greater rate of immigration than that in the early 1930s which induced Arab solidarity against Zionism." The diplomat resented the committee's assumption as though Palestine belonged to Arabs and European Jews alike.[40] For their part, the Zionists were not satisfied with the report because the AAC did not recommend the establishment of a Jewish state in Palestine.

The CFM meeting in Paris enabled Bevin and Byrnes to discuss the report face-to-face. In their 26 April conversation, Bevin told Byrnes that he was willing to permit the entrance into Palestine of one hundred thousand DPs on condition that the Jews be disarmed; he hoped that the Americans would be prepared to send soldiers to help the British achieve this objective. He was critical of the Jewish Agency, whose policy, he said, "had been to smuggle arms illegally into Palestine and to select Jews for immigration for militant purposes." Many of the Jewish immigrants, Bevin charged, "were not genuine refugees at all." (On the previous day, seven British soldiers had been killed in Tel Aviv by LHI.) More important, Bevin told Byrnes that the British government was seriously weighing the possibility of abandoning Palestine because the task of governing it was a thankless one, entailing both a great economic and military burden. Such a step, the foreign secretary warned, would enable the Russians to step in and take Britain's place.[41]

With these intimations Bevin hoped to influence the United States to take into serious consideration the constraints under which Britain was laboring. He tried to exploit both U.S. anxiety over the expansionist intentions of the Soviets in the Middle East, which had found expression in the Iran crisis, and Washington's objections to the idea of sending troops to the region. While Bevin was somewhat exaggerating the British cabinet's state of mind, both Attlee and Dalton, the chancellor of the exchequer, at the time, supported British withdrawal from the Middle East, in large part because of Britain's own economic crisis. Bevin and the chiefs of staff strongly opposed the prime minister's stand.[42]

Attlee then suggested that a committee of officials headed by Cabinet Secretary Norman Brook assess the AAC recommendations. This committee was very critical of the AAC, which it felt had not made any contribution to a solution to the problem of the Jews (proposal no. 1). The recommendation to grant one hundred thousand certificates, it claimed, was based not on an analysis of the economic and political capacity of Palestine to absorb these people but rather simply on the number of Jewish DPs living in camps in Europe and the fact that no other country was ready to take them in. The failure of the AAC to name countries besides Palestine that were willing to accept these Jews, and the fact that there were an additional five hundred thousand Jews in Europe who might want or need to migrate, it argued, would cause the Arabs to think this distribution of one hundred thousand certificates was only the first stage on the way to bringing in five hundred thousand Jews. The Brook committee was convinced that adoption of the AAC report would seriously compromise Britain's status in the Middle East and perhaps also in India. In any case, it was stressed, disbanding the illegal Zionist organizations would need to be made a precondition for any increase in Jewish immigration to Palestine.[43]

Bevin did not share the Brook committee's pessimism, and at the cabinet meeting on 29 April he remained adamant that through cooperation with the Americans it would be possible to reach a solution based on the recommendations of the AAC. He was opposed to transferring the matter to the Security Council of the UN and dismissed the predictions of violent reactions on the part of the Arabs, believing that the cabinet "should not be unduly alarmed by some initial clamor from the Arab States." In the meeting there was general agreement that the Americans should be pressed into absorbing DPs in the United States and dealing with the problem of the resettlement of European Jews as part of the overall refugee problem. The cabinet decided not to react immediately upon publication of the report, and Bevin was asked to find out how willing the Americans were to help militarily and economically in implementing the AAC's recommendations.[44]

Further Discords

The cabinet ministers, however, discounted the possibility that President Truman might decide to move ahead quickly. One day after the cabinet meeting an advance version of the speech Truman was to deliver the next day jointly with the publication of the AAC's report reached London. Of the ten recommendations contained in this report, the president endorsed only those favorable to the Zionists. The proposed statement read as follows: "I am very happy that the request which I have made for the immediate admission of 100,000 Jews into Palestine has been unanimously endorsed by the Anglo-American Committee of Enquiry. The transference of these unfortunate people should now be accomplished with great dispatch." Truman also expressed satisfaction with the committee's recommendation to abrogate the White Paper of 1939 with its limitations on immigration and acquisition of land in order to further the development of a Jewish national home.[45] Truman's decision to highlight those aspects of the report which suited him had largely to do with political considerations: from the president's standpoint, there was a danger that the press and antiadministration forces would emphasize precisely those aspects considered negative by the Zionists, while midterm elections were only six months away. Perhaps Truman also wished in this way to send the British a clear message that although his position that one hundred thousand Jewish DPs should be moved to Palestine remained unchanged, he had no interest in the political aspect of the Palestine question.

Attlee and Bevin both felt betrayed by the president's statement and decided to fight back. At Bevin's suggestion, in his speech to Parliament on 1 May the prime minister stressed that until the illegal armies in Palestine were disbanded, the Mandatory government could not absorb the large number of immigrants mentioned in the AAC report. Noting the difficulties involved, he added that the government intended to examine the extent of American willingness to share the military and financial responsibilities entailed in the implementation of the report's proposals.[46]

The prime minister's statement failed to assuage the leaders of the Arab League countries, who quickly convened their first summit meeting in Anshass, Egypt, at the end of May. They demanded that Britain put a complete stop to Zionist immigration, prevent the transfer of Arab land into Zionist hands, and grant independence to Palestine. Britain and the United States were warned that any adoption of the AAC's recommendations would be considered a hostile act not only against the Arabs of Palestine but also against the Arab countries themselves. Another emergency meeting of the council of the Arab League convened in Bludan, Syria, on 8 June. The league adopted several secret resolutions that were to go into effect in case the recommendations of the AAC were implemented. These resolutions dealt with political and economic sanctions against Britain and the United States.[47]

Bearing the diplomatic brunt of the renewed confrontation between Washington and London on the matter of the Jewish DPs, Halifax was soon sending worried reports from the U.S. capital. The demand to bring one hundred thousand Jews to Palestine was acceptable to American public opinion, but chances were meager that the United States would agree to Britain's request for American assistance in the form of soldiers and money.[48] As examples of how the press covered the renewed Anglo-American discord, Halifax reported on two typical articles, one favoring the American stand and the other the British position. Isidor F. Stone, writing in *P.M.*, claimed that Attlee's declaration had taken events back to their starting point in September 1945 when Truman had first asked the British to permit the entry of one hundred thousand Jews into Palestine. The demand that the United States share the military responsibility with Britain in the case of an Arab uprising, he argued, could have been made sooner without the need for a committee of inquiry. In Stone's opinion, the demand to disband the military organizations would lead to unlimited delay in the immigration of the one hundred thousand. He believed that raising what actually was an impossible condition put in question the sincerity of the British government and led many to think that the real purpose of the inquiry had been to delay progress.[49] Conversely, an editorial in the *New York Herald-Tribune* reflected to a great extent the thinking of the British government on Truman's policy regarding the Jewish DPs. The newspaper attacked the president for expecting that the part of the report which was to his liking would be implemented immediately while the remaining recommendations could wait and instead called on him to stop trying to make "political capital out of the miseries of the Jews and the tragedies of the Palestine dilemma without accepting any responsibility in the premises."[50]

Differences of opinion also prevailed at the U.S. State Department. General John H. Hildring, assistant secretary of state for occupied areas, assailed the delaying tactics of the British and maintained that the conditions they had set not only were inconsistent with the recommendations of the AAC but had been discussed and rejected by it. In his view, U.S. military and political interests in Germany and Austria necessitated the rapid resettlement of the Jewish DPs and the American government should pursue "an aggressive policy of needling the British to implement the Committee's recommendation for entry of 100,000 immediately and without reference to future action on any other aspects of the Report." Hildring believed that in light of Attlee's public criticism, the president should reiterate his support and announce U.S. readiness to accept responsibility for the transfer of the one hundred thousand DPs to Palestine.[51] In his response to this memorandum, Gordon Merriam, chief of the Division of Near Eastern Affairs, claimed that Hildring was ignoring the complexities of the Palestine question. He believed that the United States should adopt the report in toto, which meant also taking into consideration the position of the Arab countries, since American interests there were as great as its interests in the occupied parts of Europe. The British position should be taken into serious account, and Merriam called attention to the commitment the United States had made to refrain from taking any action that might cause a substantial change in Palestine without consulting with both the Arabs and the Jews.[52] Obviously, this discord between Hildring and Merriam had its roots in their respective areas of responsibility but had a minor effect because the Division of Near Eastern Affairs had very little influence on determining American policy toward Palestine. It was the White House that set the policy.[53]

As it happened, after the publication of the AAC report the British and Americans found themselves ironically in much the same deadlock that had led them to establish the joint committee of inquiry in the first place. Yet both sides sought to avoid an escalation in tension between them, especially in light of the increasingly strained relations with the Soviets. Bevin continued to believe that Britain could derive benefit from cooperating with the Americans in shaping a solution for the Palestine question. His optimism was apparently influenced by the recent successful cooperation between the United States and Britain in the Iran crisis, which had brought about a withdrawal of Soviet forces from that country; by the Senate approval of the British loan on 10 April 1946 (approval by the House of Representatives was still pending); and by the firm stand taken by the Americans vis-à-vis the Soviets in the discussions then taking place at the first session of the CFM in Paris.[54]

The Americans too needed the British in order to make a solution for the Jewish DPs work. The conclusions of the AAC left no doubt that Palestine was the only place to which the Jewish DPs could be transferred. Anxious to find a quick solution, the president understood that loss of the Palestine option would cause increased pressure to open the United States to the immigration of Jewish refugees. He well knew that the majority of the American public opposed such a step. This mutual dependence led the Americans and British to persevere in their search for a solution. Truman did not want to be accused of procrastination and thus was interested in speeding up the Anglo-American discussion on the question of moving one hundred thousand DPs, while the British were afraid that the moment an agreement was reached on this matter, the Americans would walk away from further deliberations on how to solve the Palestine question. London therefore insisted that it would be impossible to transfer one hundred thousand DPs to Palestine before taking decisions on the report as a whole.[55]

In the midst of these contacts with the Americans about continuation of the discussions on the committee's report (and while Congress was heatedly debating the loan so important to Britain), Bevin made another somewhat irresponsible statement. Addressing the Palestine question at the Labour Party conference at Bournemouth on 12 June 1946, Bevin caused tempers to flare by mentioning how propaganda in the United States, particularly in New York, was urging the transfer of one hundred thousand Jews to Palestine. "I hope I will not be misunderstood in America," he remarked, "if I say that this was proposed with the purest of motives. They did not want too many Jews in New York." He went on to say that he did not accept the assumption that Jews could not remain in Europe, and he observed that if one hundred thousand were allowed to enter Palestine within a short period of time, he would be compelled to send an additional division there, which he was not prepared to do.[56]

Bevin's assessment of American unwillingness to absorb Jewish DPs into the United States was shared by many in London. When, on 22 December 1945, Truman had set out U.S. policy on the absorption of DPs and refugees from war-ravaged Europe, he categorically stated that his country's contribution was limited to the scope of immigration provided for by current legislation (which, of course, had been passed long before the war), that unused immigration quotas did not accumulate, and that he was not about to ask Congress to change the law. Most of the potential immigrants were nationals of Central and Eastern European states and of the Balkans, and the quotas for these countries allowed about 39,000 persons to enter the United States each year, but two-thirds of the quota was allocated to Germany. At the same time, he hoped that congressional legislative attempts to ban or drastically limit immigration to the United States would not be successful. In other words, America's contribution to a solution for the DP problem did not go beyond allowing DPs entry within the existing immigration quotas. Jewish DPs, most of whom were Polish citizens, had little reason for optimism, since the annual immigration quota for Poland was 6,524.[57] In a public opinion poll conducted two weeks before Truman published his announcement, respondents were asked about their attitude toward increasing the scope of immigration from Europe to the United States from its prewar level. Five percent supported increasing the quota; 32 percent favored leaving the quota as it was; 37 percent were for lowering the number; 14 percent called for banning immigration to the United States entirely; and 12 percent had no opinion.[58]

Meanwhile, at a mass demonstration in Madison Square Garden, Rabbi Abba Hillel Silver, the militant Zionist leader and co-chairman of the American Zionist Emergency Council, picked up the remarks Bevin had made about New York and called them "a cheap slur on the American people and a coarse bit of anti-semitic vulgarity reminiscent of the Nazis at their worst."[59] New York mayor

William O'Dwyer also condemned Bevin's remarks and went on to criticize the British for erecting a barrier against displaced persons and holding them where there was no food, thereby causing those unfortunates added suffering.[60] The American public did not forgive Bevin for his remarks and demonstrated their resentment when the British foreign secretary visited the United States a few months later. On his arrival, dockers refused to handle his luggage, and later at a football game he attended the crowd booed him.[61] Even though he was asked about Bevin's remarks at a press conference, Truman refrained from responding to them.[62] Apparently, the president did not want public confrontation to further impair contacts on the issue between the two countries.

Halifax tried to bring Bevin to publish a declaration of sorts that might help to dispel the negative atmosphere his words had created. "Your criticism of New York," Halifax wrote Bevin, "has, of course, not only hit the nail on the head but driven it woundingly deep." The ambassador was especially concerned that antiadministration circles might try to represent Bevin's remarks as a personal affront to the president who was so closely identified with the demand that one hundred thousand DPs be transferred to Palestine.[63] The main fear in London centered on whether American Jews would take advantage of this situation to try to adversely influence the outcome of the scheduled vote on the British request of a loan in Congress. But when Secretary of State Byrnes urged Whitehall to publish a statement about Palestine in an effort to allay the criticism of Britain in Congress, the cabinet refused to do so.[64] Bevin informed Halifax that the government would be prepared to allow the entry of one hundred thousand Jews as part of a comprehensive plan that would resolve the two problems of Palestine and the European Jews. But, he observed, he did not agree with the view that Britain is "committed under the mandate to meeting exclusively in Palestine the needs of the European Jews arising out of the war which had just ended." Bevin again stressed the importance he placed on continued close connection with the American government in shaping foreign policy.[65]

Respite for Whitehall

But the remarks Bevin had made at the Labour Party conference were not the only factor that threatened to disrupt British-American contacts. On the night of 16–17 June 1946, the Palmach sabotaged eleven bridges linking Palestine with neighboring countries, causing material damage estimated at about £250,000. The following evening LHI attacked the Haifa railway workshops, and on 18 June, Irgun kidnapped six British officers. The six officers were held hostage to prevent the execution of two Irgun people who had been sentenced to death. This incident coincided with preparatory talks between an American delegation headed by Averell Harriman, American ambassador to Britain, and a British delegation headed by Cabinet Secretary Norman Brook, who were to discuss the technical aspects of transferring one hundred thousand DPs to Palestine. The high commissioner urged the cabinet to halt the discussions, which had started on 17 June 1946, until the six officers had been released, but this idea was rejected because of the considerable importance the cabinet attached to continuing the contacts with the Americans.[66]

Ten days after talks had begun, the Brook-Harriman committee submitted its recommendations. The committee stressed that it had limited its discussions to the physical and economic problems involved in transferring the DPs and had not examined the political and military repercussions that might be expected to follow. The aim had been to formulate an operative plan that could be activated without delay if it were decided to carry out this recommendation of the AAC. Because of the fear that the allocation of 100,000 certificates would encourage Jews to leave Eastern European countries en masse, it was suggested that certificates be distributed only to those DPs already present in the Western occupation zones of Germany and Austria as well as Italy. If there happened to be a surplus of certificates, these were then to go to Jews in Eastern and southeastern Europe. The Brook-Harriman report stated that the AAC's estimate of 98,000 Jewish DPs currently in Germany, Austria, and Italy was no longer up-to-date and that new data indicated there were 133,320 Jewish DPs in the three countries, of whom 84,020 were to be found in the DP camps; altogether 115,570 DPs were interested in immigrating to Palestine.[67] The Brook-Harriman proposals were of limited importance because they were dependent on Anglo-American agreement about the AAC's report as a whole, and they did little more than create the impression that discussion of the matter of the 100,000 certificates was continuing and that a solution to this problem was, from an American standpoint, the first step to be taken. The main discussions would have to tackle how to implement the report in its entirety.[68]

These discussions began two weeks later. In the meantime the Mandatory government took wide-ranging reprisal actions against the Yishuv. About seventeen thousand British soldiers took part in what was called Operation Agatha, which began on 29 June and continued for two weeks. In the course of the operation, the British entered the offices of the Jewish Agency in Jerusalem and arrested about twenty-seven hundred Jews, including four members of the Jewish Agency Executive.[69] The operation had no repercussions on the joint deliberations on the AAC report which started on 13 July. The American delegation was headed by Henry F. Grady, former assistant secretary of state, and the British delegation by Brook who, unlike his American counterpart, was thoroughly informed about all the problems surrounding the Palestine questions and European Jewry. According to the program formulated by the British cabinet, the discussion opened with a consideration of the AAC's first recommendation concerning the Jewish DPs in Europe.[70] Brook divided the subject into two spheres: first, creation of conditions that would enable the Jews to live in Europe without persecution or discrimination; and second, resettlement elsewhere of those Jews who could not be rehabilitated in Europe. As he put it, the AAC had not come up with any practical suggestion for resolving these issues. But neither had he any concrete recommendations of his own to make. Brook refrained from pressing the United States to absorb DPs above and beyond the set legal immigration quotas. Since he wanted to persuade Grady to support a British plan for the solution of the Palestine question, he preferred not to bring up sensitive matters. Also, a demand that America open its gates would almost surely have led Grady to make a similar demand of Britain. As in the not too distant past, when there had been an understanding between the two countries on this subject, the two delegations called on various other countries to take in DPs but avoided making the same recommendation to their own governments. Instead, each of the delegations reviewed the contribution its country had been making to a solution for the problem of Jewish refugees since 1933.[71]

The recommendations the Brook-Grady committee formulated did not embody a solution for the problem of the Jewish DPs in Europe, and most were inoperative. The committee thought that a new international organization ought to be established to deal with the refugee problem and further counted on the goodwill of various countries, including the British dominions, to absorb the Jewish DPs. It was also decided to continue to support the activity of the Inter-Governmental Committee on Refugees, which ever since the Evian Conference in July 1938, where it had been created at Roosevelt's urging, had contributed very little to a solution of the refugee problem. The Brook-Grady committee reconfirmed the conclusion of the AAC that the large majority of the Jewish DPs would continue to live in Europe and that therefore it was necessary to create adequate conditions to help a large number of them to resettle there. It was noted that formerly hostile countries would be compelled by the peace treaties to guarantee human rights, while for other places in Europe, the two governments would need to rely on the United Nations to take action. The delegations recommended adoption of proposals no. 2 and 6 of the AAC, which spoke of the transfer of one hundred thousand DPs to Palestine and of immigration policy afterward respectively, and also wanted to see the Brook-Harriman program implemented regarding the allocation of the one hundred thousand certificates. All this was conditional on the adoption by the two governments of the suggestion for provincial autonomy on which the two delegations had agreed. It was proposed that upon adoption of the constitutional recommendations, transfer would begin of the one hundred thousand DPs and that an attempt would be made to complete the operation within a period of twelve months (rather than five as Harriman had suggested in his talks with Brook). As part of the attempt to halt the illegal sailings, it was suggested that from the moment the first DPs were being transferred to Palestine, the number of illegal immigrants would be subtracted from the quota of one hundred thousand certificates.[72]

At its meeting on 25 July, the cabinet approved the recommendations of the Brook-Grady committee. Brook won praise from Attlee for his professional maneuvering of the Americans (more precisely, Grady) into supporting the British plan for provincial autonomy. Briefly put, this plan called for the division of Palestine into four areas: an Arab and a Jewish province, a district of Jerusalem, and a district of the Negev. Provincial governments would be responsible for the administration of internal matters while the central government, under the British high commissioner, would rule the Jerusalem enclave and the Negev region directly and also retain the sole authority for all of Palestine in such spheres as defense and foreign relations. It was decided that during the first year one hundred thousand Jewish DPs would be allowed to immigrate; thereafter the central government would regulate immigration. In other words, the plan assured the British of the continuation of the Mandate, including the use of Palestine as a base for their armed forces. What was left was to secure President Truman's approval for the committee's recommendations.[73]

While the entire plan was acceptable to Byrnes as a basis for discussions, he was less happy with the idea that transfer of one hundred thousand Jewish DPs would begin only after a Jewish-Arab agreement had been reached on the program as a whole. Afraid the interim period might last for months or even years, the secretary of state explained to Grady that in view of the president's repeated pronouncements concerning the immigration of one hundred thousand DPs, their transfer should begin at once.[74] In a meeting with Attlee and Colonial Secretary Hall, who were then in Paris for the peace conference discussions, Byrnes proposed 1 September 1946 as the final date for commencement of the DP transfer. Attlee opposed setting a specific date before the provincial autonomy plan was accepted.[75] On 31 July Home Secretary Herbert Morrison presented the plan to Parliament.[76]

Swayed by Electoral Considerations

Truman and his cabinet were at first inclined to support the provisional autonomy plan, but following intense pressure on the part of the American Zionists and mindful of the coming midterm elections in November 1946, the president changed his mind. On 7 August, he informed the British that he had decided to reject the plan. In his memoirs Truman was later to write: "I studied the proposed plan with care. But I was unable to see that anything could come out of it except more unrest. The plan made the admission of the hundred thousand conditional on its being accepted by the Arabs, so no relief was offered in that direction either. Nor was this the kind of plan that I had hoped would result. It seemed a retreat from the fine recommendations that had been made by the Anglo-American Committee of Inquiry earlier in the year. I therefore felt compelled to inform Attlee that the Government of the United States could not go along."[77] In an attempt to induce Truman to reconsider his position, Attlee decided to take advantage of what he believed to be the president's Achilles' heel—his public commitment to bring about the transfer of one hundred thousand Jewish DPs to Palestine. The prime minister emphasized that the provincial autonomy proposal would enable a substantial number of Jewish refugees to leave Europe for Palestine in the near future without endangering the peace in the entire Middle East and without placing an unsustainable military burden on Britain. American refusal to support the plan, he warned, would force the British government to suggest an alternative plan at the Jewish-Arab conference, which was due to meet at the end of the month in London, in which the proposed "tempo and extent of Jewish immigration" would have to be modified.[78]

Attlee's arguments did not have their desired effect, however, and on 12 August Truman announced that in view of opposition in the United States to the plan, he was unable to support it.[79] Trying to lessen the disappointment and frustration of the British, Truman added four days later that the American government "has not presented any plan of its own for the solution of the problem of Palestine." He hoped that the projected conversations between the British government and Jewish and Arab representatives would lead to a fair solution of the Palestine problem and that immediate steps would be taken to alleviate the situation of the Jewish DPs in Europe. He further proclaimed that the solution to the Palestine question could not solve the problem of the hundreds of thousands of European DPs and that he intended to ask Congress to pass special legislation that would allow the entry of "a fixed number" of refugees, including the Jewish DPs, into the United States.[80]

The British embassy in Washington had no doubts about the president's motives for rejecting the plan. "This deplorable display of weakness," Lord Inverchapel, the new British ambassador in Washington, wrote to Bevin, "is, I fear, solely attributable to reasons of domestic politics which, it will be recalled, caused the administration last year to use every artifice of persuasion to defer the announcement about the establishment of the Anglo-American Committee until after the New York elections." Inverchapel based his evaluation, among other things, on talks with Loy W. Henderson, director of the State Department's Near Eastern Division and the official responsible for handling the Palestine question. Henderson, whose views on the Palestine issue were not consistent with the policies of the president, attributed the latter's stance to the opposition of the American Zionist leadership to the plan. Citing the fact that the two chairmen of the American Zionist Emergency Council belonged to different political parties (Stephen Wise was a Democrat and Abba Hillel Silver a Republican), the State Department official suggested that "neither, therefore, could afford compromise without certainty that the other would at once derive political benefit from his decision. With both leaders thus solidly opposed to the joint recommendations, the administration dared not take the risk of antagonizing the powerful Zionist lobby in an election year." [81]

Inverchapel was not impressed by the president's announcement that he would act to bring the DPs to the United States. He observed that not only did this declaration not arouse any enthusiasm in Congress, but there was even word of initiatives to cut the existing quota by half. The ambassador quoted one of the newspapers to the effect that Congress supported rescue of the Jews by sending them to Palestine and that it did not intend to consider the possibility of allowing even some of them to enter the United States. [82] The American public as well failed to show any enthusiasm for the idea of increasing immigration quotas. In a public opinion poll in August 1946, 72 percent were opposed to the president's initiative, 16 percent were in favor, and 12 percent had no opinion. [83]

Inverchapel's analysis of the president's decision to reject the provincial autonomy plan seems accurately to reflect the course of events. Truman and Byrnes were at first inclined to support the British proposal. But intensive Zionist pressure coupled with the approach of the midterm elections in November 1946 led the president to dissociate himself from the provincial autonomy program, which the Zionists portrayed as part of British efforts to preserve the Mandate. A typical example of the pressure brought to bear on the president was the warning he received in early August from the New York State Democratic Committee chairman, Paul E. Fitzpatrick: "Looking only at the political side of the question, if this plan goes into effect, it would be useless for the

Democrats to nominate a state ticket for the election this fall. I say this without reservation and am certain that my statement can be substantiated."[84]

Approximately two months later, the British had to absorb another blow when Truman expressed cautious support for a Zionist program toward a solution of the Palestine question. This time as well the president presented the British with a fait accompli. On the evening of 3 October, Truman informed Attlee of his intention to publish an announcement the following day concerning the Jewish DPs and the Palestine question. He was led to do so, he claimed, by Britain's communiqué of the previous day about the postponement until 16 December 1946 of the talks that had been going on in London between the British and representatives of the Arab countries, primarily because Zionist and Palestinian Arab representatives had boycotted the meetings.[85] This postponement, wrote the president, was causing him much disappointment, and he expressed the hope that during the interim period the transfer of a large part of the one hundred thousand DPs would commence. The timing of the announcement was explained by the president's desire to address the Jews "on the eve of Yom Kippur, the Jews' annual Day of Atonement." Truman then reviewed the course events had taken since the Harrison report, emphasizing his efforts ever since the war to alleviate the situation of the Jewish DPs through the transfer of one hundred thousand of them to Palestine. Now that the conference on the Palestine question had been postponed, the president called for permitting immediate large-scale immigration to Palestine so that the DPs would not need to spend another winter in the camps. He offered the help of the United States in transferring the DPs and called on various nations, including the United States, to be more liberal in absorbing DPs. The president promised, further, to ask Congress to approve economic development aid for Palestine if a solution were found for its problem. In light of the suffering and torment that had been the lot of the Jews in the last war, Truman stressed, the plan should be implemented immediately.

Until then Truman had limited himself to speaking out on the DP problem. This time, however, he went further and also took a stand on the issue of a political solution for the Palestine question. He referred to the widespread attention both the press and public forums were giving to the Jewish Agency proposal to establish "a viable Jewish State in control of its own immigration and economic policies in an adequate area of Palestine instead of in the whole of Palestine." The president asserted that, unlike the provincial autonomy plan, a solution along these lines, which included the immediate allotment of one hundred thousand certificates, would be supported by American public opinion. "I cannot believe," Truman concluded, "that the gap between the proposals which have been put forward is too great to be bridged by men of reason and goodwill. To such a solution our government could give its support."[86] Truman's new initiative took the British completely by surprise, not in the least because during the months since his rejection of the provincial autonomy plan, the president had avoided making any comment on the Palestine question. Moreover, the information generally available to the British suggested that the president would no longer broach the subject. By the end of August, for example, Inverchapel had still reported that "Mr. Truman is held by many to have washed his hands of the Palestine question."[87]

The time span Truman left Attlee to respond was very brief indeed. The prime minister, who tried to convince Truman not to publish the announcement, said the Zionists were to blame for the postponement of the conference on Palestine until December 1946 because they had refused to participate. Attlee emphasized that the British government would neither permit commencement of the transfer of one hundred thousand Jewish DPs to Palestine nor change its immigration policies before the end of the conference on Palestine because the question of immigration was the crux of the problem, and any change in the prevailing policy would lead to a crisis of confidence on the part of the Arabs. The prime minister made it abundantly clear that the announcement the president intended to publish would not be of help to those European Jews wishing to enter Palestine and "would certainly provoke strong reaction from the Arabs and might be the occasion of serious disorder and bloodshed in Palestine." Apparently Attlee realized that to induce the president to delay publication of the announcement so as to reexamine its potential ramifications, he needed to take an aggressive stance on the matter of immigration. Still, he knew Truman was unlikely to change his mind and thus asked him at least to delete the promise to support the program the Jewish Agency had submitted to him. Attlee ended his letter by expressing concern for the difficulties the two governments could expect in dealing with the complex problem of Palestine if the president were to go ahead and publish his declaration.[88]

In the event Truman proved unwilling to delay publication of the statement even for a few hours so as to enable Attlee to communicate on the matter with Bevin, who was at the time at the peace conference in Paris, and the announcement was made public as planned on 4 October 1946.[89] "I have received with great regret your letter," Attlee wrote to Truman, "refusing even a few hours of grace to the Prime Minister of the country which has the actual responsibility for the government of Palestine in order that he might acquaint you with the actual situation and probable results of your action."[90] Attlee's frustration was all the stronger as Truman had also refused his request to omit his promise to support the political solution of the Zionists.

Several days later Truman wrote to Attlee explaining why he made the Yom Kippur statement. He pointed out that postponing the talks with the Arabs and the Jews on Palestine until mid-December 1946 without taking any decision on concrete steps to alleviate the situation of the Jewish survivors had had a most distressing effect on the morale of the displaced European Jews, who for nearly a year and a half had been waiting for a decision about their future. The declaration was timed to coincide with their annual Day of Atonement, when the Jews "are accustomed to give contemplation to the lot of Jewish people." As for Attlee's comment that Britain was the Mandatory power having responsibility for the administration of Palestine, Truman responded: "In our view the development of the Jewish National Home has no meaning in the absence of Jewish immigration and settlement on the land as contemplated in the Mandate. We therefore feel that the implementation of the Mandate, as well as the humanitarian considerations mentioned above, call for immediate and substantial immigration into Palestine."[91]

Attlee did not care much for Truman's explanations and neither did he share the president's special concern for the Jewish DPs, reminding him that the number of non-Jewish refugees was much larger than the number of Jewish DPs. The problem of the refugees, he argued, had to be treated as a whole and special treatment of the Jewish DPs was liable to jeopardize chances for an overall solution of the problem. Palestine could not solve the problem of all the Jewish DPs; distribution of one hundred thousand certificates would provide only a partial solution. Transfer of the DPs to Palestine should occur only in the framework of a comprehensive solution of the Palestine question, which until now had been impossible to achieve, largely because of the refusal of the Jews to enter into negotiations with the British government.[92]

By this time it was clear to both sides that disagreement between Washington and London had gone up a few notches in level of intensity since it no longer involved merely a U.S. rejection of a British plan on how to solve the question of Palestine or a demand to allow one hundred thousand Jewish DPs to go there. Until his Yom Kippur statement Truman had been careful to speak out only on the DP problem, but this time he had also expressed support for an alternative plan for Palestine's future, one that had been proposed by the Zionists but was wholly unacceptable to the British. Still, the declaration itself did not represent an unequivocal and clear-cut stand on a specific solution for Palestine; its main novelty was the call to bridge the gap between the Zionist approach — partition of Palestine—and the British—provincial autonomy. Yet the press interpreted Truman's statement as lending support to the Zionists' partition plan.[93]

Convinced that electoral considerations had once more guided the president, British officials saw Truman's explanations as mere pretext. State Department officials unofficially confirmed the British belief. Dean Acheson, under secretary of state, acknowledged that Truman had given in to intensive pressure from elements in the Democratic Party and Jewish organizations. The president, Acheson added, had been greatly agitated on hearing that all the candidates nominated for the forthcoming elections in New York were to come out with an open attack upon him. Inverchapel concluded, "This is probably what lies behind the action of Mr. Truman who hopes, by the issue of this statement, to stave it off. I fear that we must be prepared for something like a whirlwind here."[94] Inverchapel also learned from Acheson why the president had refused to allow Attlee "a few hours of grace": the fifth of October was the Jewish Day of Atonement and on the sixth, New York State governor Thomas Dewey had been scheduled to make a statement favoring the Zionist solution designed to attract the Jewish vote in the five key states in the East that tended to dominate the presidential elections.[95] Dewey, who had been governor of New York State since 1942, was running for a second term. He also had been the Republican candidate for the presidency in 1944 and was considered a potential presidential candidate for 1948. In his speech that he delivered at a convention of the Jewish Palestine Appeal two days after the Yom Kippur statement, Dewey in effect demanded that hundreds of thousands of Jews be allowed to enter Palestine.[96]

In his memoirs Truman contradicted Bevin's accusations that his Yom Kippur declaration had been made for partisan political reasons, arguing that "Presidents have often made statements on this holiday, so the timing was nothing unusual, and what I had said was simply a restatement of my position: namely, that I wanted to see one hundred thousand Jews admitted to Palestine."[97] The memoirs, however, concealed not only the political pressure to which Truman was then being subjected but also that his popularity had by then plummeted to the point that only one-third of the public supported him, not to mention that this was the first time he had taken a stand concerning a solution to the Palestine problem.[98]

Ambassador Inverchapel found partial comfort in the interpretations the American press was giving to the Yom Kippur statement. The majority of the press, he reported to London, drew "the obvious conclusion from the timing of the statement that the coming elections were at the bottom of it." He was especially happy with an article by James Reston of the *New York Times* that said the president had acted against the counsel of his foreign policy advisers

A demonstration of American Jews against British policy in Palestine
(Courtesy Yad Vashem, Jerusalem)

and had chosen to listen to those who were primarily concerned with a Democratic election majority. Reston claimed that because of its overriding concern with internal politics, the administration could never approach the matter of Palestine with the necessary degree of objectivity. Inverchapel noted that even newspapers usually hostile to Britain on the Palestine issue had joined in the offensive against the administration. He gave the example of a *Washington Post* editorial that, while including "a routine attack on British policy in Palestine," expressed great concern over the fact that presidential demarches were so clearly moved by election considerations that they put a strain on "bipartisan unity" in foreign policy and diminished the influence the United States should be able to exert. High policy, the *Washington Post* editorial advised, should not be put at the mercy of party politics, and for this taint to be removed, handling of the Palestine issue should be given over to the State Department.[99]

The number and painful nature of the failures the British government experienced during the summer and autumn of 1946 in its efforts to influence Washington's position on the Palestine question led T. E. Bromley, first secretary in the British embassy in Washington, to examine the sources of the Jewish community's political power. Zionist pressure was indeed highly effective, and he attributed this to the geographical proximity of Washington and New York. "Election-minded Congressmen and Senators joined in turning on the heat with the United States members of the Anglo-American Committee and the press, much of which in the east is Jewish-owned or dependent on Jewish advertisement." Since the majority of American Jews and their supporters lived on the East Coast, this meant, Bromley remarked, that "if an observer were to judge by that alone it would rightly be said that the country is behind the Zionists. This is, in fact, not the case."

The British diplomat thought that the "shrewder" Zionist leaders must realize that time was not on their side; moreover, they had to be aware that anti-Semitism was a force to be reckoned with in the United States. If their publicity campaign were to last too long or to become too strident, it would provoke a hostile reaction among American Jewry themselves. Even in New York, he maintained, Zionist activities were causing annoyance, while elsewhere in the country there was at best much indifference and at worst hostility. Strong support for the AAC recommendations came only from the coasts, east and west (the latter, particularly around Los Angeles, an area where Jewish communities were also strong). Sympathy for the Zionist demands also emanated from "idealists such as school-teachers, professors, and social workers, who are responsible for much that is best in American life," groups that generally harbored liberal views and commonly championed the underdog. To them, Bromley added, were allied those "into whom a sense of guilt has been instilled by [the] antisemitism of their neighbors." On the whole, the Zionists and their supporters, he observed, were well organized and most vociferous, but their numbers were small compared with the population as a whole.

Analysis of overall American public opinion brought Bromley to the for him frustrating conclusion that "the official attitude was due not to any widespread American feeling on the subject but to the anxiety of a weak president about approaching elections." Still, Bromley believed that the president's sentiments about the DPs were genuine and that Palestine represented the only serious source of Anglo-American political friction at the present time. He therefore cautioned the Foreign Office not to ignore U.S. public opinion on the Palestine question because "[a] policy that can be shown to override the expressed wish of the President of the United States can and will be used whenever the general climate is unfavorable to us, for the purpose of demonstrating that the British, while running to the United States for help in every emergency, are still practicing their old selfish, imperialistic, reactionary tricks and should be firmly told where to get off."

The Republicans' sweeping victory in the November midterm elections, in which they secured control of both the Senate and the House of Representatives for the first time since 1928, would, according to Bromley's analysis, only strengthen the importance of Jewish vote. (In the Senate the Republicans enjoyed a majority of 51 as opposed to 45, and in the House of Representatives, they had 245 delegates compared with 188 Democrats.) He noted the Republican victories in New York, where Governor Dewey had been reelected, receiving 650,000 more votes than his Democratic rival Senator James Mead, and the Republican candidate for the Senate, Irving M. Ives, had routed the former Jewish governor of New York, Herbert Lehman. These victories, Bromley said, were made possible by the switching of a certain percentage of traditionally Democratic Jewish voters. As the Republicans would try to retain these votes for the 1948 presidential campaign, "no present responsibilities need deter them from promising the Zionists the moon," whereas the Democratic administration would do all it could to win back the Jewish vote. "Both parties," Bromley concluded, "may over-estimate the importance of Palestine to the Jewish electorate, but in present circumstances, they will not feel able to take a chance on it." [100]

Foreign Office officials in London were equally bemused by the question of the American Jewish electorate. F. B. A. Rundall, of the northern department of the Foreign Office and formerly a consul general in New York, doubted whether the Jews could "control" any state since they numbered fewer than five million in all, "although the Zionists are apt to claim that their voting strength is decisive in certain areas and the Administration seems all too willing to believe them." Under certain circumstances, Rundall observed, if the Jews of New York State voted en bloc, their vote would carry much weight; however, there seemed little evidence that "this usually happens." Only in certain big cities, notably New York, Philadelphia, and Chicago, did the Jewish vote have real importance. [101] Rundall thereby ignored the importance of the Jewish vote in Pennsylvania (36 electoral votes), Illinois (27 electoral votes), and Ohio (27 electoral votes). Orme Sargent, Foreign Office permanent secretary, called attention to the standing of the Zionists among American Jews, who had direct channels of communication to statesmen, journalists, and shapers of public opinion. He too believed that in those cities where there was a large concentration of Jews, they constituted a political force that could not be ignored. [102]

Truman's Yom Kippur statement caused a number of Foreign Office officials to lose all hope that anything could neutralize the president's electoral considerations. They even lost confidence in the State Department, which until then was considered to have held positions similar to those of the British on such matters as the Jewish DPs and the Palestine question. A remark by Foreign Office official George Rendel typified the prevailing view: "[State Department officials] are terrified of Jewish opinion and are behaving in an even more timid and weak way than usual since the American elections." [103]

In his Yom Kippur declaration Truman had reiterated the need to adopt a more liberal approach in regard to American immigration laws and his readiness to appeal to Congress on the matter. While Bevin was cautiously optimistic over prospects that the administration would now support legislation allowing the entry of larger numbers of DPs into the United States, the embassy in Washington was more skeptical. Still, Bromley claimed that if the UN General Assembly were to advocate joint international action, "the opposition to it in the United States may be overcome, even though the anti-Semites will not fail to note the large proportion of Jews among the displaced persons." [104] When at the end of 1946, Bevin visited the United States, he kept pressing Byrnes for an increase in the immigration quotas to the United States, if possible before the beginning of the London conference that was to discuss a solution for the Palestine problem.[105] Unfortunately for him, this did not transpire.

Around this time, too, the Jewish non-Zionist organizations in the United States, under the impression that the president by now had lost interest in the transfer of one hundred thousand DPs to Palestine, began to campaign for entry of Jewish refugees into the United States. The American Jewish Committee and the American Council for Judaism set up a new body called the Citizens Committee on Displaced Persons to mobilize support among the American public and in Congress. The organization included outstanding non-Jewish figures and was headed by Earl Harrison (who, it will be recalled, had avoided suggesting in his report that the United States open its gates to the DPs) so as to stress its nonsectarian character. Within a short period of time the organization became one of the largest, most efficient pressure groups in the United States, although it failed in opening U.S. gates for Jewish DPs when most of them were still in Europe.[106]

Though he had been deeply disappointed by Truman's Yom Kippur statement, Bevin did not say so publicly, possibly so as not to endanger talks between the Zionists and the Arabs scheduled to begin in London on 27 January 1947 for a solution to the question of Palestine. Those talks indeed took place but had floundered by 13 February, when both the Arabs and the Zionists rejected the "Bevin plan." [107] The failure of the London conference and Britain's decision to transfer the Palestine question to the UN in effect concluded the hapless chapter in Britain's Palestine policies that had begun in the fall of 1945 with the initiative to set up the Anglo-American Committee. Beginning with the AAC's recommendations, none of the British proposals for a solution to the threatening crisis in Palestine had been accepted by the other parties involved, whether the United States, the Zionists, the Arab countries, or the Arabs in Palestine itself.

When the collapse of the London talks highlighted the failure of his policies in Palestine, Bevin, in a speech to Parliament on 25 February, gave full vent to his disappointment with and his bitterness toward the United States. While stating that he did not want to create any ill feelings and arguing that he had done all he could "to promote the best relations" with the United States, he accused Truman of having thwarted his efforts to find a workable solution for the problem of Palestine. "In international affairs," he continued reproachfully, "I cannot settle things if my problem is made the subject of local elections." Bevin blamed the U.S. president for having disregarded the fact that as the country's Mandatory power Britain "carr[ied] the responsibility" for Palestine. Briefly describing the history of his handling of the Palestine question, Bevin sharply criticized American policy on the Jewish DP problem, from the publication of the Harrison report to Truman's Yom Kippur statement, recalling for his audience how Attlee had telephoned him at midnight on 3 October with the information that the president was going to issue another statement on the one hundred thousand. "I begged that the statement not be issued," Bevin related, "but I was told that if it was not issued by Mr. Truman, a competitive statement would be issued by Mr. Dewey." [108]

Bevin realized that his speech would stir up a storm in the United States. He explained to Inverchapel that it was necessary to inform Parliament "how we have striven for American cooperation, and how the attitude of the United States has in fact complicated our problem." Bevin made it clear that he had still not lost hope of resolving the Palestine question without UN involvement. He was convinced that if the Arabs received sufficient assurances as to their future, they would agree to the entry of one hundred thousand Jewish immigrants into Palestine. [109] Harold F. Beeley, adviser to the foreign secretary on Palestine, conveyed a similar message in a talk with John W. Gallman, the U.S. embassy attaché in London. Beeley explained that personally the foreign secretary's views about the one hundred thousand DPs were not very different from those of the Americans and that Bevin would do his best to permit them to enter Palestine as soon as possible but that this must be done on a humanitarian basis and not as a step on the way to creating a Jewish majority in Palestine whose final goal was the establishment of a Jewish state. [110]

The White House quickly issued a statement in response to Bevin's accusations. Byrnes had wanted to criticize the British foreign secretary by name, but

Truman, somewhat surprisingly, opted for a very mild reaction even though Bevin's attack on Truman in Parliament was unprecedented in Anglo-American relations. The president in effect did little more than "merely reaffirm the attitude toward Palestine and Jewish immigration into Palestine which the United States Government has publicly expressed since the summer of 1945." [111] When he recorded this incident in his memoirs, Truman remarked: "This was a very undiplomatic—almost hostile—statement for the Foreign Secretary of the British government to make about the President of the United States." [112] Especially as Bevin, in the British cabinet, had always been the most ardent supporter of an American orientation, his harsh statement should be seen as revealing deep frustration. His foreign policy strategy was grounded on close cooperation with the United States. Moreover, the outburst had come at a highly sensitive point in time. Because of Britain's near economic collapse, the cabinet had several days earlier decided to cease aiding both Greece and Turkey. Bevin, the architect of the aid policy, expected Washington to take over Britain's role in both countries to prevent them from sliding into the Soviet sphere of influence. [113] As Truman was well aware of this, Bevin's contradictory moves puzzled him even more: "At the time that I was weighing the problem of aid to Greece and Turkey, Ernest Bevin had just made a public statement about our Palestine policy that cast a dark shadow over our relations with Britain." [114]

Bevin directed his anger at the U.S. president because it was Truman who had made the problem of the Jewish DPs a central issue in the relations between the two countries and had shaped U.S. policy on the Palestine question. [115] When he initiated the AAC, Bevin was convinced that, had it not been for electoral considerations, the president would have accepted the British solution for the Palestine problem. In his correspondence with his ambassador in Washington he had even attacked the president for cynically exploiting the Jewish DP problem for electoral purposes. But then back in the winter of 1945–46, Bevin had been prepared to take this into account, fearing that the agitation in the United States over the Jewish DPs might harm Anglo-American relations. Because he had assumed that the intrusion (as he saw it) of domestic politics into White House foreign policy would cease after the New York mayoral election, Bevin had involved Washington in formulating an overall policy on Palestine believing that the president would come around to supporting the British course. The midterm elections of November 1946, however, quickly dispelled this illusion.

The Foreign Office failed to recognize that by supporting Zionist goals Democratic and Republican politicians in fact had nothing to lose: there was no risk of antagonizing other organized groups of voters, especially since there was no Arab vote in the United States. The British refused to grasp, furthermore, the importance for American politicians of the generous donations American Jews habitually made to their campaigns. Thus it could happen that Bevin's attempt to exploit the president's public commitment to bring about the transfer of one hundred thousand Jewish DPs to Palestine boomeranged. He had wanted to snare Truman into solving the political problem of Palestine according to British interests. Instead, not only did Britain's tactics fail to move the president away from his commitment with regard to the Jewish DPs, they even resulted in Truman's, admittedly cautious, support of the Zionist plan for Palestine. Seen in this light, one would almost get the impression that Bevin's move to involve the Americans was bound to fail from the start. That is far from certain, as, for example, in the summer of 1946 he was very close to achieving his goal.

London's main mistake had been to interpret White House policy only in terms of political expediency. British officials refused to accept that many Americans, the president included, were indeed moved by true feelings of compassion toward the victims of Nazism, even though they stopped short of translating these feelings into a generous gesture enabling immigration. In the eyes of British diplomats in the United States, it was mainly American Jews who felt genuine sympathy toward the Jewish DPs in Europe, which for them transformed itself into a moral obligation to support the Zionist goals. These officials, wrongly, saw Washington's refusal to open the gates to Jewish DPs as evidence that American Jewry had only marginal power. They failed to realize that for American Jews the struggle to open Palestine's gates not only displayed their Zionist ideology but accorded conveniently with the nature of their domestic-political constraints. Embassy diplomats were bewildered by the refusal of both Democratic and Republican politicians to acknowledge the actual limited political strength of American Jewry as they saw it. Not only was this deference to the Jewish vote exaggerated, the British felt, it was also to a large extent groundless: a very large portion of the American population was indifferent to the Palestine issue, while anti-Semitism in America seemed to be on the rise.

There was bitterness, too, over the fact that the Americans were pressing the British to open the gates of Palestine to the Jewish DPs, while refusing to open their own country to the refugees, Jewish or other. With time the British came to see clearly that except for Palestine, the United States was the only practical alternative for resettlement of the Jewish DPs. The British at this point pinned their hopes on legislation submitted by William G. Stratton, congressional representative from Illinois, which called for the entry into the United States of one hundred thousand DPs annually for four years. The British Foreign Office believed that most of the Jewish refugees would be happy to resettle in the United

States, which, of course, meant that the Zionists would lose their "raw material" for illegal immigration.[116] The proposed legislation languished in committee for seven months, however, and the Eightieth Congress eventually dispersed without taking any action.[117] It was not until 25 June 1948 that a law allowing two hundred thousand DPs entry into the United States over a period of two years was finally passed. But even if it had been passed earlier, it could not have solved the problem of the Jewish DPs because it came with restrictions that reduced to a minimum the number of Jewish DPs eligible to enter the United States. It was only in 1949 that new legislation actually enabled mass entry of Jewish refugees into the United States.[118] But by then most of the Jewish DPs had already immigrated to the State of Israel. From the end of the war until the end of 1948, no more than seventeen thousand Jews actually entered the United States.[119]

It is clear that Truman's hands were bound to some extent and that he did not exercise full control over events. When he appealed to the British to allow entry of the one hundred thousand Jewish DPs into Mandatory Palestine, Truman clearly believed that as long as he did not speak out on the Palestine problem, London would have no reason not to respond favorably to his request. Although humanitarian considerations played a major role, the president also had his eye on the domestic political rewards his stance might reap him. As the Harrison report did not accept a connection between Jewish immigration into Palestine and Britain's political problem there, it only helped to reinforce this approach, not in the least because it translated the Americans' humanitarian notion into concrete terms: one hundred thousand immigration certificates. The election campaigns of 1945 and 1946, for the success of which the Democratic Party needed the Jewish vote and Jewish financial contributions, guaranteed that Truman's initiative would not be sidelined, in much the same way as the 1948 presidential campaign was to influence Truman's decision to support the UN partition plan and to recognize the State of Israel.[120] With the transfer of the question of Palestine to the United Nations, the fate of the Jewish DPs in Germany and Austria no longer featured prominently in contacts between the United States and Britain.

Truman's disregard for British interests and constraints in his shaping of Washington's policy on the Jewish DPs and the Palestine question was very much in the context of the White House's treatment of Whitehall at the time, at least until the end of 1946. It is true that the increase in political tension with the USSR demanded a united front; yet Washington insisted on reserving virtually complete freedom for its own actions and decisions and had few qualms about occasionally taking steps that could only infuriate London. And, of course, in the post–World War II reality Britain was increasingly dependent on the United States. Given this situation, Truman's policy toward the Jewish DPs had decisive repercussions for the outcome of the Zionist struggle, as the president's continuing pressure on the British to allow Jewish DPs into Palestine worked havoc on London's policy to keep any solution to the Jewish DP problem firmly separated from the political fate of Palestine. The guidelines he gave on treatment of Jewish DPs in the American occupation zones—which included opening those zones for Jews fleeing from Eastern Europe and separating Jewish DPs from the others—played into the hands of the Zionists, who claimed that regardless of their country of origin, all Jewish DPs were part of a single people, the Jewish nation, for whom Zionism was creating a state in Palestine. As the number of Jewish DPs increased, the chances that they could be resettled in Europe or overseas diminished. On the one hand, the public conflict between Britain and the United States over policy toward the Jewish DPs undermined the effectiveness of the pressure the British were trying to exert on those European countries, such as France and Italy, that were tolerating illegal movement of Jews across their territories, while on the other it meant that Eastern European countries were increasingly willing to allow, or even encourage, the Jews to leave for the DP camps in Germany and Austria.[121]

6 AMERICAN OCCUPATION ZONES OFFER ASYLUM

An Open Gate Policy

In the first months after the war there was as yet no policy regarding Jews arriving from Eastern Europe. On 13 October 1945, General Joseph McNarney, who was to replace Eisenhower as commander of the American forces in Germany by the end of November, published interim guidelines to be followed until a final policy was in place. Army commanders were told to concentrate new arrivals — "infiltrators" they called them — in separate camps, away from other European refugees and from the assembly centers of "persecuted Jews," for whom the army was responsible, and to provide them with "reasonable care until a decision is made concerning their disposition."[1] While he was visiting the DP camps in Germany in October 1945, Ben-Gurion learned that the Americans were aware Jews from Eastern Europe were moving into their occupation zones but that they did not intend to stop them. Sensing the opportunity this offered, he outlined a plan that was to bring as many Jews as possible into the occupation zones that were under U.S. command.[2] Emissaries from Palestine active at the time in Germany and Austria reported that the American military authorities were indeed cooperative.[3]

Still, the American military authorities were not interested in seeing the American zones transformed into a refuge for the Jews of Eastern Europe and thus opposed a recommendation made in November by Judge Rifkind, adviser for Jewish affairs, that every person persecuted because of race or religion be allowed to enter the American occupation zone in Germany. Headquarters in Germany warned that this would lead to the emergence of a large Jewish minority that would not be able to assimilate, not to mention the expected heavy financial burden for the military government. The lack of resources, they emphasized, would mean that the military authorities could provide such refugees with no more than "rescue from hunger, disease, and lack of shelter," and it was doubtful "whether this [limited] scale of assistance would be acceptable to a rather large section of the American press and public."[4]

Conditions in the DP camps did deteriorate when thousands of Jews began streaming in from Eastern Europe in the course of the fall and winter months. In early November 1945, the JDC complained that no camps had been set up in the eastern part of the occupation zone for Jewish DPs arriving from Poland and that, as a result, there was nowhere to house the refugees who were arriving in Munich at a rate of one hundred people per day. Small numbers of these Jews were managing to infiltrate the camps, where they were only exacerbating the situation. Because of a shortage of food supplies, circumstances in the Farenwald camp, for example, had become desperate, while most Jews arriving from Eastern Europe were aimlessly wandering around the streets of Munich, many of them in need of medical assistance, clothing, and food.[5]

When he took over from Eisenhower, McNarney showed himself to be keenly aware that the Jewish DPs issue was a sensitive one and, mindful no doubt of the stinging criticism to which his predecessor had been subjected, quickly turned to the War Department for a policy decision. While he estimated at about 550 the number of Jews arriving daily from Poland in the American occupation zones in Berlin and West Germany, McNarney reported that there were about 250,000 Polish Jews remaining in Poland and the USSR and that it was difficult to foresee how many of them would seek shelter in the American zone in Germany, which they considered the only safe option left for them in Europe. Nor was it known how many Jews from the other Eastern European countries were likely to try to enter the zone. Moreover, DPs who had agreed to go back to their countries as part of the repatriation scheme were returning to the American occupation zone accompanied by members of their families and by their friends.[6]

As an interim step, the American military authorities tried to persuade their partners in the occupation authority in Germany to share with them the burden of caring for Jewish refugees from the East. They were worried by the practice of the British and the Soviet military authorities who enabled Jewish DPs to move freely from their own into the American occupation zones. In early December 1945, when the American delegate to the Directorate of Prisoners of War and Displaced Persons of the Allied Control Council suggested dividing the Jewish refugees coming into Berlin among the four occupation zones, this idea was rejected out of hand by the other participants in the meeting. The Soviet delegate, supported by the British member, was in favor of returning the Jews to Poland. Though they did not actually want this to happen, the Soviets had to stick to their principle that all nationals from countries under their control should be repatriated. This was, of course, out of the question for the U.S. delegate, who stressed that these people could not be returned to a place where their very lives would be in jeopardy.[7]

In Washington, Secretary of War Robert Patterson turned to Dean Acheson, under secretary of state, and told him of McNarney's uncertainty as to how to treat these people and whether to grant them asylum and look after them. Although the United States had undertaken to care for those DPs in its occupation zone when the Germans surrendered, the government had nowhere undertaken to provide refuge in its occupation zone to persons claiming to be victims of discrimination in countries other than Germany. At the Potsdam Conference, Patterson noted, the United States, Britain, and the USSR had agreed to absorb inside Germany those Germans who had been Polish, Hungarian, or Czechoslovakian citizens, and he would not like to see the hard core of DPs who could not be repatriated extended. Patterson mentioned this because he thought repatriation was important and not because he did not want to grant them asylum.[8]

At a meeting at the State Department on 21 December 1945, George Warren, the department's adviser on refugees and displaced persons, reported that Generals Eisenhower and Hildring had taken it upon themselves to institute a policy of granting asylum to Polish Jews on humanitarian grounds. The War Department was now apprehensive over criticism that no doubt would follow because living conditions in the camps were already deteriorating as a result of the influx of Jews from Poland. Acheson, who worked closely with Truman, cautioned against taking a decision or any action "which would appear to be inconsistent with the spirit of the President's directive on refugees." The outcome was that the War Department was advised to continue granting asylum, pending a final decision.[9]

Within the State Department there were differences of opinion over the policy to be adopted. Acheson disagreed with the head of the department's Polish desk, Elbridge Dubrow, that steps should be taken to halt the exodus of the Jews from Poland. According to Dubrow, the exodus of the Jews from Poland was organized by the Zionists, and he did not discount the possibility that this movement was "part of a scheme to further complicate the Arab-Jewish situation in the Near East by forcing us to insist that the large number of Polish Jews in our zone in Germany be sent to Palestine." To avoid any further harm to Anglo-American relations, Dubrow proposed informing the governments of Poland, the USSR, and Czechoslovakia that after 15 January 1946, Jewish refugees would not be allowed to enter the American zone. The Polish government should be warned that if it allowed this movement to continue, the U.S. government would make sure UNRRA's extensive assistance to Poland would be cut. In instances where Jewish refugees did succeed in entering, Dubrow added, "we should care for them temporarily and as soon as practicable, return them across the demarcation lines."[10]

Unlike Under Secretary Acheson, Secretary of State Byrnes believed that the borders of the American occupation zones should be closed to infiltrating Jewish refugees. He justified this opinion by arguing that "the choice appears to be not between either granting or not granting asylum but between maintaining bearable conditions for those who have already sought asylum and permitting those conditions to deteriorate by the influx of still further refugees into the zone, where the conditions of all would be intolerable." Reports at his disposal did not confirm the refugees' tales of pogroms and physical persecution in Poland, although fear of persecution and hostile acts at the hands of the Polish population was real enough.[11] The U.S. secretary of state had recently agreed to establish the Anglo-American Committee and certainly did not want more Jewish DPs in the American zones. The War Department, however, fearing adverse public reaction in the United States if it were announced that the borders of the American occupation zones would be closed, decided not to take up Byrnes's recommendations.[12]

In the course of the winter of 1945–46 the British Foreign Office thought it might use diplomatic pressure to induce the Polish government to prevent the exodus of the Jews from its territory and instructed Halifax to check what the U.S. administration's position would be on a possible joint appeal to the Polish government and on possible cooperation between the U.S. and British military authorities in Germany and Austria against the infiltration of Jews from Poland into their occupation zones.[13] The head of the Polish desk in the State Department rejected the idea of a joint appeal to the Polish government because he feared it would simply make public the fact that the two Western powers were putting pressure on them to prevent the departure of Jews from Eastern Europe at a time when Poland was ready to allow them to leave. Cooperation between the two military authorities required interdepartmental discussion, and therefore no immediate reply was possible.[14] Halifax's impression was that American authorities thought that without serious military measures, it would not be possible to prevent the exodus from Poland and that an appeal to the Soviet authorities to prevent the movement through their occupation zones would be unproductive.[15]

From talks with American military commanders in Europe the British realized that the Americans had no intention of changing their policy. General Richard MacCreery, commander of the British occupation forces in Austria, learned from his American counterpart, General Mark Clark, that he had no intention of preventing the movement of Jews from Poland to Austria, especially since the force of thirteen thousand soldiers at his disposal was not sufficient to do so effectively.[16] In a meeting at the end of February 1946 with AAC subcommittee members Bartley Crum and Richard Crossman, Clark asserted that it was U.S. policy to open the borders and enable Jews fleeing from Poland to save their lives.[17] Official approval of this policy came on 21 March 1946, when both McNarney and Clark were informed of the War and State Department's decision not to close the borders. They had taken this decision because they feared that otherwise serious incidents would erupt between army personnel and refugees, especially as the AAC report was not yet out but also because infiltration at that time was much less than had been forecast.[18]

Failing to Seal the Borders

Shortly after the publication of the final AAC report, however, the War Department proposed that the borders of the American occupation zones be promptly closed, at least as an interim measure, because, as they saw it, news of the AAC's recommendation that one hundred thousand Jews be allowed to enter Palestine would result in Jewish refugees pouring into the displaced persons camps in the thousands. Acheson disagreed with this assessment, arguing in a memorandum to the president that since it was impossible to predict the reaction of European Jews to the report, there was no urgent need to seal the borders, especially as the humane policy adopted by the American government so far had received much praise. He also pointed to a political difficulty to the effect that "it must be borne in mind that the borders can be effectively closed only by using German border patrols." Acheson advised that the president instruct Generals McNarney and Clark "to continue the present liberal policy so long as it is consistent with maintenance of satisfactory conditions among the Jewish displaced persons in Germany and Austria." If, as a result of an increase in movement, the military authorities were no longer able to provide the refugees with adequate services, they would then be allowed to close the borders temporarily. Well aware of the president's political constraints, Acheson also proposed that prominent American Jewish leaders be summoned to a secret meeting at which the reasons behind the government's guidelines for closing the borders could be explained to them.[19]

Truman's decision to adopt Acheson's proposal was almost certainly influenced by the same blend of political and humanitarian considerations that till then had informed his policies toward DPs generally and toward Jewish DPs in particular. A few days previously the president had openly expressed his satisfaction with the AAC's recommendation to move one hundred thousand Jewish DPs to Palestine, though at the same time he had ignored all other suggestions the committee had made. The president also rejected the joint recommendation of the secretaries of the state and war to close all DP camps except for those with Jewish DPs because he did not want to upset U.S. citizens of Polish origin or the Catholic community.[20] Truman nevertheless remained hopeful that Britain would solve the refugee problem by carrying out the AAC's recommendation that one hundred thousand refugees be permitted to enter Palestine.[21]

As Acheson had suggested, the secretary of war and the under secretary of state met with Jewish leaders and explained the complicated situation to them. The Jewish leaders were asked to aid the administration in preventing the human inundation of the American zones in Germany and Austria. Following this meeting, Acheson and Patterson again instructed the commanders of the American occupation zones to leave the borders open.[22] But when in June 1946 the number of Jews leaving Eastern Europe increased, McNarney asked for permission to seal the borders of the American zone in Germany to Jewish DPs infiltrating from the British zone in Germany and from the French zones in Germany and Austria or, alternatively, to withhold from Jewish refugees arriving from the east the status of DPs the moment the population in the camps reached one hundred thousand. He estimated that this would happen in September. (At the time of McNarney's request there were fifty-four thousand DPs in the camps and another twenty-five thousand outside them.) McNarney reported on his directive to transfer non-Jewish DPs to installations where there were prisoners of war in order to make room for the Jewish infiltrators, though even then there would still be a lack of housing. Instructions at that time spoke of increasing the number of housing units at a rate of three thousand per week. McNarney estimated that by the end of 1946 the number of Jewish DPs in the American zone in Germany would top two hundred thousand. He anticipated, furthermore, an increase in hostility toward the Jewish DPs not only on the part of the non-Jewish DPs and the German population, which would have to be evacuated from their homes, but also from American soldiers.[23]

At the beginning of July, the secretaries of state and war mutually agreed to accept both McNarney's proposals. Though they would not be deported to their countries of origin, infiltrators who had managed to enter the American zones in Germany and Austria after the borders were closed would not receive the same treatment accorded to DPs.[24] One day before the decision was taken, 4 July, a pogrom occurred in Kielce, Poland. Arthur Bliss Lane, American ambassador in Poland, reported that if before the Kielce pogrom about 70 Jews had been leaving Poland illegally each week, after the pogrom at least 700 people a day were fleeing and approximately another 70,000 were expected to follow.[25] In mid-July McNarney put the scope of the movement to Germany at 5,000 per week. From Austria as well there were reports of a considerable increase in the number of Jewish infiltrators. For example, on the night of 12–13 July, 1,390 Jewish refugees had reportedly arrived in the American part of Vienna.[26]

Greatly concerned by the recent influx but at the same time well aware of the electoral importance the president ascribed to American Jews, the secretaries of war and state again summoned Jewish leaders to a meeting on 22 July to seek their acquiescence in the steps they proposed to implement. Acheson and Patterson explained that if the stream of Jews from Poland and Czechoslovakia did not slow down, the United States would be forced to close the frontier. The Jewish leaders, who were asked to help lower the number of incoming Jews to ten thousand per month, strongly opposed sealing the borders and not granting infiltrators the status of DPs. Under the circumstances, the secretaries of state and war decided to permit McNarney to bar refugees seeking to enter from the British zone in Germany and from the French zones in Germany and Austria but told him not to limit the number of refugees from East and Central Europe, who were allowed to enter the DP camps in the American zone.[27] The JDC, which had also been asked to help reduce the rate of exodus from Poland, was quick to explain that it had no connection with organizing the movement as all it did was provide food and clothing. Concerned for its legal image, the JDC did not want its name linked with any illegal activity. Still, its chairman, Edward M. Warburg, said that only armed intervention could halt the population movement.[28]

At a press conference on 9 August 1946, McNarney announced the intention of the American authorities to prevent the movement of Jews from the other occupation zones except Vienna into the American zone. In a meeting with Jewish leaders about two weeks later, McNarney observed that since the end of the war, approximately 140,000 Jews had received asylum in the American zone. He noted that he had ordered the transfer of 19,000 persecuted Jews from Austria as well as Jewish infiltrators from Berlin to the American zone of Germany.[29] The meeting had been suggested by Rabbi Bernstein, the general's adviser on Jewish affairs, who urged McNarney to act to change the impression the press had created that the army did not like the Jews and that he was about to seal the borders of the American zone before Jews arriving from the east.[30]

The decision to leave the borders of the American occupation zones open was in large measure the result of intense pressure exerted by the Jewish lobby in Washington. The secretaries of war and state, who were in agreement with McNarney and Clark about the need to close the borders, believed that the president would not countenance such a step. As a result, they did not even broach the idea to him.[31] Just then Truman, again under pressure from the Zionist lobby, had rejected the provincial autonomy plan for Palestine. Both secretaries further recognized that the midterm elections were only three months ahead.

Under the circumstances, McNarney asked the War Department to examine the possibility of moving fifty thousand Jewish DPs to Italy, thirty thousand to Austria, and twenty-five thousand to France, Czechoslovakia, Britain, and other parts of Europe. In mid-August, the American commander estimated that sixty thousand Jews could be expected during the coming three months and another forty thousand during the following nine months. Also, it was anticipated that each month the camp population would swell by an additional ten to fifteen thousand bona fide non-Jewish DPs who had till then managed to support themselves outside the DP camps. McNarney warned the War Department of the potentially severe consequences, especially given the shortage of housing and food. He observed that not only was the American zone in Germany now supporting two million more Germans than in 1939 but that another one million German DPs were expected. Like his British counterparts, McNarney feared the adverse consequences a cut in the food allocation for these Germans was likely to have.[32]

Washington decided to act on two levels. The State Department directed its representatives in Poland and Czechoslovakia to approach the governments of those countries in an attempt to regulate the movement of the refugees between their territory and the American occupation zone in Austria.[33] Concurrently, Acheson instructed the U.S. embassy in Rome to urgently discuss with the Italian government the possibility of transferring twenty-five thousand refugees from Germany to the empty DP camps in Milan and Bari. The transfer would be handled entirely by the American military authorities and by UNRRA, and the burden of supporting the refugees would not fall upon the Italians.[34] This, however, was not an easy policy to implement. Asked for its opinion of the proposal, the British government was quick to reject it. London maintained that not only would a transfer of Jews to Italy simply encourage the continued

*Jewish refugees on the way from a DP camp in Austria to one in Germany
(Courtesy Yad Vashem, Jerusalem)*

flow into the West, but Italy was also the most convenient base for clandestine sailings to Palestine.[35] The Italian government also rejected the American request. The U.S. embassy in Rome believed that the Italians were afraid that the funds for maintaining some ten thousand refugees would be deducted from the current UNRRA appropriation to Italy.[36]

To prevent the transfer of the DPs to Italy, the British frustrated subsequent American attempts to gain UNRRA council approval for increasing the supplies the organization was providing the country.[37] At the same time they tried to bolster Italian readiness to stand up to American pressure. They warned the Italians of the burden involved in maintaining the Jewish refugees once UNRRA's work was concluded.[38] Washington in the end decided to cancel the plan to move the DPs to Italy because of a lack of funds and the War Department's preference for keeping the DPs in areas where control over supplies was in the hands of U.S. military authorities.[39]

Greatly annoyed by Washington's policy, the British believed that the U.S. government and its overseas representatives were not giving sufficient thought to the dangers a mass flight of the Jews from Eastern Europe entailed. For example, they were unwittingly cooperating with the Russians to thwart Britain's efforts to carry out its mandate in Palestine.[40] While failing to influence Washington, the British hoped that the difficulties the Americans were now encountering in providing for the tens of thousands of refugees who had arrived during the summer of 1946 would eventually force the administration to reconsider its open-borders policy. London knew that the American commanders in Austria and Germany were very concerned about the refugee movement from Eastern Europe and were exerting pressure on Washington to halt it. From talks Inverchapel held with officials in the State Department, he learned that the department would have taken more drastic steps to halt the further influx of refugees were it not for the pressure that was brought to bear on the government by Jewish organizations in the United States.[41] By torpedoing the attempts these groups were making to transfer some of the Jewish DPs to other locations, London hoped to speed up the moment when the Americans would decide to give up. This was also behind their opposition to dividing the fleeing refugees among the four occupation zones. But the hopes Whitehall placed on these moves were soon to be disappointed.[42]

London further realized that because they failed to influence their government's policy, American military authorities in Germany and Austria were encouraging and assisting DPs in their occupation zones to move on to Italy and France.[43] From the French the British learned that the Americans were sending large numbers of Jewish refugees from Poland on American military trains via the French zone to Marseilles, whence they sailed for Palestine. Paris made it clear that they could not stand up to American pressure.[44]

Change of Policy?

In a determined effort to reduce the number of Jewish infiltrators, General Lucius D. Clay, who replaced McNarney in March 1947 as American commander in Germany, published an order to the effect that refugees who made it into the American zone after 21 April 1947 would no longer be accepted in the DP camps and would not receive food from American sources. But the borders of the American occupation zones would not be closed to the refugees. At a press conference, Clay indicated that the IRO plan to care for refugees in Germany was based on the number present in the country and that the military authorities intended to focus on solving the problem of those who already had been in the camps for a long time. (IRO was to begin operating on 1 July 1947.) Clay further admitted that it had never been and probably never would be possible for the American military authorities to prevent the illegal border crossings.[45]

The practical consequence of this new policy to withhold assistance from new arrivals was to place the financial burden of maintaining the Jewish refugees on the JDC. Efforts of Jewish organizations to have this order retracted failed.[46] General Geoffrey Keyes, the commander of U.S. forces in the country, cautioned against rescinding the policy, claiming that the Jewish migrants from Rumania and Hungary "are not fleeing persecution but leaving their countries because of poor crops, dissatisfaction with present governments, and the belief that the United States would furnish living accommodations, food, and immigration aid." He also thought that the new policy would force the JDC, which was already carrying the brunt of caring for the infiltrators, to act to halt this movement. Revocation of this policy, he maintained, would be interpreted by Polish, Hungarian, and Rumanian Jews as well as by the Austrian government and the other occupation authorities as an open invitation to the migrants to come to the American zone of Austria.[47] That the War Department agreed with Keyes's arguments did not mean, however, that its hopes for the new policy materialized.[48] On the contrary, as the weeks passed, the number of refugees reaching Vienna only increased. Mostly Rumanian Jews, they were adamant about leaving Rumania no matter what hardships were in store for them.[49]

The Americans, however, strictly implemented the directive not to provide food to new refugees. JDC hopes of receiving help from the IRO in maintaining the Jewish refugees quickly dissipated. Some relief for the JDC in helping the Rumanian Jews did come from the Austrian government, which, as a result of American pressure, accepted responsibility for supplying 1,550 calories daily to each Jewish refugee in the American sector of Vienna, beginning 18 August, to which the JDC then added 600 calories per person.[50]

The shortage of housing was the main problem. At the beginning of August 1947, in the camps in Vienna that were meant to hold not more than fifteen hundred persons, there were already, according to British estimate, over eight thousand refugees. The British diplomatic representative in Austria also stated that every week about a thousand Jewish refugees arrived. A British medical officer reported on the abysmal conditions in the Rothschild Hospital that was located in the American sector of Vienna and was serving as a DP camp. It had capacity for a thousand people but was now accommodating thirty-five hundred.[51] To alleviate the situation in Vienna, the *Brichah* (Hebrew: "flight," mass movement of Jewish survivors across Europe following the war; also the name of the underground organization that coordinated this flight) began moving refugees to camps in the American zones in Germany and Austria with American military authorities turning a blind eye.[52] That the Americans knew such movements were taking place is clear, for example, from a report the State Department received in mid-September from Austria saying that during the past few weeks about five thousand Rumanian Jewish refugees had moved into the

Part of Parsch DP camp near Salzburg, Austria
(Courtesy Israel Ministry of Defense, Museums Unit)

American zone there and had succeeded in infiltrating into the existing Jewish camps, the Soviets having allowed them passage.[53]

Significantly, the change in American policy toward Jews fleeing Eastern Europe in spring 1947 was not a response to British pressure but rather the consequence of constraints faced by the American occupation authorities. This is clear, for example, from the indirect encouragement they continued to give to Jewish DPs on their way to Italy and France,[54] which frustrated the efforts of the Italian and French authorities to reduce this infiltration. A memorandum of the Italian Foreign Ministry (10 April 1947) stated that the groups of Jews infiltrating into the country across its northern frontiers had come from camps in the American zone in Austria and were traveling via the French zone to Italy. By refusing to take back the Jews who managed to enter the French zone, the Americans were thwarting French efforts to prevent the movement. It was also alleged that the Americans, interested in encouraging the refugees to leave for other occupation zones, were doing almost nothing to control the departures from their zones. As a result, the French, unable to return the refugees who had entered their zone, were allowing these people to continue on to Italy.[55] When asked by the British in September 1947 to take steps to check the illegal movement of Jews from the French zone of Austria to Italy, the French responded that most of their efforts were directed toward preventing infiltration of Jews from the American zones in Germany and Austria into their own zone in Austria. This policy, they observed, was necessary since the Americans were willing to take back Jewish refugees only if they were stopped at the border.[56]

It was not only the British who were powerless against the open gate policy. Even the U.S. secretaries of war and state and the American military authorities in Germany and Austria, all of whom advocated closing the borders, were unsuccessful in this respect. The significant increase in the flight from Poland during the summer of 1946 concurred with Anglo-American contacts on the AAC's report. Until the talks ended, the White House saw no point in changing the policy of open gates and thus risking possible incidents between the Jewish refugees and the military authorities. Then later, the same considerations — midterm elections — that had led the president to reject the provincial autonomy plan and to publish his Yom Kippur statement prevented the closing of the borders. The April 1947 policy change proved inconsequential in the long run because of the directive to leave the borders open. The U.S. administration obviously feared the political consequences of taking a more drastic step. Under the circumstances, the American military authorities, seeking to minimize the number of DPs in the U.S. occupation zones and to lessen the economic burden of their upkeep, helped the refugees move on to Italy and France, even though they knew that both countries were serving as the main base for clandestine embarkations to Palestine.

Washington and "Illegal Sailings"

The inability of the British to enlist American support for their campaign against the illegal immigration was not confined to the movement overland. London suffered a similar failure in its efforts to convince the U.S. administration both to prohibit fund-raising in the United States for the illegal sailings and the sale of ships to *Ha'apala* agents and to use its influence to persuade the Zionist leadership to stop the illegal sailings. From the summer of 1946 on, public fund-raising for the illegal immigration by means of newspaper advertisements and tax exemptions for the contributions raised were important targets for pressure on the American State Department by London. It was clear to the British that not only was most of the funding for the illegal immigration coming from the United States but also that some of the fund-raising campaigns were being conducted under the auspices of American public figures.[57]

At the beginning of January 1947, Bevin instructed Ambassador Inverchapel to pursue energetically the matter of the fund-raising through newspaper ads for the illegal immigration. Byrnes expressed understanding for British arguments but observed that his hands were tied by American law, which permitted the raising of funds. Inverchapel countered that there was no justification for the tax exemption these contributions enjoyed, since the law accorded such exemptions for money given for charitable purposes, whereas here they went to underground and terrorist activities.[58] He nevertheless knew of the legal difficulties and told the Foreign Office that "unless we can prove to the satisfaction of the Attorney-General of the United States that a conspiracy is about to break the laws of the friendly country of Palestine," there was little prospect of success. U.S. officials, furthermore, informally told the British that the political considerations bearing on the problem were such as to make it virtually insoluble, "since we are not dealing with contraband goods or war material but, as the case would present itself in this country, with very unfortunate victims of Nazi persecution."[59]

An additional problem the British raised at the time was that vessels were bought and renovated in the United States and then, manned by American citizens, left for Europe with the aim of transporting illegal immigrants from there to Palestine. British suspicions were first aroused by the *Abril*, which was purchased at the beginning of December 1946 and then sailed to Europe. The State Department explained to the British embassy that the American government had no legal grounds for stopping the boat because it had violated no American law. Although an investigation of the vessel had revealed inordinately large provisions of life jackets, medical equipment, and food, this in itself did not constitute an infringement of American law.[60] Approximately two months later, the *Abril*, renamed the *Ben Hecht* and sailing for the American League for a Free Palestine of Peter Bergson, left Port-de-Bouc, France, with 626 illegal immigrants on board.[61] In mid-March 1947, word reached the British embassy in Washington that another vessel, the *President Warfield*, was being repaired so that it could participate in the illegal sailings.[62]

Further contacts he had with State Department officials in an attempt to enlist American aid in fighting the illegal departures made Inverchapel realize that, because of Zionist pressure, the State Department could not or would not act against the fund-raising for the illegal immigration via newspaper ads or against the renovation of ships for the illegal sailings in the United States.[63] For almost a year now, the British ambassador reported to London in June 1947, the State Department had avoided a written reply to the British complaints but would limit itself to expressing regrets for the absence of legal grounds to act, arguing "that the withdrawal of tax exemption facilities would stir up more trouble than it would be worth." It had further been suggested that the British government not persist in this matter so that more important British interests would not be adversely affected.[64]

The British, however, drew some solace from the appeal Truman made to the American public on 5 June to refrain from any activity that might provoke Palestinian public opinion, disturb public law and order, or incite riots there so long as the UN was discussing the Palestine problem. London hoped that this would have some repercussions on fund-raising in the United States. At a session of the Cabinet Committee on Illegal Immigration, Bevin predicted that Truman's declaration would influence such groups as the American trade unions to stop contributing and would increase the willingness of other governments to cooperate in the fight against the illegal immigration.[65] Following Truman's statement and sensing a change in the position of the State Department, Bevin appealed to the new secretary of state, George C. Marshall, to aid Britain in its campaign against the illegal sailings. Organizers of the movement, the foreign secretary maintained, were exploiting Jewish refugees "as a means of exerting political pressure on the government of Palestine at a moment when the future of that country is under consideration by the United Nations."[66]

At the beginning of August 1947, Marshall promised Bevin that ships owned by the U.S. government would not be sold to persons suspected of involvement in illegal sailings. He added that the Treasury and Justice Departments had been directed to investigate the possibility of halting the fund-raising via newspaper ads and the renovation of illegal immigration boats. Bevin's request that U.S. citizens working in the charitable and refugee organizations in Europe be instructed to take action against the illegal sailings of Jewish refugees was rejected because it would have conflicted with the law.[67] This change in the position of the State Department may well have stemmed from Marshall's support for the British position on the Palestine question and the closer relations between the two powers following Bevin's response to the proposals Marshall had outlined in the speech he had given at Harvard University at the beginning of June 1947 and which eventually led to the Marshall Plan.

When, at the end of August, they decided to deport the *Exodus ma'apilim* back to Germany, the British put the State Department in an uncomfortable position. Keenly aware of the damage it would cause to Britain's status in American public opinion, State Department officials tried to persuade the Foreign Office to reconsider.[68] John Balfour, British consul in Washington, shared their misgivings and warned that sending the illegal immigrants back to the country where the Jews had suffered the cruelest horrors would arouse a good deal of bitterness in the United States, which would spread way beyond the propaganda circles of the Zionists.[69] Balfour, of course, was also fully aware that Britain was on the verge of bankruptcy as it tried to fulfill the obligations it had undertaken as part of the conditions for its loan from the United States. The British Foreign Office, though not oblivious to the ramifications it could expect, asserted that it had no choice.[70] The embassy later reported to London that as a result of the wide press coverage given to the disembarkation of the *Exodus* illegal immigrants in Hamburg, criticism of the British, particularly from circles that usually failed to show any interest in British policy in Palestine, had sharpened considerably.[71]

A few weeks later, the British tried to recruit the help of the State Department to prevent the sailing of two illegal immigrant vessels from ports in the Balkans. In mid-October 1947, Marshall's attention was called to two ships, the *Pan York* and the *Pan Crescent*, that were about to set sail from Black Sea ports for Palestine carrying 16,500 illegal Jewish immigrants. The two vessels had American crew members and had been financed by American funds. In an attempt to exploit the escalating tension between the West and the Soviet Union and its satellites, Bevin instructed Inverchapel to stress that all illegal immigrants were arriving from countries subject to Soviet influence and that "only those well indoctrinated with the communist faith are allowed to go." The British claimed that the illegal immigration was now a factor in the Russian plan to use Palestine "as a springboard for their influence in the Middle East and the principal source of confusion and instability throughout the area."[72] The British legation in Rumania also took pains to make sure that the American diplomats in Bucharest were aware of the dangers inherent in the sailing of these vessels. They spoke of an ongoing movement of Jews from the Soviet Union to Rumania and of the Soviet involvement in this illegal movement. Many of the Jews were joining these illegal sailings. Assembly points and ports of departure were situated at vital locations along Soviet transport routes, and Soviet military trains were conveying the Jewish immigrants to the Mediterranean coast. Furthermore, the NKVD provided thousands of exit permits to these immigrants "when exit clearance for normal passengers was practically impossible to obtain."[73]

Marshall demonstrated a large measure of goodwill. He mentioned that investigations were under way concerning the *Colonel Frederick F. C. Johnson,* which was anchored in Norfolk, Virginia (Bevin had requested that this vessel's departure be prevented), and he noted that until an answer was received, the ship would remain under the watchful eye of the American Coast Guard. Bevin also was briefed on a talk which State Department official Dean Rusk had conducted with a representative of the Jewish Agency, Lionel Gelber, about the *Pan*s and the *Colonel Frederick F. C. Johnson.* Rusk had stressed that the State

Department expected the Jewish Agency to act to the best of its abilities to restrain the underground organization.[74] Moreover, Marshall himself had apprised the Jewish leaders who had been summoned to a meeting with him that if effective and immediate measures were not taken to halt the clandestine activity, he would be forced to deal with the matter in public. The secretary of state informed Inverchapel of the priority the Treasury Department was giving to a renewed investigation of the tax exemption which had been granted to the American League for a Free Palestine of Peter Bergson and other similar organizations in light of information that had since been received about the true nature of their activities.[75] British diplomats in Washington were satisfied: for the first time since they had appealed to the State Department in the summer of 1946 about halting the activity surrounding the illegal immigration, the Americans were showing some readiness to act.[76]

Within days of the UN Partition Resolution, 29 November 1947, Bevin cautioned Marshall that further illegal sailings might lead to a bloodbath in Palestine because they would provoke the Arabs into massacring Jews. If that happened, the U.S. government would have no choice but to send troops to the region, and then the Soviets might want to send in forces as well. Marshall, as Bevin anticipated, did not conceal his concern and commented that the American military was apprehensive over the possible presence of Soviet troops in Palestine. Bevin maintained that unless the illegal immigration was stopped until the British transferred control to a UN committee in May 1948, it would be impossible to get through the period in an orderly fashion. He urged the American government to restrain the Jewish Agency and if possible publicly to condemn the illegal immigration.[77]

Once again Marshall did not disappoint Bevin. On 8 December, Loy Henderson, head of the State Department's Division for Near Eastern Affairs, warned Moshe Shertok (later Sharett), head of the Jewish Agency's political department, that further illegal immigration would lead to undesirable results. Shertok diplomatically promised that the Jewish Agency would take all necessary measures to prevent the illegal immigration, but he made it clear that to achieve this goal, the Yishuv would need to have a port at its disposal, and the scope of the legal immigration would have to be expanded. Shertok further maintained that though the Jewish Agency was opposed to the sailing of the *Pans*, it might not be possible to prevent it.[78] While satisfied with the State Department's activities, Inverchapel had doubts about the effectiveness of Henderson's pressure, since "the pro-Arab reputation of the State Department did much to blunt their influence with the Zionist leaders."[79]

Despite a positive attitude toward Britain at the time, the State Department

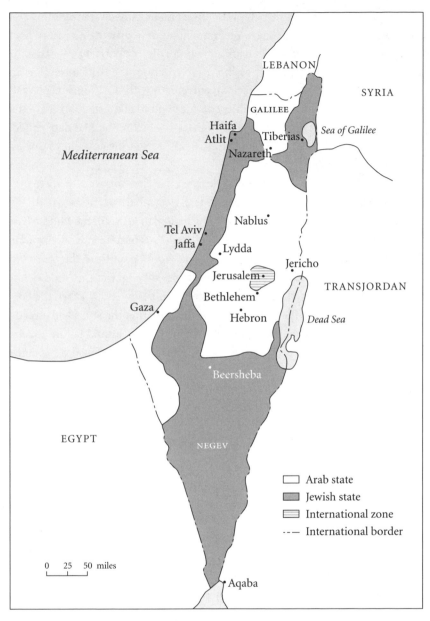

UN *Partition Resolution, 29 November 1947*

rejected a British demand that the U.S. government publicly censure the illegal immigration, in view of the UN recommendation to give the Zionists a port (no later than 1 February 1948) enabling Jewish DPs free entry to Palestine. At the same time, in deference to possible Arab reaction, the British rejected an American suggestion that they reach an agreement with the Zionist leaders to the effect that in exchange for a British commitment to allow the transfer of the illegal immigrants detained in Cyprus to Palestine before the Mandate ended, the Zionists would forgo their port and would prevent illegal sailings during the interim period.[80]

Meanwhile, when the Foreign Office learned that the *Pans* were ready to sail, it pressured the American authorities in late December 1947 to persuade the Jewish Agency to desist. As they put it, the arrival of the *Pans* in the Middle East would tax the resources of the British and push the Arabs to react violently. The Foreign Office stressed that "only the Russians would gain from the proposed operation through greatly increased disturbances throughout the Middle East and the introduction of a large number of communist agents."[81] When the Foreign Office telegraphed the embassy, it was unaware that the ships had already set sail three hours earlier. Ironically, the affair was not a total failure for the British in the American arena. American pressure had compelled the Zionist leadership to instruct *Ha'apala* organizers to prevent the sailing of vessels. The danger of antagonizing the Americans both before and after the vote on partition in the UN General Assembly was too great. When the *Pans*, therefore, sailed out, they did so contrary to the instructions of the Zionist political leadership.[82]

Until the winter of 1947–48 the State Department had shown little willingness to act on British requests that it prevent activities taking place in the United States connected with illegal Jewish immigration to Palestine, for the most part taking advantage of legal constraints to avoid confronting the problem. When this policy changed, Washington prevented the sailing of the *Colonel Frederick F. C. Johnson,* tax exemptions were reviewed in the case of organizations suspected of involvement in promoting the illegal immigration, and pressure was brought to bear on American Jewish leaders and on the Zionist leadership to prevent the sailings. This policy change resulted from the State Department's growing concern with the consequences of a British decision to evacuate Palestine. In mid-December 1947, the State Department's Near East Division, which still hoped that it would be possible to reverse the UN resolution of 29 November and prevent the creation of a Jewish state, tried to convince the British to remain in Palestine.[83] Given British concerns over the illegal immigration, particularly the anticipated sailing of the *Pans*, the State Department wanted to help Whitehall cope with the problem but only as long as this did not involve presidential action (for example, public censure of the illegal immigration) or the intervention of Congress.

If the American secretaries of war and state and American army commanders shared the British stand on the illegal Jewish immigration, it was mainly because, in their view, this was also in the interest of the United States. Not only did the flight of the Jews from Eastern Europe to the American zones in Germany and Austria place a heavy economic and administrative burden on the occupation authorities, the illegal sailings were undermining Britain's position in the Middle East, particularly in Palestine, and thus were also contrary to the growing American interests in the region. But U.S. policy was directed by Truman, who demonstrated a determined stand in everything related to the Jewish refugee problem. And none of the leading American officials was willing to confront the president on this issue.

III

THE
SOVIET
BLOC

7 | THE FLIGHT FROM POLAND

After the end of World War II the largest number of potential Jewish emigrants were in countries within the sphere of Soviet influence, as were many of the routes to the American and British occupation zones in Germany and Austria. Jewish refugees had begun arriving in the DP camps during the first few months after the war, but most moved there in the summer of 1946. During 1947 the great majority consisted of Rumanian Jews fleeing via Hungary to Austria. Thousands of these refugees and DPs subsequently took part in the illegal immigration to Palestine from the shores of Italy, France, and Greece. Ports in the Balkan countries also served as embarkation bases, and more than twenty-nine thousand illegal immigrants sailed from Rumanian, Yugoslavian, and Bulgarian harbors.

More than 160,000 Jews fled from Poland, most of them before October 1946, and they soon formed the majority of the Jewish DPs gathered in the camps in Germany, Austria, and Italy.[1] They were the main pool of illegal immigrants who would set sail from Western European ports to Palestine. In their efforts to limit the number of Jewish DPs, the British anxiously monitored the situation of the Jews remaining in Poland and discussed the Jewish exodus with the Polish government. But relations between London and Warsaw were complicated, and the internal power struggle between the Communists and anti-Communists in Poland also left its mark on the negotiations over the Polish Jews.

Conflicting interests and disagreements about Poland between Britain and the Soviet Union surfaced when the war was barely over. Having declared war on Germany in the first place because of its invasion of Poland, Britain had felt a moral obligation to help restore Poland to its original borders. But shortly after Germany attacked the Soviet Union on 22 June 1941, Stalin advised Britain that he wanted a return to the status quo ante concerning borders of the USSR, that is, annexation of the Baltic states, parts of Finland, Bessarabia, and Bukovina to the Soviet Union, whereby the Curzon Line was to serve as the border between Poland and the USSR. In fact, Stalin was determined to preserve what he had gained through his now defunct agreements with Germany.

It was clear to Britain that failure to accede to Russian demands would adversely affect Anglo-Russian cooperation. On 30 July 1941, through British mediation, the USSR and the Polish government in exile signed an agreement to settle their differences. Since the main problem—the question of the border between the two states—was left unresolved, the agreement afforded only a momentary respite. Moscow insisted on relocating its border with Poland westward, whereas the Polish government in exile adamantly opposed any border change. At the Big Three Conference in Teheran (28 November–1 December 1943) an understanding was reached: the Curzon Line would serve as the eastern border of Poland, and a Polish government friendly to the USSR would be set up. Prime Minister Churchill and Foreign Secretary Eden failed to convince the Polish government in exile to agree to a quid pro quo in the form of a modification in Poland's western border at the expense of Germany.

Not one readily to compromise in the pursuit of his goals, Stalin refused to help the Armia Krajowa (Home Army, the Polish anti-Communist underground under German occupation), which in August 1944 revolted against the Germans to try to liberate Warsaw before the Red Army entered the city. Nor did Stalin accede to Churchill's request that British and American airplanes be allowed to land at Soviet bases so that they could deliver supplies and weapons to the Home Army. About two hundred thousand Poles lost their lives when the Germans ruthlessly suppressed the uprising and destroyed the city. On 5 January 1945, in the face of Anglo-American protests, Moscow officially recognized the Polish Committee of National Liberation (known as the Lublin Committee) that had been formed on 12 July 1944 and was headed by Bolesław Bierut as the transitional government of the Polish Democratic Republic. Bierut served as president and Edward Osóbka-Morawski became prime minister.

At the Yalta Conference (4–11 February 1945) Poland's eastern border, agreed upon in principle at Teheran, was confirmed, but the question of the western border remained open. Britain and the United States conditioned their recognition of the transitional government on the inclusion of "democratic" (non-Communist) leaders and on the holding of free and secret general elections in which all democratic and anti-Nazi parties could take part. Stalin and Molotov promised to hold free elections within a short time, and on 5 July the Americans and the British recognized the Polish Provisional Government of National Unity that had been set up on 21 June. Fourteen of its twenty-one members belonged to the Lublin Committee. Key positions in the government such as president, prime minister, deputy prime minister, minister of defense, minister of the interior, and minister of finance were filled by Communists and their supporters. Stanisław Mikołajczyk, the former Polish government in exile's prime minister, was appointed deputy prime minister and minister of agriculture. Although at the Potsdam Conference (16 July–2 August 1945) it had been decided that the western border of Poland would be determined in the peace agreements, in practice the Western powers recognized the Oder–Western Neisse Line as the western border of Poland, as the Soviets had demanded. In April 1945 Moscow transferred to Poland the administration of more than 21 percent of the German territory.[2]

Postwar Poland was a country in ruins and deeply divided politically. The new regime was identified with Moscow, which had troops stationed in the country, and was regarded with hostility by large segments of the populace and by the Polish Catholic Church. Various opposition groups had organized themselves into an underground and resorted to violent action with the purpose of bringing down the new government, which had managed to assert its control primarily in the large cities but not in the rest of the country. Here armed antigovernment groups were able to operate mostly unhampered. According to figures published by the historical department of the central committee of the Polish Workers' Party, more than ten thousand soldiers, police, and other supporters of the new regime were killed by the underground, two-thirds of them during 1945 and 1946, with casualties among the underground in the three years following the war estimated at approximately seventy-five hundred dead and two thousand wounded. Elections eventually were held on 19 January 1947. According to official results, the Communist bloc received 80 percent of the votes, and the Peasant Party of Mikołajczyk received only 10 percent. The government that was set up after these elections included neither Mikołajczyk nor any other representatives of his party. Fearing for his life, Mikołajczyk fled Poland in October 1947 with the help of the American embassy.[3]

Polish Jews in the Aftermath of the War

In the struggle between the Communists and the majority of the Polish population which opposed them, including the Catholic Church, Poland's Jews were largely identified with the former. Various opposition trends were clearly anti-Semitic, and they were united in their approach as to what steps should be taken toward Jews remaining in Poland.[4] Out of the 3.25 million Jews who had been living in Poland on the eve of World War II, only about 380,000 had survived. Roughly 70 percent of these were Jews who had fled the country, principally to the Soviet Union, either before the war had broken out or during the initial months of German occupation; included among them were Jews who had been evacuated to the Soviet Union by the Red Army after Poland was split up following the Ribbentrop-Molotov agreement. Approximately 20 percent were liberated from concentration camps, forced labor camps, and death camps while the remaining 10 percent had been able to make it by assuming non-Jewish identities and hiding among Poles or as partisan fighters.[5]

Estimates of the number of Jews in Poland after the end of World War II range between fifty-five thousand in June 1945 and eighty thousand in August of that same year.[6] Most of the Polish Jews who survived the camps did not want to return to Poland. A Jewish Englishwoman who worked in the Bergen-Belsen camp almost from the day it was liberated reported that the Jewish survivors from Poland were seized by despair at the very thought of having to return to Poland, for them the scene of Jewish annihilation.[7] In a memorandum to the Anglo-American Committee, the director of the Inter-Governmental Committee on Refugees, Herbert Emerson, stated that all the Jewish DPs from Western European countries had returned to their homelands at the end of the war, but there was some opposition to returning to Hungary, Rumania, and Yugoslavia, and the refusal to return to Poland was almost universal.[8] A small number of these Jews had returned to their former homes, but in most cases, this was out of a desire to search for relatives and not to make new lives for themselves in Poland.

Disheartening reports reached the Yishuv in Palestine about the situation of the Polish Jews. In March 1945, an illegal immigration activist from Palestine, Ehud Avriel, reported how Poles felt that, with all the atrocities they had committed, the Nazis at least had to their credit the extermination of the Jews, while others regretted that despite their Prussian thoroughness the Germans had not completed the job so that approximately ninety thousand Jews were still alive.[9] Abba Kovner, one of the underground commanders in the Vilna Ghetto and a founder and organizer of the *Brichah* movement, found that the Polish people — no matter what their walk of life — were united in only one thing, their desire to get rid of the Jews; a few individuals among the Communist government elite who thought differently were an exception.[10] A similar picture was painted in a report prepared by the American Research and Analysis Branch of the Office of Strategic Services, which noted that anti-Semitism remained very strong. Christians who had rescued Jews asked the survivors not to divulge their identities for fear of being compromised. Jews were murdered or stabbed every day—on the very same day that Prime Minister Osóbka-Morawski announced the restoration of all rights to the Jews, twelve Jews had been murdered.[11]

Theoretically, the drastic reduction in the Jewish population—from 10 percent of the total population before the war to a marginal fraction afterward—should have removed the Jewish question from the Polish agenda, but in effect the opposite happened: the Nazi occupation government, through the virulent anti-Semitic propaganda it had ceaselessly spread and the shedding of Jewish blood it had sanctioned, had only further reinforced a centuries-old anti-Semitism. Many Poles had thought that they would be rid of the Jews forever, only to find that Jews were returning from the camps and from the Soviet Union. It should be remembered that after the eastern border had been adjusted and the Germans had been deported, the Jews were the only minority remaining to disturb the ethnic unity Poles felt so strongly about.

Traditional anti-Semitism was also aggravated by considerations of a pragmatic nature. During the Nazi occupation many Poles had taken possession of Jewish property. The return of the Jews meant that they might have to return such property to its former owners.[12] Moreover, while the Jews were excluded from the Polish economic system during the war years, Poles had taken control of commercial activities in which Jews had been dominant, and they were determined to hold on to their new positions. Yet the new Polish regime, confronted with the task of rebuilding the official administrative system and in need of expert staff, saw the few remaining Jews as loyal and competent people who could fill the gap. Thus a relatively large number of Jews were integrated not only into the state bureaucracy but also into the security police. Talk of Jewish control of public administration was exaggerated, but the activity of senior Jewish Communists on a national scale stood out. Jacob Berman was generally considered to be the contact person with Moscow, Hilary Minc, the economic boss of Poland, and Roman Zambrowski filled central positions in the Communist Party apparatus. The opposition soon argued that the government was being run by Jews and decided to include an anti-Jewish plank in its struggle against the government.[13]

Phase One: Summer and Winter of 1945–1946

During the first months after the war, the British embassy showed very little interest in the plight of the Jews in Poland. In the middle of September 1945 Victor Cavendish-Bentinck, the British ambassador in Poland, reported to the British Foreign Office that Jewish annihilation in Poland had been so thorough that there were almost no Jews left there. In small towns, which before the war had teemed with Jewish merchants, not a single Jew was to be found. Based on the estimates of the Polish government, he reported that in the month of August there were altogether about 50,000 Jews living in Poland and that approximately 200,000 more were expected to arrive from the USSR. Cavendish-Bentinck believed that the latter figure was exaggerated and that no more than 150,000 were likely to return. Following a visit to Auschwitz in September 1945, he telegraphed to London: "There is no doubt that all the horror stories that have been heard about the place are correct, including the extraction of fat for the purpose of manufacturing soap (or perhaps margarine?) from corpses that were burnt in electric furnaces with German efficiency." He estimated that fully six million people had perished in German concentration and death camps and that at least four million of them had been Jews.[14] During the war Cavendish-Bentinck had served as chairman of the Joint Intelligence Committee; that he found it necessary to confirm the stories about Auschwitz suggests that he knew there still were British officials who had doubts about the scope of the annihilation of European Jewry.[15]

At the end of 1945, after reports reached London from British occupation authorities in Germany and Austria about the infiltration of thousands of Jews from Poland, Britain began to take an interest in the situation of the Jews there. From interrogation of Jews who entered the British occupation zones, the British learned that they were seeking asylum from persecution in their native country that was the result of popular enmity; the government, it was maintained, did not instigate the persecution. Another forty thousand Jews were expected to leave Poland, but the winter weather would no doubt interrupt the movement. As the British Control Commission in Germany saw it, the exodus of Jews from Poland was part of a Zionist plan to increase the number of potential immigrants to Palestine in Germany before the visit of the Anglo-American Committee there.[16] The British knew that several thousand more Jews had already entered the American zones; early in December 1945 the British embassy in Prague reported that between fifteen and twenty thousand refugees from Poland, most of them Jews, had crossed Czechoslovakia on their way to the American zones in Austria and Germany.[17]

The British embassy in Warsaw believed that the departure of Polish Jews was largely prompted by anti-Jewish sentiments among 25 million Poles. Cavendish-Bentinck believed the Polish Jews had good reason to leave because the Poles remained as anti-Semitic as they had been ever since the establishment of the state of Poland after World War I. The Germans had done all they could to exterminate the Jews of Poland, yet the Polish people "appeared anxious to finish what the Germans had left undone." The flight was not the result of any policy of the regime, notwithstanding the fact that in exchange for one thousand zlotys the Polish government was issuing the Jews passports that were valid for a single crossing over the Polish border. The preferred method of departure was to obtain a transit permit to visit relatives in the Soviet zone of Germany and then simply not to return. Many Jews also left without passports via Prague, Stettin, or Berlin to the American occupied zone in Germany, where the Americans had set up camps for the refugees. Cavendish-Bentinck thought that the exodus was genuinely inspired by current persecution and fear of the future and not by political or Zionist motives—there was no evidence at this stage of direct Zionist influence. He rejected the claim of Polish authorities that the killings and other acts of violence were the work of reactionary groups that had infiltrated the country but instead attributed them to the widespread anti-Semitism among the populace and to the fact that Jews were prominent in the government and among the hated security authorities. Cavendish-Bentinck concluded that Polish Jews were unanimous in wanting to leave the country, and there was no way of stopping them from doing so. As he saw it, within a few years Poland would become one of the few countries in the world where one would not find a single Jew.[18]

The flight of Jews from Poland began to receive widespread attention after a press conference held on 2 January 1946 by General Frederick Morgan, the head of UNRRA in Germany. At the end of the official part of the press conference, intended to arouse world public opinion to the problem of the DPs still remaining in Germany, the British general addressed the issue of the Jewish refugees, declaring that European Jews had a plan to leave for Palestine. He claimed that there was no factual basis for the stories of pogroms and violence against the Jews in Poland and that such reports were part of a Jewish scheme to force the United Nations to grant the Jews a permanent home. He maintained that the Jews who were arriving daily by train from Poland to Berlin were well dressed and possessed substantial sums of money. According to Morgan, the organization that was behind the movement and encouraged Jews to abandon their comfortable living conditions in Poland was located in Poland and in Bavaria.[19] As it fell in line with London's stand, one assumes that Morgan's statement was not coincidental.

The statement caused an immediate uproar in the Jewish world, especially in the United States. The World Jewish Congress accused Morgan of trying to influence the AAC. "His allegation," it was stressed, "is sheer Nazism, even in its wording, which might well come from a speech by Hitler and his gang of Fascist anti-Semites."[20] The British Foreign Office, alarmed by the angry response of the American press, instructed its embassy in Washington to explain that though Morgan was a British subject, he was serving under the auspices of UNRRA and not the British government and that therefore he was not expressing government policy.[21]

Morgan's view that there was a clear connection between the exodus of the Jews from Poland and the Zionist struggle for Palestine, of course, was shared by Foreign Office officials, including the foreign secretary, no less than by the Control Commission in Germany and British intelligence in Palestine. Morgan's "mistake" had been that he had stated in public what others were arguing privately. Not surprisingly, therefore, Bevin defended Morgan by telling his colleagues in the cabinet that Morgan had only wished to explain that the complicated problem of the Jewish DPs exceeded the purview of UNRRA's jurisdiction; regrettably, the general's statement had included some remarks that were quoted out of context by the press. Only a few weeks earlier, Bevin himself had been the butt of a sharp attack by Jewish leaders following his remark at a press conference about the "Jews getting too much at the head of the queue." The foreign secretary believed that UNRRA should hold on to Morgan because he was an excellent administrator who had contributed much to the organization and was good at taking appropriate action.[22] Eventually, Lehman, the secretary general of UNRRA, decided not to dismiss Morgan, who had flown to New York to explain what had happened at the press conference.[23]

As a result of the turmoil Morgan's press conference had created, the British embassy in Warsaw was asked for information concerning renewed pogroms and cruelty toward Jews in Poland and for an assessment of the alleged motives behind the current mass exodus of Polish Jews: whether the departure was linked to the Palestine question or the result of actions by Poles who wished to be rid of the Jews for economic and political reasons.[24] According to Robin Hankey, the chargé d'affaires at the Warsaw embassy, it was largely economic and psychological factors that were responsible for Jews leaving the country: economic chaos and the introduction of Communist methods had made it exceedingly difficult to make money in Poland. Zionist motivation, too, played a role, and many of those who were leaving were persuaded that by their departure they would increase the pressure for the settlement of Jews in Palestine. Information concerning the organization that was arranging the Jewish exodus was hard to come by, but the movement was organized and Lodz and Katowice seemed to be its main centers.

Hankey argued that despite the killings, Polish Jews did not face physical threat on a scale that warranted mass flight. After all, pogroms were no longer occurring. Still, he admitted that Jews were afraid of living in small towns and villages because of enmity of Polish peasants, who refused to return Jewish property they had taken over during the war. Hankey moreover maintained that not all the murders of Jews had been inspired by anti-Semitism. According to the data at his disposal, about three hundred Jews had been slain in the period between the end of German occupation and November 1945. The British diplomat was unable to determine if Polish authorities had a hand in the events, let alone whether such involvement was official or stemmed from the corruption of certain government personnel. In any case, he pointed out, one bottle of vodka sufficed to get a person past the border. Hankey suggested the possibility of threatening the Polish government with postponing acceptance into Germany of Germans living in Poland—as had been decided upon at the Potsdam Conference—if the departure of Jews from Poland was allowed to continue.[25] Cavendish-Bentinck reported that, in contrast to the situation in the past, very few Polish Jews were currently asking to be admitted to the United States. This would appear to give some support to rumors that the present exodus was part of an effort to bring pressure to bear on the AAC by creating a large concentration of Jewish refugees in Germany demanding to be allowed to immigrate to Palestine.[26] In his evaluation of the situation, the British ambassador neglected to mention not only that the number of entrance visas allocated by the United States for immigration of Polish nationals was negligible but also that the United States was giving preference to DPs living in the camps.

It turned out that the embassy in Warsaw had come round to the opinion of Whitehall and of British occupation authorities in Germany and Austria that the departure of Jews was part of the Zionist struggle over Palestine. The embassy's report not only differed from previous analyses but it no longer accommodated the views of A. G. Banks, head of the embassy counselor section, who had said he could understand that Jews would want to leave a country in which they had been made to suffer unspeakable afflictions, physically and emotionally. Banks also observed that many of the survivors had been left without either kin or community so that they had no hope of rebuilding their lives and businesses in Poland.[27]

Reports in the world press of cruel and anti-Semitic acts in Poland inevitably hurt that country's image and greatly worried the new government, coming as they did just when it was seeking international legitimacy.[28] The regime recruited the Central Jewish Committee in Poland for a propaganda campaign intended to refute reports of the difficult situation of Polish Jews. The committee was established in February 1945, in Warsaw, and in April 1945 was recognized by the government as the representative organization of Polish Jews. In a January 1946 press conference, the committee's representatives argued that the reports in the overseas press of violent acts had been highly exaggerated even though they admitted that since the liberation 353 Jews had been killed by what they described as gangs, reactionary elements, undisciplined soldiers, or robbers. It was suggested that propagandists outside Poland were exploiting these terror attacks to put the government in a bad light. The committee reported that two organized pogroms in the summer of 1945, in Rezsow and Cracow, had been mercilessly suppressed by the government, and since then the murder of Jews had subsided.[29] Zionist sources put the number of murders much higher.[30]

At the British Foreign Office there was some difference of opinion as to what course of action to follow vis-à-vis the Polish government regarding the flight of the Jews. As before, George Rendel had no doubts. He argued that the Jewish movement was part of the Zionist struggle against Britain for Palestine, and therefore he proposed enlisting the cooperation of the American government in applying pressure on the Polish government to stop the Jewish exodus. Patrick P. Hancock of the Northern Department believed that applying pressure on the Polish regime would not be effective because the central government in Poland exercised very little authority in the country and that anyway the movement of Jews across the border could not be stopped.[31] Henderson, of the Refugee Department, was also convinced that there was no point in approaching the Polish government because it wanted to see the country be rid of the problem of Jews by their expulsion to Palestine. Still, he was doubtful that the Polish government had any involvement in the organization of the movement.[32]

The exodus of Jews from Poland was discussed at the meeting of the Cabinet Overseas Reconstruction Committee at the end of January 1946. As the minister responsible for the Control Office for Germany and Austria, Hynd reported that the British parliamentary delegation that had visited Poland had concluded that the Jewish departure was clearly an organized movement. He warned against allowing a large number of Jews into Palestine because that might encourage others to flee and also influence Polish Jews in the camps in Germany who had intended to return to Poland as part of the repatriation scheme to change their minds. Hynd certainly was concerned by a possible increase in the number of Jewish DPs in the British zones of occupation. For his part, Bevin had no doubt that the exodus from Poland and the illegal immigration to Palestine were directly linked to the start of the inquiry of the AAC. In his opinion, there was almost no persecution in Poland and certainly none of the sort that could justify Jews quitting the country. Bevin believed that the best way to curtail the movement was to stop the flow at the source. He was aware, however, of the difficulty in asking the Polish authorities to improve the situation of the Jews there, since the Polish government would reject the implication that there was anti-Semitism in Poland. Bevin acknowledged that no serious attempt had as yet been made to convince the Polish government to act vigorously against the movement.

Lord Nathan, the parliamentary under secretary of state for war, was dubious about the claim that an organized evacuation of Polish Jews was taking place. Himself a Jew, he explained his analysis in terms of the Holocaust. If in the past Zionist efforts had been directed to establishing a Jewish majority in Palestine by settling a million Jews in the country from a total reserve of five million, to achieve the same end at this juncture would require bringing in all surviving Jews from Europe. Nathan suggested appealing to Russia to forestall the repatriation of Polish Jews from the Soviet Union. At the end of the meeting it was decided to turn to the Polish government but to refrain from alleging that the Jews were subject to ill treatment in Poland. The committee also decided not to appeal to the Soviet government concerning this matter.[33]

Behind the Scenes: Moscow's Role

The British decided not to approach the Soviets because they were aware of the Soviet position on this issue. Within the joint Allied control bodies in Germany and Austria the Soviets were careful to deny any knowledge of or involvement in the exodus movement, and they even supported taking extreme measures against Jewish infiltrators. A typical expression of Soviet tactics may be found in the session of the Directorate of Prisoners of War and Displaced Persons in Germany at the beginning of December 1945, when the Soviet representative rejected the American proposal to split up the Jews arriving from Poland among the four occupation zones, according to the relative percentage of German refugees that each zone was supposed to absorb. This procedure would require the Soviets to absorb 41 percent of the fleeing Jews, the Americans 34 percent, the English 22 percent, and the French only 3 percent. The Soviet representative rejected the proposal and suggested, innocently, asking the Polish government not to grant visas to Jewish emigrants and to allow the Kommandatura (the Council of the Occupation Forces in Berlin) to return the emigrants to Poland.[34]

The British command in Austria was skeptical of the Soviets' claim that they were not aware of the Jewish influx into Austria: without Soviet agreement it would not have been possible for thousands of Jews to enter that country.[35] Given their involvement in Poland, the Soviets must have known that although the Jews were leaving the country illegally, the government was allowing this to happen. The suggestion that an appeal be addressed to the Polish government was probably less than candid, and the proposal to force the Jews to return to Poland should also be treated with some skepticism. The Soviets knew that the Americans would object because of the response the plight of the Jewish refugees in the DP camps had aroused in American public opinion, particularly in light of the Harrison report and Truman's stand on the issue. Moscow's position should also be appreciated in light of its overall support of repatriation, including use of force if needed. While strongly demanding the return of all Soviet nationals, Moscow could not be seen supporting a different course in public.[36]

At the beginning of January 1946 the British ambassador to Poland reported hearing rumors that the Soviet authorities were encouraging the Polish government to allow the Jews to leave for Palestine in order to implant Communism there. Since such a possibility seemed very unrealistic to him, Cavendish-Bentinck explained that he had refrained from conveying this information when it first reached him and he had first wanted to find corroborating evidence. This had come from Deputy Prime Minister Mikołajczyk, who had called his attention to the support expressed by Adolph Berman, the representative of Left Poalei Zion (Hebrew: Zion workers) in Poland, for the exit of the Jews. Berman's brother was Jacob Berman, the deputy minister in the prime minister's office and one of the most influential politicians in Poland because of his close contacts with Moscow. Mikołajczyk suggested that Adolph Berman would not have made the statement in support of Jewish emigration without Moscow's approval, and he hinted that if 120,000 Polish Jews were to leave the USSR, there were likely to be many Soviet agents among them. As the anti-Communist opposition leader, Mikołajczyk certainly was not the most reliable and objective source of information on Soviet plans and intentions. Cavendish-Bentinck remained hesitant but decided that there was no longer justification for delaying a report on the rumors.[37]

British intelligence in Austria was similarly cautious about information it had received from Polish intelligence sources in General Władysław Anders's army in Italy because here, too, the objectivity of such anti-Soviet elements was doubtful. They also resisted the assessment of the commander of the DP camp in Judenburg (Austria) that the mass movement of the Jews was being encouraged by the Soviets so as to embarrass the British authorities in their occupation zone in Austria and exacerbate the political situation in Palestine. All that the Russians were doing, they argued, was to pass on the Jewish infiltrators to the British zone because they constituted a problem for them as well.[38]

In Washington, Halifax was doubtful that an appeal to the Russian authorities would be of use. Britain's ambassador based his judgment on unofficial talks with officials from the Polish desk in the State Department from whom he had learned that Soviet military and government officials were helping the movement of Jews via the Soviet occupied zone and that an official appeal to the Soviet government would not bring about a change in their policy.[39] In the end it was this absence of substantive proof of Soviet aid to the Jewish population movement together with the considerable tension that existed between them and the USSR that apparently made the British decide not to turn to Moscow on this matter. The British further believed that the Soviets, as they were trying to penetrate into "almost all Middle East territories," were strongly tempted to support the Arab cause.[40]

Under the circumstances, it was decided to appeal directly to Poland. At the beginning of February 1946 the Foreign Office instructed Cavendish-Bentinck to make it clear to the Polish government that, despite the warning issued by the Polish foreign minister, many Jews were managing to leave Poland for the American and British zones in Germany and Austria as well as Italy and from there migrate illegally to Palestine. The British government believed that the exodus had external political causes and was aimed at increasing the difficulties the British were having in Palestine and elsewhere. Britain wanted to see vigorous measures to stop the illegal departures and also opposed Jewish emigration by means of government-issued visas.[41] An attempt to convince Washington to join Britain in making an overture to the Polish government was unsuccessful. The Americans reasoned that without serious military measures it would not be possible to halt the flight from Poland.[42]

The Poles denied any involvement in the exodus. In his conversation with Cavendish-Bentinck, Joseph Olszewski, the secretary general of the Polish Foreign Ministry, emphasized that his government was making every effort to prevent illegal departures, including those of the Jews, and that in recent months these efforts had had considerable success. Olszewski assured the ambassador that very few exit visas had been allocated to private individuals in the course of 1945 — no more than two or three hundred all told. Passports were issued only to applicants who could show that they had a visa or an entry permit to some country. Olszewski estimated the number of Jews who had left Poland since it was liberated at approximately 20,000. Cavendish-Bentinck concluded from this that the Polish government was not able to prevent the Jews from leaving the country illegally.[43] He estimated that at the very least 120,000 Jews would be leaving Poland by January 1948 and that the figure was more likely to be 170,000. The Jews were determined to leave despite the consequences, and nothing could prevent them from doing so. Contrary to the clear-cut position of the Foreign Office and to his own previous assessment, Cavendish-Bentinck now argued that there was no proof that Jews wanted to get out of Poland because of propaganda by Zionist organizations.[44]

The Anglo-American Committee Visits Poland

An opportunity to canvass the situation of the Polish Jews and their intentions was given to a subcommittee of the Anglo-American Committee that visited Poland during the second week of February 1946. Its three members met with Polish government leaders, including the prime minister and the foreign minister, and with leaders of the Polish Jewish community. Prime Minister Osóbka-Morawski told them that Poland needed its Jewish citizens, particularly because they were professional people and craftsmen. He noted that legislation had been put in place forbidding all anti-Semitic acts and claimed that it had almost totally eradicated anti-Semitism. Nonetheless, the Jews seemed to regard Poland as one large cemetery, and it was this view that instilled in them the powerful urge to emigrate. The prime minister explained that he did not intend to place obstacles in their path. He expressed the hope that the economic rehabilitation in Poland would make the country again attractive for Jews as well.[45] Polish foreign minister Wincenty Rzymowski told his guests that Jews who left Poland illegally would not be allowed to return. According to him, during the six months the government had been in office, four hundred passports had been issued to nongovernment persons.[46]

An optimistic picture about the future of the Jews in Poland was painted for the subcommittee by Władysław Wolski, the Polish plenipotentiary for repatriation questions. He reported that as part of the repatriation agreement of 6 July 1945, 110,000 Jews had registered to return to Poland, and of these, 25,000 had already arrived by February 1946. The Polish government and the repatriation authority were making every effort to keep the repatriates in Poland.[47] Wolski estimated that within five years there would be 250,000 Jews in Poland. Cavendish-Bentinck did not take Wolski's statement seriously, shrugging off his assessment that there would be 250,000 Jews in Poland as totally unrealistic, and felt that Wolski had failed in persuading the subcommittee that "the Jews would be very happy to remain in Poland if they were not being lured out by evil Zionists."[48]

In contrast, the subcommittee was impressed by the testimony of David Kahane, acting chief rabbi of Poland and chief rabbi of the Polish army with the rank of colonel. Rabbi Kahane believed that as part of the repatriation agreements, about 150,000 Jews were expected to return from the USSR to Poland, but most of the returnees would consider Poland as a springboard to safer countries. Unlike Wolski, Rabbi Kahane thought that by January 1948 there would be no more than 50,000 Jews in Poland, including about 10,000 "non-religious Jews of extreme left-wing political persuasion" and about 40,000 orthodox Jews of the older generation with deep roots in Poland. He believed that within ten years, as a result of assimilation and emigration, there would be no Jews left in Poland.

Rabbi Kahane praised the Polish Provisional Government of National Unity as well as its predecessor, the Lublin Committee, for assisting in the physical and spiritual rehabilitation of the Jews and for their efforts in defending Jews against anti-Semitism. He sharply criticized Jews who were in the Polish government, like Jacob Berman and Hilary Minc, and argued that they should not be regarded as part of the Jewish community and did not represent it. He also attacked the Central Committee of Polish Jews, saying that it and its pronouncements should be viewed as part of the Polish government's propaganda. He thought that it was not possible for Jews to resettle in Poland and rebuild life there. Anti-Semitic tendencies had intensified during the Nazi rule, the atmosphere of terror was too heavy, and pogroms were daily occurrences. Rabbi Kahane blamed reactionary elements such as the National Armed Forces (Narodowe Siły Zbrojne) for resurrecting the blood libel. He told of a case where a child had disappeared from a small town near Lublin, and two days later nine Jews were burned to death in their homes. He asserted that most of the Jews wanted to leave Poland for Palestine, which they considered to be their traditional home and the center of their faith. In his view, their Zionism was not political but rather the result of the anti-Semitic terror and the desire to fulfill the age-old religious aspiration of those in exile. If, as a consequence of injustice, they were prevented from reaching Palestine, Rabbi Kahane believed they would go to the United States, England, or any country with a reasonable climate and a chance to make a living.[49]

Members of the subcommittee received a similar appraisal from Dr. Emil Sommerstein, a Zionist leader who had been a member of the Polish Seim until the war broke out. During the war he had been a prisoner in the USSR until he was released in 1944 to become the representative of Polish Jews in the Soviet Union; he was co-opted into the Polish Committee for National Liberation established in July 1944. Dr. Sommerstein too stressed that the Polish Jews, including those who were well off economically, aspired to leave. He gave two reasons for the desire to emigrate: the first was political—growing Zionist awareness—and the second psychological—the survivors had no remaining family or friends, and community life had been destroyed so that there was no incentive to remain. Dr. Sommerstein also emphasized that the government was opposed to anti-Semitism and had used all possible means to fight it, but Jews were still being murdered.[50] The Jewish Central Committee placed four recommendations before the AAC's subcommittee: free emigration to Palestine, repeal of the 1939 White Paper, a free and independent existence in Palestine, and American and British support of a free Palestine. Members of the Central Jewish Committee were careful not to speak of establishing a Jewish state in Palestine but rather of a Jewish homeland there.[51]

The AAC's subcommittee also held discussions about the problem of anti-Semitism in Poland with Monseigneur Zdzanek, secretary to the bishop of Lodz. Zdzanek blamed the Polish lack of sympathy for the Jews on the preferential treatment the government accorded them and the fact that Jews had filled the better social positions before the war. Moreover, "whenever there is lawlessness of a racketeering nature—such as smuggling or white slavery—the Jews are the ones engaged in it." According to Zdzanek, the government and the church were doing everything possible to end anti-Semitism. Still, he, too, believed that most of the Jews in Poland wanted to go to Palestine.[52]

The report the AAC published in April 1946 stated that since the end of the war about 30,000 Jews from Poland had entered the British and American occupied zones in Germany and Austria. After the war, 80,000 Jews remained in Poland, and it was estimated that 150,000 Jews would return to Poland from the Soviet Union. Of this total figure, about 200,000 were expected eventually to leave Poland. The Jews had convinced members of the subcommittee of their desire to leave. Although the subcommittee did not think any organization was directing the exodus, it did believe that an underground system operated to transfer the Jews from "hand to hand on the way out."[53]

During the first months after the end of the war, Jews leaving Poland blended into the mass movements of other refugees and DPs who were then returning home. Some referred to this time as the "Greek period" because fleeing Jews tended to present themselves as Greeks returning home, thus merging into the waves of repatriates. The Jews constituted an inconspicuous minority in this vast population movement.[54] At first, starting in the autumn of 1944, Jewish migrants went via Rumania in the hope that from there they would be able to sail for Palestine. Until September 1945 about five thousand persons had left Poland for Rumania and Hungary.[55] After it became clear that there was no possibility of sailing from Rumania, the exodus shifted its route to Austria, Germany, and Italy.[56] By December 1945 more than thirty-three thousand Jews had left Poland.

Brichah activists and the Zionist leadership felt that the Polish government was actually amenable to the Jewish exodus and therefore did not place obstacles in its path.[57] Indeed, as early as August 1945, Osóbka-Morawski stated in public that the government would support efforts of organizations or individuals who organized Jewish emigration from Poland.[58] During his visit to the DP camps in October 1945, Ben-Gurion told General Bedell-Smith, Eisenhower's chief of staff, that the Polish government knew of the exodus of the Jews and wished to encourage it because the government could not and did not want to protect them.[59] At the beginning of 1946, however, Brichah activists sensed a change in the Polish government's position; border exits had allegedly been closed by order of Warsaw, and departure by train and as part of repatriation from Poland had also come to an end.[60]

After December 1945, it had indeed become more difficult to leave, not only because winter had set in but also because of closer inspection at the border. Steps taken by the Polish government at the border were not directed against the Jews but were part of the government's war against the underground opposition and of its efforts to establish control in the country in general and at the borders in particular.[61] It would seem that introducing tighter control at the borders did not come at any urging by Britain, since the ambassador to Poland broached the matter only at the beginning of February 1946. The British themselves did not attribute the decrease in Jewish emigration from Poland to their intervention.[62] In fact, the British had avoided turning the subject of the Jewish exodus into a major issue in the relations between the two countries and refrained from threatening retaliation, as Hankey and others had suggested. It may well have been this significant decrease in the number of Jews leaving Poland in the first months of 1946 together with the hope of arriving at an agreed solution with the United States on the Palestine question that caused the British authorities to adopt a low profile on the matter. Zionist sources estimated that during the first four months of 1946 no more than 5,700 people left Poland, perhaps even much fewer.[63] During these months when the Brichah had difficulty getting Jews out of Poland, the Soviets allowed about another 100,000 Jews to repatriate. All in all, between February and October 1946 about 170,000 Jews arrived from the Soviet Union.[64]

By the second half of May the number of Jews leaving Poland began increasing again. Within two weeks about thirty-five hundred people had left, and during June about another eight thousand followed.[65] Movement on such a scale could not have taken place without the knowledge of the Polish authorities. And indeed, Prime Minister Osóbka-Morawski at the opening of the tenth session of the Polish National Council in the beginning of May repeated that the government would not stand in the way of Jews wanting to emigrate to Palestine to realize their national aspirations.[66] At that time tens of thousands of Jewish repatriates from the Soviet Union were being gathered at special assembly points in Poland. The great majority of them had no desire to be reintegrated into the Polish nation, and their continued presence in the country was bound to have undesirable repercussions for political, economic, and cultural but also for security reasons. Quite likely, the Polish authorities were aware of the potential risks of having the repatriates remain in Poland and therefore took no overt action to prevent their departure, though without extending cooperation at an official level.[67] Probably, the renewed conflict between the British and the Americans over the Jewish refugees after the AAC had submitted its report also played a role.

Phase Two: Summer of 1946

The turning point in the Polish government's policy on Jewish emigration came with the pogrom in Kielce on 4 July. On the eve of the war, Kielce had counted close to 20,000 Jewish inhabitants, who made up more than one-third of the city's population. After the war, when the city had 50,000 inhabitants, only 200 to 250 Jews were living there, most of them having come from the Soviet Union. Many of the Jews lived at 7 Planti Street, in a building that served as the home of a group from Hanoar Hazioni (Zionist Youth). On the morning of 4 July 1946 a nine-year-old boy named Henryk Blaszczyk appeared in the police station saying he had managed to escape from the cellar of the building of the Jewish Central Committee after having been kidnapped by a Jew who had held him there for two days and had wanted to kill him. The boy added that he had seen Jews murdering Christian children. On his way to the police station the child spotted the Jew who had allegedly "kidnapped" him—a mentally ill man who was then arrested by the police. The commander of the local militia ordered his men to surround the building of the Jewish Committee. Word of these events spread rapidly through the city, and within a short time an angry mob had gathered near the building. Inside at the time were several committee workers and a group of young members of Hanoar Hazioni. A contingent of policemen, under the command of a sergeant, which was sent to disperse the mob, entered the building and confiscated the few licensed guns that belonged to the besieged Jews. The incited, impassioned mob then broke into the building and began venting its rage on people and property. At the same time rowdy mobs roamed the streets, grabbed Jews out of their homes, and murdered them on the spot. Toward evening security forces arrived in Kielce from Lodz and restored order. Among the forty-two murdered Jews was the head of the community.

The following day the Communist minister for public security, Stanisław Radkiewicz, came to Kielce, accompanied by the public prosecutor. Orders were given to convene a special military court. The head of the police force, the commander of the security forces, and the commander of the district were arrested. The court sentenced eleven people to death, to life imprisonment, or to long terms in jail. A representative of the Polish government participated in the funeral of the Jewish victims. The Polish press censured the perpetrators of the pogrom and blamed Polish reactionary circles and especially the Catholic priests, who could have opposed the rioting but failed to do so. The official government position was that the pogrom had been organized by the anti-Communist underground affiliated with Polish emigrants in the West together with the opposition group, the Polish Peasants' Party headed by Deputy Prime Minister Mikołajczyk. Moral responsibility was laid at the door of the Catholic Church. The one newspaper that had reservations, arguing that the reasons for the pogrom should be investigated, was, not surprisingly, Mikołajczyk's *Gazeta Ludowa*.[68]

Some argued that the pogrom had been the result of a provocation. There were two versions. One was that it was the doing of the opposition, which sought to foment riots within Poland and tarnish the country's international standing. This was the view adopted by the Polish government, the Polish press, and Rabbi David Kahane.[69] The other was that the Soviet and Polish governments, wishing to promote the regime's struggle against the opposition, were behind the Kielce pogrom.[70] The one thing that was clear was that it proved very easy to arouse Poles to start a pogrom against the Jews by invoking blood libel.[71]

After the Kielce pogrom, Antek Zuckermann, deputy commander of the Warsaw ghetto rebellion, and the Polish deputy minister of defense, General Marian Spychalski, came to an agreement that the Jews would be allowed to leave Poland without visas or exit permits. According to the agreement, the Zionists undertook to coordinate the exit with Polish security forces to prevent non-Jews, particularly opponents of the government, from leaving, to avoid the smuggling of national assets, particularly foreign currency, and to keep the agreement secret. Assembly and transit points were established at the frontier with Czechoslovakia, and on 30 July 1946 the Polish border was opened to all Jews wishing to leave. Although the agreement spoke of a duration of one or two months, in practice the border remained open until the end of February 1947.[72] On 7 August, Isser Ben-Zvi, a Brichah emissary in Poland, reported that "a very comfortable setting for widespread activity had been created. For a number of weeks we have the possibility of bringing out as many as we can, i.e.

the maximum possible." During the first three months beginning in July, more than sixty-six thousand people left Poland; in August alone about thirty-five thousand Jews departed.[73]

When he learned of the increased number of Polish Jews reaching the American occupied zone of Germany during the summer of 1946, Rabbi Bernstein, General McNarney's adviser for Jewish affairs, decided to visit Poland.[74] On this trip, during the last week of July 1946, he met with high-ranking officials in the Polish government including the prime minister, with the Jewish religious and secular leadership, with representatives of the UNRRA and JDC welfare organizations, and with representatives of the Polish, American, and Jewish press. In the detailed report he gave to General McNarney at the end of the visit, Rabbi Bernstein estimated that there were 160,000 Jews in Poland at the time. He described in detail the anti-Semitism prevalent in Poland and quoted the general claim of Jewish survivors that the Nazis had been able to exterminate 90 percent of the Jews of Poland because they had had the enthusiastic cooperation of the Poles, who carried out the killings under Nazi orders. He explained the flight from Poland before the Kielce pogrom by the atmosphere of terror that reigned in the country and the acts of murder that helped perpetuate it. The rabbi noted the enthusiastic cooperation of various elements in Kielce in perpetrating the brutal murders. From testimony of Jews he had the impression that the Polish government was not anti-Semitic and that energetic steps had indeed been taken to integrate Jews in the life of the country. Legislation had been introduced against racial or religious discrimination, and vigorous steps had been taken against perpetrators of the pogrom. Significant, however, was the absence of support for the government among the Polish public, which regarded it as a vassal of the USSR. He emphasized that as part of the opposition struggle against the government, it had singled out the Jews "for its most virulent attacks." Some people believed that Poland was heading toward a civil war during which the Jews would be eliminated.

The only point of light in Rabbi Bernstein's report was his description of the seventy-five thousand Jews in Lower Silesia. This region had been transferred to Poland from Germany, and its acquisition had enabled the government to distribute among the Poles and the Jews the land, the industries, and the homes of Germans who had lived in the area. There, he wrote, the Jews were not living in an atmosphere of fear, and they were not encountering violence above and beyond the level society in general was subject to.

While Rabbi Bernstein believed that most Silesian Jews would not seek to move to the American zone of Germany during the coming weeks, he thought that such a move was a possibility for most of the Jews in the other parts of

Poland, except for the Communists, Socialists, and Bundists, together constituting about 10 percent of all the Jews. He estimated that 100,000 of the 160,000 Polish Jews would emigrate within one year but rejected a plan calling for the evacuation of all Polish Jews because it had not been proven that indeed all needed to leave the country. Furthermore, the Polish government would oppose an open effort to remove the Jews from Poland since it would imply Polish laxity in keeping order in the country and defending its citizens. Such a step might bring the Jews into conflict with the government. A hysterical exodus, he feared, might lead to pogroms, acts of murder, and robbery. And finally, "a public acceptance of emigration as a direct answer to the Kielce pogrom might establish the precedent by which antisemites in other countries might initiate pogroms in order to bring about the emigration of all Jews." [75]

Rabbi Bernstein's report caused some concern among officials in the Foreign Office. George Rendel thought that the report should be treated with caution since it was based only on talks the rabbi had conducted with government circles and Jewish figures and not with "gentile sources," by which he meant members of the anti-Communist opposition. In his view, the report added weight to the demand for an international inquiry into the situation of the Polish Jews; a critical report submitted by an international delegation would probably have a more useful influence. Rendel reaffirmed British policy that opposed Jewish emigration from Poland, and he supported increased British efforts to improve the situation of the Jews in Poland.[76]

Rendel's suggestions needed time to work out, which was lacking because Whitehall was confronting immediate ongoing large-scale flight from Poland. The British legation in Czechoslovakia reported in August 1946 that a steady stream of Jews were entering the country from Poland at the rate of eighteen hundred daily and that about thirty-five thousand Jews had arrived between 1 July and 9 August with another seventy thousand expected to follow on their heels.[77] The American ambassador to Poland, Arthur Bliss Lane, informed the State Department that after the pogrom in Kielce, the daily departures had risen to seven hundred, and that about one hundred thousand more were expected to leave. He noted that the Polish border police were allowing them to pass freely.[78] In mid-August the Americans conveyed to the British the assessment of General Mark Clark, the commander of American forces in Austria, that in the coming three months some sixty thousand Jews would leave Poland.[79]

News of the massacre at Kielce produced no change in the Foreign Office's stand that the Jewish exodus from Poland was organized rather than spontaneous and part of a plan to encourage illegal immigration to Palestine so as to influence British policy there.[80] The Warsaw embassy continued to disagree with the Foreign Office's assessment of the reasons for the Jewish exodus. One of the embassy's staff, J. W. Russell, told Charles Baxter, the head of the Foreign Office Eastern Department, that 99 percent of the 120,000 Jews in Poland wished to leave the country. For most of them, he said, the target country was not important as long as they could leave Poland. A variety of groups dispersed along Poland's southern and western borders were engaged in smuggling Jews across the border. These organizations were for the most part semiautonomous and not necessarily under Jewish control; their motives were mercenary. The embassy had no evidence that "there is an overall controlling organisation or master mind behind the various local rackets." Most of the movement was headed southward in the direction of Czechoslovakia, whence it proceeded to the American zone in Germany. Russell observed that the Polish government was attempting to control the exodus but that thus far its efforts had been unsuccessful because it was very easy to leave Poland via the "green borders." He believed that conditions in Poland were intolerable for Jews and that the Kielce pogrom had changed the minds of those who until then had been reluctant to leave. Although instances of actual persecution of Jews were rare, the Jews had been living in a state of terror ever since the German atrocities, and the Kielce pogrom only reinforced this feeling. He predicted that the exodus from Poland, estimated at about a thousand persons per day, would continue unabated.[81] Unlike Foreign Office officials, who cited the infrequency of attacks on Jews as proof of their argument that the reason for flight was not the fear of persecution, Russell believed that the paucity of attacks since the Kielce pogrom did not justify concluding that the Jews could continue to live in Poland. Ambassador Cavendish-Bentinck agreed that there was no proof that the Jewish exodus from Poland was anything but spontaneous.[82]

Whitehall, however, did not agree with the embassy's analysis. At a meeting with La Guardia, then secretary general of UNRRA, Prime Minister Attlee refused La Guardia's request to allow Jews who were leaving Poland to enter the British zones in Germany and Austria, repeating the government's stance that the exodus from Poland was an "artificial movement engineered largely with a view to forcing our hands over Palestine." He also rejected La Guardia's argument that allowing one hundred thousand Jewish DPs to enter Palestine would solve the problem of the Jews from Poland. Attlee compared the American's suggestion to the hypothetical situation in which there is a sharp conflict between the "white and coloured population" in Detroit and Britain suddenly proposed sending "100,000 West African immigrants" there. The prime minister, furthermore, dismissed the allegation that the anti-Communist Polish opposition was responsible for persecuting Jews who could therefore no longer remain in Poland. "This would merely be adopting the Nazi view that there was no place for Jews in Central and Eastern Europe," he told La Guardia.[83]

The Foreign Office and the embassy in Warsaw were in agreement, however, that the Polish government was willing to allow the Jews to leave after the Kielce pogrom.[84] Word had reached the embassy of the unrestricted mass exodus of Jews from Poland without documents and with government consent. An eyewitness reported that the exodus from Poland to Czechoslovakia was taking place in broad daylight. Upon reaching the border, a group of people were seen to submit a list of names of those about to leave, along with confirmation from a Jewish organization that all people mentioned on the list were Jews. After the Polish soldiers had made sure no non-Jews had tried to slip in among the departing Jews, the group crossed the border. John Dickenson, the British consul in Szczecin, reported that every day approximately five hundred Jews were coming across the border near Kudowa. Trucks would bring Jews to Kudowa during the day; at night and without passports they would cross the border near Slone with the help of local Jewish guides. The authorities were obviously making no effort to hide the movement and even had put up a temporary customs checkpoint to deal with the traffic.[85] Kudowa was one of the assembly points and Slone one of the border crossing sites designated in Zuckermann's agreement of July 1946 with the Polish authorities.[86]

The Foreign Office was uncertain as to whether it was worthwhile submitting a protest to the Polish government. This would then have to go together with a request that the government take action against anti-Semitism and also prevent the illegal departure of the Jews. The general view was that such protests would have no results and that making them public would only annoy the Polish government.[87] Hesitation stemmed, among other things, from a discussion Cavendish-Bentinck had held in August with Olszewski, who claimed that the Polish government hoped the Jews would remain in the country, especially artisans, tailors, and jewelers, and that a special office had been established to settle repatriated Jews in the former German territories in Silesia. But the pogrom in Kielce had caused hysteria among the Jews, and the Polish government, because of the country's extensive land borders, was unable to prevent them from fleeing. It would be possible to curb the illegal exodus from Poland, Olszewski thought, by allowing a certain number of Jews to emigrate to other countries every month, but Cavendish-Bentinck had countered that no refuge could be offered to Jews now in Poland without first solving the problem of the great number of Jews in Germany, Austria, Italy, and Cyprus.[88]

From his interview with Olszewski, Cavendish-Bentinck concluded that the Poles were powerless to prevent Jews from leaving the country illegally because policy on this matter was actually determined by Moscow. He doubted if approaching Polish authorities in secret or publicly would do any good. Any attempt to suggest to the Poles that they should act against anti-Semitism in their country was likely to be met with the counter claim that it was the agents of General Władisław Anders, whose activities were being directed from London, who were fomenting anti-Semitism and violence against Jews in Poland. According to the ambassador, Britain's difficulties in Palestine met with satisfaction in the Polish government. He was very doubtful about Foreign Office attempts to bring a halt to the exodus; he believed it was unstoppable. The only element that could moderate the anti-Semitism that was impelling the Jews to leave, Cavendish-Bentinck argued, was the Polish bishops, "though they themselves are fundamentally antisemitic."[89] An additional factor that reinforced doubts in London about the wisdom of addressing an appeal to the Polish government was the latter's sharp reaction to an official protest that British and Americans had submitted on 19 August over irregularities in the referendum of 30 June and in the preparations for the first Polish general elections. The Poles accused the two Western powers of intervening in Polish internal affairs.[90]

Cavendish-Bentinck had reached his conclusions about the Polish bishopric after meetings with leading Polish clergy on the subject of anti-Semitism. When he asked the principal coadjutor of Cardinal Adam Stefan Sapieha of Krakow and Bishop Juliusz Bienik, the auxiliary bishop of Upper Silesia, that anti-Semitism or at least racial prejudice be denounced in the pastoral letter to be published at the end of the conference of Polish bishops planned for 5 September in Czestochowa, Cavendish-Bentinck was told that "owing to deep anti-semitic feeling in Poland, the bishops fear that an open condemnation of anti-semitism might weaken the Church's influence." The ambassador regarded the reply as "an excuse for evading condemnation of antisemitism in strong terms." Bishop Bienik added that there was proof that the gentile child from Kielce had indeed been tortured and the Jews had drawn blood from his arm. Stunned by this state of mind, Cavendish-Bentinck thought that only a directive from the Holy See to condemn anti-Semitism would help "to counterbalance the innate feeling of the Polish bishops."[91]

He was soon to learn that his hopes for the Holy See were misplaced. In a conversation between Darcy Osborne, British ambassador to the Vatican, and Domienico Tardini, deputy minister in the Vatican, the latter protested that the problem of anti-Semitism in Poland had been exploited and distorted for political purposes, as was proven by the Kielce pogrom. According to the Vatican official, approximately sixty thousand Jews had remained in Poland after the war, but the Soviet government had transferred to Poland about five hundred thousand Jewish Bolsheviks, many of them Russians, with the aim of fostering Communism in the country, and this had helped increase the traditional anti-Semitism of the Poles. What also did not ingratiate them with the Poles was that a large number of Jews held administrative positions throughout Poland.[92]

The Vatican's version of the causes of the Kielce pogrom reveals that there was little or no difference between Vatican anti-Semitism and that of the Polish bishops. A Vatican memorandum stated, among other things, that "the influx of Russian Jews [into Poland] coincided with the mysterious vanishing of Christian children." The Vatican totally accepted the fabrication that the child in Kielce had been kidnapped to draw his blood and expressed doubts only as to the number of Jewish victims in the pogrom. It was suggested that no more than eleven persons had been killed. Sharp criticism was directed against the trial as if this had been conducted by the Jews: "The accused were not allowed to plead 'not guilty' but were forced by the prosecutors to plead 'guilty.'"[93] Once again the Jews were to be blamed. Given the religious, political, social, and economic reality in Poland, British expectations that the Catholic establishment in Poland could be called upon to help restrain anti-Semitism were largely futile. Identified as they were with the Communists, the Jews were counted among the political rivals of the church, which in turn supported the mainly anti-Semitic opposition. Then also, the bishops feared harming their political interests.

While giving up on any help from the church, Cavendish-Bentinck, in spite of his skepticism, called Olszewski's attention to Dickenson's findings about the illegal border crossings near Slone and the indifference exhibited by the local border authorities. The ambassador alluded to the promises that had been made by the Polish government that it would prevent the departure of Jews who lacked proper permits.[94] By that time, mid-September 1946, however, there was a steep drop in the number of refugees from Poland: unlike the waves of mass departures that had been going since June, from October 1946 to February 1947 no more than approximately ten thousand Jews left Poland.[95] This was partly because the hysteria following the Kielce pogrom had died down and also because Jews who had stayed on were beginning to manage, especially those who were living in Silesia. Winter was setting in, which helped curb traffic out of the country. Also influential were reports on the difficult conditions in the DP camps and that there were no clear prospects of any solution enabling Jews to immigrate to Palestine or anywhere else.[96] At the end of February 1947, as one of the measures implemented by the regime to assert its control over the country following the victory of the government bloc in the elections of 19 January 1947, Polish borders were closed to Jewish emigration.

Throughout the rest of 1947 the British showed only the slightest interest in the situation of the Jews in Poland. At the beginning of June it was reported to Bevin that 90 percent of the younger generation of Polish Jews had left and that there were still in Poland about fifty to sixty thousand Jews, half of whom wished to join their relatives living abroad, including Palestine, though, it was emphasized, this did not need to happen immediately. The Polish government was showing goodwill toward the remaining Jews, and there was no discrimination based on race. Knowing that there had always been anti-Semitism in the country, the Polish government decided to let the problem resolve itself by not placing obstacles in the path of the departing Jews. As for the future, it was assumed that there would not be a mass exodus but that a constant trickle would continue with or without the government's agreement.[97]

About six months later, Rabbi Kahane painted a much less optimistic picture for Russell from the British embassy. According to him, there had been a change in the attitude of the authorities toward the Jews living in Poland, whom he estimated to number about ninety-three thousand. Only a very small number of Jews were being allowed to leave the country, in contrast to the earlier policy of allowing any Jew to receive a one-way emigration visa. The ideological attacks previously directed at the Catholic Church had now been broadened to include the religious Jewish communities. The Jewish population, he asserted, was no longer afraid of pogroms, but it did fear the destruction of its culture and religion by the Communist authorities, who did not permit the opening of new religious schools and who forbade religious studies in the existing ones.[98] At the beginning of 1948 Zionist sources also reported that the exit of Jews with government permission had become almost impossible.[99]

CZECHOSLOVAKIA
AND HUNGARY
COUNTRIES OF
TRANSIT

The flight route of the approximately two hundred thousand Jews from Poland and Rumania who made it to the American and British occupation zones in Germany and Austria led through Czechoslovakia and Hungary. Jews in these two countries left for the West, but their numbers were comparatively small. The Brichah was helped in achieving this success in part by the cooperation its organizers received from leading officials in these two countries of transit.

On 4 February 1945 free elections were held in Hungary in which the Smallholders Party received about 57 percent and the Communists only 17 percent of the vote. The massive presence of the Red Army (about one million soldiers) ensured that the Communists were included in the coalition and that they were assigned several ministries, including, significantly, the Ministry of the Interior, which had responsibility for the security services. The new prime minister was Zoltán Tildy of the Smallholders Party. When on 1 February 1946 Hungary became a republic, Tildy was appointed president, and Ferenc Nagy, a member of the same party, who had served as chairman of the parliament, became prime minister. Soviet marshal Klement Voroshilov, who headed the Allied Control Commission in Hungary, played a central role in the country's affairs; according to the "Percentages Agreement" Churchill and Stalin had reached in October 1944, the two powers were to exercise equal influence in the country, but in practice the Soviets retained dominance by neutralizing British and American attempts to activate the Control Commission.

In the summer of 1946, the Hungarian Communists, abetted by Russian occupation authorities, began to increase pressure on the Smallholders Party government, among other things by demanding the dismissal and arrest of several Smallholders Party officials. During the winter this pressure intensified. Although encouraged by British and American representatives in Hungary to stand fast, Prime Minister Nagy yielded to Communist demands. In February 1947, the month the peace agreements were signed, the Soviet military police arrested Béla Kovács, secretary general of the Smallholders Party. Three months later, while he was on a visit to Switzerland, Nagy was forced to resign and to remain in exile. Even though it had the support of only 22 percent of the voters, the Communist Party won the elections of 31 August 1947, whereas the Smallholders Party suffered a resounding defeat, receiving less than 16 percent of the vote. By the end of the year, of the seven "bourgeois" parties that had participated in the elections and together had won 55 percent of the vote, only the Democratic People's Party (the Catholic progressive party) survived. The British and Americans decided that it was no longer possible to influence events in Hungary. The real authority in the country remained the Red Army.[1]

Unlike in Hungary, in Czechoslovakia the Red Army forces stayed for only a few months. In accordance with an agreement between the United States, whose forces had liberated the western part of Czechoslovakia, and the Soviet Union, the armies of both powers evacuated the country in November 1945. Czechoslovakia was the only country the Communists controlled after the war in which the Communist Party had been allowed to participate in political life between the two world wars, that is, until 1938. Representatives of all the anti-fascist parties took part in the interim government set up in Czechoslovakia in March 1945, headed by the Social Democrat Zdeněk Fierlinger. With the Soviets making certain that they would not be slighted, the Communists were assigned the positions of minister of the interior, deputy prime minister, minister of defense, and deputy foreign minister. The foundations the Communists had been able to lay before the war and the public's appreciation of the USSR for the part it had played in defeating Nazi Germany found clear expression in the free elections conducted in May 1945 (six months after the retreat of the Soviet soldiers from Czechoslovakia). The Communist Party received 38 percent of the votes; its leader, Klement Gottwald, was appointed prime minister; and Eduard Beneš, who had been president of Czechoslovakia before the war, returned to that post. Jan Masaryk, the non-Communist son of the founder of the republic, Thomas Masaryk, became foreign minister.

Although Czechoslovakia tried to retain a certain degree of independence vis-à-vis the Soviet Union and even had reasonable relations with the West, there was no question as to the way it was going. During the peace conference in Paris, 29 July–15 October 1946, for example, the Czechs consistently supported Soviet positions. A year later, in July 1947, Soviet pressure forced the Czechs to go back on their agreement to participate in discussions on rebuilding Europe which the British and the French were organizing in response to the initiative of American secretary of state George Marshall. During February and March 1948 the Communists completed their takeover of the country.[2]

Czechoslovakia: Between Poland and Germany

One of the first actions of the Czechoslovakian government that was set up after the war was to deprive Czechs of German origin of their rights and their citizenship. A similar policy was adopted toward the Hungarians in Slovakia. This policy also affected Jews who in the 1930 census had declared themselves to be either German or Hungarian. Some were held in detention camps for Germans, and others became candidates for direct deportation to Germany. Reports reaching the Jewish Agency in April 1946 stated that of the forty thousand Czechoslovakian Jews, eighteen thousand were suspected of being either German or Hungarian and thus likely to be deported. If they were not deported, such Jews could expect to become second-class citizens. It was only in September 1946 that this policy was amended.[3]

Because it opposed giving minorities full civil rights, the government began to pressure the Jews, especially in Bohemia and Moravia, either to assimilate or to leave the country. Vladimir Hurban, the Czech ambassador to the United Nations, in a conversation with Eliahu Epstein (Eilat), a Jewish Agency representative in Washington, argued that the Jews could not continue to live in Europe and should choose one of two alternatives: assimilation or emigration to Palestine, where they were entitled to build their national existence with international guarantees and protection.[4] President Beneš expressed similar sentiments in his discussion with members of the subcommittee of the AAC when they visited Czechoslovakia. At the same time, however, Beneš also affirmed his intention of fighting anti-Semitism because it was harming the good name of the country.[5]

The report submitted by the AAC distinguished between the situation of the Jews in Bohemia, Moravia, and Silesia, on the one hand, and that of the Jews of Slovakia, on the other. The number in the former category was estimated at about twenty thousand, including six to eight thousand Jews from the Sub-Carpathian Ukraine who regarded themselves as Czechoslovak citizens.[6] After the liberation the state had repealed all the anti-Jewish laws, and all forced transfers of property had been abrogated, though the process of returning such property had only just begun. According to the AAC, the Council of Jewish Communities was convinced that although the Jews had not yet rehabilitated themselves economically, they would be able to integrate into the republic and become a productive element in the country.[7]

The AAC painted a gloomy picture of the Jews of Slovakia. Its report was based on a comprehensive memorandum that had been prepared by the Central Union of Jewish Communities in Slovakia for the visit of the AAC subcommittee to Czechoslovakia. It turned out that only 30,000 Jews were presently living in Slovakia, whereas in 1938 their number had been about 140,000. At the time the region was liberated by the Red Army in April 1945 there were about 5,000 Jews in Slovakia, who were then joined by approximately 8,000 from among those who had been deported between 1942 and 1945. Approximately another 10,000 Jews were transferred together with the territories that Hungary returned to Slovakia, and 7,000 more returned from various countries where they had served as soldiers or in other capacities; immigrants also arrived from Hungary. Of the 30,000 Jews, 6,000 had converted to Christianity in the hope of saving their lives; the great majority of them would return to Judaism.[8]

Jews who had returned to Slovakia, the memorandum stated, were physically and psychologically debilitated, and their economic situation was grave. Their families had been exterminated, their homes destroyed or looted, and anti-Semitism, fed by the past six years of fascist education and propaganda, was flourishing. Fear of the local population that it would have to restore the Jewish property it had taken over during the war also contributed to intensifying anti-Semitism. Rebuilding Jewish economic life was made difficult by the restrictions imposed by local authorities, the change in the economic system, and the general refusal to return Jewish property, including that being held by the state. As result, about 57 percent of all Slovakian Jews needed to be supported by the JDC. Given these circumstances, approximately 60 percent of the Jews were determined to emigrate, most to Palestine. The Central Union of Jewish Communities in Slovakia called for the immediate repeal of the White Paper and the opening of the gates of Palestine to large-scale immigration.[9]

Although the AAC adopted the description the memorandum gave of the state of the Jews, it decided not to include the solution suggested by the Central Union of Jewish Communities in Slovakia. The AAC report expressed the belief that if anti-Semitism were severely condemned by the government and by intellectuals, it would become less prevalent, and if restitution were made of seized Jewish property, "a considerable number, including many who now profess a desire to migrate, will decide to remain in the country in which they were so deeply rooted." [10]

While local Jews also participated in the *Brichah* movement, Czechoslovakia's main importance was as a country of transit between Poland and Germany. Reports reaching the British Foreign Office in December 1945 spoke of between fifteen and twenty thousand refugees, mostly Jews from Poland, who had crossed through Czechoslovakia en route to the American zones in Germany and Austria, noting that at any given moment two to five thousand Polish refugees were to be found in Czechoslovakia. C. A. Schuckburgh, from the British legation, thought that if conditions in Poland did not change, twenty thousand more Jews there would leave. He was certain that the Czech government was helping the Jews cross the country because it was afraid of anti-Semitic outbreaks as had occurred recently in Slovakia and which, it was thought, had been triggered by the arrival of Jews from Poland.[11] Schuckburgh's information was corroborated by reports of Brichah emissaries indicating that in the first months after the end of the war Jews fleeing via Czechoslovakia encountered no special difficulties and that the government evinced understanding: by mid-December about fifteen thousand had passed through Prague and about ten thousand through Bratislava, with the government supplying food and transport for the refugees.[12]

What mainly concerned the Czech government, apart from making sure none of the refugees would stay, was to be reimbursed for the food, heat, and transport it provided. Foreign Minister Jan Masaryk came to an agreement with UNRRA that the government would be remunerated for its outlays. This arrangement was in force from January to July 1946, when it was reviewed because of the increase in the scope of the exodus from Poland in June and particularly in July, after the Kielce pogrom.[13] Complications arose after a visit to Czechoslovakia at the beginning of July by the American deputy director general of the UNRRA Relief Services. Mary Gibbons claimed that UNRRA was not obliged to bear these costs. Organizers of the *Brichah* feared that if money were not found to pay for railroad tickets to transport the fleeing Jews from one side of the country to the other, the Czech government might change its policy.[14]

These apprehensions proved to be unfounded. The outcome of the Brichah contacts with the local Czech authorities in the summer of 1946 was that the latter agreed to allow the passage of five thousand persons each week and even put a train at their disposal for the daily transport of about fifteen hundred people. The Brichah activists were far from meticulous in observing the limitations of the quota, and when possible they as much as doubled it.[15] For their part, Czech authorities were careful to keep a detailed list of the transports and the food given to the refugees, expecting UNRRA to compensate them for their expenses. In the end, the Czech government received about $250,000, approximately half of the expenses involved.[16]

Zionist elements, without exception, lauded the support and assistance Czech foreign minister Jan Masaryk gave to the exodus via Czechoslovakia. Other Czech officials from the lower echelons up to some of the government ministers supported the movement and provided assistance. Of particular significance is that in the government that took these decisions the Communists held most of the key posts, including that of prime minister. It can be assumed that this transit movement, which concerned most of the Polish Jewish repatriates from the Soviet Union, would not have been allowed without clearance from the Soviets.[17] Reasons behind it were far from altruistic. A report on the movement of Jews through Czechoslovakia during 1946, prepared by the Czechoslovakian Repatriation Department, stated that assistance for the movement of Jews was provided for the sake of security and the health of the nation and to prevent the transients from settling in Czechoslovakia and infiltrating into the country's economic life. Another consideration was the desire to gain the sympathy of the foreign press, especially in America.[18] By assisting the Jewish refugees, the Czech government hoped to gain the support of the U.S. Jewish community, to which the Czechs too attributed extensive political influence. Such support would be timely because relations between the two countries had begun deteriorating in summer 1946 as a result of the anti-Western positions adopted by Masaryk at the peace conference in Paris. James Byrnes, U.S. secretary of state, ordered his office to prevent Czechoslovakia from exploiting $41 million of the $50 million line of credit it had been accorded. Also, negotiations between Czechoslovakia and the Export-Import Bank for a $150 million loan were halted.[19]

By the summer of 1946, Britain's apprehension that the migration via Czechoslovakia had the full knowledge and concurrence of the national government strengthened. In early August, Schuckburgh told the British Foreign Office that approximately eighteen hundred Jews were crossing the border from Poland to Czechoslovakia each day and that most came in groups organized by UNRRA and the JDC. The British diplomat stressed that the Czech government had set the condition that not one of these Jews was to remain in the country.[20] The Foreign Office received further confirmation of Schuckburgh's report from that of UNRRA's Mary Gibbons at the end of her visit to Czechoslovakia. She wrote that Jews were crossing the border with the agreement of Polish and Czech border guards and were transported by train by the Czechs to Bratislava, where the Soviets helped them cross the border to the American zone.[21]

The Foreign Office also discovered that not only did the Czech government allow the movement of the Jews through its territory, but the illegal migration in Europe altogether was being managed from Czechoslovakia. A comprehensive report in August 1946 on the illegal immigration to Palestine spoke of a Jewish organization in Prague, called Brichah, with branches in Bratislava, Belgrade, Budapest, Bucharest, Zagreb, and Trieste. The organization had semiofficial status in Czechoslovakia and had been set up to encourage the movement of the Jews from these regions to Palestine.[22] Copies of the protocols of Brichah meetings in Czechoslovakia held toward the end of 1945 that had fallen into the hands of British intelligence in Palestine revealed that the Czech government was assisting the Jewish refugees crossing the country.[23]

Because they could not effectively close off the border with Poland, Schuckburgh understood the motives of the Czech authorities in helping the Jews. They had arranged two assembly points, one at Nachod and the other at Bromov, to supervise those entering and to prevent epidemics. At Nachod, the Czech authorities assembled and registered the refugees, administered inoculations, and gave them food. A daily train took the Jews from Nachod across the country to Bratislava. Each day about eight hundred refugees passed through Nachod and five hundred through Bromov. Schuckburgh pointed out that although UNRRA was not involved in bringing the Jews, from the moment they arrived it cared for them and encouraged them to continue on to UNRRA's camps in Germany, Austria, and Italy. Between 1 July and 9 August, approximately thirty-five thousand Jews had entered Czechoslovakia from Poland, and of these, about thirty-two thousand had already left from Bratislava. While the Red Army allowed the entrance to Austria of six hundred persons per day, the American authorities permitted three hundred persons to enter the American zone of Germany each day. Schuckburgh believed that an additional seventy thousand persons could be expected.[24]

Unofficially, Schuckburgh was informed by Dr. Hubert Ripka, Czech deputy foreign minister, that the government would find it difficult to stop the movement of the Jews. Ripka explained that his government was unwilling to anger Jewish public opinion in the United States at a time when Czechoslovakia was asking the administration for a loan. The Czech also mentioned humanitarian considerations, citing the fact that pogroms were continuing in Poland, and feared that stopping the movement would lead to unhampered infiltration of migrants, which might endanger public health. While Schuckburgh believed that there was no point in asking the Czech government to halt the migratory transit, which he described as "an authorized and 'legal' movement of Jews," he recommended that the Foreign Office urge the Czechoslovakian government to check the illegal activity of the Jewish organizations, intensify its supervision on the Polish border and in the area of transit, and carefully list the names of those entering.[25] He further suggested that an effort be made to convince the

The Brichah Movement (From Encyclopedia of the Holocaust, *editor in chief Israel Gutman, Yad Vashem, Jerusalem and Sifriat Poalim Publishing House, Tel Aviv, 1990*)

Czechs to transfer the refugees to the American and Soviet occupation authorities, believing that the latter would put an end to this movement. The Foreign Office decided not to follow up this suggestion because it felt the Soviets and the Americans could not be relied on to prevent further Jewish movement.[26]

Schuckburgh's treatment of the exodus from Poland as a legal movement met with dissent in the Foreign Office. He was instructed to deliver a letter to the Czech government emphasizing that when a movement was considered legal, travelers possessed valid passports and visas for the country of destination. Czech attention was to be called to accepted international practice according to which those infiltrating into a country without documents were returned to the country of origin and not transferred to a third country as Czechoslovakia was doing.[27] At the beginning of September, before Schuckburgh was able to deliver this missive, the secretary general of the Czech Foreign Ministry, Dr. Arnošt Heidrich, showed him a dispatch from Masaryk, who was then participating in the peace conference in Paris. The communiqué reported that General McNarney, commander of the American occupied zone in Germany, had promised to allow one hundred thousand Polish Jews to enter the American zone during September and October. Schuckburgh found it difficult to believe that this information was reliable, and he suggested that the Czech delegation in Paris might have been misled by interested parties who wanted to open up the borders of Czechoslovakia to Jewish immigration from Poland. Dr. Heidrich agreed not to take any steps before hearing the British Foreign Office's reactions.[28] McNarney denied that he had ever made such a suggestion and said he did not intend to organize groups of Jews to be sent to the American zone but added that he would not prevent any Jew from entering the occupation zone.[29]

Although skeptical that it could influence the Czech authorities to stop the passage of Jews through Czechoslovakia, London decided to ask the Czech government for help, explaining that the illegal immigration served to swell the ranks of the illegal militias in Mandatory Palestine and increase the danger of a civil war there, which in turn could jeopardize peace throughout the Middle East. The Czech government was told that an efficiently organized and well-financed underground of Jewish agents was running the illegal movement in Europe from its center in Czechoslovakia and was asked to "take immediate action to tighten up their control arrangements at the Polish border and throughout the transit area" and to carefully observe international regulations that prevented the entrance or passage of migrants unless they possessed the appropriate documents.[30] Schuckburgh had low expectations for this appeal because of the policy the American authorities in Vienna were following. Not only were they ready to accept six hundred Jews daily from Bratislava, but General Clark, commander of the American occupied zone in Austria, suggested to Czechoslovakia that a new route be opened to Austria through Linz if the daily stream of emigrants increased to more than six hundred. This policy of the American military authorities, Schuckburgh maintained, gave the Czechs "an unanswerable reply to our protests." [31]

Surprisingly, at first it seemed that the British protest had brought about some results. A few days after it was tendered, a member of the Czech Foreign Ministry informed Schuckburgh that the government had closed its border with Poland in the face of infiltrating refugees, but this had caused pandemonium at the border when fifteen hundred Jews had managed to enter Slovakia. The official said that an attempt might be made to send them back. Since the decision to close the border was not mentioned in the local press, Schuckburgh concluded that the government hoped to avoid publication of this step.[32] Very quickly it turned out that the border closure was only temporary. Czech government officials explained to a JDC official that, in addition to British pressure, the step had been taken because many refugees who lacked permits had begun reaching Prague. But following contacts between Jewish leaders and representatives of the government, the border was reopened on 5 October, after being closed for three weeks.[33] Czech authorities not only permitted the crossing of their country but also negotiated during that same period (from the end of August) with both Rabbi Bernstein, McNarney's adviser on Jewish affairs, and Israel Jacobson, director of the JDC in Czechoslovakia, about temporary housing for ten thousand Polish Jews in the homes of Germans who had been deported from Sudetenland. Czech prime minister Gottwald agreed to the plan in mid-November 1946 after receiving assurances from the Americans that they would accept these refugees in their occupation zone in Germany if no other asylum were found for them.[34] Although the plan was not put into practice because of the sharp drop in the number of Jews leaving Poland during the winter of 1946–47, it clearly demonstrated Prague's priorities.

During 1947–48, when Poland closed its borders, there was only a limited movement of Jews via Czechoslovakia, and it was coordinated with government institutions.[35] This time, Czech authorities also helped the Zionists diplomatically and militarily. There was a Czech representative on UNSCOP who was among those who supported the partition of Palestine, and the Czechs would be the first of the Slavic bloc to declare their support for the partition (3 October 1947). Moreover, in February 1948 representatives of the Jewish community in Palestine signed their first arms contract with the Czech authorities. Altogether,

Czech policy was compatible with the Soviet campaign to undermine Britain's stand in the Middle East.[36]

Hungary: Between Rumania and Austria

By the end of 1945, of the 762,000 Jews who had been living in Hungary when the German army entered the country on 19 March 1944, approximately 144,000 remained. Of these, about 97,000 were living in Budapest and the rest in the provinces.[37] In the first months after the war the *Brichah* movement made its way from Hungary to Austria as part of and concealed by the general refugee wanderings. In Hungary there was a local organizational infrastructure of Zionist youth movements which had acquired much experience in the course of the war in smuggling Jews into Hungary until the country's occupation by the Nazis and from Hungary to neighboring countries after the occupation.[38] From May 1945, Brichah organizers in Poland stopped sending people to Rumania and instead sent them directly to Budapest, whence they continued to Graz, Austria. In mid-August 1945, Yona Rosen, a Brichah emissary in Hungary, reported that thus far about 7,000 persons had gone through Hungary. A trickle of fleeing refugees also moved from Hungary to Yugoslavia and from there to Italy.[39] According to Yehuda Talmi, another Brichah emissary in Hungary, by April 1946 more than 40,000 Jews had left the country, including approximately 10,000 Hungarian Jews.[40] Rosen described the activity in Hungary right after the war as having been conducted quasi-officially. Two reasons inspired government policy: first, the absence of any other solution for Jewish refugees sojourning in Hungary (the same consideration also applied to some of the local middle-class Jews, who constituted a burden on the authorities); and, second, the desire to harm British interests. According to him, in the winter of 1945–46, when there was no railroad traffic whatsoever, the authorities placed the necessary number of trains at the disposal of Brichah activists. The Soviet and Hungarian security forces kept track of the activities of Brichah emissaries and in most cases placed no obstacles in the way of departing Jews. Furthermore, the Red Army allowed the refugees to cross the border from Hungary into the Soviet occupation zone in Austria.[41]

British diplomats in Hungary not only were unaware of the movement through the country but, until the spring of 1946, believed that the general situation of Hungarian Jews was good and that there was no cause for worry that they might wish to emigrate. Shortly after the war, the British minister Alvary D. Gascoigne rejected claims that Jews who had been deported from

Hungary and had returned after the war found it impossible to reorganize their religious and community lives there.[42] As he saw it, Hungarian Jews enjoyed political and economic freedom and Jews were serving in leading political, administrative, and commercial positions in the country. He listed several well-known Jewish figures in Hungary: Mátyás Rákosi, the Communist Party leader; Ernő Gerő, who was minister of transport; Joseph Révai, a leading Communist journalist (the ideologist of the Communist Party); and Zoltán Vas, the mayor of Budapest. Gascoigne did acknowledge that the Hungarian population harbored anti-Semitic feelings but attributed these to "the 'terror policy' of the Political Police which is supposed (not without some reason) to be instigated by the Jews who are anxious for revenge against their 'former persecutors,' and also on account of the Jewish 'black market' activities which cause prices to rise to fantastic levels." Cooperation of the Jews with the Russians, harming the interests of Hungary as a sovereign state, also contributed to increased enmity toward them, said Gascoigne. He believed that the Jews had no desire to leave and noted the small number of requests to emigrate to Palestine. The Soviet authorities and the Hungarian government, he averred, were not inclined to allow emigration. He predicted that if the power of the Communists were weakened as a result of the departure of the Soviets, anti-Semitism might become more severe and that this would be followed by demands that Jews be allowed to leave the country for Palestine and elsewhere.[43]

British representatives were confirmed in their belief of the sound status of the Jews in Hungary by a lecture delivered by István Balogh, under secretary in the Hungarian Prime Minister's Office, to a Jewish gathering in November 1945. Balogh denounced the steps that had been taken against the Jews in Hungary in the past and emphasized that the new democratic government would do its best to compensate the Jews for the suffering and injustice they had experienced. He assured his audience that the government had not completed its task and that it recognized the need to take action for the sake of the Jews. Balogh promised that past events would not be repeated and that Jews who continued to live in Hungary would be regarded as brothers by all Magyars.[44]

The British were able to glean a more realistic assessment in the spring of 1946 from the testimony of Lajos Stöckler, the president of the Jewish community, who represented Hungarian Jews before the AAC's subcommittee. Stöckler stated that 77 percent of the Hungarian Jews wished to emigrate, 54 percent preferring Palestine and 23 percent hoping to move to other countries such as the United States, Australia, and South Africa. Jews living in the provinces were almost totally dependent on the support of the local governments, whereas half of the Jews in Budapest were being fed in soup kitchens and three-quarters were suffering from a serious lack of suitable clothing.[45] At first British representatives in Hungary did not take this report seriously, but W. M. Carse, British consul in Hungary, soon learned that of the 140,000 Orthodox Jews in Hungary, about 40 percent had expressed a desire to emigrate to Palestine and 30 percent to other places abroad. Unlike Hungarians who simply wanted to improve their economic situation by moving abroad, Carse maintained, the motive for many Jews to leave was anti-Semitism. He confirmed the difficult economic situation. Carse reported that in Budapest 40,000 Jews were being fed in soup kitchens, 36,000 were receiving financial assistance, 14,000 were receiving funds to buy clothes, and 8,500 were living in poor houses. In the provinces the percentage of Jews receiving welfare payments was even higher.[46]

Carse's appreciation of the situation clearly contradicted Gascoigne's analysis. Although expressing doubts as to the accuracy of these data, Gascoigne admitted that as a result of anti-Semitism the Jews were increasingly apprehensive about their future. Non-Communist Jews feared that if the Soviets were to depart and the Communist regime collapse, "they might well be made to suffer, as Jews, for the nefarious activities of the Jewish officialdom in Hungary at present." The desire to leave Hungary, he maintained, was not unique to the Jews.[47] The change in the British evaluation was not sparked by a sudden deterioration in the situation of Hungarian Jewry. Gascoigne had for a long time been reporting on the better situation of the Jews and may well have been influenced by the perception to that effect prevalent among the Hungarian public. That he criticized the Jews for what he saw as their negative behavior, especially their cooperation with the Communists, suggests that he identified with complaints directed at the Jews by anti-Communist and anti-Semitic elements. It seems that Gascoigne, like some of his colleagues (for example, A. C. Kendall in Rumania), tended to accept the stereotype of the Jews as black market profiteers.[48]

At the same time, British representatives in Hungary also remained unaware of the departure of thousands of Hungarian and other Jews from the country without official permits. In reports sent to London, no mention is to be found of the movement of Jews through and from Hungary. Such reports came from other sources. For example, on 15 October 1945 the British command in Austria reported that during the previous six weeks about five thousand Jews from Poland and Hungary had infiltrated into the British zone in Austria.[49] Interrogation of a group of Jews who had reached the Troflach camp in Austria on 28 December 1945 revealed that an organization called Deportiertesheim, active in Budapest and run by Hungarian Jews, was behind the movement of the Jews to Austria. Hungarian, Soviet, and Austrian border guards had allowed the group to continue on their way, even though no one carried identity papers, when they realized that these were Jews wanting to reach Graz. British intelligence in Austria believed that the Hungarian Red Cross was helping the Jewish refugees in Budapest to leave the country and was even furnishing them with forged documents. The main route continued from Budapest to Milan via Vienna, DP camps in the British zone of Austria, Salzburg, Innsbruck, the Brenner Pass, and Milan.[50] In spite of these sporadic reports, as late as March 1946, British intelligence had to admit that it did not have sufficient reliable information about Jewish emigration from Hungary.[51]

Though it could not visit Hungary because of Soviet opposition, the AAC pointed out in its report that it had been shown evidence of the involvement of Zionist organizations in Hungary and Rumania in moving people to the American zones of occupation in Germany and Austria. According to the testimony of an American officer, American military authorities were permitting the JDC to organize the arrival of Jewish groups from Hungary. AAC members believed that only 25 percent of the Jewish population would remain in Hungary and that the United States was their most favored destination, but since actual prospects for immigration there appeared slim, between fifty and sixty thousand Jews said they would want to move to Palestine.[52]

When finally in the spring of 1946 the British learned of the movement through Hungary they immediately tried to stop it. At a meeting of the Allied Control Commission in Hungary in May 1946, the American and British representatives joined together in pressing their Soviet colleague on the issue. The American, General William Key, asserted that the Hungarian government was aware of the extensive illegal movement through the country but was doing nothing to prevent it. Both Key and the British delegate, Major General O. P. Edgecumb, asked the Russian marshal Voroshilov, the chairman of the Control Commission, to instruct the Hungarian government to take steps to halt the flow. Voroshilov explained that that would be difficult to achieve, adding that to the best of his knowledge the Hungarian authorities had reinforced the border police. He presumed, however, that some individuals could have managed to leave with the help of forged documents.[53] Key may have raised the issue because the American military authorities in Germany and Austria were just then trying to reduce the number of Jews reaching the DP camps, as President Truman had rejected recommendations to close the American occupation zone to Jewish refugees from the East and to close down those DP camps where non-Jews were living.

A few weeks later, the British military mission in Hungary discovered that the headquarters of the Brichah was located in Budapest, that during the last two weeks of July it had organized the passage of one thousand Jews to Germany, and that Jews also had been sent eastward to Bulgaria and to Rumania, all a clear indication that the Soviets and the Hungarian government were allowing the Jews to cross the border even without official documents. Responsibility for the border police was in the hands of General George Pálfi-Oesterreicher, "a communist and close collaborator with NKVD." [54] In his memoirs, Yehuda Talmi relates how through the mediation of Vas, the organization's emissaries reached an understanding with Pálfi-Oesterreicher about the departure of the Jews and coordinated the selection of departure points for Austria and Yugoslavia with him. [55]

At the next meeting of the Allied Control Commission, in mid-August, General Edgecumb again raised the subject of the illegal border crossings from Hungary to Austria and demanded that the Hungarian government make every effort to put an end to them, adding that he was aware of the difficulties and especially the huge bribes involved in this traffic. Lieutenant General Vladimir P. Sviridov, Soviet representative and acting chairman of the commission, reported that the Hungarian minister of war had decided to expand the Border Police from 5,000 to 10,000 men. Sviridov noted that every month the Border Police arrested approximately 1,000 persons trying to cross the border illegally. He recounted an instance when 520 people had been taken from a train after their documents were found to be forged. According to the Soviet general, the Hungarian government was concerned about the border crossings, especially as speculators were attempting to flee following government steps to stabilize the currency. He displayed forged transit permits found in the possession of an organization that had been selling such permits and said he would impress upon the Hungarian ministers of war and the interior the need to make all possible efforts to prevent the illegal movement of Jews. [56] Sviridov further denied Edgecumb's claim that Russian lorries were helping the Jews move illegally from Hungary to Austria. [57] The Soviet general's somewhat conciliatory attitude may have been owing to the peace discussions that were going on in Paris, and he may also have been trying to reduce the tensions between him and his colleagues in the Control Commission over a list of Soviet demands he had presented to the Hungarian government without coordinating his action with his Western partners. [58]

London meanwhile concluded that it ought to discuss the illegal movement with the Hungarian authorities. On 16 August, Alexander K. Helm, who had replaced Gascoigne in July, met with Hungarian prime minister Nagy. Helm, who later said he had expressed himself very assertively, stressed that he had considerable proof of the illegal migration via Hungary and of the fact that

Budapest served as the central transit point. Moreover, the Hungarian authorities and the Hungarian Red Cross were providing Brichah organizers with the necessary documents. The prime minister, who appeared not surprised at the news of the cooperation of the Hungarian authorities, promised Helm his government's assistance. Nagy, however, hinted at his inability to guarantee that his instructions would be carried out.[59] As a member of the Smallholders' Party, the prime minister enjoyed only limited ability to determine policy because the Communists controlled the ministries of the interior and police. At the same time, Nagy's government was under increased pressure from the Soviets, with the help of local Communists. Moreover, Soviet soldiers guarded the border between Hungary and the Soviet occupation zone in Austria, and the Hungarian commander of the Border Police, Pálfi-Oesterreicher, fully cooperated with the Russians and the Zionists. Only Hungary's western frontier and particularly the area facing the British zone of Austria, Helm reported to London, were at present strongly patrolled by Frontier Guards or Soviet troops.[60]

At the same time the British Foreign Office was undecided as to whether it was worthwhile approaching the Hungarian government on the subject of persecution of the Jews. The British representatives in Hungary were asked to check whether there was evidence that the persecution of the Jews was indeed being inspired by the government and to recommend steps the Hungarian government might take to improve the situation.[61] The Foreign Office believed that the situation of the Jews in Hungary and Rumania was similar to that of the Jews in Poland.[62] Helm reported to the Foreign Office that there was no information to the effect that the government was encouraging persecution of Jews and that most of the Jews who had recently left Hungary were not Hungarians at all but rather Yugoslavian and Rumanian Jews who had traveled across Hungary. The anti-Jewish feelings in Hungary stemmed largely from the political and economic power that was in the hands of the Jews: "Not only do the Jews fill five important Government portfolios, but they occupy key positions in the Civil Service, and big business is largely in their hands. So long as they are dominated by Rákosi and his colleagues, the Hungarian Government would seem powerless to remedy this situation even if they wished." Helm believed that under the circumstances the Hungarian government was unable to improve the situation so that there was no point in turning to the Hungarian foreign minister. Like Gascoigne a year earlier, he believed that if the Soviets were to retreat and the Communists were ousted, the condition of the Jews would deteriorate significantly.[63]

The pressure exerted by the British on the Soviet military authorities in Hungary and on the Hungarian regime did have some results, at least in the short term. Talmi noted that after receiving permission from the Red Army in Hungary to transport two groups, one of one thousand persons and the other of eight hundred, to Austria, Brichah organizers were informed that, because of intensive British activity, it was not possible to continue the transfer.[64] Apparently, the change in Soviet and Hungarian policy coincided with the discussions at the peace conference in Paris (29 July–15 October 1946) on the peace agreements with Hungary. The Soviets stood to profit most from the peace treaties, among other reasons because the accords would bring about the dispersal of the Allied Control Commissions in Hungary, Rumania, and Bulgaria and enable them to consolidate their control of southeastern Europe. It is reasonable to assume that in ad hoc fashion the Soviets wished to limit the areas of friction with London, especially in what were, to them, peripheral matters. Moreover, their objective of aggravating the problem of the Jewish DPs in Germany was being achieved at that time by the relocation of Jews leaving Poland via Czechoslovakia.

Meanwhile, a change also occurred in the attitude of the Hungarian Jews. The improved economic situation in the country after the currency had been stabilized in August 1946 neutralized what for Hungarian Jews was the primary factor impelling them to leave. Economic stability also brought about a decrease in the attacks against Jews. The economic situation had been a central reason for the anti-Semitic outbreaks in 1946 that resulted in the pogrom on 22 May 1946 in Kunmadaras, in which three Jews were killed and many more injured, as well as the pogrom in Diósgőyr on 30 July. The economic crisis and the incitement against Jews who allegedly were running the black market had provoked an increase of violence against the Jews in the summer of 1946, and this, in turn, had induced some Hungarian Jews to move to the DP camps. But in autumn 1946 and throughout 1947 only a small number of Hungarian Jews expressed an interest in leaving the country.[65]

Deterioration in the economic situation in Rumania in 1947 led many Jews to flee that country. The movement from Rumania via Hungary to Austria reached a peak during the summer months of 1947. During July and August more than eight thousand persons left Rumania.[66] After the discovery of a transit camp with eight hundred Jews in one of the residential neighborhoods of Budapest, British representatives asked the government to investigate the matter. The deputy minister of the interior promised, at the beginning of September, that the camp would no longer be used to house illegal migrants and that the authorities were investigating two or three other suspected camps as well. He said the Hungarian government was acting to the best of its ability to stop the infiltration and was trying to return all the illegal immigrants to where they had come from. The problem, he averred, was that action was also needed on the other side of the border. In the absence of Rumanian supervision of the border, Hungary had difficulty single-handedly preventing the illegal movement. The deputy minister of the interior stressed his point by noting the cooperation between the Yugoslavian and Hungarian governments which had brought about an end to the border crossings between the two countries.[67] Cooperation between the Rumanian and Hungarian governments to prevent crossings on their common border was achieved at the end of 1947, mainly for internal reasons. Altogether close to nineteen thousand Jews crossed over from Rumania into Hungary during 1947.

THE BALKANS
PORTS TO PALESTINE

Approximately two-fifths of all illegal immigrants who set out for Palestine after the war embarked from Balkan ports. For the majority, who were Rumanian citizens, Yugoslavia and Bulgaria served as the main embarkation ports. To stop this movement at the source, the British had to engage not only with the Rumanian authorities but also with Moscow and the Russian military delegation in Rumania—according to the October 1944 Percentages Agreement between Churchill and Stalin, the Soviet Union was accorded 90 percent of the influence in Rumania. This meant, among other things, that the Soviets were able to enforce their rule over the country quicker even than in Hungary. On 6 March 1945, following the intervention of Andrei Y. Vyshinski, vice-commissar for foreign affairs, a Communist-dominated government was installed. It was headed by Petru Groza, and principal ministries were held by the Communists. As in Hungary, here, too, the Soviets took advantage of the large Red Army present in the country.

Claiming it was not representative, both London and Washington refused to recognize Groza's government. In Rumania and Bulgaria the Americans insisted on free and open elections, inclusion of representatives from the non-Communist opposition parties in the government, and unhindered access to all journalists. The result was the breakup of the first session of the Council of Foreign Ministers that had met in London in September 1945 to prepare the peace agreements with formerly belligerent countries. In the second session of the CFM in Moscow (December 1945), the Soviets agreed that the Communist-dominated governments of both Rumania and Bulgaria would be broadened. Co-option of two ministers from the democratic opposition parties paved the way for the Western powers to recognize the Groza government in February 1946.

In the Rumanian elections held on 19 November 1946, the government bloc "won" about 90 percent of the votes. The Western powers limited themselves to publishing a sharp censure of the way the elections had been conducted. The British thought it was futile to demand that new elections be held, since no change was to be expected. About three weeks later the Allies agreed on the final wording of the peace agreements with formerly belligerent countries, including Rumania and Bulgaria, and in February 1947 the treaties were signed. In the summer of 1947 the Communists moved rapidly to complete their takeover of Rumania. Leaders of the non-Communist parties, led by Iuliu Maniu, head of the Peasant Party, were dismissed from the government and arrested. The Rumanian government rejected British and American protests against persecution of opposition leaders and violations of civil rights, which they saw as Western intervention in Rumanian internal affairs. At the end of November, Maniu was sentenced to life imprisonment. With the deposition of King Michael approximately one month later, on 30 December 1947, the entrenchment of Communist control was complete. In the elections held three months later (28 March 1948), the Communists gained 405 out of the 414 seats in the Rumanian Parliament.[1]

Rumania: The Main Thrust

When the war ended there were some 430,000 Jews in Rumania. Except for Soviet Jewry, this was the largest remaining nucleus of Jews in countries that had been under Nazi control. About 420,000 Rumanian Jews had been killed in the Holocaust. After Rumania was occupied by the Red Army in August 1944, the British feared a renewal of the illegal sailings from Rumanian ports, which had served since 1939 as the main base for illegal immigrant embarkations. In fact, after a two-year lapse, the sailings of Jews from Rumania had already begun in March. During 1944, 4,699 persons sailed from Constanta to Turkey. Of these, 345, sailing on the *Mafkura*, died when that ship sank in August. Early in 1945, British diplomats in Bucharest reported that more than 100,000 Jews had registered for immigration to Palestine. As part of their efforts to prevent emigration from the Balkans and especially from Rumania, the British announced to the Turkish government in December 1944 that they were abrogating their commitment to find shelter for any Jew who reached Turkey.[2]

Apprehensive of Rumanian policy on Jewish emigration, British representatives in Bucharest closely monitored the situation of Rumanian Jews after the war, the extent of their reintegration in the country, and the attitude of the authorities and the local population toward them. A comprehensive report dispatched at the beginning of August 1945 by the British minister in Rumania, John Le Rougtel, divided the Jews into two categories. The first included some 250,000 persons who had lived in Rumania throughout the war and had been subjected to persecution by the Rumanian fascists and the Nazis. The second group included Rumanian Jews who had been banished from the country and had managed to return, as well as nonlocal Jews who, after the armistice, had entered Rumania from concentration camps in Poland, Hungary, Austria, and Slovakia. Their number was estimated at 150,000. The first group was generally "not very badly off." The situation of the poor among them was no worse than that of the rest of the population, whereas "the richer Jews control the Stock Exchange and have already largely regained their manipulation of industry and trade." Although many Jews had lost their property, they proved more able than gentile Rumanians to rehabilitate themselves. Le Rougtel sounded a critical note in describing the behavior of Jews whose property had been returned to them and who were now renting it out at speculative prices. He thought that the Jews in his first category could be absorbed in Rumania and that if they wanted to emigrate to Palestine this was out of fear that the Russians, who were beginning to show renewed signs of anti-Semitism, would allow the Rumanians again to discriminate against the Jews. Prosperity of the Jewish community was dependent on foreign trade, and the future in that sphere was uncertain.

As Le Rougtel saw it, the situation of the Jews in the second category was bleak indeed. The only way to rehabilitate Jews who had returned from the camps was to exchange their present abysmal surroundings for places where they could gain back their self-respect. Jews who had fled to Rumania from neighboring countries could be returned without much difficulty. Many of these refugees had been persuaded to cross into Rumania by Zionist emissaries active in Hungary, Austria, and Slovakia and had been promised easy immigration to Palestine, while others had entered the country in the wake of the Red Army in the hope of being able to take up some trade or other. Le Rougtel believed that about sixty thousand Jews needed to be removed from the country so as to enable a normal existence for the others. Because the Soviet authorities were not granting exit visas, there had been no emigration from Rumania since the beginning of 1945. But if the Soviet Union were to change its position, the Rumanian government would not object to large-scale Jewish emigration for two reasons: "First because of the liability which these populations present, and secondly, because of the native prejudice against the Jews." The British concluded that those in need of emotional and physical rehabilitation wished to reach Palestine, whereas most of the Jews who wished to emigrate were not necessarily interested in settling Palestine but rather saw the country as a springboard for other places, especially the United States.[3]

Approximately three months later, London was informed that anti-Semitic feelings were on the rise in Rumania following reports of alleged Jewish activity on the black market—then the only market functioning—and of Jews who had joined the secret police. In contrast to reports from Zionist sources on the growing support for Zionism among the Jewish public, Colonel A. C. Kendall, head of the consular section in Rumania, averred that a majority of the Jews in Rumania realized that the Zionists were actually harming Jewish interests because they tended to subordinate everything to Zionist ideology. He felt that compared with the situation right after the war, the place of Palestine in Jewish public opinion had receded since it had meanwhile become clear that at this stage mass emigration to Palestine was not a possibility; reports of economic stagnation there contributed to the depressing atmosphere. Kendall complained that the subject of emigration to Palestine served the Communist interest as a means of stirring up anti-British feelings among the Jews.[4]

A different picture of the standing of Zionism in Rumania was painted by the British press officer there. He described how Bevin's speech on 13 November 1945 on the Labour government's policy for Palestine and on the decision to set up the AAC had provoked a mass protest rally in Bucharest in which ten different Jewish organizations had taken part and all speakers had attacked Bevin and protested against his policies in Palestine. Subsequently, a petition demanding the abrogation of the White Paper and the establishment of a Jewish state in Palestine had been sent to the British mission in the name of Bucharest Jewry, signed by Alexander Shafran, the chief rabbi of Rumania.[5]

British apprehensions about renewed illegal sailings from Rumania in the winter of 1944–45 subsided when it emerged that at least for the time being the Soviets opposed the departure of Jews, including those who had received immigration visas for Palestine from the local British representatives.[6] It was only a year after the war that the first ship of immigrants, the *Smyrna,* sailed from a port in the Soviet sphere of influence. The Soviets held up the embarkation of the *Smyrna* until March 1946 in large measure because of their efforts to get the Americans and British to recognize Groza's government, which they did in February 1946.[7]

It was on 4 April 1946 that the British delegation in Rumania reported to the Foreign Office in London that a Greek boat, the *Smyrna,* carrying 1,500 illegal immigrants, was expected to set sail from Constanta within forty-eight hours. Soon after, two more vessels were to bring another 2,500 immigrants from Rumania to Palestine. The British military mission in Rumania was asked to activate the Russian, British, and American representatives of the Allied Control Commission in Rumania in an attempt to prevent the sailings.[8] Soviet military authorities in Rumania explained to the British that no one without exit visas approved by the Allied Control Commission and the Rumanian government would be permitted to depart.[9] Several days later, the *Smyrna,* renamed the *Max Nordau,* sailed with 1,666 illegal immigrants on board.[10] The Soviets countered a protest lodged by the British military mission by saying that since all the passengers had visas for Mexico, there was no reason to prevent the ship from leaving harbor.[11]

Within a few weeks Adrian Holman, who replaced Le Rougtel as British minister in Bucharest, learned that the ship's passengers had not possessed Mexican visas at all but that, at the request of the Rumanian Red Cross, the Rumanian Ministry of the Interior had issued collective travel documents to Mexico. Mexico had no representative in Rumania, and no other country represented it there. A Rumanian master mariner told Holman that he had been offered $2,000 to sail the boat to Palestine, that the vessel's crew consisted of Communists, and that Communist emigrants had been given preference when the passenger list was made up. Holman also discovered that all expenses entailed in the sailing of the *Max Nordau* had been financed by one Moshe Averbuch (Agami), who had received the money from American sources.[12] (Averbuch was a Zionist emissary from Palestine who had been in charge of the illegal sailings from Rumania.)

Given what they knew of Soviet plans for the Middle East, the British were puzzled that the Soviets had given permission for the ship to set sail. General Alan Cunningham, then high commissioner in Palestine, speculated as to the Soviet motives: "Possibly this was an example of a tactical mistake in this new field which is attributable to Soviet ignorance of the Arab world . . . alternatively, the opportunity of causing embarrassment to Great Britain may have proved too tempting to resist." The British legation in Rumania was convinced that the Jewish Agency's efforts to establish a route of passage via Constanta enjoyed the active assistance of the Russians and that Soviet and official Rumanian considerations in allowing Jewish emigration were political and not economic or humanitarian. The aim was to add to Britain's difficulties in Palestine.[13] The Soviets viewed the establishment of the AAC as an attempt by two Western powers to prevent Russia from taking part in formulating policy in the Middle East, so Moscow naturally looked for indirect ways to influence events in Palestine.[14]

Two factors led the chiefs of staff in London to the conclusion that local contacts were insufficient and that authorities in Moscow should be asked directly to halt the illegal sailings from Rumanian ports. One was the failure of the British military mission in Rumania to have the Soviet military authorities prevent the sailing of the *Max Nordau;* the other was the news that Jews were being brought from all over Europe to Constanta and other southern European ports.[15] Though the Foreign Office did not place great hopes on these overtures, it believed that a direct appeal to the Soviets would help strengthen Britain's status in the Arab countries. Sir Maurice Peterson, British ambassador in Moscow, was given information from British diplomats in Rumania to the effect that "the Russians are not only conniving at, but are actively assisting in this traffic."[16] Because he believed, however, that the Soviet authorities would refuse the request and would direct him to the Rumanian government with the advice that Rumania was a sovereign state, Peterson proposed first turning to the authorities in Bucharest and only afterward asking the Soviet government to use its influence.[17]

As in Hungary, the Allied Control Commission was the main forum for the British to launch their protests against the illegal embarkations from Rumania. There was no doubt in London that the Soviets, aided by local Communists, were determining government policy. At a session of the Allied Control Commission in Rumania on 20 July 1946, the British representative, Air Vice-Marshal Donald Stevenson, asked the head of the Soviet delegation, General Ivan Susaikov, to prevent the embarkation of the *Agia Anastasia.* The Soviet officer claimed that he did not have the authority to interfere with embarkations from Rumania and that his job ended with providing permits to those persons whom the Rumanian government was willing to let go. Susaikov similarly dismissed Stevenson's protests about the *Max Nordau* by replying that the destination of departing vessels was not his affair and that for all he cared, "they might go to the bottom of the sea." He had been told that the people on the *Max Nordau* were sailing to Mexico, and it could not be put at his door if in the course of the trip the ship changed destination and decided to make for Palestine. As Ambassador Peterson had anticipated, Susaikov added that in anything pertaining to Jewish embarkations the British political mission ought to turn to Rumania's Foreign Ministry.[18]

Holman strongly rejected Susaikov's suggestion and told the Foreign Office in London that "ultimate control of all movements in and out of Roumania still rests with the Allied Control Commission and therefore proposed approach to the Roumanian government would not only be ineffective but also serve generally to acknowledge a right which we do not in effect admit and which that government has so far not attempted to claim in principle." According to Holman, not only did the captain and crew of the *Smyrna* (*Max Nordau*) know that the passengers were illegal immigrants sailing for Palestine, but the captain had informed the Soviet port authorities in Constanta of the ship's true destination. Under the circumstances, he argued, the Soviet authorities should be asked to prevail on the Rumanian government to prevent the illegal sailing of Jews.[19]

London at that time preferred not to turn to Moscow because of the tension prevailing between the two countries. There had been confrontation (March–May 1946) between the West and the Soviets over Iran—from which Stalin was eventually forced to withdraw his troops—and seemingly insurmountable disagreements that had led to the interruption of the meetings of the CFM in Paris (26 April–17 May 1946) for one whole month. The cabinet decided, therefore, instead of appealing to Moscow to turn directly to the Rumanian government with the demand that it prevent the sailing of a boat that, according to reports, was preparing to sail from Constanta with two thousand people on board.[20]

That the Soviet military authorities in Rumania had no inclination to stop the sailing of the Jews was made abundantly clear once more at the end of July, when the head of the Soviet administrative section of the Allied Control Commission, Colonel Borisov, informed Kendall that he had distributed 440 exit visas to Jews who intended to sail to Costa Rica on the *Agia Anastasia.* In so doing he was violating a Soviet promise to consult with the British before providing exit visas to Jews.[21] Kendall vigorously protested against what he called "Soviet collusion with the enemy country in illegal measures directed against her ally Great Britain." He claimed that he had proof the Jews intended to sail to Palestine and accused Borisov of aiding and abetting the illegal immigration. Borisov rejected Kendall's demand that the ship not be allowed to sail until Costa Rica confirmed the validity of the visas, saying that the validity of transit visas or the visas to final destinations was not his affair. In the circumstances, Holman decided to approach the Rumanians directly. He demanded that the Rumanian Foreign Office vet all requests to leave Rumania, since officials in the Rumanian Ministry of the Interior (under Communist control) were overlooking the fact of invalid visas.[22]

Actually, the British legation in Rumania had information indicating that the Rumanian Communists were cooperating closely with the Zionists. Among the Rumanian personalities responsible for assisting the Zionists was Emil Budnaras, secretary general of the Council Presidium and head of the Secret Political Police, who, it was said, had the full confidence of the Soviets. He was assisted by the head of the State Security Department and the head of the Alien Control Department of the Ministry of the Interior. Budnaras was thought to be the link between the Zionists and the Soviets. According to Holman, the Rumanian Ministry of the Interior was following Budnaras's directives in allowing the movement, while ignoring the Foreign Ministry, which was responsible for issuing passports and visas. The Foreign Ministry was headed by Vice-President Gheorghiu Tatarescu, an anti-Communist and anti-Semite.[23]

While admitting that the situation of the Jews was difficult, Kendall did not portray them as powerless victims. In a report he presented to London in mid-July 1946, he noted an increase in anti-Semitism and the spread of the allegation that all the Jews were traitors and should be killed at the first opportunity. He attributed this wave of anti-Semitism to the intensive involvement of the Jews in the Central Committee of the Communist Party, thought by most Rumanians to be a Trojan horse. He was inclined to understand the Jewish motivations for cooperation with the Soviets since the Rumanians, "smitten with racism," had difficulty understanding that "the Jews, whom they have consistently repudiated and to whom they have never given equal status, cannot justly be called traitors to a country that has always disowned them. Roumanians fail to realize that it is only natural that the Jews should collaborate very closely with the Russians who liberated them from the degrading regime to which Roumania had subjected them and whose presence in Roumania is the only guarantee that they, the Jews, will not be subjected to further outrages."[24]

At the same time, Kendall had prejudices of his own. He did not absolve the Jews from responsibility for the situation they were in but thought that the Jews were their own worst enemy. They were devoid of any sense of political responsibility. Worse still, in his eyes, was their greed, which drove them remorselessly toward the excess that drew upon them the hatred of their neighbors. Kendall noted that the Rumanian government had taken several initiatives to improve the situation of the Jews. It had repealed anti-Jewish legislation and granted the Jews civil and national equality; it had compensated the Jews as far as possible for damages suffered in the course of the war; Jewish property had been restored to its owners; schools and other cultural institutions had been returned to the Jewish community; Jewish mobilization was permitted on a basis of equality; Jewish employees were returned to their previous positions in the government administration and the public service; moreover, Jews were given preference in public service and in the universities. The Jews, for their part, in Kendall's view, were discriminating against the Christians, who were employed by Jewish firms or institutions in menial posts. Jews held almost all the key governmental positions, especially in the police, in finance, and in supply. A Christian who was interested in solving a problem in one of these ministries had to employ a Jewish intermediary. The stock exchange and the black market were controlled by the Jews, and the Christian population of the cities had to obey Jewish dictates.

Kendall attacked the local Jewish press for purveying anti-British positions that enjoyed the enthusiastic support of the Rumanian government. He alleged that the Jewish press had turned the subject of Jewish immigration to Palestine into a political issue rather than an economic or humanitarian one. Kendall estimated the number of Rumanian Jews whose emotional and economic rehabilitation was dependent on their emigration at less than forty thousand, including the Jews who had returned from Germany, Poland, or Russia.[25]

Meanwhile, British pressures, based in part on evidence showing that the visas to Costa Rica had been forged, elicited a promise from the Soviet representatives in Rumania that they would for a short while delay the departure of the *Agia Anastasia*.[26] Not willing to settle for this noncommittal response, London decided to appeal directly to Moscow. This decision was influenced by progress made at the second session of the CFM in Paris (15 June–12 July 1946) in drafting the peace treaties, thus enabling the convening of the peace conference plenum at the end of July. Furthermore, London was worried by the presence of the 440 Jews with exit visas for Costa Rica on board the *Agia Anastasia*. Whitehall feared that the stream of illegal immigrants from Rumania was likely to grow if nothing was done to counter the impression that there were no obstacles on the way to Palestine. There was at that time a considerable increase in the number of illegal immigrants who succeeded in actually reaching the shores of Palestine, and the cabinet was under heavy pressure to intensify the struggle against this movement.[27]

At this point Ambassador Peterson reported to the Soviet Foreign Ministry on the methods, including the use of forged visas, employed by the organizers of the illegal immigration. He told of the British protest submitted to the secretary general of the Rumanian Foreign Ministry, who had admitted that the departure of the Jews was taking place without his approval. Peterson likewise mentioned Borisov's objection to taking steps to prevent the departure of the *Agia Anastasia*. The Soviet government was asked to instruct its representatives in Rumania not to allow the exit of Jews whose documents were not in order and who intended to violate the laws of Palestine.[28] At the same time, the British delegation in Rumania continued to apply pressure on the local authorities. Holman told the Rumanian foreign minister that certain officials in the Ministry of the Interior and the Council Presidium were collaborating with the Jews, possibly with Soviet agreement. Holman warned Tatarescu that if the *Agia Anastasia* were to set sail, "he must not be surprised if he had a rather frigid reception in Paris." Tatarescu promised to do all he could to prevent the illegal departure of Jews. Aware of the political reality in Rumania, Holman did not stop at discussing the matter only with the foreign minister; he also urged the prime minister to prevent the sailing of the *Agia Anastasia,* calling Groza's attention to the fact that the Ministry of the Interior in general and Colonel Budnaras in particular were involved in the illegal emigration.[29]

The British warning that Rumania's interest might suffer at the peace conference because of its policy toward the illegal emigration appeared to have achieved its purpose. The Rumanians wanted to improve the conditions of the peace treaty and needed the goodwill of the two Western powers, among other things, concerning their disagreement with the Hungarians about Transylvania.[30] At the conference, the Rumanian foreign minister, who headed his country's delegation, was able to tell Hector McNeill, minister of state at the Foreign Office, that the Rumanian government had decided to prevent the Jews from sailing on the *Agia Anastasia* even if it were found that the passengers' visas were legal. When, only a few days afterward, the Rumanian government found that the visas to Costa Rica had been invalid, but visas to Ethiopia that the passengers on the *Agia Anastasia* had meanwhile received appeared to be valid, the ship was forbidden to sail.[31]

Nevertheless, London's low regard for and distrust of the Rumanian authorities led to another appeal to Moscow. At first the Soviets delayed their reply, hiding behind formalistic excuses. But the British embassy in Moscow adopted a firm position, stressing that "in matters of this kind where unscrupulous and interested parties were clearly out to twist the regulations to their advantage and to deceive the British and the Soviet authorities we had expected that the Soviet government, in view of their professed concern for the interests of the Middle Eastern peoples, would have adopted a cooperative instead of legalistic attitude." British pressure on Moscow eventually had the desired effect.[32] Toward the end of October 1946 the Soviets announced that the visas to Ethiopia of the Jews who were about to sail on the *Agia Anastasia* were forged and that therefore they were not allowing them to sail.[33]

It is likely that the decision of the Soviets to prevent the *Agia Anastasia* from sailing had nothing to do with the fact that the visas were forged but in this case, too, was connected with the deliberations of the peace conference in Paris (29 July–15 October 1946) and with their anticipated continuation in the CFM, which was to meet in New York between 4 November and 12 December 1946. So as to give the British no excuse to cause trouble, the Soviets and the Rumanians elected to avoid creating additional conflicts until the peace agreements were signed. The pressure the British had exerted in the case of *Agia Anastasia* and their intensified struggle against illegal sailings — deporting illegal immigrants to Cyprus — left no doubt as to the importance the British ascribed to the matter. Moreover, the Rumanians, interested in ridding themselves of certain numbers of Jews, as well as the Soviets, as ever eager to increase British difficulties in Palestine, could achieve their objectives by means of Jewish sailings from another Communist country that was not a former belligerent country— Yugoslavia.

Yugoslavia: Interim Sailing Base

It is not surprising, then, that when in the middle of 1946 the future of Rumania and Bulgaria was being discussed at the Paris peace conference, Yugoslavia became the only base for embarkation in the Balkans. Relations between London and Belgrade were strained, and the Yugoslav authorities exhibited much enmity toward the Western powers who had opposed Yugoslav demands to be given control over the region of Venezia Giulia and the port city of Trieste, both of which had been transferred from Austria-Hungary to Italy after World War I. Tension reached a peak at the Paris peace conference when, within a few days during the month of August, the Yugoslavs shot down two American transport planes flying from Italy to Austria. A few weeks previously British destroyers sailing through the straits of Corfu had been fired on from the Albanian shore, and the Yugoslavs had been involved in this attack. British soldiers were the main obstacle preventing Yugoslavia from realizing by force its territorial claims, including a revision of the border with Austria in the area around Slovenian Carinthia and Styria (a region of three thousand square kilometers and two hundred thousand inhabitants).[34]

During the first year after the war the British evinced little interest in the illegal migration of the Jews through Yugoslavia. In fact, except for four weeks beginning in mid-June 1945, when about five thousand persons had traversed Yugoslavia on their way to Italy, the movement through Yugoslavia continued on a much smaller scale.[35] A January 1946 report of British Intelligence in Austria noted that some groups of Jewish DPs coming from Hungary were going on via Yugoslavia to northern Italy,[36] and the authors of a comprehensive report in March on the illegal traffic to Palestine mentioned that they had at hand very little information about the illegal movement in Yugoslavia.[37] At the beginning of April, the British Foreign Office was informed of a group that included 219 Hungarian, Rumanian, and Polish Jews who had crossed the border from Yugoslavia to Italy in the disputed region of Venezia Giulia.[38] Attempts of the Allied authorities in this region to convince the Yugoslav government to deport these people to their lands of origin came to nothing, and thus the headquarters of the Allied forces in Italy was compelled to transfer them to DP camps inside the country.[39] Headquarters thought that the migration of Jews arriving in Yugoslavia from Austria, Czechoslovakia, Rumania, Germany, and Poland was taking place with the active help or at least the knowledge of the Yugoslav authorities. Still, apprehensive over the possible outbreak of violent confrontations with the detained refugees, Allied military authorities refrained from returning them to Yugoslavia.[40]

Nevertheless, the British Foreign Office did not ignore this incident and at the beginning of June 1946 instructed the embassy in Belgrade to ask the Yugoslav government to prevent the transit of Jews without permits to Italy.[41] G. L. Clutton, first secretary at the British embassy in Yugoslavia, preferred that the appeal to the Yugoslav authorities be made jointly with the American embassy.[42] Washington's approval was delayed, and on 1 August 1946 the Foreign Office in London instructed its embassy in Belgrade to appeal urgently to the Yugoslav government without waiting for the Americans.[43] What apparently triggered British anxiety was the arrival of the *Haganah* in Palestine at the end of July. This vessel had sailed from Yugoslavia with 2,678 immigrants, the largest contingent yet to arrive on a single ship. Clutton gained the impression from his talk with General Vlatco Velebit, deputy foreign minister, that at most the Yugoslavs would confine themselves to trying to prevent Jews from entering Yugoslavia but not from departing the country.[44] He made it clear to the Foreign Office that there was no difficulty in passing through Yugoslavia illegally because of its topography and the possibility of purchasing exit visas. Crossing the border to Italy was being managed by the Yugoslav Jewish community, which was well organized and was able to care for and if necessary even conceal Jewish refugees who were in the country without proper documents. Clutton explained that while the Yugoslav authorities opposed the departure of the local Jews, they allowed Jews from other countries, especially Rumania, to sail.[45]

Of the approximately eighty thousand Jews who had lived in Yugoslavia before the war, only about eleven thousand remained.[46] When Yugoslavia was liberated, Josip Broz Tito initiated a vigorous propaganda campaign in Italy to convince the Yugoslav Jews to return. The first ones who returned discovered that it was very difficult to recover the property that had been taken from them and no less difficult to find work. Some of the returnees went back to Italy and settled there, and those who stayed warned friends and relatives to stay away because of local anti-Semitism. By the middle of 1946, almost five thousand Yugoslav Jews who had fled to Italy during the war had managed to gain a foothold there.[47] The AAC put the number of Jews wishing to emigrate from Yugoslavia at more than three thousand, of whom the large majority allegedly preferred to move to Palestine.[48]

Although London had doubts about its ability to influence the policy of the Yugoslavian government, which till then had shown no willingness to co-operate, it was decided toward the end of August to appeal once again to the Yugoslav Foreign Ministry.[49] The situation in Palestine had become more difficult after an increasing number of illegal immigrants had arrived there in the summer of 1946, resulting in a lack of internment facilities. A memorandum delivered to the Yugoslav Foreign Ministry spoke of substantial evidence showing that the illegal movement through Yugoslavia was being organized by an underground network of Jewish agents in Europe. The Yugoslav government was asked to prevent illegal immigrants on their way to Palestine from entering the country.[50] At the beginning of October, the Yugoslav Foreign Ministry promised that the government would pay particular attention to illegal border crossings in the Venezia-Giulia district, adding that thus far it had received no requests from DPs asking to cross through Yugoslavia en route to Palestine.[51]

The British embassy in Belgrade was not impressed. The British ambassador in Yugoslavia, Charles Peake, was certain that the local authorities were aware of the movement across Yugoslavia and of the existence of two camps located near Zagreb housing 5,000 Jews who planned to sail from Yugoslavia.[52] At that time, the fall of 1946, London feared that the *Agia Anastasia,* whose departure with illegal immigrants from Rumania it had managed to prevent, would attempt to embark illegal immigrants at one of the Adriatic ports such as Split in Yugoslavia. Because of the tension between the two countries, the Foreign Office was uncertain of the course it should pursue.[53] Before London had made a decision, two vessels sailed from Bakar on 2 November 1946. The *Knesset Yisrael* had more than 3,000 immigrants from Rumania on board and the *Agia Anastasia* about 600, mostly from Hungary. The plan was for the *Agia Anastasia* to transfer its passengers to the *Knesset Yisrael* near the shores of Palestine to prevent the ship from being confiscated and its foreign crew detained. But two days after it sailed out, the engine of the *Agia Anastasia* cracked, and the ship sank. All the passengers were transferred to the *Knesset Yisrael,* which returned to the port of Split to take on additional provisions. On 26 November that vessel, carrying 3,548 passengers, was intercepted in Palestinian waters by British patrol boats.[54]

When he met again with General Velebit in mid-November, Peake was unaware of the sailing of the *Knesset Yisrael.* The ambassador declared that given the Yugoslav government's strict control at the borders, he found it difficult to believe that it was ignorant of the illegal emigration of Jews. In an attempt to spur the authorities into action, Peake claimed that this illegal movement was enabling opponents of the regime to leave the country disguised as Jews. Velebit was quick to disavow all responsibility and maintained that the government viewed this population movement as contrary to its interests and was thus interested in bringing it to an end. He observed that it was difficult to deal with the movement since it was taking place throughout Europe and was ably managed by a central organization whose activities were difficult to monitor. Peake replied that the memorandum he had submitted specified methods that could help stop the passage via Yugoslavia, and he asked what steps the authorities intended to take. Velebit told Peake of a Greek vessel (he was referring to the *Rafiah,* formerly the *Athnai*) that had reached Split carrying an unknown number of Jews who had to be allowed to disembark. Peake asked Velebit to prevent these people from boarding any other boat.[55] Ten days after their conversation, the *Rafiah* sailed with 785 illegal immigrants from Rumania. This voyage ended tragically when, on 7 December, the vessel sank near the isle of Sirna in the Dodecanese and eight passengers drowned. Five days later the survivors were removed to Crete by two British ships and then transferred to Cyprus.[56]

Peake, who felt he had been deceived, complained to Marshal Tito in mid-December that the passengers of the *Rafiah* had been allowed to sail from a Yugoslav port despite Velebit's assurances. Tito responded that Yugoslavia had no interest in helping Jewish emigration to Palestine. He pointed an accusing finger at La Guardia, secretary general of UNRRA, who had visited Yugoslavia the previous August and had urged Tito to assist the movement. This, he said, was also why transit camps, which were receiving supplies from UNRRA, had been set up in the country. Peake tried to discover whether La Guardia had made the continuation of assistance to Yugoslavia conditional on that country's aid to the Jewish movement. According to Peake's report of the meeting, Tito avoided a direct answer but tried to create the impression "that he had been subjected to a species of blackmail." Tito explained that the Jews were permitted to remain in the camps and that even though individuals fled from time to time, there was no possibility of putting them in camps. The ambassador responded that it was not a matter of a few individuals but rather of a continuous, systematic flow directed by an organization. Tito did not accept this argument, and Peake promised to bring him evidence.[57]

From their interrogation of the Greek crew of the *Rafiah,* the British learned not only that the Yugoslav port authorities in Bakar had observed the embarkation of the illegal immigrants (who had arrived by train from Zagreb) but that the ship had been openly refueled by the Yugoslavs and that no attempt had been made to conceal the identity of the passengers or their destination.[58] Clutton was quick to put this information in a letter to Tito at the end of December 1946. When the British note was tendered, Velebit claimed that he would be very surprised "if in fact another ship was to sail, for although at the request of UNRRA the Yugoslav authorities had accommodated Jewish displaced persons in the camps, the Marshal had given instructions that transit traffic was to cease."[59]

In contrast to previous equivocal commitments, this time the Yugoslavs did indeed keep their promise. On 12 March 1947, Peake informed the Foreign Office that since the contacts with the authorities in Belgrade at the end of 1946 there had not been any illegal movement of Jews via Yugoslavia. The ambassador noted that although Clutton had not received a reply to his December note to Tito, the impression was that members of the Yugoslav government were opposed to continued transit traffic via that country. Peake believed that the authorities had taken the necessary measures and therefore advised the Foreign Office to refrain from again urging the Yugoslav government to act against the illegal migration.[60] The British political mission in Hungary confirmed the ambassador's assessment that, according to the local deputy minister of the interior, the Yugoslav authorities were cooperating in closing the border between the two countries and that as a result the illegal passage had ceased.[61] Clutton's assessment of the situation turned out to be accurate. Fifteen months were to pass from the embarkation of the *Rafiah* until, on 18 February 1948, another boat, the *Bonim Velohamim* (Hebrew: Building and Fighting), would set sail from the shores of Yugoslavia.

Zionist sources confirm the change in Yugoslavian policy. Reports to Palestine throughout 1947 mentioned that the Yugoslav authorities were adamantly opposed to continued sailings of illegal immigrants from that country and that it was no longer possible to refurbish vessels in Yugoslav ports. Ehud Avriel, assistant to the head of the organization behind the clandestine illegal sailings, Ha'mossad Le'aliya Bet (Organization for Immigration B), who was in close touch with members of the Yugoslav government, correctly analyzed the Yugoslavs' motives when he reported that the local authorities wanted to alleviate the tension with the British. The main source of tension with Britain continued to be the disagreements over Venezia Giulia, Carinthia, and Greece, and Yugoslav assistance to the illegal emigration did not help to ease the situation. While throughout 1947 there was no change in the pro-Soviet orientation of Yugoslav foreign policy, Tito, anticipating conflict with the Soviet Union, may have wanted to demonstrate a measure of goodwill toward the British, especially as relations with the Americans were worsening. Cessation of the sailings was an expression of this trend. Furthermore, that there was a Yugoslav representative on UNSCOP had prompted the Yugoslav government to decide that it could not probe the Palestine question and at the same time aid the illegal emigration. Nevertheless, the Yugoslavs told the Zionists that they would halt activities for the duration of the summer but would renew contact with them in September 1947. (UNSCOP was to present its report on 31 August 1947.)[62]

British embassy contacts in Yugoslavia about the illegal Jewish emigration were held for the most part with General Velebit. Conversations between the latter and Eliahu Epstein (Elat), Jewish Agency representative in Washington in June 1947, provide an insight into the position of the Yugoslav government at that time toward the future of the Jews in Europe. The two officials, who were on friendly terms, first met in Cairo in December 1943 when Velebit served as a general in Tito's army. The two then discussed parachuting into Yugoslavia Jews from the Yishuv and giving medical assistance to Tito's partisans. In 1947, as Epstein relates, Velebit tried to convince him of the friendly intentions of his government and of the other governments in the Slavic bloc toward the Zionists. He believed that only a small minority of Hungarian, Rumanian, or Bulgarian Jews would be able to adapt to the changing conditions in these countries because so few of them had shown an interest in integrating into the new social and economic model being implemented there. According to Velebit, the Rumanian and Hungarian governments hoped for the largest possible emigration of Jews to solve the problem of anti-Semitism, which was being exploited by antigovernment elements. He believed, Epstein adds, that no less than one or one and a half million Jews would need to leave Central Europe and that this was a historic opportunity for the Zionist movement to realize its objectives. The Soviet government and its allies had reached the conclusion that only Palestine could absorb the Jews of Central Europe since there was no other country in the world that was ready to take in large numbers of Jews. Velebit expressed the hope that the Yugoslav representative in UNSCOP could be of assistance to the Zionists (this did not happen).[63] Velebit's remarks must be seen in light of the speech Andrei Gromyko had given at the special session of the UN General Assembly on 14 May in which he expressed USSR support for the partition of Palestine into two independent states, one Jewish and one Arab, in case a binational state proved unworkable.[64]

Halting the departure of vessels carrying illegal immigrants from Yugoslavia came after the peace agreements with formerly belligerent countries, including Rumania and Bulgaria, were signed in February 1947. This meant that the British had less leverage on the Rumanian authorities, and the latter no longer had any reason not to allow sailings from their country. As it happened, by March 1947 the Rumanian authorities were already exerting pressure on Ha'apala emissaries to renew the sailings from Rumanian ports. Probably this also was related to the British cabinet decision, in February 1947, to transfer the Palestine question to the United Nations. But at that time the organizers of the illegal emigration put off immediate embarkations out of tactical considerations. They feared that as soon as one more ship sailed from Rumania (as in the case of the *Max Nordau*), the British would renew their pressure on the local authorities, who would then be compelled to put a stop to further maritime departures. The aim therefore was to take a maximum number of Jews out of the country at a single time. Such an operation, of course, necessitated larger ships. That was the reason the organizers preferred to wait until all preparations for such a large-scale undertaking were in place.[65]

The Hunger Flight

This situation, however, was aggravated when in the course of 1947 there was a further downturn in the economic situation in Rumania. Jews who had returned to Rumania after the war were particularly affected. Reports reached the Yishuv of severe hunger, adding to the need to extricate as many people as possible. A letter sent at the beginning of February 1947 reflects the seriousness of the situation: "After the long-lasting and destructive war, the country was hit by two consecutive years of drought, with the result that today we are suffering the epitome of real hunger. . . . I can only tell you this: in Iasi, Galati, Botosani, and other places where Jews are living, people are starving to death. This is not mere rhetoric or an exaggeration but simple fact. People are dying of hunger, and the Jewish communities are helpless and unable to help." The letter went on to say that because of the hunger and Jewish black market activity, anti-Semitism had increased "in the most alarming manner" and that the Jews were being accused of causing all the ills that had fallen upon the country. It was underscored that hatred of the Jews was not being encouraged by the authorities. Under such circumstances, "the majority of Rumanian Jewry wishes to leave and is ready to depart under any circumstances, no matter what the difficulties or obstacles."[66]

As a result of the hunger, Jews began, on their own initiative, to cross the Hungarian border in order to reach the DP camps in Austria. During the first months of 1947 this movement was spontaneous and was not directed or organized by any Brichah emissaries. The number of those fleeing was estimated at between four and five hundred persons each month, and they usually reached Budapest penniless. So as to prevent this movement from causing difficulties with local authorities, the JDC rented a building to house the Rumanian refugees. With the help of Brichah emissaries, these Jews were then moved from Hungary to Austria. The determination of some Rumanian Jews to leave the country at any price led to incidents with Rumanian border patrols, in the course of which dozens of Jews were arrested.[67] At the beginning of May, Zionist emissaries from Palestine in Rumania reported back to Palestine that "the situation of the Jews has taken a serious turn for the worse in recent weeks, and hundreds of people are streaming toward the western border. Neither we nor the police have as yet succeeded in overcoming and controlling this phenomenon. Clearly it causes serious damage to our entire venture and lowers our prestige in the eyes of the authorities." Despite the border incidents, the Zionist activists believed that there had been no change in the intentions of the Rumanian government to be rid of the Jews.[68]

The British embassy in Rumania was not unaware of the incidents and was of the opinion that government policy toward the departure of the Jews had changed. In mid-May 1947 the embassy reported on a statement published in the local press by the Jewish Democratic Front, which embodied all Jewish associations supporting the government. The statement criticized the illegal border crossings by Rumanian Jews and declared that families who had sold their property in order to leave Rumania found themselves abandoned and penniless in the neighboring countries. It also stressed that the JDC in Hungary would no longer assist Jews arriving there. Those wishing to go to Palestine were advised to apply to the authorized organizations, which would arrange their departure in accordance with the laws of the land. Adrian Holman, the British minister, thought that this statement indicated that the Communist Party was retreating from its hitherto friendly attitude toward the illegal emigration from Rumania. Holman reported that the JDC had even begun to bring many Jews who had been staying in camps in eastern Hungary and western Rumania back to their homes. The change in policy, he thought, ensued from the difficulties the organizers of the illegal immigration were having in acquiring ships in France and Italy. The presence of thousands of Jews without legal documents or means of livelihood in Hungary, Austria, and Italy created severe economic and security problems, which were moving the governments of these countries to prevent further movement.[69] In his assessment, Holman failed to take into account the despair that drove many Rumanian Jews to leave the country and the inability of the local leaders to stop their hasty departure overland.[70] Several weeks after he had sent his analysis, during July and August alone almost eighty-five hundred Jews had crossed the border. All in all, approximately nineteen thousand people left Rumania and reached Vienna during 1947.[71]

Britain's greatest worry, however, continued to be the departure of the Jews by sea. In the summer of 1947 the British became aware of preparations to renew the sailings from the Balkan countries. At that time, tension between the Soviets, on the one hand, and the British and Americans, on the other, was increasing. Stalin, who had decided not to join Marshall's recovery initiative for Europe, began to extend Soviet control over the countries within Moscow's sphere of influence. The Rumanian and Bulgarian Communists accelerated their control with the removal of anti-Communist opposition leaders, paying no heed to British and American protests against the persecution of the leaders of non-Communist parties and breaches of civil rights. It was under these pressing circumstances that the British set out to prevent resumption of the illegal embarkations from Communist bloc countries. For the first time since the war, the British had to consider that illegal sailings might take off from Bulgarian ports. Until the peace treaty was signed and until the new Communist government received recognition from the British and American governments, the Bulgarians refused to allow Rumanian Jews to sail from Bulgarian ports, and they opposed the emigration of Bulgarian Jews.[72] But in the fall of 1947 the Bulgarians changed their policy, and within three months, more than nineteen thousand Jews, mostly of Rumanian origin, had set sail from Burgas.

Bulgaria: Final Sailing Base

In mid-August 1947, the British representatives in Rumania and Bulgaria were asked to warn the two governments of a suspicious ship, the *Paducah*, that was about to pick up illegal Jewish emigrants in one of the two countries. It was mentioned that the Uruguayan visas the passengers might carry were most probably forged and that, in any case, the ship itself was in no condition to take passengers as far as South America.[73] Holman was of the opinion that decisions concerning emigration were in the hands of the Soviets and that it was therefore necessary to gain their support.[74] This being the case, on 25 August Brigadier E. R. Greer, the British representative to the Control Commission in Rumania, took the matter up with Soviet general Susaikov, and the following day Frank Roberts, the British minister in Moscow, approached the Soviet deputy foreign minister, Andrei Vyshinski.[75] Following publication of an article in the Rumanian newspaper *Timpul* reporting that six thousand "legal" Jewish emigrants were about to set sail for Palestine in two Panamanian vessels from Constanta, and based on information that had reached the British legation in Rumania concerning a large group of young Jews heading for the Rumanian shores of the Black Sea, Holman again exhorted the Rumanian Foreign Ministry not to allow these people to sail.[76]

At the same time, the British mission in Bulgaria turned to the local Foreign Ministry, where the acting general secretary informed them of his government's intention to prevent passengers from embarking or disembarking from the *Paducah.* He emphasized, however, that international law required his government to provide the vessel with fuel.[77] A few days later, on 24 September 1947, John Sterndale-Bennet, the British minister in Bulgaria, called the attention of the Bulgarian Foreign Ministry to reports of large numbers of Jews heading for a Bulgarian port. The *Northland* was then anchored at Burgas, and the Bulgarian authorities were asked to deal with it as they had promised to do with the *Paducah.*[78] Two days later the two vessels, renamed the *Geula* (Hebrew: Redemption) and *Medinat Hayehudim* (Hebrew: The State of the Jews) and carrying more than four thousand Jews from Rumania, set sail. That same day, the Rumanian Foreign Ministry informed the British legation in Bucharest that it had no knowledge of vessels supposedly taking illegal emigrants on board in Rumanian territorial waters and that it did not know of illegal movement organized from Rumania.[79] On 2 October both ships were intercepted by the British and all illegal immigrants deported to Cyprus.

Until the latter had been interrogated, the British legation in Bulgaria remained uncertain whether the operation had been carried out with the consent of the local authorities. Nevertheless, Sterndale-Bennet decided to meet with the Bulgarian foreign minister without waiting for authoritative information because the *Pan Crescent,* which the British had unsuccessfully attempted to sink while it was being overhauled in Italy, was reportedly entering the Dardanelles strait.[80] Vasil P. Kolarov, the Bulgarian foreign minister, maintained that the Bulgarian authorities wanted to prevent illegal sailings to Palestine but that the Jews had shown them valid visas and transit permits to other countries. To the British representative's comment that it was necessary to check whether these visas were indeed genuine, the minister replied that his government had no diplomatic relations with most of the countries that were supposed to have issued them (Syria, Lebanon, and Egypt). When his attempts to secure a commitment that in the future the Bulgarian government would help prevent illegal movement were met with evasion, Sterndale-Bennet expressed the hope that the Bulgarian government did not intend to aggravate the already strained relations between the two countries.[81]

Relations between the two countries, however, did worsen when despite British and American protests the leader of the Bulgarian anti-Communist Peasant Party, Nikola Petkov, who had been arrested in June 1947, was executed by hanging on 23 September. In Rumania, Iuliu Maniu, leader of the opposition Peasant Party, had been given a life sentence. In general, the steps taken by the Bulgarian Communists to achieve their goal were more brutal than in Rumania. In Bulgaria, unlike in Rumania, the Communist Party enjoyed the support of a large part of the public; and unlike the situation in Poland, Rumania, and

Father on Medinat Hayehudim *showing the dead body of his baby to guarding British soldiers (Courtesy Yad Vashem, Jerusalem)*

The Medinat Hayehudim *following capture by the British at Haifa port*
(Courtesy Yad Vashem, Jerusalem)

Hungary, there were no anti-Soviet feelings. After Soviet forces occupied Bulgaria in September 1944, the Fatherland Front coalition government included the Communists, the Agrarians, and the Social Democrats. The Communists took the key positions, including the Interior and Justice Ministries, and then exploited their position to oust their political rivals. Within six months close to twelve thousand people had been brought to trial and convicted; of these, more than two thousand were put to death. Both the Agrarian and Socialist Parties boycotted the first elections that were held after the war (on 18 November 1945). As a result, the Communists gained almost 90 percent of the vote. In the summer of 1946, the Communists began to harass their rivals in the military. The minister of defense was forced to resign and top-ranking generals were imprisoned. In the elections called by the Communists for 27 October 1946, only 99 of the 465 delegates to the National Assembly did not belong to the Communist front. Georgi Dimitrov, former head of the Communist International, was appointed prime minister. In February 1947 Britain recognized the Bulgarian government. But when in the year following the elections the opposition, including the Peasant Party, was eliminated, both the British delegation in Bulgaria and officials in London believed that because of the brutality of their acts, there could be no talk of normalizing relations between the two countries.[82]

Meanwhile, the British learned that the *Geula* and the *Medinat Hayehudim* had sailed with the knowledge and assistance of the local authorities. Shaike Dan (Yeshayhu Trachtenberg), the Zionist emissary who was handling the contacts with the Bulgarian authorities, noted years later that the two vessels had been given final permission to sail only after the Bulgarians had been paid the money that had been agreed upon between them.[83] British intelligence officials believed that the Soviets had had a hand in the sailing of both ships and that this was yet another stage in the anti-British campaign the USSR was conducting in the Middle East.[84] While in London British officials debated whether to return the illegal immigrants to the Balkan countries, the British legations in Rumania and Bulgaria strongly rejected their forced "repatriation." Holman was particularly apprehensive about a confrontation with the Soviets.[85]

Shortly after the two ships had sailed, the British begun another campaign, this time in regard to the *Pan* vessels. From the beginning of October 1947, reports reached the Foreign Office in London that extensive carpentry work was being done on the *Pan Crescent,* then lying at anchor in Constanta, and that the port authorities were extending assistance. The assumption was that illegal immigrants would soon be arriving at the port. Holman was skeptical as to whether the strong protest he had sent to the authorities would have an effect.[86] Meanwhile, on 11 October, the *Pan York* arrived in Constanta, and this inaugurated a new series of British appeals to the Rumanian and Bulgarian governments.[87] The Rumanian Foreign Ministry informed the British legation that it was exerting pressure on the Ministry of the Interior to prevent Jews from boarding the boats in Rumania.[88]

The British mission in Rumania thought that the Zionists were attempting to bring as many Jews as possible out of Rumania because they realized that the agreement between them and the Communists would continue as long as it served Communist aims and that the day was not far off when they themselves would become a target of Communist attacks. Kendall, the head of the consular section, stressed that the 450,000 Jews of Rumania represented the largest Jewish community in Europe and that the Zionists were afraid of losing these Jews. The understanding with the Communists was being exploited for the purpose of moving Jews to regions under Zionist influence. There were no restrictions on leaving Rumania for Hungary, whereas the Hungarian authorities were taking efficient measures to ensure that those who had taken flight would not remain in Hungary but would continue westward. Kendall anticipated that the stream of Jews from Rumania to Austria, Germany, and Italy would increase. This was why several Zionists were staying in Bucharest to hold discussions with the Central Committee of the Communist Party: Joseph Schwartz, JDC European head; Moshe Sneh, member of the Jewish Agency Executive (and its *Ha'apala* liaison); and Moshe Averbuch (Agami), organizer of the illegal emigration from Rumania to Palestine. Kendall observed that the Communist Party was interested in being rid of most of the Jews currently living in Rumania as they were seen as "non-assimilable, inadaptable, and incorrigible racketeers and individualists." "If by assisting their departure they can also present the West with yet another problem and lay hands on the very important Jewish assets in Roumania," he continued, "then they will encourage the migration by every means in their power."[89]

Reports of British intentions to turn over the Palestine Mandate to the UN organization, Kendall emphasized, were causing much concern in Jewish circles and in their eyes made the question of bringing the Jews out of Rumania even more urgent. He told of four instances known to him personally of Jews whose families had lived in Rumania for three generations and who had recently sold two industrial enterprises and a private bank to the Communist Party; these businesses, he claimed, were sold at 15 percent of their real value so the owners could "get away before it was too late."[90]

At the beginning of December 1947, British representatives in Rumania reported a change in the policy of the authorities regarding Jews leaving the country. Kendall mentioned an article published in the Rumanian press about the exposure of a Jewish organization in Bucharest specializing in the forgery of emigration documents and visas. People arrested had included the head of the organization and a technical expert. According to Kendall, the Rumanian and Hungarian governments had decided to prevent the border between the two countries from being crossed since there were many political opponents of the regimes among the emigrants; the authorities also sought to prevent the smuggling of foreign currency and precious stones and metals out of the country. Kendall thought that the appointment as foreign minister of Ana Pauker (a Jew), who opposed the illegal Jewish movement, was also connected to the change in policy. Holman also attributed the arrest of a group of Jews attempting to cross the border to Hungary at the end of November to the new foreign minister's opposition to the departure of the Jews.[91] Brichah activists reported that the border between Rumania and Hungary was now blocked and that two hundred people had been arrested and returned to Rumania.[92] Clearly, there had been a change in government policy concerning the departure of Jews overland. In December 1947, legislation was passed stipulating that illegal emigrants returned to Rumania would lose their citizenship and that their property would be confiscated.[93]

These measures did little to convince the Foreign Office in London that the Rumanian authorities could now be counted on to cooperate in halting the *Pan* boats.[94] Following the sailing of the *Pan*s from Constanta (on 22 and 23 December 1947) without passengers to an unknown destination,[95] J. E. Cable, of the Foreign Office, argued that if Jews boarded the ships in Bulgaria, as had been in the case with the *Geula* and *Medinat Hayehudim*, "we shall know that the changed attitude of the Roumanian government is of purely local significance. If, on the other hand, they leave the Black Sea empty and are forced to try their luck in Italy or some other non-Communist country, we shall have to revise our ideas about the Communist policy toward Jewish illegal immigration."[96] It very quickly became clear that there had been no change in Communist policy. The ships had set sail for Bulgaria, and approximately twelve thousand Jews were currently en route there in eight trains.[97]

Sterndale-Bennet appealed urgently to Bulgarian foreign minister Kolarov demanding that people be prevented from boarding the ships and pointing out that Bulgarian Jews were among those about to embark.[98] The appeals were ineffective, and on 27 December a Russian pilot guided the *Pan*s, with 15,632 illegal immigrants aboard, out to open waters.[99] After the ships had sailed, the British reached an agreement with representatives of the Yishuv that the ships would proceed directly to Cyprus. Both sides wanted to prevent a confrontation between the illegal immigrants and British soldiers that might result in many casualties.[100]

About three weeks after the *Pan*s sailed, the British legation in Bucharest reported that the curtain had come down sooner than expected on the departure of Jews from Rumania. Discussions between the Central Committee of the Communist Party and the Zionists and the JDC concerning the mass exodus of Jews from Rumania had produced only the sailing of the *Pan*s. The legation believed that the Soviets were no longer interested in maintaining their truce with the Zionists in Rumania. It emerged that Chief Rabbi Shafran had left the country, and there was much evidence that "those who carried the Zionist movement into the Communist camp in Roumania are now themselves being denounced as 'international agents.'"[101] Zionist sources also reported in mid-January 1948 that the Rumanians were forbidding the departure of the Jews by sea in addition to the already existing measures against overland departure.[102]

Negotiations with the Bulgarian authorities proved extremely complicated and frustrating for Britain. The Bulgarian foreign minister, for example, vigorously rejected the sharp protest submitted to him by Sterndale-Bennet in the end of 1947.[103] According to Kolarov, emigrants coming from Rumania and Hungary who claimed they were en route to Panama all possessed regular valid passports, and the Bulgarian authorities had neither reason nor desire to cast doubt on the legitimacy of passports issued by countries with which Bulgaria maintained friendly relations. The foreign minister dismissed the allegations that Bulgarian citizens were to be found among the emigrants, noting that Bulgarian Jews had been forbidden to sail on the *Pans*.[104] As for the UN decision (17 November 1947) concerning the illegal emigration to which Sterndale-Bennet had referred, Kolarov explained, not without irony, that the Bulgarian government was not a member of that organization and thus was not necessarily aware of its decisions regarding Palestine. The Bulgarian government had not been invited to participate in deliberations on the Palestine question and had not been informed about the UN recommendations, nor had it been asked to assist in their implementation. Under the circumstances, Kolarov argued, it was surprising to hear the Bulgarian government criticized for ignoring the UN decision.

The matter of the United Nations Organization was particularly sensitive for the Bulgarians (and for the Rumanians and Hungarians as well). Requests in August and October 1947 by the three previously belligerent countries to join the UN had been rejected by the Security Council. Kolarov expressed his annoyance to Sterndale-Bennet as follows: "It is well known that certain Great Powers, contrary to all spirit of equity and to the express obligation undertaken by them, did their utmost to reject admission of Bulgaria to the United Nations at the last session." Kolarov declared that only admission to the United Nations would ensure Bulgaria's cooperation with the organization.[105] The exchange of accusations between the two countries continued for several more weeks. British protests did not prevent a group of twelve hundred members of Zionist pioneer youth movements in Bulgaria from crossing the border to Yugoslavia and sailing from Bakar on the *Bonim Velohamim* on 18 February 1948.[106]

The British by now no longer had the leverage of sanctions against Bulgaria. The absence of economic and other ties between the two countries enabled the Bulgarian government to ignore the British pressure.[107] Even Bulgaria's eventual admission to the UN was not dependent on its relations with Britain but rather on an overall agreement between the USSR and the United States and Britain. The main incentive for the Bulgarians to allow the sailings from their ports was most probably the hard currency received in payment from the *Ha'apala* organizers.[108] Still, it can be assumed that the sailings from Bulgaria, which entailed coordination with the Rumanian authorities, took place with the approval of the Soviets and possibly at their behest.

With Moscow's Blessing

The mass departure of approximately 280,000 Jews by land and sea from Soviet bloc countries could only have occurred with the knowledge and consent of Moscow. During the first year after the war various British officials were still uncertain about the extent of Soviet involvement in the *Brichah* movement, but by the summer of 1946 they had no doubts whatever that the movement was taking place with Moscow's support. The Foreign Office argued that the Soviets were not only encouraging the Jews to leave but were also training Jewish youths for underground activity in Palestine and helping them to reach their destination and that Jewish Communists were shown preference in the sailings to Palestine.[109] These assertions fit the wider British assessment that the Soviets were out to undermine Britain's status in the Middle East and seeking a foothold in the area. The British were well aware that Moscow had been piqued when the two Western powers had excluded the Soviets from their efforts to resolve the conflict in Palestine. The illegal immigration was regarded as part of the Kremlin's efforts to cause a rupture not only in London's relations with the Arab states but also with the United States.

It is clear that the British Foreign Office had difficulty in finding out exactly what role the USSR was playing in the Polish and Czechoslovakian decisions to allow the migration to take place. The assumption was that the Polish and Czech governments, which were subject to Soviet influence, were coordinating their positions with Moscow. For example, the Communist ministers in the Czech government, including Prime Minister Gottwald, were found to support a policy that permitted Jewish refugees to move across the country, while the Soviet military authorities in Germany allowed them to enter their occupation zone. Moreover, most of the refugees at that time were Polish Jews whom the Soviets had permitted to return to Poland as part of the repatriation program, even though they knew that most of the Polish Jews, including the repatriates, were moving on to the DP camps in Germany and Austria and to ports of embarkation in Italy. It may also be that the renewed movement of thousands of Jews from Poland via Czechoslovakia (starting in the second half of May 1946), which had the consent of the authorities, was connected to the publication of the AAC's report at the end of April. When the AAC was set up, it had seemed that the problem of the Jewish DPs was about to be solved, but now Anglo-American disagreement over the issue again reared its head and the Soviets realized the potential advantage for them in exacerbating the DP problem. Polish prime minister Edward Osóbka-Morawski's declaration on 8 May that his government was willing to allow those Jews wishing to emigrate to Palestine to leave the country only reinforced this assumption.[110]

The Soviets systematically rejected British charges that they were involved in the sailings. When they were accused of facilitating the activities of the *Brichah* movement, they pointed a remonstrative finger at the United States, whose policy regarding Jewish DPs and Zionism was no secret. The Soviets exploited the disputes between the Americans and the British on this matter. In the joint Allied Control Commissions, they supported positions and recommendations on Jewish migration consistent with those of the British, which ostensibly placed them on the side of the British against the Americans. These Soviet tactics were based on the knowledge that the Americans would oppose any proposal to close the gates of their occupation zone in the face of Jewish refugees or to return them to their countries of origin. For example, in a session of the Allied Control Commission in Austria at the end of September 1946, the American delegate accused the Soviets of aiding the Jews to reach the American zone of Vienna. The Soviet representative argued in response that the Americans were helping one hundred thousand Jews to reach Palestine while the Soviets were ready to do whatever was necessary to halt the stream of emigrants to Austria. When the British delegate then moved for a decision to close the borders and block illegal Jewish emigration, the Soviets supported the proposal, and the American delegate opposed it.[111] In taking this stand the Soviets also followed their principal position that all East European citizens must be repatriated, if necessary by force.

Summing up, it was only in August 1946 that the British began launching a diplomatic campaign against the flight of Jews from Soviet bloc countries. More or less regular reports of the exodus from Poland via Czechoslovakia had begun reaching London at the end of 1945. A short time afterward the population flow significantly abated, and consideration of the problem was sidetracked. Only from the British headquarters in Austria was there word of the movement of Jews from Hungary, and the assessment did not reflect the real situation, as the British mission in Hungary continued to report to London until March 1946 that there was no fear of an exodus of local Jews. There were almost no reports of the departures via Yugoslavia until the spring of 1946. British lack of awareness can be explained both by the social and economic turmoil in these countries and the fact that during the first months after the war the exodus took place under the cloak of the general mass movement of people in which the Jews constituted only an insignificant proportion. This, in turn, explains why at the time the British did not ascribe high priority to the problem of Jews leaving Central and Eastern European countries and no special personnel were assigned to deal with it. Furthermore, London hoped that contacts with the Americans, first in the Anglo-American Committee and later between delegations of the two countries, would lead to a joint program first to resolve the Palestine question and then to provide a solution for the Jewish refugee problem.

It was only when contacts with the Americans on the Palestine issue had failed to bring the desired results and *Ha'apala* vessels began reaching Palestine in increasing numbers in late July and August that London realized the need to start a diplomatic campaign against the illegal emigration of the Jews. The Soviets' initially positive response to British pressure concerning the illegal sailings from Rumania and the illegal flight from Hungary was temporary, dictated by the proceedings of the peace conference in Paris. The Soviets ascribed great importance to reintegrating these two Communist-dominated former enemy states into the international community and to bringing about the dispersal of the Allied Control Commissions in the two countries. Actually, however, there was no change in policy toward the departure of Jews from countries in the Soviet sphere of influence, as demonstrated by the mass exodus from Poland via Czechoslovakia in summer 1946 and the sailings from Yugoslav ports. The tactic of the Soviet satellite countries was to transfer the point of embarkations from one country to another according to the prevailing diplomatic wind, which was why, for example, Rumanian and Yugoslavian security forces cooperated in transporting Rumanian Jews to Yugoslavia. Given the intensive Soviet involvement in Rumania and the close ties between Belgrade and Moscow at the time, it may be assumed that the Soviets both knew and approved of the operation.

Yugoslavia was a suitable alternative to Rumania and Bulgaria since it was not a formerly belligerent country and thus its dependence on Britain's stance in the peace conference deliberations was minimal. (This was also true in the case of Poland and Czechoslovakia.) Yugoslav willingness to allow *Ha'apala* sailings during the second half of 1946 ended British attempts to use the discussions on the peace agreement as leverage on Communist bloc countries to prevent illegal embarkations. Even though the ship sunk, the *Agia Anastasia* incident reflects the difficulties Britain faced in its efforts to prevent illegal sailings from regions in the Soviet sphere of influence.

British officials, though not always ready to admit so in public, recognized that anti-Semitism in Poland, Rumania, and Hungary played a part in motivating the Jews to abandon these countries. After the war the Communist governments in these three countries not only opposed anti-Semitism but also accorded the Jews opportunities that had previously not been available to them, and Jews came to hold key positions. At the same time, the anti-Communist opposition, which enjoyed the political support of the West, was largely anti-Semitic and used anti-Semitism in its struggle against the Communists. Under these circumstances, British officials realized that there would be no point in asking the Communist authorities to fight anti-Semitism.

During 1947 British influence was further eroded because of the signing of the peace agreements (February 1947), increased tensions between East and West, the consolidation of Communist control in Soviet bloc countries, and a severe economic crisis in Britain itself. Throughout the year, especially the second half, Rumania and Bulgaria were the main bases for Jewish departures, with Rumania supplying the illegal immigrants and Bulgaria the ports of embarkation. The intensive pressure applied by the British on the Rumanians led to the relocation of ports of departure from Rumania to Bulgaria, which had nothing to lose by antagonizing the British. More than thirty-eight thousand Jews left Rumania during that period by land and sea.

The mass exodus of Jews from countries under Soviet influence was made possible in large part through a rare convergence of the interests of those countries themselves and the USSR, of the Jews in those countries, and of the Zionist movement. The Polish authorities did not wish to hold Jewish repatriates against their will, particularly as their departure suited internal needs of the regime, while the Hungarian and Czech authorities did not object to the departure of the local Jews because they were determined that all alien Jews must leave the country. In the case of Rumania, the desire to be rid of Jews combined with the incentive it was offered in the form of the hard foreign currency the Zionists provided. The Bulgarians as well were offered financial inducements. For their part, the Yugoslavs were mainly motivated by their hostility to the British, although sympathy and solidarity with the victims of Germany also played some role. The desire to harm British interests was common to all Soviet satellites. In view of the Anglo-American disputes about policy toward Jewish DPs, it was logical for the Soviet Union both to try to exacerbate the problem of Jewish refugees in Germany and Austria and to allow tens of thousands of Jews to sail to Palestine. The Soviets' support, since the second half of 1947, for the establishment of a Jewish state there was part of this strategy. The Kremlin was well aware of the difficulties the illegal immigrants were causing the British in Palestine and the implications for London's relations with the Arab states. The sailing of the *Pans* after the UN had already passed its partition resolution was intended, among other things, to serve Soviet interests in the Middle East. Moscow wished to signal to the British what they could expect if they went back on their decision to leave Palestine — hundreds of thousands of Jews still in Communist bloc countries constituted a significant potential threat to the British. When the emigration of Jews from Communist bloc countries was eventually halted, it was not the result of British pressure but rather stemmed from the internal political considerations of the Communist regimes seeking to entrench their rule.

IV

ITALY
AND
FRANCE:
DELAYING
TACTICS

ITALY
CONTRARY
MANEUVERS

More than half of the illegal immigrants who sailed for Palestine between the end of the war and May 1948 embarked from Mediterranean ports. Most of them had come from Eastern and Central European countries and had reached Italy and France either through the Allied occupation zones in Germany and Austria or through Yugoslavia. That a total of almost thirty-seven thousand Jewish refugees were able to depart from Italian and French ports relatively unhindered is one indication that Britain's diplomatic campaign against the *Ha'apala* movement was not much more successful here than in the Soviet bloc countries.

Italy was the main base for the illegal sailings after World War II. Of the fifty-six *Ha'apala* ships that sailed between the end of the war and the establishment of the State of Israel, thirty-four set out from Italy, carrying more than twenty-one thousand persons, or about 30 percent of the total. Britain's campaign to halt the movement was waged on two fronts: the first against the Jews infiltrating into Italy from the north, and the second against Jews who had made it into Italy and from there attempted to sail for Palestine. The Italians themselves were much more concerned about the Jewish influx of the Jews into the country than about their departures by sea.

Relations between Britain and Italy during the first two years after the war were characterized by mutual dislike, if not hostility. This may have been in part because Britain was not prepared to show much leniency toward Italy's wartime record. Italy had declared war on Britain and France on 10 June 1940 and eighteen months later had joined Germany in declaring war on the United States. On 8 September 1943 Italy surrendered unconditionally to the Allies (about six weeks after Benito Mussolini's government had been overthrown), and on 13 October it declared war on Germany. After the war, the Big Three Allies were divided over how to treat Italy. Differences prevailed also between the two English-speaking powers. At the Potsdam Conference, Truman proposed that Italy be released from the restrictions placed on it after its surrender and that it be allowed to join the United Nations. In support of his suggestion, the U.S. president stated Italy's readiness to join the Allies in the war against Japan. Churchill was less conciliatory. Opposing Truman's proposal, he recalled Italy's attack on Britain at the time of the fall of France, the fierce North African campaign Italy had waged, and the heavy casualties the British fleet had suffered in battles against the Italian navy in the Mediterranean. It was eventually agreed at Potsdam that the peace treaty with Italy would be the first to be dealt with by the Council of Foreign Ministers that was to prepare the peace settlements with the former enemy countries. America's lenient attitude toward Italy was due in no small part to electoral considerations, that is, the president's wish to gain the Italian and Catholic vote in upcoming elections.

The first CFM, convened in London on 11 September 1945, dispersed after three weeks without reaching any agreement. The Western powers objected to Soviet demands that the USSR be awarded trusteeship over Tripolitania for a ten-year period, that the whole of Venezia Giulia, including the city of Trieste, be transferred to Yugoslavia, and that Italy pay heavy war reparations to the Soviet Union. Although the three Western powers were not in accord about the future boundary between Italy and Yugoslavia and the future of Italy's colonies, they all opposed the Soviet demands, in particular any arrangement that would give the Soviets a foothold in the Mediterranean region, the Middle East, or North Africa. The controversy over the terms of the Italian peace treaty remained unresolved during the first session of the CFM in Paris (25 April–16 May 1946). The Americans defended Italian interests. A compromise was reached at the second session of the CFM in Paris according to which Trieste would be internationalized and the decision about the future of the colonies would be postponed for one year while their administration would be left in British hands in the interim. For their part, the Soviets were to receive reparations of $100 million.

The peace agreement that was signed in February 1947 forbade the Italians to possess tanks, submarines, and bombers. Italy's army was limited to 250,000 soldiers, including 65,000 *carabinieri*, and its navy and air force to 25,000 personnel each. Most Italian navy ships were to be divided between the United States, Britain, France, the Soviet Union, Greece, and Yugoslavia. Italy was to pay $360 million in war damages. Britain received control over Tripolitania,

Eritrea, and Italian Somalia, while Albania and Ethiopia regained independence. In Europe, Italy was obliged to relinquish territory to Greece, France, and Yugoslavia. It was also compelled to demilitarize its frontiers and dismantle its fortifications. The Italian Constitutional Assembly approved the treaty on 31 July 1947.[1]

Politically the postwar situation in Italy proved most problematic. In December 1945, Alcide de Gasperi, leader of the Christian Democrats, formed a coalition government in which the Communists participated. The first postwar elections were held six months later, in June 1946. The Christian Democrats received 35 percent of the votes, the Socialists 21 percent, and the Communists 19 percent. The Socialists and Communists established a united front. Following a plebiscite on 2 June the Italian monarchy was terminated; King Umberto abdicated and left the country. In January 1947 the Socialist Party split, and a majority of its members together with its leader, Pietro Nenni, joined the Communist Party. On 13 May 1947, de Gasperi formed his fourth government, this time without the Communists. Communist Party representatives participated in September in the founding congress of the Cominform. During the winter of 1947–48 Western leaders began to fear that the Italian Communists might exploit the difficult economic situation and the evacuation of the last British and American troops from Italy in December 1947 to sabotage the Marshall Plan, topple the government, and mount a Communist coup d'état by means of strikes and demonstrations. Thus the elections set for April 1948 were seen as a test of strength for de Gasperi's pro-Western orientation in light of the escalation of the Cold War. Both the United States and the Soviet Union tried to influence the choice of the Italian voters. De Gasperi's Christian Democrats secured about 48.5 percent of the votes compared with 31 percent for the Communists and Socialists. Holding 305 of the 574 seats in the Chamber, the Christian Democrats had been able to secure an absolute majority.[2]

The fragility of the political system stemmed partly from Italy's deteriorating economic situation. Italy had suffered greatly from the battles that had taken place in the country toward the end of the war; a large proportion of its industry, transportation infrastructure, schools, hospitals, and railroad stations had been destroyed. The Italian merchant fleet, which in 1938 had been the fourth largest in Europe, had shrunk from 3.5 million tons to only 450,000 tons. Agricultural production dwindled in 1945 to 60 percent of 1938 levels, and industrial production at the end of 1945 was one-quarter of what it had been during the period just before the war. The national debt at the end of the war was more than six times the amount it had been in 1939, and prices in 1945 were twenty times what they had been before the war and were still rising. Inflation and unemployment reached astronomical proportions. As a result, between the time of Italy's surrender and the end of the war, the country was completely dependent on foreign assistance. The United States supplied it with most of its vital food provisions, and later UNRRA provided most of the foreign aid. The Americans, who financed about 75 percent of the organization's budget, played a central role in setting the scope and selecting the recipients of the UNRRA assistance. After UNRRA's activity was terminated at the end of June 1947, Washington extended assistance to Italy until Marshall Plan aid became available.[3]

British-Italian relations began to improve in the second half of 1947, at the time that tensions were increasing between the West and the USSR. The Italians felt resentment toward Britain following the British stand on the peace arrangements with Italy and the transfer of the Italian colonies to British control. The Italian Left was hostile toward the British for ideological reasons as well. Moreover, Italy was an occupied country under the supervision of the Anglo-American Commission, and the Italians were bitter because Britain objected to rescinding some of the restrictions that had been imposed. What caused Britain to change its approach were fears that Italy would fall into the Soviet sphere of influence. At the end of October 1947, Italian foreign minister Count Carlo Sforza was invited to London. This was the first visit to Britain of an Italian minister since the war. A communiqué at the end of the visit spoke of the renewal of friendship between the two countries and announced their intention to conclude a series of agreements dealing with commerce, shipping, air transport, and culture. A trade agreement was duly signed between the two countries in February 1948.[4]

The La Spezia Episode

With the conclusion of the war, Italy began attracting Holocaust survivors and Eastern and Central European Jews as soon as it became known that the Palestinian Jewish Brigade was stationed in that country. Brigade soldiers helped Jewish refugees who had managed to reach Italy in the migratory wave that swept Europe at the end of the war and also assisted in smuggling Jews across the Austrian border into Italy. Zionist sources estimated that about fifteen thousand Jewish refugees had entered Italy during the three summer months of 1945.[5] With the coming of autumn and winter, the number of infiltrators into Italy declined markedly, mainly because of rumors about hunger and shortages in the camps. The arrival of huge numbers of refugees within a short time, the worsening economic situation in Italy, and the difficulties in receiving help from the JDC were some of the reasons why the situation in the camps deteriorated so soon. Moreover, the Jewish Brigade was transferred at the end of July 1945 to Belgium. But the movement never came to a complete halt, and by early January 1946 Brichah emissaries had managed to transfer most of the refugees from the British zone in Austria to Italy. At the same time, limited movement continued from Rumania and Hungary to Italy via Yugoslavia.[6]

Allied authorities in Italy knew of the movement of Jewish refugees into Italy, but their attempts to stop the infiltration were unsuccessful. According to Philip Broad, the British resident minister in Caserta, the Allied military authorities believed that this movement was "part of a very large organization which aims at using Italy and Austria as a transit camp between Central Europe and Palestine." The British diplomat thought that stopping the migration would require the cooperation of the Allied occupation forces in Austria, especially of the French authorities, who had been allowing the movement of the Jews through their occupation zone to Italy. The possibility of returning the infiltrators to Austria should not even be considered since it would require the use of force, and the Allied Commission (which included the Americans) would not countenance such a move. Although Broad was doubtful whether the Jewish refugees were entitled to UNRRA assistance, he recommended that Britain assist them; otherwise, hunger would drive them into crime.[7] British intelligence estimated the number of Jewish refugees in Italy in October 1945 at twenty thousand.[8]

The British embassy in Rome anticipated that the illegal movement via Italy would intensify by the end of January 1946, when most of the refugee camps would come under UNRRA supervision. UNRRA was already managing four camps in southern Italy, and according to Noel Charles, the British ambassador, the "organization within the camps is in the hands of Jewish committees which hold themselves responsible to the Palestine office in Bari [that is, the Zionists] rather than to their camp managers." Charles also told of "an elaborate organisation throughout Italy which receives parties of illegal immigrants after they have crossed the northern frontiers, arranges for their despatch to camps in the heel and their illegal embarkation for Palestine." The ambassador recommended that Spurgeon M. Keeny, UNRRA director in Italy, be asked to refrain from extending assistance to the illegal Jewish movement and that Jewish Brigade personnel still posted in Italy be transferred to other places. He also thought that the Allied command should cooperate more closely with the Italian security authorities in controlling those entering Italy and that the Italian fleet should be allowed to patrol along the Italian coasts. This last recommendation stemmed from the Italians' claim that they were unable to control departures from the country because the navy was prohibited from patrolling the shores.[9]

Brichah: *On the move (Courtesy Israel Ministry of Defense, Museums Unit)*

Success in the struggle against illegal sailings depended in large part on the cooperation of the Italian authorities. But given Britain's general attitude toward postwar Italy, during the first months after the war various British officials in London had reservations about involving the Italians at all. London also feared that the Italians would predicate their assistance on a relaxation of the military restrictions that had been imposed, particularly on the fleet. Whitehall preferred to use British forces stationed in Italy to take preventive measures in the ports of embarkation. This proposal was countered by Britain's headquarters in Italy, which claimed that it was impossible to stop the illegal sailings to Palestine since most of the Italian ports were not under military control. They urged that the Italian government be asked to prevent vessels involved in the illegal movement from sailing from Italian ports.[10] Following interdepartmental consultation in London in mid-October 1945, it was decided not to seek the cooperation of the Italian government for the time being, in part because doing so would require supplying them with information about ships involved in the illegal movement. Such information might well be leaked to those organizing the sailings, who then could use it to their own advantage.[11]

Reservations, however, evaporated with the detention on 17 January 1946 of the *Enzio Sereni*, which had sailed from Italy with 911 Jewish refugees.[12] With the approaching visit of the Anglo-American Committee Bevin very much wanted the situation in Palestine to remain quiet. At the end of January 1946, the Italian government was asked by Britain to pass legislation that would prohibit its citizens from taking part in any acts connected to the illegal movement.[13] Such legislation was problematic because of the opposition of the Italian left-wing coalition partners to British policy in Palestine. Ambassador Charles was doubtful whether Prime Minister de Gasperi, who had taken office in December 1945, could muster the necessary support for such legislation. But he also thought the Italian government would be unable to comply with the British request for fear of angering the Americans.[14] Aware of the interest in the fate of the Jewish refugees exhibited by the White House, members of Congress, and the American press, the Italians indeed tried to avoid taking steps that would provoke adverse reactions among them. Italy was dependent on American economic assistance and American defense of its interests in the peace treaty deliberations. The Italians were also aware that the British were not making much headway in their efforts to enlist American cooperation against the illegal movement from Austria to Italy.[15] Furthermore, Britain was very unpopular in Italy because of its adamant opposition to the French proposal that Cyrenaica and Tripoli be returned to Italy.

The first direct confrontation between British authorities in Italy and *Ha'apala* organizers and the illegal immigrants themselves occurred after the arrest on 3 April of twelve hundred Jews of "Polish extraction" by Italian police in La Spezia. According to the Allied forces headquarters in Italy, these Jews had all been brought to the port in British military vehicles and had with them food for ten days which had been taken from British army supplies. Headquarters also reported that Jewish soldiers serving in the Palestinian Transport Company of the British army had been involved and that three of them had been arrested.[16] Charles was quick to conclude that the Italian government was ready to assist the British.[17] What the ambassador could not yet have known was that the arrest of the illegal immigrants by the Italians had actually happened by mistake (see below). British Foreign Office officials preferred not to involve British forces stationed in Italy but to leave the issue to the Italian authorities. Very quickly, however, the incident developed into a serious crisis following an announcement by the detained illegal immigrants in La Spezia of a hunger strike and of their intention to sink the boat with all on board if an attempt were made to remove them forcibly to the shore. (The Jewish refugees earlier had been able to board the boat with the connivance of the Italians.)

Harold Laski, chairman of the British Labour Party and himself a Jew, who was then in Italy as the guest of the Twenty-fourth Congress of the Italian Socialist Party, managed to defuse the escalating tension between the British and the illegal immigrants. The latter were headed by Yehuda Arazi (head of the illegal

immigration activities in Italy), who pretended to be a refugee and was leading the struggle in La Spezia. On a visit to the ship on 19 April, Laski reached
an agreement with Arazi that the hunger strike would be suspended and that
the illegal immigrants would not do anything drastic until Laski had met with
Bevin within ten days' time.[18] Meanwhile, Colonial Secretary Hall rejected the
Jewish Agency's request that a special immigration quota be granted to the illegal immigrants in La Spezia. He also refused the alternative suggestion that the
illegal immigrants be given the November–December 1945 quota, which the
Jewish Agency had not exploited at the time in protest against British policy.
Hall warned Attlee that granting the illegal immigrants in La Spezia a special
quota would constitute a breach of the assurance given to the Arabs that until
the AAC's report, Jewish immigration to Palestine would be limited to fifteen
hundred persons per month, including illegal immigrants. Hall, still unaware
of the real circumstances behind the arrest of the illegal immigrants, argued
that if they were allowed to sail, the Italians would no longer cooperate in the
struggle against the illegal sailings. He considered the hunger strike announced
by leaders of the Yishuv to be a political move intended to force the British to
accede to their demands. Hall's analysis was accepted by the prime minister.[19]

As the British soon discovered, the real reason why the Jews were arrested
by the Italian police was a case of mistaken identity. The police commander in
La Spezia had been told that Italian fascists were planning to leave the country
secretly. When his agents came upon the convoy of Jewish refugees, they believed they were arresting those Italian fascists. According to Charles, the police
commander told a Jewish Agency representative that had he known they were
Jewish refugees, he would not have interfered.[20] Charles, who feared the incident might end in bloodshed, called upon his government to decide between
"the risk of violence and bad publicity, on the one hand, and some immediate further concession, on the other." He favored the second alternative. The
ambassador did not dismiss the possibility that Italian naval authorities in La
Spezia would allow the Jews to sail after all.[21] Unhappy with the predicament
they found themselves in, the Italians did not hide their fear of further incidents if the refugees remained in La Spezia.[22] The Mandatory government in
Palestine, which was also apprehensive over the refugees' threats to commit sui-
cide in public if their departure for Palestine was not approved and over the
agitation in Palestine, was in favor of allowing the illegal immigrants to enter
Palestine as part of the monthly quota.[23]

In the confrontation between the British authorities and the *Ha'apala* organizers and Jewish refugees in La Spezia, it was the latter who triumphed. On
8 May the *Dov Hoz* and *Eliahu Golumb* sailed with 1,014 illegal immigrants on

board. The event and the timing were significant. For the British, success in their struggle against the illegal sailings depended largely on preventive measures in the ports of embarkation with the cooperation of the local authorities. In La Spezia the British lost the opportunity to establish a precedent. The incident, which took more than four weeks (from 3 April to 8 May 1946), brought home to the Italians and to other governments what was in store for them if they complied with British demands to prevent *Ha'apala* vessels from departing. Moreover, the wide and sympathetic coverage in the Italian and world media of the struggle of the Jewish refugees trying at all costs to reach Palestine served the propaganda needs of the Zionists (the report of the AAC had been published only a few days before the final resolution of the La Spezia incident). The way the British dealt with the La Spezia incident was influenced not only by the sensitive relations with the Italian authorities but also by the fact that illegal sailings were as yet limited in number and stopping them less urgent because the British at this stage were still hopeful of reaching an agreement with the Americans over the Palestine question.

Meanwhile, the British were working to prevent infiltration of Jews into Italy. Most of the frontier between Austria and Italy passed through the British and French occupation zones but also, for a short stretch, through the American zone. An April 1946 report of British intelligence in Austria noted that since the British maintained rigorous border controls, Jewish refugees from northeastern Europe refrained from entering the British zone of Austria. Rather, from Vienna they moved via the American and Soviet occupation zones to Bavaria and from there to northern Italy via the French zone. This route was chosen because conditions in the American zone were more amenable to the movement of Jewish DPs.[24] The British embassy in Rome was unhappy over the laxity the Italians displayed in their control of the mountain passes, even though in some instances Italian border patrols had prevented the entry of groups of Jews whose laissez-passer documents were found to be unsatisfactory.[25] An inspection carried out by the British at the beginning of July 1946 in the Resia Pass showed that Italian border authorities had no idea who was permitted to enter the country and who not; they did not even know what authority they had in this matter and what documents Allied military personnel needed in order to cross the border. Any person wearing a uniform of one of the Allied powers and presenting some document that appeared to be official was allowed to cross the border. Similarly, any civilian showing the Italian border guards some document signed by a British or American officer was also allowed to enter.[26] That this was no exaggeration is shown by the way Brichah emissaries transferred refugees into Italy with forged laissez-passer documents while disguising them as Allied soldiers or members of the various relief organizations; the Zionist activists clearly took advantage of the large number of military units in Italy, which were allowed to issue travel permits, as well as the numerous relief organizations whose members frequently crossed international frontiers.[27]

The Italians rejected British criticism. The Italian Ministry of the Interior maintained that until April 1946 the border passage had been under the control of Allied soldiers; thus it was they who should have prevented Jewish refugees from entering the country. Furthermore, even after control was transferred to them, the Italians argued, they were unable to stop the infiltration because authority to permit entry and exit remained in Allied hands. The plethora of official and quasi-official Allied bodies allowed to grant travel permits made it difficult for Italian border authorities to fulfill their duties.[28] The Italians tried to take advantage of the importance the British clearly attached to the struggle against the Jewish infiltrators in order to pressure London into partially restoring their sovereignty—by allowing them to monitor their own frontiers even before the peace agreements were signed—but also to let the British help them by transferring foreign refugees to other countries. As far as the Italians were concerned, the Jewish refugees were not the main problem. Of the approximately 158,000 refugees and DPs in Italy at the end of 1946, only an estimated 20,000 were Jewish.[29]

Even more disturbing from the British point of view was the Italians' ineffective control of the country's ports. Charles was of the opinion that the Italian port authorities did nothing to prevent illegal vessels from sailing and that the security police, because they were anxious to be rid of foreign refugees, would never try to confirm the validity of the travel documents embarking passengers were carrying. The British Foreign Office again consulted with the ambassador about how advisable it would be to ask the Italians to pass legislation forbidding any involvement of their citizens in the illegal movement. Charles thought the Italian government probably would not be willing to enact legislation against the illegal Jewish emigration and suggested that it not be pressed on this matter.[30] It was at that time that the Italians became aware of the conditions of their peace agreement and were particularly angered by the decision of the CFM (at the end of June and beginning of July) to postpone for one year the determination of the future of the Italian colonies and until then leave them under British control.[31]

Differences of opinion soon arose between Charles and London over the best way to deal with the illegal sailings from Italy. He disagreed with the suggestion of the chiefs of staff to the cabinet that pressure be exerted on the Italian government and instead advocated reinforcing the British security field units in Italy, allowing them to arrest suspects, and increasing the frequency of Royal Navy patrols along the Italian coast. Charles was aware that his recommendations would "look particularly retrograde as regards Anglo-Italian relations."[32] The Foreign Office had reservations about the ambassador's suggestion of expanding the authority of British security field units—it might be thought that Britain was still acting as though Italy were an occupied enemy country. The office also feared the effect such a step would have on the Americans, their partners in supervising the Italians, who wanted to relax Allied control and grant maximum freedom of action to the Italians.[33]

By this time, the British had changed their policy in Palestine and no longer had reservations about deporting illegal immigrants to detention camps in Cyprus. On 18 August 1946, 1,391 illegal immigrants who had been arrested on the shores of Palestine were transferred to Cyprus. These were all illegal immigrants who had sailed from Italy and the first to be so deported. In a memorandum he sent to the Italian Foreign Ministry immediately following the deportation, Charles stressed that intensifying control over the Italian land frontiers would make it easier for the authorities to prevent the illegal sailings. The ambassador underscored Britain's desire to help the Italian government deal with the infiltrators and noted that instructions had been given to British authorities in Germany and Austria to increase surveillance in the British occupation zones.[34] London preferred to avoid submitting a sharp protest in light of the growing Italian bitterness toward Britain. The steps taken by the British in their occupation zones were of very marginal importance because the movement was taking place for the most part through the American and French occupation zones. British overtures to the Italian authorities did not bring the desired results, and *Ha'apala* ships continued to set sail from Italian ports. Between mid-August and the end of October 1946, six *Ha'apala* vessels arrived in short succession on the shores of Palestine, all having set sail from Italy. Except for the small *Amiram Shohat*, they were all intercepted and their passengers deported to Cyprus.

UNRRA and the JDC

Among the British targets in the campaign against the illegal movement of Jews into and out of Italy were the UNRRA and JDC welfare organizations, some of whose personnel were assisting *Brichah* and *Ha'apala* organizers. The British were concerned about the lack of Italian control of the UNRRA camps housing Jewish refugees who had infiltrated into Italy, since it was clear to them that those in the DP camps and in the *Hachsharot* (vocational training) farms run by the JDC constituted the reservoir of illegal immigrants for the sailings.[35] London wanted the Jews to leave the camps because Whitehall believed that as long as UNRRA continued to feed and house them there, the infiltration would continue. Therefore, the British Foreign Office wished UNRRA to end assistance to them. At a meeting of the Committee of the Council for Europe, UNRRA, in mid-December 1946, British representative George Rendel protested that only 22 percent of the assistance dispensed by UNRRA to refugees in Italy was given to non-Jews even though the Jews constituted only a small percentage of the DPs and refugees in Italy.[36] In his view, "it looked as though UNRRA had been very much concentrating on relief of Jewish refugees to the exclusion of non-Jewish refugees." Since it was not to be expected that the Jews in Italy would return to the countries from which they had come, they should be classified as "non-repatriables." UNRRA policy stipulated that assistance to that category was to be limited in time, and therefore, Rendel seemed to be implying, aid to such Jews should be stopped. He warned of the danger that the camps would become bases for illegal sailings to Palestine and emphasized the importance of avoiding suspicion that the organization was abetting or encouraging the illegal movement.[37] But Rendel's attempts to end UNRRA assistance failed.

The Italians were careful not to assert their authority over the camps for fear of losing UNRRA aid and angering the American Jewish community.[38] London believed that only an appeal from the United States could persuade the Italian authorities to act energetically. When Irgun members bombed the British embassy in Rome (31 October 1946), it provided Bevin with the excuse he needed to ask Byrnes to urge the Italian government to exercise its authority in the camps. Bevin argued that the UNRRA camps in southern Italy "virtually represent an extreme Zionist enclave on Italian territory; the inmates are known to be drawing excessive quantities of rations and clothing from UNRRA which provide them via the black market with large supplies of Italian money; and the camps are believed to be full of hidden arms." Bevin maintained that no one knew how many Jews were staying in them but that there was no doubt that the camps were serving as illegal immigration training sites.[39] At the beginning of January 1947 the British and Americans separately appealed to the Italian government to take charge of UNRRA camps in which the Jewish refugees were concentrated.[40] In its note, the U.S. government expressed concern at reports that DP camps in Italy "may be in use as centers and screens for perpetrators of acts of terrorism." The Italian government was asked to increase its efforts to control DP camps and the movements of DPs in Italy, "so as to prevent irregularities which might contribute in any way to further acts of terrorism."[41]

Instead of responding, the Italian Foreign Ministry complained to the Allies about the latter's lack of supervision of the UNRRA camps in Germany and

Austria and about the involvement of Allied authorities in the Jewish infiltration into Italy. The ministry warned that no improvement would take place "if the Allied authorities do not prevent their subordinate authorities from interfering with the action taken by Italian authorities, particularly as regards the entry into Italy of foreigners, whether Jewish or not, and if they do not facilitate the general removal of the refugees who in the past have entered Italy." [42] Still, the Italian Foreign Ministry realized that some action was needed to assuage the British. Accordingly, toward the end of March 1947, the Italians informed the British embassy that the infiltration of Jewish refugees into Italy had not stopped and that with improved weather conditions it could be expected to expand. The number of DPs in Italy who were receiving aid from UNRRA had increased since November 1946 by approximately six thousand. Despite more frequent patrols, the Italian police force was having difficulty in guarding the border because of its length, because of insufficient resources, and because of the assistance the infiltrators were receiving from people affiliated with UNRRA and the JDC and sometimes even from Allied soldiers. These illegal immigrants were not really DPs since they had abandoned their homelands of their own free will and thus were not entitled to UNRRA assistance. Moreover, such aid "contributes indirectly to encourage further clandestine immigration into Palestine." The Italian Foreign Ministry reported that it had instructed its embassy in London to urge the European headquarters of UNRRA to deny assistance in Italy to those who had suddenly abandoned the DP camps in Austria or Germany or to those who had willingly left their homelands and to take measures in the UNRRA camps in Germany and Austria to make it impossible for the refugees to infiltrate into Italy. The Italians further announced that they would start concentrating the infiltrators in special camps until a decision was reached about their future. Britain was asked to support the Italian demands submitted to UNRRA. [43]

Charles welcomed the Italian initiative and especially the willingness of the Italian government to declare in an official letter that UNRRA was aiding the illegal Jewish movement. The ambassador advised his government to give its wholehearted support to the protest the Italian government had made to UNRRA. He also urged the British Foreign Office to prepare for the transfer of authority from UNRRA to IRO to prevent the new organization from serving as a cover for organizers of the illegal movement. The ambassador's suspicions in that direction had been aroused when he heard that the top leadership of UNRRA in Italy was due to move to IRO. [44]

UNRRA was only part of the British problem in Italy. According to Ambassador Charles, most of the illegal Jewish activity in Italy was occurring under the auspices of the JDC, which was using most of its budget to finance infiltration into Italy and subsequent illegal sailings. Charles stressed that, given the decisive role the JDC played in the illegal movement, everything possible should be done to curb its power. He was aware of the sensitive nature of the matter for Anglo-American relations and of the apprehension that a British attack on the JDC would be represented as an attempt on the part of the British to prevent aid and assistance to persecuted Jews. Therefore, he advocated preventing the JDC from taking part in IRO as it had in UNRRA.[45]

Italy's readiness to protest to the European headquarters of UNRRA about the assistance the latter's personnel were rendering the illegal Jewish movement probably was motivated by its efforts to reenter the international community following the signing of the peace treaty—the Italians were well aware of Britain's ability to obstruct their acceptance in various international organizations. The fact that UNRRA was to end its work within a few weeks and disband also had some influence. At that point Rome no longer had to worry that attacking the organization might harm the country's interests. Moreover, complaining to UNRRA was the easiest and most elegant way to dissociate itself from what was happening in the camps and to avoid the risk of incidents with Jewish DPs.

Charles's satisfaction with the Italian government's gesture of goodwill, however, was short-lived. The hiatus in *Ha'apala* sailings from Italy lasted four months and ended in March 1947 with the embarkation of two vessels, the *Shabtai Lujinsky* and the *Moledet* (Hebrew: Homeland). This time the British embassy in Rome firmly warned the Italian Foreign Ministry that if any more illegal immigrants were to sail from Italy, the British government would demand that they be returned to Italy. Charles pointed out that according to information available to the British, the organizers of the illegal sailings intended to send a large number of Jews to Palestine during the next two or three months.[46] Britain's recently announced decision to transfer the Palestine question to the United Nations was coupled with fears of an inundation of illegal immigrants into Palestine. London was also furious with the Italians over rumors that Prime Minister de Gasperi had acceded to the request of Rafael Kantoni, head of the united Jewish community in Italy, to allow ten thousand Jews to enter the country.[47]

It fell to Francesco Fransoni, secretary general of the Italian Foreign Ministry, to respond. The Italian government, he claimed, was just as interested as the British government in ending the exploitation of its country and preventing Jews from infiltrating via its northern frontiers, but it could not act to that end because of the armistice and peace agreements, which forbade Italy to maintain a sufficiently large military and police force. It was not the fault of the

Italian government that the military authorities of the United States and France in Germany and Austria were encouraging the illegal movement of Jews to Italy. When the Jews reached Italy, Fransoni continued, they were received immediately in the UNRRA camps, where the standard of living was much higher than that of the local Italian population. Their preferred status made it easier for them to sail from Italian shores while the shortage of police personnel was preventing the authorities from adequately monitoring the country's shoreline.[48] The Italians did not conceal from the British the fact that because of increased infiltration into Italy, prevention of the illegal sailings would be against Italy's interests, since there were no alternative routes of departure and the number of Jewish refugees in the country was rising steadily. They repeated their appeal to the British to support the Italian request vis-à-vis UNRRA and to grant preference to Jews presently in Italy in Palestine immigration quotas.[49]

Despite Fransoni's critical tone, the British embassy in Rome was encouraged by the Italian reaction. Charles believed that the Italian authorities, including the prime minister and the foreign minister, were now interested in accommodating Britain. Until then, he maintained, the Italian government had demonstrated "extreme reluctance" to stop Jewish refugees from leaving Italy. British satisfaction derived in part from the instructions issued by the head of the Division of Public Safety and General Affairs at the Ministry of Interior, Dr. Giuseppe Migliore, to the police department to do all it could to prevent infiltration from Austria, including permission to shoot to kill if necessary. Migliore even suggested to the British that all infiltrators entering Italy starting from a certain date be concentrated on the island of Ustica and kept there until it became possible to return them to their own countries or to transfer them somewhere else. The plan was intended to prevent new infiltrators, whose arrival was expected with the advent of summer, from intermingling with groups of refugees already in the camps. Migliore thought that the plan would facilitate monitoring of the movement of refugees in Italy. He emphasized that there would be room on the island for six thousand persons and that therefore it would be necessary to remove refugees from the island on a regular basis.[50]

Confounding British Strategies

The British embassy was also optimistic because the Italians had instructed the port authorities throughout the country to monitor and report on vessels suspected of being involved in illegal sailings and to delay supplying them with fuel. The ambassador was present when Fransoni appealed to the naval chief of staff as well as the minister of the merchant navy to make every effort to delay the departure of the *President Warfield* (later known as the *Exodus*), then anchored in Portovenere near La Spezia. Bevin explained to Sforza, the Italian foreign minister, that he considered it to be of the utmost importance to prevent the ship from sailing to Palestine. While appreciating the importance the British ascribed to this ship, the Italians were willing to delay the sailing only for several days.[51] This was not enough for London, and Charles made it clear to the Italians that if the *President Warfield* were eventually to sail for Palestine, Britain would demand that the Italian government take back the passengers once they were intercepted. The ambassador also hinted that relations between the two countries could be harmed.[52] British pressure caused the Italian authorities to delay the boat's departure for several weeks and to prevent anyone from going on board.[53] Eventually, on 12 June 1947, the authorities allowed the *President Warfield* to sail, without Jewish refugees, accompanied by an Italian warship until it had entered French territorial waters.[54]

The *President Warfield* was not the only source of difficulties. At the beginning of May, the British embassy in Rome learned that local authorities in Palermo had provided coal to an illegal immigration ship (the *Anal*) although only a few weeks earlier the British had asked the Italians to prevent fuel from being supplied to vessels involved in illegal sailings.[55] In response to British protests, the secretary general of the Italian Foreign Ministry argued that international law obliged them to furnish the ship with at least as much fuel as was needed to reach the nearest port. Fransoni, however, also admitted that the Italian government had been eager to be rid of the ship and its unwanted passengers.[56] On 13 May 1947, the *Anal,* renamed the *Yehuda Halevi,* was detained on the shores of Palestine. The vessel, which had set out from Algeria, had been anchored for three days at Palermo. The coal provided there, Charles protested to the Italian Foreign Ministry, had enabled the vessel to complete its journey to Palestine.[57]

By spring of 1947 London had decided to start deporting illegal immigrants detained on Palestinian shores back to their ports of embarkation. The Foreign Office was inclined to activate this policy first toward Italy and then broaden its application to other countries.[58] Implementation, however, necessitated obtaining the agreement of the Italian government. London knew of Italian concern over the expected American reactions, especially by the influential Jewish community there, if Italy were to help Britain in the struggle against the illegal sailings. The Italian government, Charles stated, "is terrified of doing anything which would annoy the Government or public opinion in the United States upon whom Italy depends so much in a material sense for its food, fuel, etc."[59] In an effort to soften Italy's opposition, Bevin called Sforza's attention to the

announcement Truman had made on 5 June 1947 calling on the American public to act in accordance with the decision taken by the United Nations on 15 May
1947 and to avoid any moves that might hurt efforts to resolve the Palestine
issue. He also warned the Italians, who wished to join the UN, not to ignore the
memorandum sent by UN general secretary Trygve Lie asking countries to take
stringent measures to prevent the passage or embarkation of Jews attempting
to enter Palestine illegally.[60]

With summer approaching, British fears increased concerning the infiltration of large numbers of Rumanian Jews into Italy seeking to sail from there to
Palestine. At the beginning of June, Charles informed Sforza that most of the
infiltrations into Italy occurred in the Bolzano region, from the French occupation zone. Noting Italian ineffectiveness, Charles expressed concern over the
success of relatively large groups in entering the country despite intensified
monitoring of the borders and the daily deportation of Jewish groups back to
Austria. He warned that if drastic action were not taken, organized mass infiltration could be expected. Charles promised Sforza British support for any
appeal about controlling the movement of the Jews that the Italian government
might address to the neighboring countries.[61]

British embassy officials, however, were skeptical about the willingness and
ability of the Italian authorities to stop the infiltration via the northern border
and to supervise the Jewish refugees in the country. The whole Italian administration, Charles maintained, "is chaotic and corrupt by our standards and their
police force is inadequate." Moreover, the Communist and other elements in
the Italian administration were "most glad to see the Allies embarrassed in this
way." Migliore's plan to concentrate the infiltrators on the island of Ustica, it was
maintained, appeared impractical because the chances that the United Nations
or the British government would agree to guarantee the removal of infiltrators
from Italy seemed meager. Embassy personnel believed that public opinion,
especially in the United States, would not allow the Italians "to establish a concentration camp for Jews administered with the degree of severity necessary to
prevent escapes." The inevitable conclusion was that until the American and
French occupation authorities cooperated, the Italians would not attempt to
close their frontiers.[62]

Charles's skepticism was not misplaced. Although the Italians agreed to enlist the help of an English expert in the struggle against Jewish infiltration, they
made it clear that intensified steps to monitor the frontier would be of no use
as long as the French were allowing refugees detained at the Italian border to
enter the country by another route. Migliore suggested to the British ambassador "that all illegal Jewish entrants in the Austrian frontier zone should be

handed over to the authorities of the British zone who could keep them in properly supervised camps and, where possible, return them to refugee camps in Germany from which they originated." The message was clear: since Britain was not able to convince the French and the Americans to take back the Jewish infiltrators, Britain should shoulder the burden if it wanted the cooperation of the Italians. Charles, aware of the implications of Migliore's proposal, was of the opinion that in view of the illegal mass emigration from Rumania and the anticipated increase in pressure on the Italian borders, perhaps it was advisable for Britain to accept refugees who had been infiltrated into Italy into the British zone in Austria in order to gain the cooperation of the Italians.[63] British military authorities in Austria strongly opposed this suggestion, arguing that since the French and the Americans were allowing Jews to leave, the burden that could be expected to fall on the British zone would be very heavy. W. H. B. Mack, the advisory British political representative in Austria, observed that since June 1946 the illegal immigration of Jews via the British zone had stopped almost completely and that there were now only eighteen hundred persons in Admont Camp.[64]

Although infiltration into Italy continued during the summer of 1947, the feeling in the British embassy in Rome at the beginning of August was that the Italian Foreign Ministry was keen to display goodwill and a readiness to cooperate.[65] Zionist sources indicated that the heavy pressure exerted by the British on the Italian authorities had begun to have an effect by spring 1947. Both national and local authorities stopped aiding organizers of the movement, which meant that they were forced again to act clandestinely, as they had done during the first year after the war.[66] That the Italians had joined the British and French initiative following Marshall's speech at Harvard and wanted to avoid unnecessary confrontations with Britain also played a part. The British, however, realized that willingness of the Italians to act decisively against infiltrators into the country was one aspect of the problem; the other was their ability to do so. A British expert, sent to check out the Italians' method of monitoring their border with Austria, asserted that the Italian border police were not equipped to cope with the organized Jewish movement, especially as movement organizers had different and much greater means at their disposal than did the border police.[67]

News of the impending sailing of an alleged seventeen thousand illegal immigrants from the Black Sea (the *Pan* vessels) meant that the capacity of the camps on Cyprus would soon be overstretched. Britain braced itself for an all-out attempt to prevent additional embarkations from other places. Italy was considered to contain the highest risk, since the number of potential illegal immigrants there was estimated at twenty-eight thousand, and the seven vessels then anchored in Italian ports and suspected of involvement in the illegal sailings had a capacity of about thirteen thousand places.[68] The British Foreign Office and the British embassy in Italy decided to take advantage of Sforza's planned visit to Britain at the end of October to ensure Italian help in preventing the illegal sailings. G. J. Ward, the British chargé d'affaires, told Sforza of Bevin's personal interest in the illegal sailings and warned that any serious incident could put a damper on his visit. According to him, as long as a large number of illegal vessels were anchored in Italian ports, the threat of such an incident persisted.[69]

Vittorio Zopi, the director of political affairs in the Italian Foreign Ministry, asserted that the Italian government had no legal authority to detain suspicious ships for an unlimited period of time when it was clear that they did not intend to violate the law by taking on board Jews from inside Italy. Zopi referred to the *Exodus* affair. Ward responded that the Italian government had enabled the Jews to transform Italy into a "workshop for fitting out" illegal ships. This policy, he stressed, was tantamount to allowing the Jews to sail from Italian shores. As the circumstances were sensitive, Zopi eventually promised to take action to delay the controversial vessels in the ports but emphasized the difficulty in detaining ships that were flying foreign flags.[70] It was clear to the British Foreign Office that to encourage the Italians to check the illegal embarkations, it would be necessary to prevent more Jews from entering Italy.[71] Subsequent efforts were directed at the American and French military authorities in Austria to convince them to take action to halt the infiltration of Jews into Italy.[72]

Despite the success of Sforza's visit to London and the tokens of goodwill on the part of the British, Italian willingness to assist the British in their struggle against the illegal movement did not markedly increase. British intelligence reported that after a period of limited activities during September, the illegal movement had reached the worrisome number of about a thousand border crossings during October 1947 and that if not for the dearth of space in the IRO camps in Italy, the Jewish organizations would have accelerated the infiltration. It was presumed that the rate of infiltration was dependent on the number of departures and that therefore the Jewish organizations were doing all they could to increase the frequency of the sailings.[73] Zionist sources confirmed this assessment. At the beginning of November a *Ha'apala* emissary reported, "Entry to Benjamin [Italy] continues. In October about 1,800 persons entered. The situation in the camps is terrible beyond description. Still, the slow stream continues. The fact that the exit is not progressing makes the situation unbearable."[74] In mid-November, Jacob L. Trobe, director of the JDC in Italy, put the number of Jews who had entered Italy during the previous half year at ten thousand. The JDC itself set up a camp for Jewish infiltrators at Chiari near Milan.[75]

During the winter of 1947–48, Victor A. Mallet, the new British ambassador in Rome, had to report that the Italian authorities refused to stop ships if there was no legal basis to do so and that they might well oppose the return of illegal immigrants who had sailed from Italy and been deported from Palestine.[76] At the beginning of December 1947, Mallet protested to the Italian Foreign Ministry for having allowed one of the ships, the *Giovanni Maria,* on the list of vessels suspected of involvement in the illegal immigration submitted to Zopi about two months previously, to set sail, though admittedly without passengers.[77] At the end of the month, the *Giovanni Maria,* now called the *Kaf-Tet Benovember* (Hebrew: 29 November, the day the UN passed its partition resolution), carrying 680 passengers, was intercepted along the shores of Palestine after having sailed from Corsica. Only five days previously another ship, the *Lo Tafhidunu* (Hebrew: You Can't Intimidate Us), that also had sailed from Italy, had been detained carrying 884 passengers.

In its reply to the British protest, the Italian Foreign Ministry argued that the ability of the Jewish immigrants to evade Italian control and to set sail for Palestine was not all that surprising since these were people "who have already succeeded in eluding the vigilance of the public of other states in Central Europe and the Allied military occupation authorities themselves in Germany and Austria and since not infrequently these elements succeeded in landing in Palestine without even the British Forces being able to prevent them."[78] Fransoni maintained that the success of a few ships in sailing from Italian ports should not be interpreted to mean that the Italian government lacked good intentions or that it had not taken a clear decision to prevent such sailings. Rather, it was due to the extensive resources at the disposal of the Jewish organizations, on the one hand, and the lack of policemen and resources in Italy, on the other.[79]

In their contacts with the British, the Italians kept referring to the power and sophistication of the Jewish "organization" responsible for the illegal movement. Mallet reported to London that the vice-director of political affairs in the Italian Foreign Ministry, for example, was doubtful as to "the success of any attack on such a powerful organization, and whether any legal or other action which could be taken against the organizers would achieve more than a momentary interference with their plan."[80] As the Italian authorities, including Foreign Ministry officials, maintained some connections with *Ha'apala* organizers in Italy (particularly with Ada Sereni, who since April 1947 was responsible for the *Ha'apala* in Italy), this description may well have been a deliberate exaggeration intended to explain the Italians' lack of success and their unwillingness actually to prevent the sailings.[81]

In any case, from the end of 1947 until the establishment of the State of Israel in May 1948, Italy was again the main embarkation base, in terms of the number of vessels leaving from its ports. In mid-February 1948, disappointed by the continuing infiltration into the country, the British informed the Italians of their decision to recall the British liaison officer who had been sent to advise them in their struggle against the infiltration of Jewish refugees. The British government, the ambassador noted, had reached the conclusion that the hopes it had placed on the appointment of the liaison officer had not been realized, through no fault of the person himself.[82]

Summing up, from the end of World War II until the establishment of the State of Israel, close to fifty thousand Jewish refugees clandestinely entered Italy, and of these twenty-one thousand sailed for Palestine. The British very quickly grasped the connection between infiltration into Italy and the illegal embarkations, and securing the northern border became a central link in the campaign against the illegal sailings from Italy. As most of the countries from or through which the illegal movement was being conducted were within the Soviet sphere of influence, Britain was physically cut off from the arena of events. Italy was under semi-British control and tens of thousands of British soldiers were stationed there, yet this was not enough to prevent the infiltration of Jewish refugees and the illegal sailings. Not only were the British unable to activate British soldiers against the illegal movement, since this would have been interpreted as an infringement of Italian sovereignty, but they could not ignore the positions of the Americans, their partners in supervising Italy. Moreover, British hints of potential harm to the relations between the two countries were not enough to make the Italians invest more than minimal efforts in preventing the movement.

While the Italian authorities were interested in preventing Jewish refugees from entering the country, they attached only secondary importance to the struggle against such infiltration because the burden of supporting the refugees did not have to fall on their shaky economy. Also, it was clear to them that the Jews entering Italy intended to continue to Palestine. It was precisely the *Ha'apala* embarkations from Italian shores that meant they could expect the Jewish refugees to leave the country again. The Italians also feared further incidents such as that of La Spezia which could adversely affect their standing with the United States. The British understood that among the prime factors influencing Rome's position were the extensive political power that the Italians attributed to the Jewish community in the United States and the dependence of the Italian government on American political and economic assistance. The Italian authorities were well aware that UNRRA, which was furnishing Italy with large amounts of provisions, was headed by political figures whose main field of activity was New York and who did not hide their sympathy for the Jewish refugees.

Washington's position in the matter is made clear by the British failure to convince the Americans to prevent the refugee movement via their occupation zones and by the American objections to accepting back Jewish infiltrators who had been arrested in Italy or in the French zone. American policy not only made it easier for Jewish DPs to continue on their way; it also gave legitimization to French willingness to allow them to continue on to Italy through the French zone in Austria and to refuse to accept back those who were detained there. Sympathy for the Jewish refugees, bitterness toward the British occupation authorities in Italy, and indignation over London's attitude toward Italy even though it had joined the Allied side in 1943 also influenced the willingness of some important Italian officials and of the "man in the street" to help the Jewish infiltrators and the *Ha'apala*. To this should be added the opposition of various circles in Italy, especially among the Left, to what they saw as Britain's imperialist policies in Palestine.[83] The continuing decline in British power, especially during 1947, as evident in the serious economic crisis and the gradual disintegration of the empire, undoubtedly made it easier for the Italians to ignore London's demands. When relations improved between the two countries, it had only a limited effect on the Italians' treatment of the Jewish refugees.

FRANCE
MANIPULATIONS

Approximately one-quarter of the ships participating in illegal sailings after the war sailed from French harbors. Some of the Jewish refugees heading for Palestine entered France via the Allied occupation zones in Germany and Austria, while others came through Belgium. *Ha'apala* vessels, furthermore, were fitted out and provisioned in French ports. Overall relations between Britain and France clearly affected British efforts to bring the French authorities to act with determination against the illegal Jewish migration. Disagreements between Britain and France over the shape of the postwar world were a main factor clouding their relations for many months after the war.

Policy toward Germany constituted the main bone of contention. The French wanted to prevent Germany once and for all from being able to regain its military-industrial capacity. They were in favor of separating the region of the west bank of the Rhine, detaching the industrial region of the Ruhr with its five million inhabitants from Germany, and integrating the Saar with its mines into the French economy. The British objected to these proposals — separation of the Ruhr, the economic heartland of Germany, would have negative repercussions on the British occupation zone but also, and far more important, on the economy of Europe as a whole. In addition, London feared creating conditions for German irredentism. But the French remained set against a unified Germany and torpedoed British efforts to establish a central economic administration in Germany as had been decided at the Potsdam Conference. These disagreements about Germany were compounded by French resentment at having been ejected from Syria and Lebanon by the British.

Whitehall's strategy was to strengthen relations with Paris. Bevin regarded an Anglo-French alliance as the cornerstone of his foreign policy. London's efforts at Yalta to have an occupation zone in Germany allocated to the French and to have France included among the great powers—thus making it the fifth permanent member of the UN Security Council—stemmed in large measure from the British belief that as soon as the Americans withdrew their forces from Europe, France was the only power remaining in Western Europe that could share the burden of defending Western interests. Together the two countries were to form a counterweight to Germany or Russia while their cooperation could also help improve Britain's position vis-à-vis the United States. General Charles de Gaulle, however, made acceptance of Bevin's, and earlier Churchill's, initiative for an alliance between the two countries conditional on settlement of the disagreement over Germany and the Levant. But even when De Gaulle suddenly resigned, on 20 January 1946, and the problem of the Levant was resolved at the beginning of March, this did not bring about an improvement in relations between the two countries. The main obstacle at the time was France's demand that an independent state be established in the Ruhr. The differences between the two countries continued during the first session of the Council of Foreign Ministers (in April–May 1946) and the peace conference that followed in Paris. Relations between Britain and France took a turn for the better at the end of 1946, culminating in the signing at Dunkirk, on 4 March 1947, of a treaty of "alliance and mutual assistance" between the two countries. French-British cooperation further expanded after Secretary of State Marshall's speech on 5 June 1947 when the two foreign ministers, Bevin and Georges Bidault, led the nations of Western Europe in responding favorably to Marshall's initiative.

As with Italy, both London and Washington were concerned after the war about the instability of the political situation in France and the possibility that the Communists would gain control. In the October 1945 elections, the Communist Party emerged as the largest party with 151 delegates and five million voters (receiving 26 percent of all the votes cast) while in the elections of June 1946 the Mouvement Républicain Populaire (MRP) came up as the leading party, with Bidault serving as both premier and foreign minister. About five months later, in the November elections, the Communists regained the lead, receiving 28 percent of the vote, while the MRP received 26 percent and the Socialists 18 percent. Only in the middle of January 1947 did a coalition government of the three large parties headed by the Socialist Paul Ramadier take office. But this lasted only four months, and in May 1947 the Communists joined the opposition. By October–November 1947 the situation was critical. The Communists, who had failed in their efforts to return to the coalition, began, apparently on instructions of the Cominform, to organize mass strikes, forcing

Premier Ramadier to resign on 19 November. Léon Blum, the veteran Socialist leader, failed in his attempts to gain a parliamentary majority, and MRP representative Robert Schuman was appointed premier, serving in that office until July 1948.[1]

Asylum for Jewish Refugees

French policy of granting temporary asylum to thousands of Jewish refugees and laissez-passers to additional refugees inevitably piqued London, for whom these Jews were all potential candidates for illegal sailings to Palestine. Reports reaching London made it clear that French consuls did not bother to ascertain whether applicants for transit permits already had visas for their final destinations.[2] The French argued that their government had no legal basis for refusing to issue transit permits in cases where the country of destination had declared its willingness to accept the immigrants. Brichah activists were quick to exploit this policy. Forging entrance visas for destination countries and thus obtaining French laissez-passers without difficulty, they were able to transfer large groups of refugees to French ports from where they then sailed to Palestine.[3]

Given British pressure, toward the end of August 1946 the French informed the British of new regulations for the issuing of laissez-passers via France to individual Jews and for the temporary absorption of groups of Jewish immigrants. This policy, the French told the British, was intended to reconcile "its humanitarian duty toward Jewish refugees with that of preventing illegal immigration into countries of ultimate destination." In an agreement reached with the Jewish Association for Assistance to Exiles and Refugees (L'Assistance aux Déportés et Réfugiés), which served as the representative of all Jewish organizations in France, the association took upon itself to ascertain that every Jew entering France received a personal entrance visa for a specific country of destination. The number of persons in this category who would be allowed to stay in France at any given time was limited to one thousand. A maximum quota of seven thousand was also set for Jewish immigrants arriving in groups. Quai d'Orsay stressed that these steps were sufficient to deal with attempts at illegal emigration from France.[4]

Unable to convince France to stop granting temporary asylum to Jewish refugees, the British scuttled an attempt by the French to transfer some of their own obligations for the support of such refugees to the Inter-Governmental Committee on Refugees. IGCR director Herbert Emerson (a British citizen) rejected requests from voluntary organizations in France that eight thousand refugees, mostly Polish Jews, who had made it into France, be recognized as displaced persons and granted financial assistance.[5] London hoped that the financial burden of supporting the refugees would force the French to change their policy. From the British point of view, entry of Jewish refugees into France was only one aspect of the problem. Another was the movement of Jewish refugees via the French occupation zones in Germany and Austria. Reports reaching London during the summer of 1946 spoke of assistance extended by the French military authorities in Austria to Jewish DPs moving toward Italy.[6] Contacts between London and Paris on this matter had already taken place at the beginning of 1946 when the British realized that since the end of the war about thirteen thousand Jewish DPs had reached Italy via the French occupation zone.[7] The French were not living up to their commitment to intensify their surveillance of the border between their zone and that of the Americans and to refrain from issuing laissez-passers to Italy without being shown the necessary documents.[8] Not interested in having more DPs in their occupation zone, the French, on the one hand, allowed Jews to move on to Italy while, on the other, they supported the British in their disputes with the Americans on policy toward Jewish infiltrators from the east. For example, at a session of the Directorate of Prisoners of War and Displaced Persons in mid-September 1946, the French delegate rejected the American request that the burden involved in supporting the Jewish refugees arriving from Eastern Europe be shared and, instead, urged that everything possible be done to stop the illegal movement.[9]

London remained unimpressed by these declarations, knowing what policies the French were pursuing in practice (the Soviets had adopted similar tactics of maintaining a discrepancy between the declarative and the practical level). For example, the Italian Foreign Ministry complained at the time to the British that the French authorities "do not show themselves sufficiently rigorous in forbidding the passage over into Italy, whereas they are rigorous as regards passage in the opposite direction, even when the Italian authorities request the expulsion of an alien caught immediately after having clandestinely crossed the frontier; therefore, this frontier does not constitute any obstacle."[10] For their part, the French accused the American authorities of allowing refugee movement via their occupation zones and making it difficult for them to cope with the problem. They even claimed that the Americans were running military trains to France carrying Jewish refugees who had no transit permits or visas to any countries of destination at all.[11] Some of these charges were well founded. The American military authorities, wishing to reduce the number of Jewish DPs staying in their occupation zones, encouraged and aided the refugees to move on to Italy and France.[12]

Quai d'Orsay vs. the Interior Ministry

For the British the main problem with the illegal movement via France was that the refugees embarked from French ports. The first *Ha'apala* ship to sail from France after the end of the war was the *Tel Hai,* which the British apprehended on 27 March 1946. Interrogation of the ship's crew revealed that the passengers had boarded under the supervision of French policemen and that before that the vessel had been overhauled in Marseilles. Furthermore, 548 of the 743 illegal immigrants had been transferred to Marseilles from Belgium just before the ship's departure. The British embassy thought the Jewish Agency headquarters in Paris was in touch with the organizers of the passage.[13] About three months later, on 1 July, the British intercepted a second vessel that had sailed from French shores with 999 passengers on board. London decided to register a protest despite the opinion of the British embassy in Paris that the French would not make a serious effort to help in the struggle against the illegal departures. At the end of July the embassy warned the director of the Afrique-Levant Department at Quai d'Orsay that Anglo-French relations would deteriorate if the illegal sailings continued. The embassy's note further warned of the negative influence such sailings might have on France's status in North Africa, "if the French government were thought to be aiding illegal immigrants to Palestine."[14] A few days afterward, the *Yagur,* carrying 754 passengers, sailed from Marseilles. Whitehall realized that the prevailing cool relations with France made it impossible to convince the French authorities to prevent the sailings of Jews to Palestine.[15]

After several weeks of a temporary lull in the *Ha'apala* sailings from France, October 1946 brought the departure from La Ciotat of the *Latrun* carrying 1,252 passengers. Before the vessel's embarkation the French authorities in Marseilles had promised the local British consulate that if the refugees appeared not to have valid documents, they would not be allowed to sail.[16] Shortly after the *Latrun*'s interception, the British discovered that the Ethiopian visas in the possession of the vessel's passengers were all forged and that an officer from the French Political Police (Renseignements Généraux) had supervised the departure of three of the four vessels that had sailed thus far from France, including the *Latrun.*[17] Quai d'Orsay attributed the *Latrun*'s sailing to the lack of coordination among French authorities and to the readiness of the French Ministry of the Interior — under the control of the Socialists — to cooperate with the organizers of the illegal sailings. Quai d'Orsay officials even hinted that corruption might have played a role in the incident. The Ministry of the Interior was also alleged to be obstructing transfer of the refugee camps inland from their locations near the Mediterranean coast.[18]

Quai d'Orsay's attempt to shift responsibility for the illegal sailings to the Interior Ministry was linked to the internal political struggle. Between October 1945 and November 1946 three elections had taken place. Georges Bidault, the leader of the MRP, who had served as prime minister and foreign minister since June 1946, failed to exercise his authority over his government. Moreover, Interior Ministry officials, including the minister, Edouard Depreux, appeared sympathetic toward the Zionist efforts to transfer Holocaust survivors to Palestine. In addition to the sympathy they felt toward the Jews for their suffering during the war, some of the party leaders had fought alongside the Jews against the Nazis or like them had been imprisoned in the camps and felt obliged to help them. Jewish personalities who were active members of the French Socialist Party and had friendly relations with the Socialist leadership also played a part, as may have the Socialist nature of the Zionist movement itself.[19]

When word reached the British embassy that renovations were taking place on vessels suspected of involvement in the illegal sailings, the French authorities were asked to monitor the movements of several ships, to close the camp at La Ciotat, and to avoid setting up more refugee camps near the shores of the Mediterranean.[20] Within two weeks of the French promise (on 19 December 1946) to keep the suspicious ships under close observation, two of them were permitted to leave. The French Foreign Ministry, "as usual" in Ambassador Duff Cooper's words, placed the blame on the Interior Ministry "for the failure to implement the undertakings given by the French government and their slowness in conducting investigations." Despite the commitment made by the French government, illegal sailings were continuing as before, the ambassador complained. On 18 January 1947 the *Ha'apala* ship *Lanegev* (Hebrew: To the Negev), one of the vessels under British suspicion, set sail from Sète. Those on board possessed Cuban visas whose validity, Quai d'Orsay claimed, had not been checked by the Interior Ministry. Ten days later the French were asked to delay the departure of the *Ulua,* which had dropped anchor in Le Havre after having sailed from Marseilles to Sweden, where it had picked up six hundred illegal immigrants. The French legation in Stockholm informed Quai d'Orsay that the Cuban visas held by the passengers had been forged. After a delay of several hours, the French Interior Ministry, afraid, according to Cooper, it would be obliged to allow the passengers to remain in France, permitted the vessel to continue its voyage to Palestine.[21] Two weeks after the *Lanegev* sailed from Sète, the *Hama'apil Ha'almoni* (Hebrew: The Anonymous Immigrant), about which the French had also been alerted, left from the same place.[22]

While failing to respond to British demands regarding the illegal sailings, at the beginning of 1947 Quai d'Orsay proposed to the British that tripartite talks be held with the Americans about the illegal immigrants passing through France. The British embassy in Paris attributed the French initiative to apprehension in Paris that the coming of spring would bring renewed infiltration into France in the wake of the anticipated mass influx of Jewish DPs into the American occupation zone in Germany.[23] Before the meeting, disagreements arose between the British and the French over the latter's wish to ratify the agreement that had been signed with the Jewish organization L'Assistance aux Déportés et Réfugiés allowing eight thousand Jewish refugees to stay temporarily in France. The British regarded these refugees as candidates for illegal sailings from France and therefore wanted this arrangement abrogated.[24] Raymond Bousquet, the director of administrative affairs at Quai d'Orsay, explained to Ashley Clarke, the British minister in Paris, that the French government could not renege on its commitment to the Jewish organizations. He added that the Socialist government attached great importance to humanitarian considerations and was even more sympathetic to Jewish migrants from the east than were the Communists. As long as a Socialist minister headed the Interior Ministry, he emphasized, "it was to be expected that these persons would receive benevolent treatment."[25]

Clarke explained to the Foreign Office in London that though Quai d'Orsay was very interested in helping the British, the lack of coordination between the French Foreign and Interior Ministries made the commitments previously given by Quai d'Orsay appear excessive.[26] The British embassy in Paris found itself facing a peculiar situation whereby Quai d'Orsay did not evade the criticism and protests of the embassy but said it could do little and instead pointed an accusing finger at the Interior Ministry. Zionist sources confirmed these charges of the French Foreign Office. According to them, Interior Minister Edouard Depreux (in office from June 1946 until November 1947) as well as other officials in his ministry were allowing Jewish refugees to enter France and to sail from its ports.[27]

As it happened, the considerable improvement in Anglo-French relations during the first weeks of 1947 under the lead of the Socialists was not reflected in the struggle against the illegal movement. Only a few days after the Dunkirk agreement had been signed, the *Ben Hecht,* with 626 passengers, was intercepted off the coast of Palestine. At a meeting of the Cabinet Defence Committee in mid-March, Prime Minister Attlee declared that in light of the alliance and the Anglo-French friendship treaty, Britain expected the active assistance of the French government in preventing the illegal sailings to Palestine.[28] The Foreign Office countered that it did not pin much hope on its appeal to the

French because of the extensive political influence it attributed to the Zionists and because of the known policies of the French Interior Ministry.[29] Despite Foreign Office reservations, the Defence Committee decided to register a very sharp protest with the French.[30]

Cooper called the attention of Bidault to reports that between April and June 1947 organizers of the illegal movement were intending to dispatch about fifteen thousand Jews to Palestine in an attempt to influence the deliberations of the United Nations Organization, which was about to consider the Palestine question. (The British had decided in February to transfer the Palestine question to the United Nations.) The British ambassador stated that "the illegal Jewish immigrant traffic is not a spontaneous exodus of refugees but a carefully organized Zionist campaign to force the hand of His Majesty's Government and increase the proportion of Jewish population in Palestine." Cooper further noted that the headquarters responsible for the Jewish population movement was located in Marseilles, and three ships were currently being renovated there. He found it regretful that the French government did little to prevent the departure of the illegal immigration vessels from French ports and emphasized that the British government expected French cooperation in the spirit of the agreement that had just been signed between the two countries.[31]

Contacts he had with Quai d'Orsay personnel reinforced Cooper's perception that while the French Foreign Ministry headed by Bidault advocated compliance with British demands, the Socialist ministers, especially Interior Minister Depreux and Transport Minister Jules Moch, were "strongly pro-Jewish and so far [have] refused to cooperate in measures to stop the traffic."[32] Only a few days after the appeal to the French, the *Theodor Herzl,* carrying 2,641 passengers, sailed from Toulon. The British learned that the illegal immigrants had been brought from Belgium to France on a special train, which, they concluded, would not have been possible without the cooperation of the French authorities. This vessel also appeared on the list that had been given to the French of ships suspected of involvement in the illegal sailings. It was the fourth vessel sailing from France since the beginning of 1947 to be apprehended by the British on the shores of Palestine. In the course of the first four months of the year, altogether eight vessels carrying a total of 9,237 persons were intercepted by the British. More than half of these illegal immigrants had sailed from France.[33]

The French government, which discussed the British requests on 21 April, made its cooperation conditional on British acquiescence to several demands: the recruitment of twenty-five thousand Germans from the British occupation zone in Germany to work in France; British commitment to take back into their occupation zone in Germany illegal immigrants who had entered France without permits; and allocation of part of the Palestine immigration quota to the occupation zones of the three Western powers in proportion to the number of immigrants present in each zone.[34] Cooper, who of course recognized that the first demand had nothing to do with the issue at stake, explained to London that Bidault was in a minority in the cabinet when it came to acceding to British demands concerning the Jewish refugees and therefore the French foreign minister "needed some more ammunition with which to persuade his colleagues to reconsider it." In other words, in exchange for German labor from Germany the French government might treat British demands "in a sympathetic manner."[35] British diplomats in Paris were convinced that French premier Paul Ramadier was not prepared to help the British.[36]

The French request for Germans to be recruited to work in France because of the lack of manpower there aroused sharp opposition in the Foreign Office in London. One of the officials described the French demands as extortion, and another emphasized the need to oppose at all costs French attempts to tie future cooperation with the British against the illegal immigration to negotiations over the transfer of German labor.[37] The British Foreign Office was afraid that accommodating French demands would adversely affect efforts to expand the productive labor force in the British zone and might disrupt British efforts to convince various countries to recruit displaced persons from Germany and Austria as workers. London was also apprehensive about the hostile reaction to be expected in Germany if the French were allowed to put Germans to work in France. Therefore, the Foreign Office instructed the embassy in Paris to oppose any attempt to link the question of Jewish migration to the subject of German labor.[38]

Misgivings further arose from the French demand that all refugees who entered France without permits be transferred to the British occupation zones. The French meant this to apply not only to those who came from the British zones but also to those who came from the American occupation zones, if the Americans refused to take them back. British occupation authorities in Germany saw this as a French attempt to obtain "'carte blanche' to return any undesirables who arrive in France to the British zone."[39] The Foreign Office decided that only those illegal immigrants who had set out from the British occupation zones would be accepted back and rejected the French proposal that immigration certificates be allocated to refugees in the American occupation zones and to those who were allowed to enter France as part of the French quota of eight thousand. The latter suggestion confirmed their apprehension that French policy enabled thousands of Jews to enter the country virtually unhindered.[40] The Foreign Office was influenced also by its belief that the French were not making special efforts to help the British in their struggle against the illegal movement. Accordingly, it was decided to allocate only twenty-five certificates per month to the French zone out of the quota of fifteen hundred.[41] London's distrust of French cooperation was clearly demonstrated in the case of the *Exodus,* which on 13 June 1947 had entered French territorial waters from Italy.

The *Exodus* Affair

On 11 July 1947, one day before the opening of the International Conference on European Reconstruction called by Bevin and Bidault to discuss the plan proposed by U.S. secretary of state Marshall for European recovery, the *Exodus* slipped out of Sète with 4,530 passengers on board.[42] Not only had the French authorities received advance notice about the ship, but Bevin had personally asked Bidault to act with determination to prevent the ship's sailing, emphasizing that the arrival of the *Exodus* in Palestine would endanger the peace not only there but throughout the Middle East.[43] Stunned by this failure, Bevin addressed a sharp protest to Bidault, complaining that not only had the ship been allowed to depart from France, but the local authorities had also permitted four thousand illegal immigrants to board it even though the ship's license forbade it to take on passengers or to sail in bad weather. Moreover, the number of illegal immigrants was the largest ever to sail on such a vessel. He attacked movement organizers for exploiting the plight of the Jews for the sake of profit, accusing them of encouraging Jews throughout Europe to sell their property and pay exorbitant prices for tickets to sail to Palestine under conditions that endangered their lives. Bevin informed Bidault of the British intention to make an example of this ship and to force it to turn back to France with all on board. Bidault, who favored assisting the British in their campaign against the illegal sailings, gave his consent to the disembarking of the illegal immigrants onto French soil.[44] Bidault's immediate acceptance of Bevin's demand, without first receiving his government's approval, was directly related to the Conference on European Reconstruction and his desire to avoid a confrontation with Bevin under such sensitive circumstances. Bevin, however, wanted more than just Bidault's promise and thus complained to French premier Ramadier of the injustice of French behavior toward the British. Skeptical of French assurances, Bevin warned that "the indulgence shown to Jewish immigrants by French authorities might well have repercussions in French North Africa,"[45] a veiled threat of Britain's ability to harm French interests in Africa.

While the British Foreign Office believed that the French government would accede to the British request, so as not to embarrass Bidault, who might otherwise resign, it was also aware of the possibility that Ramadier might oppose Bidault's commitment.[46] If this happened, the Foreign Office believed that Britain would be faced with a choice between two alternative courses of action. One would be to present the French with a fait accompli based on the oral commitment made by Bidault. Such a step, however, might dampen France's future willingness to cooperate in the struggle against the illegal embarkations. A second possibility would be to deport the illegal immigrants to Cyprus. The Foreign Office feared that such a course would be an admission of failure of the campaign against the illegal sailings and would put an end to the plan to return illegal immigrants to their ports of departure.[47]

Ambassador Cooper warned against the removal by force of what he called "these miserable creatures" in France. Such a step, he stressed, "is likely to provide anti-British propaganda to which French public opinion may well be receptive in view of memories of German persecution of Jews under occupation." The man in the street, Cooper argued, "is totally ignorant of Palestine problems and sees only in these illicit immigrants survivors of a persecuted race seeking refuge in their national home." [48] Moreover, the French prime minister and many of his fellow cabinet ministers were not in accord with British policy on this matter. The ambassador pointed out that Foreign Minister Bidault was the only one exhibiting a willingness to help Britain, and this was because of his desire to strengthen the friendship between the two countries. But even Bidault's support, Cooper concluded, was uncertain because of difficulties in Germany and his standing in the government.[49]

Meanwhile, on the morning of 18 July British soldiers boarded the *Exodus*, which had reached Palestinian waters, while British destroyers continuously rammed the ship. After a bloody struggle that cost the lives of three Jews and in which about two hundred others were wounded, seventy of them seriously, the *Exodus* illegal immigrants were transferred onto three other ships for deportation. The following day, this convoy of three vessels with the *Exodus* illegal immigrants on board sailed from Haifa. Cooper was asked to inform the French of the departure of the vessels for France, based on the understanding reached with Bidault. The ambassador was told that a final decision as to the destination of the ships, either Cyprus or France, would be made at a later stage and that in any case the French were not to be given an inkling that a possibility of taking the illegal immigrants to Cyprus was being considered. This, of course, was intended to force the French to make their position clear.[50]

Eventually, on 21 July, the director of administrative affairs in the French Foreign Ministry announced that it had been decided to allow the ships to drop

Exodus 1947 *after surrender (Courtesy Yad Vashem, Jerusalem, Sifriat Poalim, Tel Aviv)*

anchor in Villefranche. Because the immigrants had sailed from France and possessed personal passports and valid visas for Colombia, however, the British government was asked to organize the continuation of their trip to Colombia in the deportation vessels. In other words, France would serve only as a transit point. British minister Clarke rejected this idea on the grounds that the deportation vessels were not suitable for crossing the ocean and that they were needed in Palestine. He asked Bousquet to see whether the French government would be willing to transport the refugees to Colombia.[51] Nevertheless, very quickly it was found that the Colombian visas were forged and that the Colombian government had no intention of absorbing the refugees.[52]

The French government, under heavy pressure from the British, decided at its meeting on 23 July to permit the illegal immigrants to disembark in France and to supply all their needs. But the government made it clear that it was unequivocally opposed to the use of force to offload the illegal immigrants.[53] This decision was a compromise between Bidault, who felt that France must respond to the British request, and the Socialist minister of the interior Edouard Depreux, who made it clear that he would refuse to make the refugees disembark by force. Although the French cabinet in general and Depreux in particular were motivated first and foremost by humanitarian reasons, it can be assumed that the decision was also influenced by the government's concern over possible bloodshed, as had occurred during the transfer of the illegal immigrants from the *Exodus* to the deportation vessels. The French, dependent on American economic assistance, were aware of Washington's sensitivity to the situation of the Jewish DPs. For his part, Bidault, mainly concerned with relations with Britain, thought that his government was making a mistake by obstructing the British on this issue when much more important matters were on the agenda. The French foreign minister did not hide his views from the British and pointed an accusing finger at the Socialist ministers, especially Depreux and Jules Moch, the transport minister, whom Bidault claimed were subject to the influence of Léon Blum.[54] Blum, who had laid the foundations for the Dunkirk treaty of "alliance and mutual assistance" signed by the two nations in March 1947, was among the sharpest critics of British behavior during the *Exodus* affair.[55]

The French cabinet decision again aroused Cooper's fears of the possible repercussions if British soldiers were to attempt to remove the illegal immigrants by force. In an effort to prevent a confrontation, Cooper suggested to his government that the refugees be offered two alternatives: either to disembark and enjoy the protection of the French government or else to put out again to open sea.[56] The second alternative was not acceptable to the Foreign Office because it meant simply offloading the illegal immigrants in Cyprus, whereas Britain wanted to use the *Exodus* to set an example. Cooper was asked to inform the French that Britain presumed that French agreement to allow the return of illegal immigrants to France also entailed consent to have them offloaded by force if that should prove necessary. If the French rejected this argument, the ambassador was to state instead that Britain's right to demand that the illegal immigrants be allowed to disembark in France followed naturally from its right to return them to France.[57] Cooper, who was looking for ways to prevent confrontation in case the illegal immigrants refused to disembark, came up against the obdurate stand of the British Foreign Office, which insisted on offloading the illegal immigrants on French soil.[58]

The three deportation vessels reached Port de Bouc on 29 July. Efforts to convince the illegal immigrants to disembark of their own free will had little effect. All in all, during the three weeks that the ships were anchored at Port de Bouc, no more than 130 refugees disembarked, most of them sick and old people or pregnant women about to give birth. The British consulate in Marseilles informed London that without the cooperation of the French authorities and in light of the hostility of the local population, it would not be possible to use force to offload the illegal immigrants. But local French port authorities refused to help the British bring the illegal immigrants ashore while French newspapers of all political leanings leveled scathing criticism at Britain.[59] Differences of opinion continued between Bevin and Cooper over how to handle the situation. While Cooper, aware of the resolute opposition of the Socialist ministers, including the premier, to disembarking the illegal immigrants forcibly, thought that there was no point in appealing to them, Bevin unequivocally rejected the ambassador's suggestion that the deportation vessels withdraw from French waters as soon as possible. He instructed him to tell the French authorities in no uncertain terms that Britain attached great importance to seeing Bidault's commitment to take back the illegal immigrants honored.[60]

About three weeks after the *Exodus* had sailed from Sète and two days after the deportation vessels arrived at Port de Bouc, Bevin began to recognize that the move he had initiated was wrong. On 31 July, he reported to the cabinet on the impasse in France and on his intention to deport the illegal immigrants to one of the British colonies or to the British occupation zone in Germany. In any case, Bevin emphasized, they would not be taken to either Cyprus or Palestine.[61] This stance, if not inspired by a feeling of spite, may have been Bevin's way of reducing the extent of his failure. At the same time he remained hopeful that the difficult situation on the deportation ships and the prospect of enjoying French hospitality might break the illegal immigrants' will. Obsessed with subduing the organizers of the illegal sailings, Bevin paid little attention to the damage caused to Britain in the international arena and world public opinion. In contrast, Ambassador Cooper was keenly aware of and greatly concerned about the harm events were causing to relations between the two countries and to Britain's status in French public opinion in light of their recent reconciliation. He desperately wanted to bring the incident to an end as quickly as possible and suggested on 11 August that the illegal immigrants be informed of a final deportation destination and given a limited amount of time to make a decision.[62]

So far, however, no decision had been made on where the deportees would be taken. The Colonial Office made it clear that it would be impossible at such short notice to absorb a large number of Jews in any of the colonies and that their deportation to a distant destination would be interpreted as a total failure to put the principle of deportation back to ports of embarkation into practice. Under the circumstances, the Colonial Office thought that Germany "has the advantage that accommodation exists and, provided the French authorities maintain their offer of hospitality, we should have a chance of returning the Jews to France through the British zone [in Germany]." Moreover, this would achieve the objective of deportation to the country from which the illegal immigrants had sailed. Following the advice of Ambassador Cooper, it was decided to inform the illegal immigrants of the intent to deport them forcibly to Hamburg and to give them forty-eight hours to disembark voluntarily in France. The Jewish Agency was also to be informed of the British plan so as to enlist its cooperation in convincing the illegal immigrants to disembark.[63] On 21 August, approximately six weeks after the *Exodus* had sailed from Sète, the illegal immigrants on the deportation vessels were informed that if they persisted in their refusal to disembark, they would be deported to Germany.[64]

British hopes of negotiating a compromise were unsuccessful. The position of the Jewish Agency was conveyed to the British by Léon Blum one day after the illegal immigrants learned of the deportation destination. The former French premier told Cooper that if the British government were to commit itself to allowing the illegal immigrants at Port de Bouc to enter Palestine within a definite period of time, the Jewish Agency would advise them to disembark. When Cooper asked whether that meant a period of three or four years, Blum replied that the agency was thinking of two or three months. Marc Jarblum, a leader of the Fédération des Sociétés Juives, the organization of Jews of Eastern European origin in France, and a prominent member of the Socialist Party, suggested to Cooper that the *Exodus* passengers be allotted half of the monthly immigration quota to Palestine (750 certificates) for a period of six months. He may have had in mind the arrangement made earlier in the La Spezia incident. Knowing of Bevin's determination on this issue, Cooper proposed permitting the people who voluntarily disembarked to apply for permission to enter Palestine, with the *Exodus* sailing not being held against them. The ambassador explained to Jarblum that this was his own private suggestion and would need London's approval. Jarblum rejected the proposal out of hand.[65]

When he learned of the decision to deport the illegal immigrants to Germany, the high commissioner in Palestine, Alan Cunningham, urged the government to look for another solution because he was greatly worried about the repercussions of such a step on the security situation in Palestine. On the very same day the three deportation vessels had reached Port de Bouc, three members of the Irgun caught by the British during the break-in at Acre prison in Palestine (Avshalom Haviv, Yaakov Weiss, and Meir Nakar) had been hanged there. When, in response, the Irgun had hanged two British sergeants it had been holding as hostages, British soldiers and police had run amok in the streets of Tel Aviv with the result that five Jews had been killed and twenty-four injured.[66] While appreciating the high commissioner's difficulties, both the Colonial and Foreign Offices were willing to give the refugees on board the deportation vessels, which had already sailed from Port de Bouc on 22 August, another opportunity to disembark in France.[67]

After it became clear that the illegal immigrants refused to disembark, the

Foreign Office hoped it would be possible to return them from the British zone in Germany to France. The French made their agreement to accept the *Exodus* passengers conditional on the latter's voluntary return. The Foreign Office debated whether to try also to return illegal immigrants who refused to go willingly.[68] Cooper strongly opposed any attempt to force the illegal immigrants to return to France, warning that the entire operation would fail if it were discovered that the British were not acting in keeping with French conditions.[69] On 8 September, the illegal immigrants were taken ashore at the port of Hamburg. British attempts to return the *Exodus* illegal immigrants to France were again thwarted, this time by the condition the French placed on accepting the refugees. The illegal immigrants preferred to wait in the DP camps in Germany until they could go to Palestine rather than accept the French offer.

Along with the contacts concerning the *Exodus* illegal immigrants, the British continued to alert the French to suspected illegal departures being planned by vessels anchored in French ports. In a memorandum to Bidault on 12 July, Bevin called attention to five ships, two of which, the *Bruna* and the *Luciano,* were about to sail that same day. Bidault was asked to take all necessary measures to prevent their departure. Four days later, the *Shivat Zion* (as the *Luciano* was now called) sailed from Algeria with 411 passengers and the *Yad Hallalei Gesher Haziv* (formerly the *Bruna*) from Italy with 685 passengers. In the same memorandum Bevin mentioned two more suspicious vessels, the *Paducah* and the *Northland* (under the Panamanian flag). Only a few days later the embassy discovered that both ships had been refueled. Following heavy pressure exerted by the British embassy, the French authorities informed their captains that they would not receive permits to transport passengers. The local authorities then allowed the *Paducah* to sail without passengers. Feeling hoodwinked, the British sent a sharply worded protest to Quai d'Orsay. The note emphasized that a delay in the departure of the *Northland* until the Panamanian government reached a decision about cancellation of the ship's license would be seen as proof of French readiness to help Britain in its struggle against the illegal sailings.[70]

Several days after he had received the sharply worded note, Bidault explained to Cooper that he had no intention of defending or making excuses for his government's actions. He also did not view the sailing of the *Exodus* as serious enough to create a government crisis over, as in any case the government would not survive until October 1947 and he himself (Bidault) would then be appointed premier.[71] Given the deep crisis in the political system in France at this time, the British realized that despite Quai d'Orsay's support of their demands, its ability to influence government policy on the matter of Jewish illegal immigrants was limited.

As it happened, Bidault did not become the prime minister and illegal sailings continued. On 26 September 1947, two *Ha'apala* boats, the *Geula* (the renamed *Paducah*) and the *Medinat Hayehudim* (the renamed *Northland*), sailed from Bulgaria, carrying over four thousand passengers between them.[72] Those two ships were not the last to refuel in France and sail from Bulgaria with Rumanian illegal immigrants. At the beginning of October, S. E. Kay, the consul general in Marseilles, reported that the local authorities had allowed the *Pan York* to refuel and take on 148 tons of food in spite of British requests to the contrary. The consul emphasized to his embassy in Paris that because the illegal sailings had now shifted to the Communist bloc countries, allowing the ships to refuel and take on supplies meant assisting the movement.[73] This was highlighted when, on 26 December 1947, the *Pan York* sailed from Bulgaria with 7,557 illegal immigrants on board.

During this entire period Jewish refugees continued to infiltrate into France and Italy through the French zone in Austria. The Italians complained to the British that the French military authorities were making it difficult to return illegal immigrants detained in Italy. Even when the French were prepared to take back those apprehended, it was of no use because they did nothing to prevent the same people from infiltrating again by another route.[74] The French did not deny the facts, but they blamed the Americans.[75] At a joint meeting of the Western Allies in Austria in mid-November 1947, called to discuss the Jewish infiltration, the French representative stressed the difficulty of monitoring the borders of the French zone, which were over a thousand kilometers long, with only eight hundred guards. Participants in the meeting were told that the main route from Austria to Italy passed through the American zone to the French zone and from there to Italy via the Brenner and Resia Passes. The movement into France went from the American zone in Austria to the American zone in Germany and from there to France. The French representative clearly stated that if the movement were to be halted, the commander in the American zone in Germany had to cooperate.[76] In other words, if London wanted to put an end to this movement, it ought to negotiate with the Americans and not with the French authorities. By then, there were approximately forty thousand Jewish refugees in France who had arrived there since the end of the war.[77]

Summing up, most of the sixteen thousand illegal immigrants who sailed from French ports had reached France from DP camps. Such a massive movement could not have happened without the concurrence of the French authorities. The British knew that some officials, including government ministers, especially among the Socialists, were allowing the Jewish refugees to enter the country and sail from France to Palestine. British arguments that the illegal sailings were primarily a political maneuver as part of the Zionist struggle and that the Zionists were cynically exploiting innocent people found no receptive ears. Memories of the Holocaust were still fresh, especially among those Socialist leaders who had fought against the Nazis and had suffered at their hands. Socialist policies appear to have been contradictory, since while Socialist government officials were aiding the Jewish refugees in reaching Palestine, party leaders like Blum and Ramadier were working for an accord with Britain and toward improved relations between the two countries. The Socialists could live with the paradox of rapprochement with Britain, on the one hand, and helping the Jewish refugees, on the other, because the Jewish DP issue was a marginal factor in overall Anglo-French relations.

The considerable improvement in relations between the two countries in the course of 1947 and increased British pressure on the French authorities did produce a decline in the scope of the illegal sailings from French shores for several months. Increased tension between the West and the Soviet Union in light of the failure of the CFM in Moscow (March–April 1947) and the challenge that Marshall had set before the nations of Western Europe brought about closer relations between Britain and France, who took it upon themselves to organize and lead this bloc. These circumstances made it difficult for the French authorities to ignore British pressure. The *Exodus* incident, which caused tension between the two countries at a most sensitive time, impelled the French to bring about a lull in departures from French ports. Reports from Zionist sources reveal that after the *Exodus* sailed, the increased pressure on *Ha'apala* organizers from French government officials made it necessary to turn to clandestine operations.[78]

Still, the change in French policy was not drastic and certainly did not halt the illegal sailings. Between the signing of the Dunkirk treaty and the establishment of the State of Israel, more than 10,000 illegal immigrants sailed in eight vessels from French ports, in comparison with 5,800 in seven ships previously. Moreover, during the first six months of Schuman's government, four ships with a total of 2,720 passengers managed to sail. The interior minister at the time was the Socialist Jules Moch, who in his previous position as transport minister had proffered much assistance to the illegal departures. Throughout 1947, furthermore, the French authorities permitted ships suspected of involvement in illegal sailings to refuel, take on provisions, and sail, albeit without passengers, despite British demands.

There was considerable similarity in the positions of the French and Italian authorities in their contacts with the British, despite the difference in their international status. Officials in the governments of the two nations had analogous feelings toward both the British and the Jewish DPs. Britain's difficulties in Palestine did not make Paris and Rome unhappy. The French and the Italians were careful to deny any responsibility for the infiltration of Jews into their countries and instead put the blame on the Americans, challenging the British to influence American policy. Both France and Italy conditioned their help against the infiltration on a British willingness to take into the British occupation zone Jewish refugees who had been arrested, even if the latter had come from the American zone (as was the case for most of those fleeing via that route) and on an increase in the quota of certificates for Jewish DPs in their own territory. The two countries also demanded a quid pro quo which had no real connection with the illegal immigration, the French asking that German labor be sent to France and the Italians seeking the deportation of non-Jewish refugees who had infiltrated into the country.

London did not retaliate against the French and Italians but made do with sending sharp protests from time to time and threatening possible harm to bilateral relations. Although annoyed by the illegal sailings, Britain preferred not to impair its relations with France and Italy, especially in 1947. Britain was aiming at closer cooperation among the nations of Western Europe, in view of increasing tension with the Soviet Union and its satellites. France had a central role to play in the Western camp. At the end of his talk with Ramadier (22 September 1947, two weeks after the *Exodus* illegal immigrants had been forced ashore in Hamburg), Bevin announced: "We've made the union of Britain and France this morning."[79] Nor were the British interested in placing further obstacles in front of the French and Italian authorities who were forced to deal with an internal Communist challenge (the Communist Parties of both countries had participated in the founding conference of the Cominform in September). Furthermore, the British were aware of the decline in their international standing and their deterrent ability since the end of the war, especially during the course of 1947. They thus had no alternative but to accept the fact that even unremitting pressure on the French and Italian authorities would bring them only sporadic success. Under the circumstances, the fight against the illegal immigrants remained theirs alone.

CONCLUSION

When following World War II thousands of Jewish refugees began streaming into DP camps in Germany, Austria, and Italy and from there tried to reach the shores of Palestine, the British explained their efforts as an integral part of the Zionist endeavor to establish a Jewish state. Of geopolitical importance in Britain's overall imperial policy, Palestine had been under British Mandatory rule since 1922. Now, after the war, the British Labour government was convinced that, if Britain was to retain its position in the Middle East, it was vital to secure the cooperation of the Arab countries in the region. As the latter had made Jewish immigration into Palestine a test case of Anglo-Arab relations, Whitehall decided to limit Jewish immigration until it had formulated a comprehensive policy to solve the Palestine question.

The Zionists counteracted by, among other things, dispatching tens of thousands of illegal immigrants from various European ports to Palestine—the *Ha'apala* movement—while directing larger numbers of Jewish refugees from Eastern Europe to DP camps in Germany and Austria—the *Brichah* movement. To halt these movements effectively the British needed the cooperation of the East and West European governments and particularly the backing and collaboration of the Americans. Neither the *Brichah* nor the *Ha'apala* movements would have reached the proportions they did without the active or even passive assistance they received from American and European officials.

For Britain the international constellation proved awkward. Relations with the United States had cooled considerably during the first months after the war, as London became economically and politically more dependent on Washington, while relations with the USSR and its satellites were marked by tension and confrontation over the shape of the postwar world. There were significant differences with Italy and France over geopolitical issues. Moreover, Britain had come out of the war in a severe economic crisis that reached its peak in 1947 and inevitably harmed its international standing and impaired its deterrent capability.

A mainstay of its policy became Whitehall's decision to keep the problem of the Jewish DPs separate from the Palestine question. From this then followed London's refusal to acknowledge that the Jewish DP problem could not be dealt with as part of the general DP problem resulting from the war. Cabinet ministers and, in particular, the prime minister and the foreign secretary were against according the Jewish DPs preferential treatment and special consideration, claiming that the suffering of the Jews was no different from that of other peoples. That is, the Jewish DP problem was to be solved as part of the overall refugee issue, which included the return of the Jews to their countries of origin or resettlement overseas. The Holocaust, in which about six million Jews had perished, played only a marginal role when officials began formulating their policy toward Jewish survivors. In Whitehall's official stand the Jews were a religious community, not a nation — recognizing them as a nation would have been tantamount to accepting the Nazi theory that the Jews were a separate race. Much of this attitude, which was shared by Attlee and Bevin, can be explained by Whitehall's efforts to safeguard British interests in the Middle East. As it contradicted the position Labour had taken up toward the Zionist movement during World War II, the shift was overwhelmingly inspired by similar geopolitical considerations that, in 1938, had led the Conservatives, then in power, to retreat from their support of the plan to partition Palestine into an Arab and a Jewish state and from their support for Zionism.

Britain's main obstacle proved to be the American attitude. When Truman demanded that one hundred thousand Jewish DPs be allowed to enter Palestine and publicly expressed his interest in the plight of the Jewish DPs, the cabinet, under Bevin's lead, decided to involve the Americans in trying to find a solution for the Palestine problem, assuming that they would eventually come around to supporting British proposals. Whitehall expected the problem of the Jewish DPs to be resolved as part of such a joint policy. London may also have wanted to reduce the criticism to which Britain was being subjected by prominent American political figures and by the press concerning its policies toward Jewish DPs. Moreover, many Americans, the British knew, believed they were motivated by reasons of empire. Whitehall was apprehensive of damage to British standing in the United States and of the harm to Anglo-American relations at a time when Britain was negotiating for American economic assistance. Britain also needed U.S. support to further its objectives in the international arena, especially in blocking the expansionist ambitions of the USSR. When, in October 1945, they invited the United States to participate in setting a Palestine policy, the British were aware that during the first months after the war the Americans had often ignored British opinions and needs and Bevin recognized that the president was exploiting the Jewish DP problem for electoral purposes. Last but not least, Bevin's initiative coincided with his desire to prevent an American return to isolationism, as had happened after World War I, and to involve the United States actively in molding the postwar world.

Bevin's strategy eventually failed, even though the U.S. State and War Departments supported Britain's policy in Palestine. Truman himself was at first amenable to the provincial autonomy plan that would have ensured the continuation of the British Mandate over Palestine, but the American Zionist lobby put pressure on the president to reject the plan. By August 1946 the Jewish DP problem, which had prompted Truman's intervention, had become much more severe than it had been one year earlier. At the time Harrison submitted his report, there were fewer than sixty thousand Jews in Germany and Austria, a number that could have been resettled had Britain given priority to the problem during the first months after the war. Truman made his public commitment to securing the transfer of one hundred thousand Jewish DPs to Palestine during the campaign for the New York municipal election in November 1945. In other words, the critical stage was reached during the summer and autumn of 1945. By the summer of 1946 it was no longer possible to resolve the problem of the Jewish DPs without transferring the large majority of them to Palestine. The U.S. midterm elections of November 1946 assured that the president would not renege on his commitment. Moreover, the Democratic Party needed the financial contributions and votes of the Jewish community and this led Truman, in his Yom Kippur statement, to take a stand on the wider question of a solution to the political problem of Palestine. From the point of view of the White House, Palestine remained the most convenient destination for Jewish DPs, especially as Truman recognized the strong opposition in Congress to any change in U.S. immigration policy.

American policy toward the Jewish DPs significantly undermined Britain's campaign against the *Brichah* movement and, to a lesser extent, also against the *Ha'apala*. That London failed in its insistence on keeping the Jewish DP problem and the Palestine question separate and on treating all Jewish DPs the same regardless of their country of origin had much to do with the American attitude. Following Truman's demand that one hundred thousand Jewish DPs be allowed to enter Palestine, the Americans began assembling the Jews in separate camps, opened the gates in the American occupation zones to Jews fleeing from countries under Soviet influence, and accorded them DP status with all the preferential treatment this entailed. American military authorities in Germany and Austria, furthermore, indirectly encouraged and assisted DPs in the American zones in reaching ports of embarkation in Italy and France. At the same time, Washington refrained from censuring the illegal Jewish immigration into Palestine and refused to prohibit fund-raising in the United States for the *Ha'apala*. Washington's policy helped the Zionists to situate the problem of the Jewish DPs and the *Ha'apala* at the center of their struggle. Equally important, the American policy encouraged the Soviets and East European and Balkan countries to allow Jews to leave and fleeing Jews to pass through because they could be certain that the refugees would be accepted in the DP camps in the American zones and thus would not become "stuck" en route. Similarly, that they could count on at least temporary asylum in the American occupation zones made it easier for Jews in Eastern European and the Balkan countries to decide to leave their countries of origin.

Open disagreements between the United States and Britain concerning policy toward the Jewish DPs undermined the efficacy of the pressure the British tried to exert on Soviet bloc countries to prevent the exodus of Jews and their embarkation for Palestine. Whenever the Soviet Union found itself confronted with a united and determined Anglo-American front on questions that did not touch on the future of the Communist governments in its satellite countries, it generally took Western demands seriously and sometimes would retract or change its plans. Furthermore, the sensitivity the White House and members of Congress demonstrated on the subject of the Jewish DPs was seen in Europe, on both sides of the Iron Curtain, as an expression of the political power the Jewish community in the United States commanded. Accordingly, some European governments sought to avoid confrontation with the Jewish DPs so as not to harm their own interests in the United States, or even helped them in the hope of facilitating economic support from the United States either directly or indirectly through, for example, UNRRA.

That about 280,000 Jews were able to leave by land and sea from countries under Soviet influence could only have happened with the knowledge and agreement of the governments of these countries and of Moscow. Poland, Rumania, Czechoslovakia, and Hungary were generally not averse to seeing part of their Jews go, especially as many of them refused to adjust to the Communist system. Britain's main diplomatic ammunition against the USSR and its satellites was to delay recognition of the new governments which Moscow had set up in Rumania and Bulgaria and to stall the peace treaty discussions with former enemy countries that now were subject to Soviet influence. The British did not hesitate to threaten Rumania and Bulgaria with retaliatory measures for assisting the illegal sailings in part because they did not have any significant interests there; more substantially, of course, there were the immediate political repercussions the influx of Jewish immigrants was having on the situation in Palestine, if not in the entire Middle East. (No action, however, was ever taken.) Wishing to retain a certain degree of influence in Poland and Czechoslovakia, however, London was careful not to aggravate its relations with them by unduly emphasizing the problem of the emigration of the Jews. In the final analysis, the problem of the Jewish DPs was secondary in London's overall policy in this region.

Until the summer of 1946, the British effort in countries under Soviet influence focused on preventing embarkations of Jews from Rumania, which London regarded as having the largest potential for illegal sailings. When the Anglo-American contacts on a solution for the Palestine question—and thereby of the Jewish DP problem—reached a deadlock, London undertook a comprehensive diplomatic campaign against the *Brichah* movement that after a lull during the winter of 1945–46 had significantly stepped up its activities. But the effort began too late; by the summer of 1946 tens of thousands of Jews had already gathered in the DP camps, and the Soviets had by then entrenched their control over Eastern and Central European countries.

London, meanwhile, was convinced that by prodding the Jews to head for the DP camps the Soviets were trying to exacerbate the problem of the Jewish DPs and thus widen differences of opinion between Britain and the United States about an acceptable solution and ultimately harm Britain's standing in the United States. London saw these moves as part of an overall effort by the Soviets to undermine Britain's position in the Middle East by having it ousted from Palestine and to obtain for themselves a foothold in the region. The Soviets did allow Polish Jews who had fled to the USSR during the war to return to Poland and Jews from other countries under the USSR's influence to move to Germany and Austria (the mass exodus from Poland via Czechoslovakia in the summer of 1946 could not have taken place without Soviet concurrence), but the Soviets did not push the Jews to leave—most Jews did not need encouragement in this direction, either by local authorities or by the Zionists.

In Poland as well as Czechoslovakia the Communists held most of the ministerial posts, including that of prime minister, and they also controlled the army and the security forces. The movement via Hungary to the Soviet zone of Austria necessitated the agreement of the Soviet military authorities who controlled the Austro-Hungarian border. It is possible that during the first months after the war, Moscow was unaware of the scope of the Jewish exodus and of its political potential. Yet it may be assumed that the Harrison report, the Anglo-American differences over Truman's demand to permit one hundred thousand Jewish DPs to enter Palestine, and the criticism of British policy toward the Jewish DPs voiced in the United States alerted Moscow to the advantage it could gain from aggravating the Jewish DP problem. This assumption is confirmed by the tactics the Soviets adopted in the joint control bodies in Germany and Austria, where they clearly exploited the Anglo-American differences about policy toward Jews arriving from Eastern Europe.

Before the peace agreements of February 1947, the British were able to persuade the Soviets and the Rumanian authorities to stop the sailings from Rumanian ports and, during 1947, succeeded in bringing about the cessation of illegal sailings from Yugoslavia. The departures from Bulgaria of Rumanian Jews during the winter of 1947–48 almost surely had the consent of the Soviets because Moscow wished to increase pressure on the British at a critical juncture in the Palestine conflict. Since the difficulties the illegal sailings created for the British were well known (for example, the *Exodus* episode), it was eminently reasonable for Russia to let the sailings continue. It also fell in line with Soviet support, since mid-1947, for the establishment of a Jewish state. The deterioration in relations between the two blocs during the second half of 1947 sharply reduced Britain's ability to exert pressure on the Soviet satellites, particularly Bulgaria, which allowed *Ha'apala* ships to sail from Black Sea ports.

As it happened, the interests of the various parties promoting the exodus of the Jews coincided in these sailings. The Rumanian authorities did not mind being rid of another several thousand Jews and could use the foreign currency they received from the Zionists. Rumania's Jews, many of them Zionists, were confronting a desperate economic situation and increasing anti-Semitism and were glad to leave a country in which Communist control had become total. The Bulgarian authorities were primarily motivated by financial gain, and the Zionists wanted to bring out as many Jews as possible before the Iron Curtain came down completely and to continue to apply *Ha'apala* pressure on the British. Transferring the departure base from Rumania to Yugoslavia, from there to Bulgaria, and then back to Yugoslavia (as dictated by international circumstances) enabled these states to outmaneuver the British during discussions on the peace agreements and to disrupt British efforts to prevent Jews from embarking in countries under Soviet influence.

Last but not least, the British came to realize that there was not much difference between the response of the Italian and French authorities and those in the Communist bloc, at least until the Cold War began escalating during the second half of 1947. In its attempts to prevent Jewish DPs from entering Italy and France and from there departing for Palestine, London was no more successful than in Eastern Europe. In fact, until February 1947, several of the former enemy countries that were now under Communist control were more responsive to British pressure. Britain came up against Italian and French government officials aiding and abetting the Jews in their efforts to reach Palestine. London attributed this willingness to aid the Jewish refugees to the sympathy government officials and wide circles of the general public in both these countries felt toward the Jewish survivors, on the one hand, and the resentment many entertained toward Britain because of its stand on geopolitical issues, on the other. The difficulties the British encountered in the Middle East as a result of the illegal sailings can hardly have been a source of regret in Rome and Paris. Furthermore, that the American military authorities allowed and even helped Jewish DPs to move on from U.S. zones to France and Italy made it easier for both countries to claim that they could not be held responsible for Jewish infiltration across their frontiers.

When relations with Britain improved during 1947, France and Italy were more willing to act against the infiltration of the Jewish DPs. No decisive change occurred in Italian and French policies toward illegal sailings, however, because these helped empty the countries of Jewish refugees. Furthermore, dependent as they were on American economic assistance, both countries wished to avoid a confrontation with the American Jewish community, a consideration that the British believed carried weight, especially with the Italians. The La Spezia affair, furthermore, alerted the Italians to the risk involved in confronting the organizers of the illegal sailings and the illegal immigrants.

In the course of 1947, when relations between Britain and the Soviet Union and its satellites deteriorated and there was genuine concern that France and Italy could come under Communist threat—especially after the Communist Party was ousted from the coalitions in both countries in May 1947—Britain decided to act with caution and restraint. In Britain's scheme for closer cooperation among the countries of Western Europe, France, together with Britain, was to constitute the nucleus of the West European bloc. The illegal sailings were not regarded as important enough to warrant creating a severe crisis, and although French and Italian authorities did take sporadic steps to limit the Jewish infiltration and the illegal sailings, all told, more than thirty-seven thousand Jewish refugees sailed from French and Italian ports between 1945 and 1948.

Finally, there was the problem of the Jewish DPs in Britain's own occupation zones. As part of its policy of keeping the problem of the DPs separate from the Palestine question, Britain continually placed obstacles before Zionist leaders and organizations who wished to help the Jewish survivors in the British occupation zones; refused to single out the Jewish DPs from the other DPs in separate camps; withheld recognition from a united representative body of all Jewish DPs and German Jews; opposed the appointment of Jewish liaison officers; and was in favor of reintegrating the Jews in their respective countries of origin, even if that country was Germany. But the British found it difficult to implement this policy as a whole and were forced to compromise. Apart from inducing Whitehall to be more flexible, British Jewry had little influence on the policy the government decided to follow. Even though publicly the British refused to acknowledge that the Jewish DPs constituted a special category, they did separate them from other DPs, appointed an adviser for Jewish DP affairs, including those of German Jews, and in effect arrived at a special policy vis-à-vis the Jewish DPs. London was also ready to allow one hundred thousand Jewish refugees to immigrate to Palestine if its comprehensive plan for a solution of the Palestine question were accepted. Still, until the UN partition resolution of 29 November 1947, London maintained that the Jewish DP problem should be resolved as part of the general DP issue, for example, through repatriation or resettlement overseas. Whitehall, in fact, entertained cautious hopes that a change in the American immigration policy would solve the problem of the majority of the Jewish DPs.

In this struggle over the illegal sailings there were no clear winners. The Zionists succeeded in having tens of thousands of illegal immigrants set sail for Palestine, but more than 70 percent of them were intercepted before they could get there and deported to Cyprus. Although the deportations failed to discourage the *Ha'apala* activities, the latter were never able to induce a change in Whitehall's immigration policy. Britain continued to try to stifle the movement until the end of the Mandate, even though the Mandate government realized that this policy stopped the moderate majority of the Yishuv from containing Jewish terrorist activities, thus impairing the ability of the British army in Palestine to deal with the Irgun and LHI. The British were also aware that deportation to Cyprus was not in itself sufficient to end or even limit the scope of the illegal sailings and that in the confrontation over the illegal immigration the Zionists were gaining support in world public opinion, especially in the United States. For the British, however, not aggravating relations with the Arab states and avoiding predictably disruptive reactions on the part not only of the Palestinian Arabs but of all Arab countries was of greater importance than the advantages that could be derived from acceding to Zionist demands. Whitehall remained adamant in its refusal to increase the immigration quota or to halt the deportations to Cyprus because these almost certainly served the purpose of obviating any retaliatory reaction by the Arabs in Palestine.

While the illegal sailings did have some impact on those who determined the Palestine policy in London, there were other factors that in the course of 1947 led the British cabinet to make two far-reaching decisions — one, to transfer the Palestine question to the UN, and the second, to evacuate Palestine. The first decision was taken in mid-February 1947, following the failure of the second stage of the London conference with the Arabs and the Zionists. Given the dominance the electoral factor played in shaping President Truman's Palestine policy, Bevin was compelled to include in his proposed solution for the Palestine question a provision for the entry into Palestine of about one hundred thousand Jewish DPs (the "Bevin Plan"). The Arabs rejected the plan, fearing that it would lead to the establishment of a Jewish state in part of Palestine and to further Jewish immigration. The difficulties entailed in the struggle against the illegal sailings did not feature in the cabinet discussions that preceded this decision. The cabinet's decision of 20 September to withdraw from Palestine was prompted by the UNSCOP majority recommendation that Palestine be partitioned into an Arab and a Jewish state. The UNSCOP report ended British hopes of tabling a plan for the solution of the Palestine question that would be acceptable to both the Arab countries and the Americans. The cabinet realized, furthermore, that to postpone a decision much longer would mean a continuation of both the illegal sailings and Jewish terrorist attacks. The *Exodus* episode and the terrorist acts of LHI and the Irgun (especially the hanging of two British sergeants) influenced members of Parliament, public opinion, and the press in Britain, all of whom increased their pressure on the cabinet to evacuate Palestine. Already facing a severe political and economic crisis at home, the cabinet could not muster the will and the motivation to persist in the face of the difficulties and dangers it could expect if Britain continued to hold on to Palestine. In fact, the decisions to leave India and to halt the aid to Greece and Turkey already reflected a different, more realistic attitude and demonstrated Britain's recognition of the need to adapt itself to the realities of the postwar situation.

Zionist efforts, in the form of the *Ha'apala,* to bring to Palestine as many Jewish DPs as possible not only helped the Zionist movement to attract world opinion to its cause at a time when Washington and European governments were preoccupied with rehabilitating their countries and their battle over the shape of the postwar world, but in the eyes of many in the West, also imbued their efforts with a considerable degree of moral and political legitimacy. Although genuine sympathy toward the survivors of the Holocaust prevailed among officials in the different countries, in the end it was political not humane considerations that played a decisive role when the Great Powers enabled the Zionists to establish a Jewish state in Palestine.

NOTES

ABBREVIATIONS
In addition to the abbreviations found in the text,
the following are used in the notes:

ABC	American-British Conversations
ADM	Admiralty
ASW	Assistant Secretary of War
BGA	Ben Gurion Archives
BMM	British Military Mission
CAB	Cabinet
CCAC	Combined Civil Affairs Committee
CGC	Classified General Correspondence
CIGS	Chief of the Imperial General Staff
CO	Colonial Office
ETO	European Theatre of Operations
FO	Foreign Office
FRUS	U.S. Department of State, *Foreign Relations of the United States: Diplomatic Papers*
FSCC	Formerly Security-Classified Correspondence
GFHA	Ghetto Fighters House Archive
GRDS	General Records of the Department of State
HA	Archive of the Haganah
HIA	Hoover Institution Archives
HP	Information Center of the Ha'apala Project
JA	Archive of the Joint Distribution Committee
JTA	Jewish Telegraphic Agency
LA	Labour Movement (Histadrut)
LPA	Labour Party Archive
LSE	London School of Economics
NACP	National Archives, College Park
OF	Official File
OSS	Office of Strategic Services
P&O	Plans & Operations
PREM	Prime Minister
PRO	Public Record Office
PSF	President's Secretary's Files
RG	Record Group
RL	Franklin D. Roosevelt Library, Hyde Park, N.Y.
SACMEC	St. Antony's College, Oxford, Middle East Center

T	Treasury
TL	Harry S. Truman Library, Independence, Mo.
WA	Weizmann Archives
WHOF	White House Official File
WJC	World Jewish Congress
WO	War Office
YIVO	Institute for Jewish Studies
YVA	Yad Vashem Archives

PREFACE

1. PRO, FO371/52571/E11651, Lord Inverchapel, British ambassador in Washington, to Bevin, no. 2775, 26 November 1946.

INTRODUCTION

1. The Labour Party had gained 393 seats and 48 percent of the poll against 210 seats and 39.6 percent of the poll of the Conservatives and allies. The Liberals held 12 seats. Morgan, *Labour in Power,* 36–44, 144–45; Eatwell, *The 1945–1951 Labour Governments,* chap. 2; Pelling, *Labour Governments,* chap. 2; Childs, *Britain since 1945,* chap. 1.

2. Brenchley, *Britain and the Middle East,* chap. 1; Pelling, *Labour Governments,* 62–67; Morgan, *Labour in Power,* 180–81.

3. Ovendale, *The English-Speaking Alliance,* chap. 2; see also below, Part II.

4. PRO, FO371/44457/AN260, Halifax to Bevin, no. 1039, 9 August 1945; see also Louis, "American Anti-Colonialism," 395–420.

5. Hamby, *Man of the People,* chap. 19; Hathaway, *Ambiguous Partnership,* chap. 9; Harbutt, *Iron Curtain,* 99–116; Edmonds, *Setting the Mould,* chap. 5; see also Kimball, *Forged in War,* chap. 9; Mayers, *The Ambassadors and America's Soviet Policy,* 156–63.

6. Hathaway, *Ambiguous Partnership,* chap. 12; Taylor, *Britain and the Cold War,* chap. 6; Edmonds, *Setting the Mould,* chap. 8; see also Dobson, *US Wartime Aid to Britain.*

7. Bullock, *Ernest Bevin,* 198–200.

8. Louis, *British Empire,* 54–73; Bullock, *Ernest Bevin,* 206–13, 234–39, chap. 7; Harbutt, *Iron Curtain,* 267–80; Messer, *End of an Alliance,* chap. 11; Kuniholm, *Origins of the Cold War,* 304–50.

9. Quoted in Hamby, *Man of the People,* 387; Kuniholm, *Origins of the Cold War,* chaps. 5–6; Rubin, *Great Powers in the Middle East,* chap. 11; Gaddis, *Long Peace,* chap. 3.

10. Hathaway, *Ambiguous Partnership,* chaps. 13, 15; Hamby, *Man of the People,* chap. 22; Donovan, *Conflict and Crisis,* chap. 30; Hogan, *Marshall Plan;* Stoler, *George C. Marshall,* 161–68; Cromwell, "Marshall Plan," 233–49; Watt, "Britain, the United States and the Opening of the Cold War," 43–60.

11. Louis, *British Empire,* pt. 3, chap. 9; Ovendale, *Britain, the United States,* chap. 1; Bullock, *Ernest Bevin,* 34–36, 154–57, 250–53.

12. PRO, CAB21/2086, Cabinet, Defence Committee, D.O. (46) 47, 2 April 1946, and Cabinet, Defence Committee, D.O. (46) 80, 18 June 1946; see also Hyam, *Labour Gov-*

ernment, doc. 277–78; Saville, *Politics of Continuity,* chap. 3; Ovendale, *English-Speaking Alliance,* 98–101.

13. Louis, *British Empire,* pt. 3, chap. 6.

14. Bullock, *Ernest Bevin,* 348–51.

15. Morgan, *Labour in Power,* 218–28; Louis, *British Empire,* 257–61.

16. Michael J. Cohen, *Palestine,* chaps. 2–4; Porath, *Palestinian Arab National Movement,* chaps. 7–10.

17. Sherman, *Island Refuge,* 95–96, 100–111, 264–65, chap. 5; Wasserstein, *Britain and the Jews,* 7.

18. Michael J. Cohen, *Palestine,* chap. 5; Rubin, *Arab States,* 66–116.

19. Zweig, *Britain and Palestine,* chaps. 1–2.

20. PRO, CAB65/10, War Cabinet Conclusions, 27 November 1940; Zweig, *Britain and Palestine,* 70–78; Wasserstein, *Britain and the Jews,* 60–76.

21. Ofer, *Escaping the Holocaust,* 147–66; Wasserstein, *Britain and the Jews,* 143–57.

22. Wasserstein, *Britain and the Jews;* Gilbert, *Auschwitz and the Allies;* Bauer, *Jews for Sale?,* chap. 10; Breitman, *Official Secrets;* Kushner, *The Holocaust and the Liberal Imagination,* pt. 2. On American policy during the war, see Wyman, *Abandonment of the Jews;* Breitman and Kraut, *American Refugee Policy;* Feingold, *Politics of Rescue;* Penkower, *The Jews Were Expendable.*

23. Michael J. Cohen, *Palestine,* chap. 9; Michael J. Cohen, *Churchill and the Jews,* 227–60; Gorni, *The British Labour Movement and Zionism,* chaps. 8–9. On the assassination of Moyne, see Heller, *Stern Gang,* pt. 3, chap. 6.

CHAPTER ONE

1. Proudfoot, *European Refugees,* 98–106, 133–47.

2. Ibid., app. B, chaps. 7–9; Dinnerstein, *America and the Survivors,* 9–13; see also Woodbridge, *UNRRA.*

3. Marrus, *The Unwanted,* 298–313; Ziemke, *U.S. Army,* 115–29, 200–206, 237–41, 342–45; Bullock, *Ernest Bevin,* 21–23, 147–49; Deighton, *Impossible Peace,* chap. 1; Willis, *French in Germany,* chaps. 4–5; Smyser, *From Yalta to Berlin,* chaps. 1–2; Oppen, *Documents on Germany under Occupation,* 13–66.

4. PRO, FO371/51095/WR2020, Joint Staff Mission, Washington to Allied Military Staff Special Operations, 2 July 1945; PRO, FO1032/311, notes on meeting held at Frankfurt on 18 July 1945; NACP, RG 59, 800.4016 DP/6-145-800.4016 DP/7-3145, Robert Murphy, political adviser, SHAEF, to secretary of state, no. 682, 24 July 1945, and Murphy to secretary of state, no. 508, 22 June 1945; NACP, RG 338, U.S. Army Command, ETO, Historical Division, ADM no. 109, DPs, SHAEF report, no. 35, 18 May 1944; Proudfoot, *European Refugees,* 147–52, 158–88; Jacobmeyer, *Vom Zwangsarbeiter zum Heimatlosen Ausländer,* chap. 5; Marrus, *The Unwanted,* 313–17.

5. These statistics refer to those DPs who lived in camps or in areas closely supervised by the army or by UNRRA. But there were other DPs who preferred to stay outside the DP centers. NACP, RG 59, 800.4016 DP/10-145-800.4016 DP/10-3145, Murphy to Byrnes, no. 1199, 26 October 1945; Proudfoot, *European Refugees,* 238–39; Dinnerstein, *America and the Survivors,* 18–23.

6. PRO, FO1032/311, Political Division, Control Commission, "Displaced Persons Assembly Centers—Discipline," 31 July 1945; Proudfoot, *European Refugees,* 220–23; Wyman, *Europe's Displaced Persons,* 78–79.

7. NACP, RG 165, War Department, General and Special Staff, ABC Decimal File, 1942–48, File no. ABC 383.6 (16 June 43), note by the Secretaries, C.C.A.C. 187, Repatriation of Polish Nationals, 9 May 1945, enclosure A.

8. *FRUS,* 1945, 2:1188–90, Arthur Bliss Lane, the American ambassador in Poland, to Byrnes, 25 August 1945; ibid., 1191, Lane to Byrnes, 25 August 1945; ibid., 1191–92, Acheson to the chargé d'affaires in Poland, 14 September 1945; Ziemke, *U.S. Army,* 413; Zink, *American Military Government in Germany,* 105–8, 121–22.

9. PRO, FO371/51098/WR2409, discussion with U.S. delegation to the UNRRA Council, 3 August 1945; PRO, FO371/51098/WR2307, memorandum by Paul Mason, head of the Refugee Department, FO, 2 August 1945; Stoessinger, *The Refugee and the World Community,* 51–52, 57, 60–76.

10. PRO, FO181/933/6, FO to Moscow, no. 1640, 4 April 1945; *FRUS,* 1945, 5:1110–11, memorandum of conversation by the Chief of the Division of Eastern European Affairs Elbridge Dubrow, 27 December 1945, and 1108–9, memorandum by the State-War-Navy Coordinating Committee, 21 December 1945. On the repatriation of Soviet refugees, see Elliot, *Pawns of Yalta,* 102–14; Bethell, *Last Secret.*

11. PRO, FO371/51128/WR3682, Lieutenant General B. H. Robertson, chief of staff British zone, to the permanent under secretary of state, Control Office for Germany and Austria, 8 December 1945, and Gottlieb, Control Office, to Ian Henderson, Refugee Department, FO, 12 December 1945; Montgomery, *Memoirs,* 356, 381–82, 391–92, 411–14.

12. PRO, FO371/51128/WR3682, Douglas Mackillop, the new head of the Refugee Department, FO, to Gottlieb, 22 December 1945, and memorandum by Mackillop, 14 December 1945. On Britain's relations with the Polish government in exile, see Kacewicz, *Great Britain and the Polish Government in Exile;* see also chap. 7.

13. PRO, FO1052/7, message from the British foreign secretary to all members of the Polish Forces under British Command, 3 March 1946; PRO, FO1052/7, "Treatment of Repatriated Members of the Polish Armed Forces," 3 March 1946.

14. PRO, FO1052/7, Report on Reaction of Polish Troops to Foreign Secretary's Statement and Warsaw Government's Terms, 31 March 1946.

15. NACP, RG 59, 800.4016 DP/11-1745-800.4016 DP/11-3145, Patterson to Byrnes, 29 November 1945, and Kenneth C. Royall, acting secretary of war, to Acheson, 19 January 1945.

16. NACP, RG 59, 800.4016 DP/11-1745-800.4016 DP/11-3145, Byrnes to Patterson, 28 December 1945.

17. NACP, RG 107, ASW, FSCC of Howard C. Petersen, December 1945–August 1947, ASW 383.7, Refugees and DPs, Patterson to Byrnes, 1 February 1946; NACP, RG 59, 800.4016 DP/2-146-800.4016 DP/2-3146, Patterson to Byrnes, 26 February 1946; ibid., Patterson to Byrnes, 14 March 1946; Elliot, *Pawns of Yalta,* chap. 5; Tolstoy, *Secret Betrayal,* chap. 4.

18. *FRUS,* 1946, 5:143, Byrnes to Winant, 21 February 1946.

19. PRO, FO945/389, War Office to Control Commission for Germany, Berlin, no. 469, 15 March 1946.

20. PRO, FO945/389, Control Commission for Germany, Berlin, to War Office, 24 March 1946.

21. *FRUS*, 1946, 5:148-49, Gallman to Byrnes, 1 March 1946; NACP, RG 59, 800.4016 DP/3-146-800.4016 DP/3-3146, British embassy in Washington to Byrnes, 13 March 1946.

22. *FRUS*, 1946, 5:143-47, Gallman to Byrnes, no. 2407, 28 February 1946, and 148, Gallman to Byrnes, no. 2419, 28 February 1946.

23. NACP, RG 59, 800.4016 DP/3-146-800.4016 DP/3-3146, Byrnes to Tayler Wood, 15 March 1946.

24. NACP, RG 59, 800.4016 DP/3-146-800.4016 DP/3-3146, Byrnes to Halifax, 16 March 1946.

25. TL, WHOF: OF 127, memorandum for the president by Byrnes, 12 April 1946.

26. NACP, RG 59, 800.4016 DP/9-145-800.4016 DP/9-3146, Charles Rozmarek, president of the Polish-American Congress, to Byrnes, 22 September 1945; TL, WHOF: OF 463, Rozmarek to Truman, 8 October 1945, and Truman to Rozmarek, 25 October 1945; TL, WHOF: OF 127, memorandum for the president by Edwin A. Locke Jr., 15 April 1946; Dinnerstein, *America and the Survivors,* 53; Wyman, *Europe's Displaced Persons,* 82-83.

27. Divine, *Foreign Policy and U.S. Presidential Elections,* 109-12, 138-43.

28. NACP, RG 107, ASW, FSCC of Howard C. Petersen, December 1945-August 1947, ASW 383.7, Refugees and DPs, note for the Press, no. 268, 22 April 1946; *FRUS*, 1946, 5:155, Byrnes to Patterson, 23 April 1946; TL, WHOF: OF 127, Truman to Cardinal Samuel Stritch, Archbishop to Chicago, 25 April 1946.

29. NACP, RG 107, ASW, FSCC of Howard Petersen, December 1945-August 1947, ASW 383.7, Refugees and DPs, McNarney to Eisenhower, 1 May 1946.

30. NACP, RG 107, ASW, FSCC of Howard Petersen, December 1945-August 1947, ASW 383.7, Refugees and DPs, memorandum for the secretary of war, 27 May 1946.

31. TL, PSF, 1945-53, File: Germany, Patterson to Truman, 11 June 1946; Ziemke, *U.S. Army,* 409-13, 435-37.

32. NACP, RG 107, ASW, FSCC of Howard C. Petersen, December 1945-August 1947, ASW 383.7, Refugees and DPs, McNarney to War Department, no. S-5309, 7 June 1946, memorandum for the secretary of war, 27 May 1946, and Murphy to secretary of state, no. 1326, 23 May 1946; NACP, RG 59, 800.4016 DP/4-146-800.4016 DP/5-1546, memorandum of a meeting, 9 May 1946.

33. *FRUS*, 1946, 5:179, Acheson to the minister in Switzerland, 14 August 1946, and 176-78, vice-consul at Geneva to Byrnes, 7 August 1946. At that time, the Polish DPs constituted about half of all the DPs. Of the 471,000 DPs living in the American zone and the approximately 368,000 in the British zone, the number of Polish DPs in the two occupied zones together was estimated at about 400,000 persons. PRO, CAB133/83, report of the Fact-Finding Sub-Committee on Jewish DPs problem in Germany, Austria and Italy, 21 June 1946; PRO, FO1005/840, Combined Repatriation Executive, Berlin, 26 June 1946, app. A, D, and Combined Repatriation Executive, Berlin, 6 July 1946, app. A; PRO, FO945/360, memorandum "Future Policy for the Disposal of Displaced Persons in the British Zones of Germany and Austria," 23 July 1946; NACP, RG 107, ASW, FSCC of Howard C. Petersen, December 1945-August 1946, ASW 383.7, Refugees and DPs, memorandum for the under secretary of war, July 1946, and Murphy to the State De-

partment, 19 June 1946; NACP, RG 59, 800.4016 DP/6-146-800.4016 DP/6-1746, Murphy to secretary of state, 11 June 1946.

34. Balabkins, *Germany under Direct Controls*, 99–109; Rothwell, *Britain and the Cold War*, 316–21; Backer, *Priming the German Economy*, 47–59; Zweiniger-Bargielowska, "Bread Rationing in Britain," 57–85; Marshall, "German Attitudes to British Military Government," 659–60.

35. PRO, T220/143, memorandum "The Refugee Problem," 26 June 1946; see also Penrose, "Negotiations on Refugees and Displaced Persons," chap. 6; Proudfoot, *European Refugees*, 260, 399–401.

36. PRO, FO945/360, minutes of a meeting, 27 June 1946; PRO, FO371/57766/WR2018, memorandum "Future Policy for the Disposal of Displaced Persons in the British Zones of Germany and Austria," 23 July 1946; Jacobmeyer, *Vom Zwangsarbeiter zum Heimatlosen Ausländer*, 159–61.

37. Carden, "Before Bizonia," 535–55; Marshall, "German Attitudes to British Military Government," 655–68; Balfour, *West Germany*, 126–31.

38. Schechtman, *Postwar Population Transfers*, 307–11; Schechtman, *The Refugee in the World*, chap. 2; Marrus, *The Unwanted*, 325–31; Schulze, "Growing Discontent," 33; Wyman, *Europe's Displaced Persons*, 19–20.

39. PRO, FO371/51125/WR3052, Lieutenant General Robertson to Sir Eric B. B. Speed, 6 October 1945; Montgomery, *Memoirs*, 400–403, 411–15; Jacobmeyer, *Vom Zwangsarbeiter zum Heimatlosen Ausländer*, 170–78, 185, 188–89.

40. At the beginning of 1947, only 71,000 of 136,000 DPs who were fit to work did so. This latter figure consisted of 88,000 males, of whom two-thirds worked, and 48,000 women, of whom but one-third were employed. Jacobmeyer, *Vom Zwangsarbeiter zum Heimatlosen Ausländer*, 184–85. Proudfoot gives different data. Proudfoot, *European Refugees*, 254–56; Wyman, *Europe's Displaced Persons*, 113–14; Carden, "Before Bizonia," 537–38.

41. PRO, PREM8/522, minutes of a meeting on "Displaced Persons in Germany and Austria," 17 September 1946; PRO, FO371/57766/WR2046, memorandum for the Cabinet Overseas Reconstruction Committee, O.R.C. (46) 76, 27 July 1946.

42. TL, WHOF: OF 423, UNRRA's monthly review, no. 26, October 1946; Stoessinger, *The Refugee and the World Community*, 52.

43. Proudfoot, *European Refugees*, 283–84.

44. PRO, FO371/66656/WR558, Parliamentary Question, 19 February 1947; PRO, FO371/66656/WR430, Zonal Executive Instructions, no. 2, "Treatment of Displaced Persons," 30 January 1947; Jacobmeyer, *Vom Zwangsarbeiter zum Heimatlosen Ausländer*, 86, 159–61, 183; Proudfoot, *European Refugees*, 284–85, 294.

45. PRO, FO371/57778/WR3943, memorandum "Refugees and Displaced Persons," March 1947; PRO, FO371/66667/WR644, memorandum "Displaced Persons in Germany," 21 April 1947; PRO, FO943/203, Control Office for Germany and Austria to Control Commission for Germany, 11 January 1947.

46. NACP, RG 59, 800.4016 DP/7-147-7-3147, American embassy, London, to Byrnes, 24 July 1947; see also PRO, FO371/66673/WR3598, memorandum for the secretary of state "The Refugee Problem," 8 October 1947; PRO, FO371/61956/E9456, brief for the United Kingdom delegation, 2 October 1947.

47. PRO, FO371/57776/WR3692, New York to FO, no. 1950, 25 November 1946; PRO, FO943/203, Control Office for Germany and Austria to Allied Commission for Germany, 11 January 1947; PRO, PREM8/522, memorandum for the prime minister, 18 December 1946; see also Cronin, *Great Powers Politics,* 39–42.

48. NACP, RG 59, 800.4016 DP/12-1246-800.4016 DP/1-1547, Rozmarek to Truman, 31 December 1946; ibid., 800.4016 DP/3-1647-4-3047, Rozmarek to Truman, 21 March 1947.

49. NACP, RG 59, 800.4016 DP/3-1647-4-3047, Acheson to Rozmarek, 2 April 1947, and memorandum of conversation, 18 March 1947.

50. *FRUS, 1947,* 2:253–55, Marshall to Truman, 15 March 1947, 412–17, report of the Coordinating Committee to the Council of Foreign Ministers, 28 March 1947, and 429–33, report of the Special Committee to the Council of Foreign Ministers, 2 April 1947.

51. PRO, FO371/66673/WR3598, memorandum for the secretary of state "The Refugee Problem," 8 October 1947. On IRO, see Holborn, *World's Refugees;* Proudfoot, *European Refugees,* chap. 13; Marrus, *The Unwanted,* 340–45; Stoessinger, *The Refugee and the World Community,* 85–155.

52. PRO, FO371/61956/E9456, brief for the United Kingdom delegation, 2 October 1947; Truman's Library, a microfilm project of University Publications of America, WHOFs, 1945–53, reel 18, memorandum "Transfers of Population," 27 October 1947.

53. *FRUS, 1947,* 2:253–55, Marshall to Truman, 15 March 1947.

54. PRO, FO371/61956/E9456, brief for the United Kingdom delegation, 2 October 1947; PRO, FO371/66673/WR3598, memorandum for the secretary of state "The Refugee Problem," 8 October 1947; Dinnerstein, *America and the Survivors,* 132–35; *The DP Story,* 9–19; Bennett, *American Immigration Policies,* 76–79, 85–92.

55. Hartmann, *Truman and the 80th Congress,* 175–79; Dinnerstein, *America and the Survivors,* chaps. 7–8; *The DP Story; Whom We Shall Welcome.*

56. Proudfoot, *European Refugees,* 422–36; Stoessinger, *The Refugee and the World Community,* 108–41; Wyman, *Europe's Displaced Persons,* chap. 8; Genizi, *America's Fair Share,* chap. 7; Jacobmeyer, *Vom Zwangsarbeiter zum Heimatlosen Ausländer,* 168–75; Vernant, *The Refugee in the Post-War World,* 33–38.

57. PRO, FO371/66673/WR3598, memorandum for the secretary of state "The Refugee Problem," 8 October 1947; Bauer, *Flight and Rescue,* 75–76, 319.

CHAPTER TWO

1. YIVO, Leo S. Schwartz Papers, 13/111, chaplain to the editor of the *Jewish Chronicle,* 20 April 1945; PRO, FO371/51117/WR1357, Jane E. Leverson to the Jewish Committee for Relief Abroad, 6 May 1945; NACP, RG 338, U.S. Army Command, ETO, Historical Division, ADM 109, Displaced Persons, SHAEF report, no. 35, "2,500,000 'Displaced Persons' Found in Two Months in Germany," 18 May 1945; Lavski, "The Day After," 36–59; Reilly, *Belsen,* chaps. 1, 5; Kemp, "British Army," 134–48; Königseder and Wetzel, *Lebensmut im Wartesaal,* 173–77; Bridgman, *End of the Holocaust,* 47–60.

2. PRO, FO371/51116/WR1224, Sidney Silverman, chairman of the British section of the WJC, to under secretary of state for foreign affairs, 25 April 1945, and Paul Mason, head of the Refugee Department, FO, to the Marquess Reading, 5 May 1945; PRO, FO371/51117/WR1224, Mason to the under secretary of state, War Office, 5 May 1945; PRO,

FO945/599, Chaim Weizmann, head of the Zionist movement, to James Grigg, secretary of state for war, 21 June 1945; PRO, FO1052/281, F. C. Bovenschen, permanent under secretary of state for war to Lt. General A. E. Grasett, assistant chief of staff, 19 May 1945. About the Jewish organizations, see Bolchover, *British Jewry and the Holocaust*, 23–30, 34, 38. For noncomplimentary appreciation of the Anglo-Jewish community response to the distress of Jewish DPs, see Reilly, *Belsen*, chap. 4; on British Jewish response to the Holocaust, see Bolchover, *British Jewry and the Holocaust*.

3. PRO, FO1052/281, Grasett to Bovenschen, 26 June, 24 May 1945.

4. PRO, FO1049/81, A. V. Anderson, director of civil affairs in the War Office, to Major General S. W. Kirby, Main Headquarters, Control Commission Germany (British Element), 28 July 1945.

5. PRO, FO1052/281, Weeks to Marquess Reading, 26 July 1945; see also PRO, FO371/51120/WR2332, Brigadier G. W. Britten to Anderson, 27 July 1945.

6. PRO, FO945/599, Major General R. H. Dewing to the under secretary of state, WO, 18 August 1945; PRO, FO371/51122, Dewing to Anderson, 27 July 1945.

7. PRO, FO371/51120/WR2318, minute by Henderson, 8 August 1945. On Harrison's report, see chap. 4.

8. PRO, FO1049/195, George Rendel, FO, to William Strang, FO, 24 August 1945; PRO, FO371/51122, minute by Henderson, 24 August 1945; PRO, FO371/51123/WR2724, Brodetsky to P. J. Noel-Baker, minister of state, FO, 6 September 1945; PRO, FO945/599, *Jewish Chronicle* clippings, 13, 20 July, 10 August 1945.

9. PRO, FO945/599, Major General G. W. R. Templer to Directorate of Civil Affairs, WO, 6 September 1945.

10. PRO, CAB120/660, Attlee to Truman, no. 9, 16 September 1945; Cesarani, "Great Britain," 605–13; see also chap. 5.

11. PRO, FO945/599, minute, 10 September 1945; Wasserstein, *Vanishing Diaspora*, 9–12. For a different interpretation of Whitehall's stand, see Reilly, *Belsen*, 85–88, 92–93.

12. PRO, FO371/51123/WR2783, minute by Henderson "Treatment of Jewish Displaced Persons in Germany," 14 September 1945, and minutes by Mason, 14, 16 September 1945; PRO, FO371/51123/WR2724, Mason to A. G. Brotman, secretary BDBJ, 20 September 1945.

13. PRO, FO371/51120/WR2163, Easterman to Henderson, 16 July 1945, and minutes by Mason, 18 July, 21 August 1945; PRO, FO371/51121/WR2511, minute by Henderson, 17 August 1945; PRO, FO371/51123, memorandum by Mason "Claim of World Jewish Congress to be represented at meeting of Jewish organizations in British zone in Germany to be held at Bergen-Belsen on September 23rd," 19 September 1945, and Eva Reading to Lt. Colonel Hammer, WO, 14 September 1945; PRO, FO371/51124, Lord Nathan to Noel-Baker, 26 September 1945; PRO, FO371/51125/WR3052, Weizmann to Lord Nathan, 1 October 1945, and Bovenschen to Sargent, 10 October 1945; PRO, FO371/51125/WR3052, minute by Mason, 15 October 1945, and Sargent to T. J. Cash, 24 October 1945; YV, o-70, File 1, minutes of the Central Jewish Committee Presidium in Bergen Belsen, 12 August 1945; Rosensaft, "Our Belsen," 42.

14. PRO, FO1052/284, Eva Reading to Montgomery, 20 September 1945.

15. PRO, FO371/51125/WR3078, report on "Jewish Congress" at Höne Camp, 25–27 September 1945.

16. PRO, FO371/51124/WR2991, Brodetsky to Attlee, 21 September 1945; PRO, FO371/51125, Brotman to Bevin, 11 October 1945.

17. PRO, FO371/51125/WR3065, Easterman to Henderson, 12 October 1945; PRO, FO371/51124/WR2966, Silverman to Mason, 3 October 1945.

18. PRO, FO1052/281, Kenchington to deputy chiefs of staff, 29 September 1945.

19. PRO, FO371/51125/WR3052, Robertson to Speed, 6 October 1945; PRO, FO371/51125/WR3043, Brotman to Bevin, 9 October 1945; PRO, FO371/51128/WR3775, Templer to the Marchioness Reading, 26 October 1945.

20. PRO, FO371/51124/WR2947, Cadogan to T. J. Cash, WO, 24 October 1945, and minute by Mason, 15 October 1945; PRO, FO371/51127/WR3420, Strang to Rendel, 13 November 1945. On the appointment of a Jewish adviser in the American zone, see chap. 4.

21. PRO, FO1052/281, "Segregation of Jews," 19 November 1945.

22. PRO, PREM8/627, Cabinet Defence Committee, D.C., 12th meeting, 5 November 1945; PRO, FO371/51127/WR397, Hynd to Bevin, 12 November 1945; PRO, FO371/45383/E8598, Archibald Nye to Arthur Street, 9 November 1945.

23. YV, 0-70, File 1, minutes of the first meeting of the Central Committee Presidium, 24 June 1945; Friedlander and Milton, *Archives of the Holocaust*, vol. 10, part 2, document no. 245, Report on the Belsen camp by Maurice Eigen, JDC representative in Belsen, 21 August 1945; Rosensaft, "Our Belsen," 33–34; Bauer, *Out of the Ashes*, 61–62, 99–100, 130; Reilly, *Belsen*, 171–76; Lavski, "Liberated but Not Free," 23–31; Bentwich, *They Found Refuge*, 143.

24. Lavski, "Liberated but Not Free," 26–27; Reilly, *Belsen*, 84–85.

25. PRO, FO371/51128/WR3668, FO to Washington, no. 12651, 17 December 1945; see also YV, 0-70/18, minutes of the Central Jewish Committee meetings, 8 December 1945, 16 January 1946; Rosensaft, "Our Belsen," 45.

26. The political adviser to Britain's commander in chief in Germany stressed in May 1946 that to recognize "any single committee as representing the interests of German and non-German Jews alike would imply that we recognised Jews as a separate nationality which would be contrary to our policy as we understand it." PRO, FO371/57691/WR1354, political adviser to commander in chief in Germany to FO, no. 605, 18 May 1946.

27. PRO, FO371/51127/WR3453, Halifax to FO, nos. 7802, 7803, 22 November 1945.

28. PRO, FO371/51127/WR3366, Eva Reading to Lord Jowitt, the lord chancellor, 8 November 1945; PRO, FO945/543, Acarbit Vienna (Allied Control Commission for Austria) to WO, no. 9295, 27 November 1945; PRO, FO371/57684/WR36, Mack to Bevin, no. 28, 19 December 1945; PRO, FO945/599, report of the treatment of the Jews in the British zone of Austria, January (?) 1946. On the Hanover incident, see PRO, FO1052/284, Control Commission for Germany, British Element, "Jewish 'Demonstration' in Hanover," 19 December 1945; PRO, FO1052/281, Easterman to J. J. Lawson, secretary of state for war, 23 December 1945; Reilly, *Belsen*, 96–97.

29. PRO, FO945/599, Parliamentary Debate, 20 December 1945; PRO, FO371/51128/WR36, minute, December 1945.

30. BGA, Chronological Documentation Division, report of Ben-Gurion on his visit in the camps, 27 November 1945; see also CZA, Z-4/302/30, minutes of the Zionist Council meeting in London, 22 October 1945; HA, 14/52, Ernest Frank to Merkaz Lagolah

(Center for Jewish Diaspora), 20 January 1946; WA, Weizmann to Attlee, 16 April 1946; LA, minutes of the Executive Committee of the Histadrut (General Labor Federation of Jewish workers in Palestine), Hadasa Bimko's report, 8 May 1946; Gelber, *Standard Bearers,* 457, 509–10.

31. PRO, FO1052/284, report on a visit by Judge Rifkind to Höne camp on 20 December 1945; see also Brenner, *After the Holocaust,* 98–99.

32. PRO, FO1052/285, memorandum relating to Jews in Berlin and British zone, 10 February 1946; see also YIVO, Schwartz Papers 41/496, report of Harry Viteles and Brotman, 29 March 1946; Reilly, *Belsen,* 176–78.

33. PRO, FO945/655, Acarbit Vienna to Troopers (War Office), no. 7758, 18 October 1945, and Acarbit Vienna to WO, no. 9238, 25 November 1945.

34. PRO, FO688/81, File no. 48, Hilary Young, Political Division, Control Commission for Germany, to Robin M. A. Hankey, British embassy, Warsaw, 5 December 1945. On the flight to Berlin, see Bauer, *Flight and Rescue,* 130–42; Königseder, *Flucht nach Berlin,* 43–62.

35. PRO, FO1005/838, note by the secretariat, Directorate of Prisoners of War and Displaced Persons, 7 December 1945; PRO, FO943/699, Bercomb (Control Commission for Germany, Berlin) to WO, 8 December 1945; YIVO, Schwartz Papers, 9/63, Philip Skorneck, JDC, director for Berlin, to Captain Vlcek, Welfare Section, Office of Military Government of the United States for Germany, 6 December 1945.

36. On the Anglo-American Committee, see chap. 5.

37. PRO, FO371/51128/WR3648, minute by Henderson, 11 December 1945.

38. PRO, FO371/57684/WR93, Rendel to Hammer, WO, 9 December 1945.

39. Ibid.; on Rendel, see Rendel, *The Sword and the Olive;* Klieman, *Divide or Rule,* 71–72.

40. PRO, FO371/57686/WR267, Cabinet Overseas Reconstruction Committee, O.R.C. (46) 2nd meeting, 25 January 1946, and Troopers to Bercomb, 28 January 1946; PRO, FO371/57684/WR75, record of a meeting at Refugee Department, 8 January 1946.

41. See chap. 7.

42. See chap. 4.

43. PRO, FO371/57686/WR258, Parliamentary Question, 23 January 1946; see also PRO, FO945/384, Brodetsky to Hynd, 23 January 1946; YV, 0-70/16 (59/18), A. Skeffington, Hynd's private secretary, to N. Barou, secretary of the WJC, 16 March 1946.

44. PRO, FO945/384, brief for the Chancellor, app. B, "Colonel Solomon's Work as a Jewish Adviser," 23 April 1947; PRO, FO945/378, minutes on Jewish adviser in Germany, 24 May 1946. On Solomon, see Bentwich, *They Found Refuge,* 95–96.

45. PRO, FO1049/626, Steel to P. H. Dean, German Department, FO, 8 October 1946.

46. PRO, FO945/384, notes by Solomon on a "Proposal for the Resettlement of Jews at Present Residing within the British Zone, Germany," 8 May 1946. On Solomon's first meeting with the Central Jewish Committee in Bergen-Belsen, see YV, 0-70, File 1, minutes of the Central Jewish Committee in Bergen-Belsen, 17 April 1946.

47. PRO, FO945/485, Acarbit Vienna to WO, 8 April 1946.

48. Ibid., memorandum by R. S. Crawford, permanent secretary, Control Office, 6 May 1946; PRO, FO945/590, WO to Acarbit Vienna, 11 May 1946; PRO, FO945/381,

Major General Sugden, WO, to Wilberforce, 8 July 1946, and Wilberforce to Sugden, 2 August 1946.

49. PRO, FO371/52526/E4928, Crawford to parliamentary under secretary, Colonial Office, 26 May 1946; PRO, FO945/378, Trafford Smith, Colonial Office, to Crawford, 19 June 1946; PRO, FO945/384, Hynd to Arthur Creech Jones, secretary of state for the colonies, 15 October 1946, and Creech Jones to Hynd, 29 October 1946; see also the following chapter.

50. PRO, FO945/723, memorandum by Hynd, O.R.C. (47)23, 10 April 1947; PRO, FO371/57770/WR2713, Allied Commission for Austria to Control Office for Germany and Austria, 29 July 1946; see also YIVO, Schwartz Papers, 41/496, report no. 341 of Shlome M. Gelber, 28 June 1946; YV, 0-70/16(59/21), Skeffington to Barou, 26 June 1946; YV, 0-70/6(3/17), Rosensaft to La Guardia, 23 August 1946; HP, Rosensaft testimony, no. 297; Hirschmann, *The Embers Still Burn,* 170; Königseder and Wetzel, *Lebensmut im Wartesaal,* 182–85.

51. PRO, FO371/57769/WR2522, Henderson to Crawford, 5 October 1946, and minute by Edmonds, 24 September 1946; PRO, FO371/66736/WR1004, minute by Rendel, 20 March 1947, and minute by Wilkinson, April 1947.

52. The overwhelming number of them left because of the Kielce pogrom. See below, chap. 7.

53. PRO, FO945/723, Bercomb to Confolk, 3 August 1946.

54. Air Marshall Sholto Douglas, commander in chief of the British Zone in Germany, made this policy public at a press conference on 9 August. PRO, FO371/57693/WR2177, statement by Douglas, 9 August 1946, and FO to Geneva, no. 662, 8 August 1946.

55. PRO, FO945/723, Confolk to Bercomb, no. 662, 8 August 1946; PRO, FO945/372, Confolk to Bercomb and Acarbit Vienna, 8 August 1946; PRO, FO371/55131/C9235, Confolk to Acarbit Vienna, 8 August 1946.

56. See chap. 3.

57. PRO, FO943/543, Allied Commission for Austria to Control Office for Germany and Austria, 19 August 1946; PRO, FO945/372, Allied Commission for Austria to Control Office for Germany and Austria, 31 August 1946; PRO, FO945/494, Control Commission for Germany, Berlin, to Control Office for Germany and Austria, 31 August 1946.

58. PRO, FO945/372, Confolk to Acarbit Vienna, no. 351, 31 October 1946; PRO, FO945/494, Confolk to Bercomb, no. 250, 23 October 1946.

59. YIVO, Schwartz Papers, 14/128, Joseph J. Schwartz, head of JDC operations in Europe, to Moses A. Leavitt, 11 September 1946; ibid., report of David Wodlinger, the JDC representative in the British zone, on the JDC activities in the British zone, 8 December 1945–20 September 1946.

60. YV, 0-70/6 (3/17), Rosensaft to La Guardia, 23 August 1946; PRO, FO945/723, Marcus Schloimovitz, BDBJ, to Control Office for Germany and Austria, 6 September 1946.

61. PRO, FO371/57693/WR2199, *New Chronicle,* 14 August 1946; TL, WHOF: OF 423, UNRRA's Monthly Report, no. 26, October 1946, and La Guardia, Broadcast, 1 September 1946; see also Kochavi, "Anglo-American Discord," 529–51.

62. PRO, PREM8/384, note of La Guardia's interview with the prime minister, 5 September 1945, and memorandum for the prime minister, 4 September 1946; PRO, FO371/57696, memorandum by Rendel, 2 September 1946.

63. See chap. 7.

64. Hirschmann, *The Embers Still Burn,* 144; *New York Times,* 18 August 1946.

65. PRO, FO371/58119, Geneva to FO, no. 33, 15 August 1946; PRO, FO371/58118/UR6932, Geneva to FO, no. 20, 13 August 1946, Geneva to FO, no. 25, 14 August 1946, and FO to Geneva, no. 53, 15 August 1946; *New York Times,* 21 August 1946; Hirschmann, *The Embers Still Burn,* 66, 125–26, 129–30, 137–38, 142–43; HP, interview with Philip S. Bernstein, adviser on Jewish affairs to General McNarney.

66. See chap. 7.

67. PRO, FO371/57770/WR2562, Morgan to the under secretary of state, FO, 14 September 1946, and memorandum by Mason, 23 September 1946.

68. *New York Times,* 9 August 1946.

69. PRO, FO371/57769/WR2506, memorandum by Rendel, 24 August 1946.

70. PRO, FO371/57771/WR2889, McNeil to General Hildring, 30 September 1946; PRO, PREM8/384, McNeil to Attlee, 4 October 1946; PRO, FO371/57773/WR3039, record of conversation with Colonel Wood, 7 October 1946.

71. PRO, FO371/57697/WR313, New York (Rendel) to FO, no. 71, 21 October 1946; PRO, FO371/57774/WR3258, Crawford to Edmonds, 31 October 1946.

72. PRO, FO945/723, Control Commission, Lubbecke to Control Office, London, 10 December 1946, Shloimovitz to Allied Control Commission for Germany, 5 September 1946, and draft letter to Shloimovitz, 6 September 1945; NACP, RG 200, Duker/Dwork Papers, OSS R&A Jewish Desk, papers cuttings, 20 December 1946.

73. PRO, FO1049/368, Political Division, Lubbecke to I. T. M. Pink, Political Division, Berlin, 19 November 1946.

74. PRO, FO945/371, Shloimovitz to Hynd, 24 September 1946, and Silverman to Skeffington, 8 January 1947; YV, 0-70 (47/7), Solomon to Rosensaft, 21 January 1947; PRO, FO945/723, Hynd to Brotman, 31 December 1946.

75. Ibid., Rosensaft to Solomon, 31 January 1947; YV, 0-70, File 1, minutes of meeting of the Central Jewish Committee in Bergen-Belsen, 31 January 1947. Solomon participated in that meeting; PRO, FO1049/798, Control Commission for Germany and Austria to Arthur G. Kenchington, chief PW and DP Division, British Element, Control Commission, 11 February 1947.

76. PRO, FO945/723, Control Office, London to Berlin (Robertson), 26 February 1947.

77. Ibid., memorandum by Hynd, O.R.C. (47) 23, 10 April 1947.

78. PRO, FO945/467, extract from the conclusions of the 4th meeting of the Cabinet Overseas Reconstruction Committee, 23 April 1947.

79. PRO, FO945/723, Lemgo to FO (German Section), 9 May 1947; YV, 0-70/5 (7/18), brief notes of interview with Mr. Friedenberg of PW & DP Division, 28 May 1947.

80. PRO, FO945/399, Gilmour Jenkins, Control Office for Germany and Austria, to Robertson, 24 December 1946; PRO, FO1049/890, Jenkins to Robertson, 14 February 1947; YV, 0-70/5(715), minute of a meeting with Hynd, 25 November 1946; Easterman, "Liberated—But Not Freemen," 80–84.

81. YV, 0-70/5 (7/18), minutes of discussion between Rosensaft and Friedenberg, 28 May 1947; PRO, FO945/399, minutes of a meeting to discuss Jewish problems in the British zone of Germany, 18 June 1947; YV, 0-70, File no. 1, minutes of meetings of the Central Jewish Committee, Bergen-Belsen, 10, 20 May 1947.

82. PRO, FO945/399, minutes of a meeting between Lord Pakenham and Silverman, 16 June 1947, and minutes of a meeting to discuss Jewish problems in the British zone of Germany, 18 June 1947; PRO, FO945/731, FO (German Section) to Berlin, 23 June 1947, Berlin to FO (German Section), 27 June 1947, and Major General Brownjohn, Control Commission for Germany (British Element) to Jenkins, 12 July 1947; PRO, FO945/399, FO (German Section) to Berlin, 2 July 1947, and Lord Pakenham to Silverman, 21 July 1947; YV, 0-70/9 (47/13), Solomon to Rosensaft, 15 August 1947.

83. PRO, FO945/384, memorandum for the chancellor of the duchy of Lancaster, 23 April 1947.

84. PRO, FO945/599, minute, 14 May 1945.

85. PRO, FO1052/281, Weeks to the Marquess of Reading, 26 July 1945; PRO, FO1032/311, comments on letter from Lord Reading to the deputy high commissioner, 25 July 1945.

86. PRO, FO371/51123/WR2783, minute by Henderson on the treatment of Jewish DPs in Germany, 14 September 1945.

87. PRO, FO371/51125/WR3052, Robertson to permanent under secretary, WO, 6 October 1945; PRO, FO371/46959/C3275, minute, 9 November 1945; PRO, FO371/57688/WR638, Jewish Telegraphic Agency, 3 March 1946.

88. YV, 0-70/16(59/21), Barou to Skeffington, 8 March 1946, and Skeffington to Barou, 26 June 1946; see also NACP, RG 200, Duker/Dwork Papers, OSS R&A, Jewish Desk, Folder 88, Box 5 of 13, daily digest of WJC activities, 22 March 1946; YIVO, Schwartz Papers 41/496, report of Harry Viteles and Brotman, 29 March 1946; JA, 7-A, File no. C-48.009, Viteles to Dr. Joseph Schwartz, 2 April 1946; YV, 0-70, File 1, minutes of meeting of the Central Jewish Committee, Bergen-Belsen, 22 July 1945.

89. PRO, WO267/32, Dean to Robertson, 5 July 1946; PRO, FO371/55705/C13546, memorandum on resettlement of persons of Jewish nationality in Germany, 30 October 1946.

90. PRO, FO945/399, Jenkins to Robertson, 24 December 1946; YV, 0-70/5 (7/15), minutes of conversation between Hynd and representatives of the DPs, 25 November 1946.

91. PRO, FO945/723, memorandum by Hynd, O.R.C. (47)23, 10 April 1947.

92. PRO, FO1049/891, Major General V. J. E. Westropp, Headquarters, Control Commission for Germany, to FO, 30 May 1947.

93. PRO, FO938/287, report of Solomon on Jewish affairs in the British zone of Germany, November 1947.

94. PRO, FO1049/891, notes of a meeting on 22 October 1947; see also Brenner, "East European and German Jews," 61–62; Stern, *Whitewashing of the Yellow Badge*, chap. 2.

95. PRO, FO1052/73, Westropp to Foreign Office, 13 January 1948; PRO, FO1049/891, Chief Political Division, Berlin, to Central Secretariat, Lubbecke, 30 December 1947. Wolheim was born in Berlin in 1913. In March 1943 he was deported to Auschwitz

together with his wife and child. Only he was to survive. When the Germans evacuated Auschwitz in January 1945, he was forced to march (the "death march") to Sachsenhausen, where he stayed until April 1945. Brenner, *After the Holocaust*, 95–96.

96. PRO, FO1052/73, Westropp to FO (German Section), 20 April 1948, and E. B. Boothby to Headquarters, Control Commission for Germany, 2 March 1948.

97. PRO, FO371/61956/E9456, brief for the United Kingdom delegation, New York, 2 October 1947.

CHAPTER THREE

1. See Introduction.

2. Wasserstein, *Britain and the Jews of Europe*, 340–41.

3. WA, John Martin to Moshe Shertok (Sharett), 25 August 1945, and Shertok to Martin, 28 August 1945; LPA, 24/45, minutes of the secretariat, Bernard Joseph, 20 September 1945.

4. PRO, CAB119/148, memorandum on Palestine, 11 June 1945; PRO, FO371/45379/E6953, Cabinet, Palestine Committee, P.(M)(45) 1st meeting, 6 September 1945; PRO, CAB129/2, Cabinet, Palestine Committee, C.P. (45)156, report of the lord president of the council, 8 September 1945.

5. PRO, CAB95/14, memorandum by the secretary of state for the colonies, P.(M)(45) 10, 1 September 1945.

6. PRO, FO800/475, Grafftey-Smith to FO, no. 471, 14 October 1945; PRO, FO800/1475, FO to Jedda, no. 492, 12 October 1945. About the Arab League, see Louis, *British Empire*, 128–46; Gomaa, *Foundation of the League of the Arab States*, part 3; Porath, *In Search of Arab Unity*, chap. 5.

7. PRO, CAB95/14, note by the secretary of state for India and Burma, P(M)(45) 14, 6 October 1945.

8. Khalidi, "Arab Perspective," 108–9.

9. About the diplomatic campaign, see chaps. 6, 9, 10, and 11.

10. PRO, AIR20/496, Middle East to A.M.S.S.G., 23 August 1945.

11. PRO, FO371/45379/E6404, Chiefs of Staff meeting, C.O.S.(45) 206th meeting, 24 August 1945; PRO, AIR20/4962, Chiefs of Staff Committee, C.O.S. (45) 563 (0), note by the War Office, 5 September 1945.

12. PRO, FO371/45379/E6745, C. in C., Middle East, to Cabinet Offices, 1 October 1945; PRO, FO371/45382/E8066, F.O.L.E.M to C. in C. Mediterranean Station, 26 September 1946.

13. PRO, FO371/45382/E8066, memorandum by Rendel, 12 October 1945.

14. SACMEC, Alan Cunningham's Papers, box 1, file 1, Hall to Cunningham, no. 1767, 10 November 1945; PRO, FO371/45382/E8212, Hall to Cunningham, no. 546, 13 November 1945; PRO, CO537/1822, note on points raised with secretary of state by high commissioner, 14 November 1945; on the *Patria* and the *Struma*, see Introduction.

15. SACMEC, Cunningham's Papers, box 1, file 1, Cunningam to C. in C., Middle East, no. 550, 27 November 1945; Charters, *British Army*, 52–56.

16. PRO, FO371/45407/E9197, Cunningham to CO, no. 1665, 23 November 1945; PRO, FO226/306, MIDEAST to H.M. minister, Beirut, 23 November 1945; PRO, FO371/45407/E9012, C. in C., Middle East, to War Office, 24 November 1945; PRO, WO169/19745,

Fortnightly Intelligence Newsletter No. 2 for the period 8–23 November 1945. The 20 *ma'apilim* had gone from Greece to Palestine on board the *Berl Katznelson*, together with another 191 who had been able to make it ashore. Six Greek crew members were also detained. The *Palmach* were the striking forces of the Haganah.

17. PRO, FO371/45407/E10197, Cunningham to CO, no. 1817, 21 December 1945.

18. PRO, WO169/19745, HQ Palestine, "Situation in Palestine," 19 December 1945; PRO, FO371/45407, minute by R. S. Howe, 31 December 1945; see also PRO, WO169/19745, Fortnightly Intelligence Newsletter No. 3, issued by British Troops in Palestine and Transjordan (for period 24 November–7 December 1945); PRO, FO371/45407/E10197, Cunningham to colonial secretary, no. 1817, 21 December 1945. About the Palestinian Arabs' stand, see Nevo, "Arabs of Palestine," 3–38.

19. PRO, CAB129/5, Cabinet meeting, 1 January 1946; PRO, FO371/45407/E10160, FO to British ambassador, Cairo, 2 January 1946.

20. PRO, FO371/52507/E879, Creech Jones to foreign secretary, 23 January 1946; see also PRO, PREM8/627, Hall to the prime minister, 15 January 1946; Michael J. Cohen, *Palestine and the Great Powers*, 96–100.

21. PRO, WO169/23021, Fortnightly Intelligence Newsletter no. 5, issued by HQ British Troops in Palestine and Transjordan (for period 22 December 1945–4 January 1946); PRO, WO169/19745, HQ Palestine, "Situation in Palestine," 19 December 1945.

22. PRO, FO371/52508/E1034, Lord Killearn to FO, no. 150, 31 January 1946.

23. Naor, *The Ha'apala*, app.

24. PRO, WO204/49, Chiefs of Staff Committee, note by the secretary on illegal immigration into Palestine, 23 February 1946.

25. PRO, FO371/52513/E2663, Trafford Smith to Colonel C. R. Price, 23 March 1946; PRO, FO371/52514/E3272, memorandum for the chiefs of staff on illegal immigration into Palestine, 2 April 1946; PRO, FO371/52519/E3969, minutes of a meeting in the War Office to consider preventive action against illegal immigration, 27 April 1946.

26. See chaps. 9 and 10.

27. PRO, FO371/52524/E4533, CO to Cunningham, no. 841, 13 May 1946; PRO, FO371/52522/E4261, Cunningam to CO, no. 768, 7 May 1946.

28. See chap. 5.

29. PRO, FO371/52527/E4995, Chiefs of Staff Committee, C.O.S.(46) 150(0), note by the War Office, 28 May 1946.

30. PRO, FO371/52528/E5405, colonial secretary to the secretary, chiefs of staff committee, 1 June 1946; SACMEC, Cunningham's Papers, box 1, file 1, Cunningham to General Paget, 3 June 1946.

31. PRO, FO371/52537/E6383, Cunningham to CO, no. 1104, 5 July 1946. About the "Black Saturday," see Michael J. Cohen, *Palestine and the Great Powers*, 81–90; Charters, *British Army*, 117–20.

32. PRO, CAB128/6, Cabinet meeting, 1 July 1946.

33. Bethell, *Palestine Triangle*, chap. 8.

34. SACMEC, Cunningham's Papers, box 1, file 1, Cunningham to CO, no. 1197, 25 July 1946, and Cunningham to CO, no. 1212, 25 July 1946; PRO, WO216/194, C. in C., Middle East, to WO, 24 July 1946; PRO, CAB104/275, report by the Joint Planning Staff, J.P.(46) 137 (Final), 23 July 1946.

35. PRO, CAB128/6, Cabinet meeting, 25 July 1946; on the Morrison-Grady Plan, see chap. 5.

36. PRO 128/6, Cabinet meeting, 29 July 1946; PRO, FO800/485, FO to Paris, no. 714, 29 July 1946.

37. PRO, FO371/52545/E7266, Paris to FO, no. 409, 30 July 1946.

38. PRO, CAB128/6, Cabinet meeting, C.M.46, 30 July 1946; see also PRO, CAB129/12, Chiefs of Staff, 118th meeting, 29 July 1946; PRO, FO371/52627/E7681, Hall to Wooly, no. 281, 29 July 1946; LSE, Hugh Dalton Diaries and Papers, vol. 34, 1 August 1946; Bogner, *Deportation Island,* part 1, chap. 2.

39. See chap. 5.

40. PRO, CAB128/6, Cabinet meeting, 1 August 1946.

41. PRO, FO371/52550/E7611, memorandum for the secretary of state, 6 August 1946.

42. PRO, FO371/52627/E7704, Cabinet meeting, C.M.(46)77th conclusions, 7 August 1946; PRO, CAB128/6, memorandum to the cabinet by the colonial secretary, C.P.(16)310, 5 August 1946; PRO, CAB129/12, colonial secretary to Cunningham, no. 1413, 5 August 1946.

43. PRO, FO800/485, FO to Washington, no. 7903, 12 August 1946; see also chap. 5.

44. PRO, FO371/52628/E7879, FO to Paris, no. 859, 11 August 1946; PRO, WO275/63, "Deportation," 13 August 1946; Schaary, *Cyprus Detention Camps,* 45–51, 321–25.

45. PRO, FO371/52628/E7943, Cunningham to CO, no. 1297, 10 August 1946; PRO, FO371/52628/E7946, Cunningham to CO, no. 1309, 13 August 1946.

46. PRO, FO141/1104, Azzam to Cambell, 12 August 1946.

47. PRO, FO371/52629/E8123, Bagdad to FO, no. 660, 17 August 1946; PRO, WO275/63, Fortnightly Intelligence Newsletter no. 22 issued by HQ British Troops in Palestine and Transjordan (for period 5–18 August 1946); PRO, ADM1/19615, commander, Royal Navy, to national officer in charge, Port Said, 11 September 1946.

48. Although at their meeting on 7 August 1946, Field Marshal Montgomery, chief of the imperial general staff (CIGS), had pointed out that additional locations would be necessary, no discussion of this issue took place before the deportation decision was taken. PRO, CAB128/6, Cabinet meeting, 7 August 1946.

49. PRO, CO537/2339, Cunningham to CO, no. 515, 9 March 1947, and no. 348, 16 February 1947.

50. PRO, FO371/52629/E8268, Wooly to CO, nos. 339, 340, 19 August 1946; PRO, FO371/52628/E7943, Wooly to CO, no. 33, 18 August 1946.

51. PRO, FO371/52630/E8515, Gater to T. Haddon, 24 August 1946; PRO, FO371/52631/E8739, General Hollis to Gater, 27 August 1946; PRO, FO371/52631/E8637, extract, Chiefs of Staff Committee, C.O.S.(46) 131 meeting, 30 August 1946.

52. PRO, FO371/52630/E8371, Chiefs of Staff Committee, C.O.S.(46) 217(o), note by War Office, 21 August 1946, and General Dempsey to VCIGS, 22 August 1946; PRO, WO216/194, VCIGS to Dempsey, 23 August 1946.

53. PRO, FO371/52631/E8282, Trafford Smith to Baxter, 3 September 1946; PRO, FO371/52631/E8789, Baxter to Trafford Smith, 10 September 1946.

54. PRO, FO371/52631/E8791, Cunningham to CO, no. 1445, 6 September 1946.

55. PRO, FO371/52631/E8797, CO to Wooly, no. 360, 3 September 1946, and Wooly to CO, no. 1445, 6 September 1946.

56. PRO, CAB127/280, CO to Mitchell, no. 360, 7 October 1946; PRO, CO537/1808, Mitchell to Creech Jones, 21 November 1946. The Colonial Office continued to believe that of all existing alternatives, Kenya was the best. See PRO, CO537/1808, minute, 6 December 1946. About the opposition to bringing Jewish refugees into Kenya before World War II, see Sherman, *Island Refuge,* 105–6.

57. PRO, FO371/52645/E9846, notes of meeting of the Palestine Conference Committee, 1 October 1946; PRO, FO371/52644/E9394, minutes of the 6th meeting, 29 September 1946; Levenberg, *Military Preparations,* 54–63.

58. CZA, Z-4/302/31, minutes of a meeting in the Colonial Office, 8 October 1946; Rhodes House, Oxford, Arthur Creech Jones Papers, box 60, file 5, Creech Jones to Bevin, 11 October 1946.

59. SACMEC, Alan Cunningham's Papers, box 1, file 2, Cunningham to CO, no. 2120, 19 October 1946; PRO, FO371/52551/E10554, Cunningham to CO, no. 1719, 21 October 1946; see also WA, Creech Jones to Weizmann, 4 December 1946.

60. PRO, WO261/564, Fortnightly Intelligence Newsletter issued by H.Q. British troops in Palestine and Transjordan for the period 9–22 November 1946; see also, for example, the contacts over the *Knesset Yisrael* which had sailed from Yugoslavia at the end of November 1946 with 3,845 *ma'apilim* on board. CZA, Z-4/302/31, report on a meeting with the colonial secretary on 29 November 1946; CZA, S-25/2600, memorandum on conversation with the high commissioner, 27 November 1946.

61. PRO, CAB127/280, Cunningam to CO, no. 1721, 21 October 1946; PRO, FO371/52638/E11634, Cunningham to CO, nos. 2003, 2004, 29 November 1946; PRO, FO800/486, FO (Creech Jones) to New York (Bevin), no. 2678, 3 December 1946; PRO, CO537/1768, Cunningham to CO, no. 1817, 5 December 1946; PRO, CAB127/281, Chiefs of Staff meeting, C.O.S.(46) 163th meeting, 20 November 1946; PRO, CO537/2391, Cunningham to CO, no. 2453, 12 December 1946.

62. PRO, FO141/1104, Azzam Pasha to R. J. Bowker, chargé d'affaires, British embassy, Cairo, 7 December 1946.

63. PRO, CO537/1727, Cunningam to CO, no. 2023, 3 December 1946; PRO, CO537/1727, Cunningam to CO, no. 2187, 24 December 1946.

64. Michael J. Cohen, *Palestine and the Great Powers,* 217–21; Ovendale, *Britain, the United States,* 191–95.

65. PRO, CAB129/17, Cabinet meeting, 14 February 1947, and memorandum by the secretary of state for foreign affairs and the secretary of state for the colonies, C.P.(47) 59, 13 February 1947; see also Jones, *Failure in Palestine,* chap. 5; Jasse, "Great Britain and Palestine," 558–69.

66. PRO, CAB129/17, memorandum by the secretary of state for foreign affairs and the secretary of state for the colonies, C.P.(47) 59, 13 February 1947; PRO, CAB128/9, Cabinet meetings, 14, 18 February 1947; PRO, FO371/61767/E1442, Washington to FO, no. 996, 15 February 1947; *FRUS,* 1947, 5:1048–49, Acheson to Henderson, 15 February 1947; PRO, CO537/2339, Cunningham to CO, no. 569, 16 March 1947; Rhodes House, Creech Jones Papers, box 60, file 1, memorandum by the secretary of state for the colonies, C.P.(47)95, 19 March 1947.

67. PRO, CO537/2333, Cunningham to CO, no. 348, 16 February 1947.

68. PRO, FO371/61905/E2114, Baghdad to FO, no. 230, 10 March 1947; PRO, FO371/

61905/E2055, Jedda to FO, no. 97, 9 March 1947; PRO, FO371/61905/E2125, Cairo to FO, no. 610, 9 March 1947; PRO, FO371/61905/E2144, Damascus to FO, no. 64, 8 March 1947; PRO, FO371/61905/E2056, Beirut to FO, no. 171, 8 March 1947.

69. PRO, FO371/61905/E2852, Cunningham to CO, no. 544, 13 March 1947.

70. PRO, WO32/10260, extract from the minutes of the 7th meeting of the Defence Committee, 12 March 1947.

71. Ibid.; PRO, CO537/2339, Cunningham to CO, no. 515, 9 March 1947, and CO to Cunningham, no. 500, 12 March 1947; PRO, CAB128/9, Cabinet meeting, 20 March 1947.

72. PRO, CAB104/275, report by the joint intelligence subcommittee, COS committee, 10 April 1947.

73. PRO, DEFE4/3, secretary, Chiefs of Staff Committee, to the CO, 11 April 1947; PRO, WO32/10260, extract from the minutes of the 11th (47) meeting of the Defence Committee, 16 April 1947; see also PRO, T220/195, Cunningham to CO, no. 1263, 2 July 1947.

74. PRO, FO945/467, minutes of a meeting of the Cabinet Committee on Illegal Immigration, GEN. 180/2nd meeting, 13 May 1947; PRO, FO371/61807/E4098, memorandum for the foreign secretary, 12 May 1947. About the decision to establish Cabinet Committee on Illegal Immigration, see PRO, FO371/61806/E3491, Bevin to Attlee, 2 May 1947.

75. PRO, CO537/2485, the Governor of Cyprus to CO, 3 June 1947. About British interests in Cyprus, see Louis, *British Empire,* 205-25.

76. PRO, CO537/2485, Winster to CO, no. 325, 26 June 1947; on the camps in Cyprus, see Bogner, *Deportation Island,* part 5; Schaary, *Cyprus Detention Camps,* 123-30.

77. PRO, CO733/476/6, Cunningham to CO, no. 1259, 1 July 1947, and CO733/476/6, Cunningham to CO, no. 1316, 12 July 1947.

78. PRO, FO371/61839/E2082, Cunningham to CO, no. 489, 5 March 1947, and CO to Cunningham, no. 468, 7 March 1947; PRO, FO371/61802/E2141, Higham to Beith, 6 March 1947; PRO, FO371/61839/E2082, Cunningham to CO, no. 509, 8 March 1947. On Peter Bergson (Hillel Kook), see Michael J. Cohen, *Truman and Israel,* 38-43.

79. PRO, FO371/61803/E2445, Charles to FO, no. 664, 19 March 1947, and FO to Rome, no. 651, 24 March 1947; PRO, ADM1/20779, Charles to Sforza, 1 April 1947; see also chap. 10.

80. PRO, FO945/494, Duff Cooper to FO, no. 392, 12 May 1947; PRO, ADM116/5561, Cabinet, Illegal Immigration Committee, I.I.P.(47) 4th Meeting, 16 May 1947; see also chap. 11.

81. PRO, FO371/61808/E4522, FO to Charles, no. 1099, 27 May 1947.

82. PRO, FO371/61809/E4688, Charles to FO, no. 1210, 30 May 1947; PRO, FO371/61811/E5001, memorandum for the foreign secretary, 7 June 1947.

83. PRO, FO945/467, minutes of the Cabinet Committee on Illegal Immigration, Gen. 180/2nd meeting, 13 May 1947; see also PRO, ADM116/5561, CO to Cunningham, no. 1109, 30 May 1947; for a detailed discussion of the *Exodus* affair, see chap. 11.

84. PRO, FO371/61815/E6272, Bevin to Bidault, 12 July 1947; PRO, FO371/61815/E6218, Cooper to FO, no. 682, 12 July 1947.

85. PRO, FO371/61823/E7770, Bevin to Maurice Edelman, 4 September 1947.

86. Louis, *British Empire,* chap. 5; Freundlish, "The Hearings and Recommendations

of UNSCOP in Palestine," 51–72; Pappé, *Making of the Arab-Israeli Conflict,* 16–41. On the Arab reaction to UNSCOP, see Mayer, "Arab Unity of Action," 338–39; Nevo, "The Arabs of Palestine," 7–8, 26–27; Levenberg, *Military Preparations,* 116–23.

87. PRO, CAB128/10, Cabinet meeting, 29 September 1947; PRO, CAB129/21, memorandum by the foreign secretary for foreign affairs, C.P.(47) 259, 18 September 1947; Louis, "British Imperialism," 1–31; Louis, *British Empire,* 473–77; Jones, *Failure in Palestine,* 282–92; Ovendale, "Palestine Policy," 73–93; Bullock, *Ernest Bevin,* 446–50, 475–78; Michael J. Cohen, *Palestine and the Great Powers,* 268–76; Kollat, Michael J. Cohen, Ilan, Gavriel Cohen, and Heller, "Discussion," 93–140; Burridge, *Clement Attlee,* 264–67; Gavriel Cohen, "British Policy on the Eve of the War of Independence," 99–128.

88. PRO, FO945/494, note by the chairman, Cabinet, Illegal Immigration Committee, I.I.P.(47)72, 22 September 1947, and I.I.P.(47) 81, 10 October 1947; PRO, ADM1/20793, CO to Palestine, no. 2276, 26 September 1947; PRO, FO371/61829/E9052, minute by Beith, 25 September 1947.

89. PRO, DEFE5/6, CO to the secretary, chiefs of staff, C.O.S.(47) 206 (o), 27 September 1947.

90. PRO, FO371/61829/E9149, Bucharest to FO, no. 1055, 2 October 1947; PRO, ADM1/20793, Sofia to FO, no. 1247, 3 October 1947; see also chap. 9.

91. PRO, FO371/61830/E9564, minute by J. E. Cable, 6 October 1947.

92. PRO, CAB104/277, note by the acting chairman of the Cabinet Committee on Illegal Immigration, I.I.P.(47) 80, 10 October 1947; PRO, FO371/61850/E9830, CO to Palestine, no. 2428, 11 October 1947, Cunningham to CO, no. 1908, 12 October 1947, and minute by Beith, 16 October 1947; PRO, FO371/61850/E9376, Cunningham to CO, no. 1848, 3 October 1947.

93. PRO, FO371/61850/E9830, minute by Beith, 16 October 1947.

94. PRO, PREM8/859, Part 1, memorandum for Attlee, 27 October 1947.

95. Ibid., meeting of the Cabinet Committee on Defence, 1 November 1947.

96. PRO, AIR23/8342, commanders in chief, Middle East, to Ministry of Defence, 17 November 1947; PRO, DEFE7/387, note by the secretary, chiefs of staff committee, 18 November 1947; PRO, AIR20/8109, memorandum by the chiefs of staff, C.O.S.(47) 240 (oo), 21 November 1947; PRO, DEFE4/8, minutes of meeting of chiefs of staff committee, C.O.S.(47) 145th meeting, 21 November 1947; PRO, AIR20/8109, extract from conclusions of chiefs of staff meeting, C.O.S.(47) 146th meeting, 24 November 1947.

97. PRO, FO371/61833/E11733, CO to Cunningham, no. 3155, 6 December 1947, and Cunningham to CO, no. 2356, 7 December 1947; PRO, FO371/61850/E11733, CO to Cunningham, no. 3167, 6 December 1947; PRO, FO371/61833/E11788, memorandum by Beith, 10 December 1947, FO to Washington, no. 13177, 20 December 1947, and note for the Colonial Office about the policy of H.M.G. with regard to Jewish immigration, 10 December 1947; PRO, AIR20/8109, FO to secretary, chiefs of staff, 22 December 1947.

98. PRO, FO371/61833/E12231, Inverchapel to FO, no. 7167, 23 December 1947; see also chap. 6.

99. PRO, FO371/61833/E12231, memorandum by Harold Beeley, 30 December 1947, and FO to Washington, no. 323, 9 January 1948; PRO, FO371/61890/E11271, Jedda to FO, no. 389, 29 November 1947.

100. PRO, AIR20/81097, Ministry of Defence to G.H.Q. MELF, December 1947; Michael J. Cohen, *Palestine and the Great Powers,* 259.

101. PRO, FO371/68521/E5820, CO to United Kingdom Delegation, New York, no. 152, 11 May 1948; PRO, FO371/68513/E85, Cyprus to CO, no. 7, 22 January 1948.

102. Naor, *The Ha'apala,* app.; see also Stuart A. Cohen, "Imperial Policing against Illegal Immigration," 275–93.

103. See chaps. 9, 10, and 11.

CHAPTER FOUR

1. HA, File 14/160, report of Martin Hauser on Jewish DPs in Germany and Austria, 20 June 1945; YIVO, Leo Schwartz Papers, file 11/89, report of Rabbi Abraham J. Klausner, 24 June 1945; NACP, RG 165, War Department, General and Special Staff, ABC Decimal File 1942–48, file no. ABC 383.6, notes by the secretaries, Combined Civil Affairs Committee, "Repatriation of Polish Nationals," 9 May 1945; Genizi, *Adviser on Jewish Affairs,* 11–14.

2. Quoted in Grobman, *Rekindling the Flame,* 65.

3. TL, WHOF: OF 127, memorandum for the president by Morgenthau, 23 May 1945; TL, WHOF: OF 127A, memorandum for the president on "Earl G. Harrison's mission to Europe on refugee matters," 21 June 1945; NACP, RG 59, 800.4016 D.P/6-1945, Joseph G. Grew to Harrison, 19 June 1945; RL, War Refugee Board, 1944–45, box 9, file: Earl G. Harrison Mission, memorandum for the president, 21 June 1945; Dinnerstein, *America and the Survivors,* 34–44; Sachar, *Redemption of the Unwanted,* 198–99.

4. NACP, RG 59, 800.4016 DP/7-245, Grew to Schwartz, 30 June 1945; HP, Schwartz testimony; PRO, FO371/51096/WR2168, Halifax to FO, no. 5030, 18 July 1945.

5. RL, War Refugee Board, 1944–45, box 9, file: Earl G. Harrison Mission, Harrison to Morgenthau, 28 July 1945; NACP, RG 59, GRDS, File no. 52D408, Records Relating to IGCR, Miscellaneous Subject File, 1942–47, file IGC-Earl G. Harrison, Murphy to Byrnes, no. 197, 21 July 1945; PRO, FO371/51098/WR2341, J. S. M. Washington to A.M.S.S.O., 3 August 1945.

6. NACP, RG 59, GRDS, Decimal File 1945–49, 800.4016 DP/8-3145, Morgenthau to Grew, 1 August 1945.

7. Chandler and Galambos, *Papers of Eisenhower,* vol. 6, no. 256, note 1.

8. Kochavi, *Prelude to Nuremberg,* 80–87, 158.

9. NACP, RG 43, Records of U.S. Participation in International Conferences, Commissions and Expositions, Records of the Anglo-American Committee of Inquiry Re Palestine, 1944–46, AACI Reports, Liaison Office, "Special Camps for Stateless and Non-Repatriables," 22 August 1945; Chandler and Galambos, *Papers of Eisenhower,* no. 256; Blumenson, *Patton Papers,* 2:743, 747; Genizi, *Adviser on Jewish Affairs,* 19–20; Nadich, *Eisenhower and the Jews,* 36, 41–47.

10. PRO, FO371/54380/E7251, report of Earl G. Harrison, 24 August 1945; see also Pimlott, *Hugh Dalton,* 388–91.

11. See, for example, Clay, *Decision in Germany,* 232. About Patton's reaction to Harrison's report, see Blumenson, *Patton Papers,* 752; Nadich, *Eisenhower and the Jews,* 116; HP, Schwartz testimony.

12. Heymont, *Among the Survivors of the Holocaust,* 5.

13. Ibid., 9.

14. *Public Papers of Truman, 1945,* no. 152; PRO, FO371/51125/WR3048, Truman to Eisenhower, 31 August 1945. In his memoirs Truman wrote: "The Harrison report was a moving document. The misery it depicted could not be allowed to continue, and I sent a message to General Eisenhower, asking him to do what he could about improving conditions in the camps" (Truman, *Years of Trial and Hope,* 164). On the American press reaction, see NACP, RG 338, U.S. Army Command, Secretary, General Staff, 1944–45, CGC, 000.71, AGWAR to United States Forces European theater, 1 October 1945.

15. TL, PSF, Subject File Foreign Affairs, Palestine, file Palestine-Jewish Immigrants, Eisenhower to Truman, no. S 23374, 14 September 1945; TL, WHOF: OF 127A, Eisenhower to Truman, 18 September 1945; Chandler and Galambos, *Papers of Eisenhower,* no. 335; Blumenson, *Patton Papers,* 754. About American policy in its occupation zone in Germany, see Gimbel, *American Occupation of Germany;* Ziemke, *U.S. Army,* chaps. 20–24; Backer, *Priming the German Economy.*

16. Nadich, *Eisenhower and the Jews,* 25–26, 48–49; Genizi, *Adviser on Jewish Affairs,* 22–26.

17. CZA, S-6/4685, reports of Nadich, 16, 27 September 1945; Nadich, *Eisenhower and the Jews,* 120–27, 147–49.

18. YIVO, Schwartz Papers, 9/63, report of Nadich, 22 October 1945; Nadich, *Eisenhower and the Jews,* 222–27; Chandler and Galambos, *Papers of Eisenhower,* no. 419. About Rifkind's activities, see Genizi, *Adviser on Jewish Affairs,* 35–56; see also CZA, S-25/5232, report of Rifkind, 8 April 1946; BGA, Ben Gurion Diary, 29 October 1945.

19. Heymont, *Among the Survivors of the Holocaust,* 13, 19, 24.

20. BGA, Chronological Documentation Division, Ben-Gurion's report of his visit in the camps, 6 November 1945; CZA, minutes of meeting of the Executive of the Jewish Agency, vol. 42/1, 2 November 1945, Ben-Gurion; LPA, minutes of meeting of the Political Department, 26/45, 22 November 1945, Ben-Gurion; Avizohar, "Ben-Gurion's Visit to the D.P. Camps," 253–70.

21. BGA, Chronological Documentation Division, Bedell-Smith to Ben-Gurion, November 1945; *FRUS,* 1945, 2:1207, Murphy, the U.S. political adviser for Germany, to Byrnes, 17 November 1945.

22. See note 20; BGA, Chronological Documentation Division, Ben Gurion to Pola (his wife), 9 February 1946.

23. NACP, RG 59, GRDS, File no. 52D408, Records IGCR, Miscellaneous Subject File, 1942–47, file Harrison's report, Eisenhower to Roosevelt, 8 October 1945; on the press reaction, see NACP, RG 338, U.S. Army Command, Secretary, General Staff, 1944–45, CGC, 000.71, AGWAR to United States Forces European Theater, 17 October 1945.

24. For report on Harrison's reaction, see PRO, FO371/51125/WR3132, Halifax to FO, no. 6972, 19 October 1945.

25. Chandler and Galambos, *Papers of Eisenhower,* no. 409; PRO, FO371/51126/WR3266, Halifax to FO, no. 537, 11 November 1945, and Halifax to FO, no. 542, 2 November 1945.

26. Heymont, *Among the Survivors of the Holocaust,* 13; NACP, RG 107, ASW, FSCC of Petersen, December 1945–August 1947, ASW383.7, Refugees and DPs, memorandum for

Rabbi Philip S. Bernstein, 13 May 1946, and Index and Book, address by Rabbi Bernstein, 1 October 1946; HP, Bernstein testimony. In his final report in August 1947, however, Rabbi Bernstein praised the American commanders for their cooperation. JA, box 6-A, file C-45.069, report of Rabbi Bernstein, 20 October 1947; Genizi, "Philip S. Bernstein," 139–76; Abzug, *Inside the Vicious Heart,* 152–56.

27. Blumenson, *Patton Papers,* 743, 745, 751–52, 754, 759–60, 788; see also Schwartz, *Redeemers,* 38–39.

28. CZA, Z-4/302/30, minutes of meeting of the Zionist Executive in London, 22 October 1945, Moshe Shertok; HA, 14/502, Ernest (Ephraim Frank), emissary from Palestine, to Mordechai Surkiss, 20 January 1946; YIVO, Schwartz Papers, file 9/63, memorandum for Judge Rifkind, 13 December 1945; Bauer, *Flight and Rescue,* 81–82; Schwartz, *Redeemers,* chap. 6.

CHAPTER FIVE

1. PRO, FO371/45380/E7251, Truman to Attlee, 31 August 1945; *FRUS,* 1945, 2:716–17, memorandum by Truman to Churchill, 24 July 1945, and 719, Attlee to Truman, 31 July 1945.

2. Truman, *Years of Trial and Hope,* 162; *Public Papers of Truman, 1945,* no. 106, paragraphs 8, 18; *FRUS,* 1945, 7:722, Byrnes to Pikerton, the Consul General at Jerusalem, 18 August 1945; PRO, FO371/45379/E6062, Balfour to FO, no. 5715, 19 August 1945; see also Donovan, *Conflict and Crisis,* 315.

3. Michael J. Cohen, *Palestine and the Great Powers,* 57.

4. On the expected repercussions of the introduction of U.S. forces into Palestine, see *FRUS,* 1945, 8:742–43, memorandum by the War Department to the Department of State, 19 September 1945.

5. *FRUS,* 1945, 8:739, Attlee to Truman, 14 September 1945, and 740–41, Attlee to Truman, 16 September 1945.

6. TL, WHOF: OF 204, Robert F. Wagner to Truman, 3 July 1945; Stevens, *American Zionism,* 129–31; Hamby, *Man of the People,* 405; McCullough, *Truman,* 596–97; Benson, *Harry S. Truman,* 63–64; Jones, *Failure in Palestine,* 43–46.

7. PRO, FO371/45380/E7599, Halifax to FO, no. 6593, 3 October 1945.

8. Ganin, *Truman, American Jewry and Israel,* 99–103; Michael J. Cohen, *Truman and Israel,* 59–86; Divine, *Foreign Policy,* 105–8, 143–44; Kaufman, *Non-Zionists in America,* 145; Feingold, *A Time for Searching,* chap. 8; Dinnerstein, *Antisemitism in America,* chap. 7; Bauer, *American Jewry and the Holocaust.*

9. Such accusations angered Foreign Office officials, who maintained that the British government was not responsible for the suffering and death of European Jews; furthermore, it supported the different proposals to rescue the Jews. See, for example, PRO, FO371/45383/E8517, minute by Henderson, 8 December 1945.

10. PRO, CAB95/14, Halifax to Eden, 1 July 1945; see also Dinnerstein, *Uneasy at Home,* chap. 9.

11. NACP, RG 59, GRDS, Office of the Near Eastern Affairs, Top Secret, Palestine, 8 January 1945–24 September 1945, Stettinius to Truman, 18 April 1945; TL, PSF, Subject File, Foreign Affairs, Palestine, file Palestine 1945–47, Grew to Truman, 28 May 1945, 16 June 1945, and memorandum for the secretary of state, 31 August 1945.

12. PRO, FO226/277, minutes of a meeting held at the Foreign Office, 10 September 1945.

13. PRO, FO371/45380/E7599, Halifax to FO, no. 6593, 3 October 1945.

14. PRO, CAB128/1, Cabinet meeting, 4 October 1945; PRO, WO32/10260, extract from the conclusions of the 40th meeting of the cabinet, 11 October 1945; PRO, FO371/45382/E8068, note for the secretary of state, 6 October 1945; PRO, CAB95/14, note by the secretary of state for foreign affairs and the secretary of state for the colonies, P(m)(45) 15, 9 October 1945; PRO, CAB129/3, report of the lord president of the council, C.P.(45)216, 10 October 1945.

15. PRO, PREM8/627, part I, FO to Washington, nos. 10267, 10268, 12 October 1945.

16. *FRUS*, 1945, 8:771–75, Halifax to Byrnes, 19 October 1945.

17. Ibid., 779–83, memorandum of conversation between the secretary of state and the British ambassador, 22 October 1945; PRO, PREM8/627, part I, Halifax to FO, no. 7013, 22 October 1945, and Halifax to FO, no. 7037, 24 October 1945.

18. Ibid., FO to Washington, no. 10730, 25 October 1945, and FO to Washington, no. 10861, 29 October 1945, and Halifax to FO, no. 7264, 31 October 1945; PRO, PREM8/627, FO to Washington, no. 10755, 26 October 1945; *FRUS*, 1945, 8:810–12, Halifax to Byrnes, 5 November 1945; PRO, FO371/45383/E7422, Halifax to FO, no. 7422, 6 November 1945; PRO, FO371/45383/E7423, Halifax to FO, no. 7423, 6 November 1945; PRO, PREM8/627, part I, Halifax to FO, no. 7444, 7 November 1945; PRO, FO371/45383/E8539, FO to Washington, nos. 11263, 11264, 8 November 1945; *FRUS*, 1945, 8:826, Byrnes to Winant, 17 November 1945; NACP, RG 59, GRDS, Office of Near Eastern Affairs, General Records, Palestine Documents Relating to Anglo-American Committee of Inquiry, vol. 1, memorandum of conversation between Byrnes and Halifax, 19 November 1945; *FRUS*, 1945, 8:829–31, Halifax to Byrnes, 20, 24 November 1945, 831–32, Byrnes to Halifax, 25 November 1945, 833, Bevin to Halifax, 27 November 1945, and 839–40, Byrnes to Halifax, 10 December 1945.

19. PRO, PREM8/627, Halifax to FO, no. 7157, 27 October 1945; *FRUS*, 1945, 8:800, Byrnes to Halifax, 27 October 1945.

20. PRO, FO371/45382/E8160, Halifax to FO, no. 7157, 27 October 1945.

21. See Introduction.

22. PRO, FO371/45383/E8342, FO to Washington, no. 994, 1 November 1945.

23. PRO, FO371/45382/E8177, FO to Washington, no. 10861, 29 October 1945. In the New York City elections, the Democratic candidate, William O'Dwyer, won.

24. PRO, FO371/45383/E8341, FO to Cairo, Bagdad, Jedda, and Beirut, 30 October 1945.

25. Bullock, *Ernest Bevin*, 129–37; Messer, *End of an Alliance*, chap. 7.

26. *Hansard, Commons*, vol. 415, cols. 1930–34; see also PRO, FO371/45387/E9270, Bevin to John Singelton, 25 November 1945.

27. Quoted in Bullock, *Ernest Bevin*, 181–83.

28. See, for example, WA, Wise and Silver to Truman, 15 November 1945.

29. PRO, CAB120/660, Attlee to Truman, 16 September 1945; see also PRO, FO371/45383/E8450, "Notes for the Secretary of State's Press Conference," 9 November 1945.

30. Bullock, *Ernest Bevin*, 164–70; see also Morgan, *Labour in Power*, 208–9; Saville, *Politics of Continuity*, 88.

31. *Public Papers of Truman, 1945,* no. 187; *FRUS,* 1945, 8:819–20, Byrnes to Winant, 13 November 1945.

32. PRO, FO371/52568/E2198, Washington to FO, no. 344, 25 February 1946.

33. PRO, FO1052/282, General V. D. Sokolovsky to General Robertson, 5 February 1946; PRO, FO181/1010/2, Vladimir Dekanozov, Soviet Foreign Office, to Frank Roberts, chargé d'affaires, British embassy, Moscow, 15 February 1946; PRO, FO371/52507/E761, Roberts to FO, no. 651, 16 February 1946; *FRUS,* 1946, 7:581; George F. Kennan, chargé d'affaires, American embassy, Moscow, to the secretary of state, 19 February 1946; PRO, FO371/52512/E1894, Parliamentary Question, 27 February 1946; Nachmani, *Great Power Discord,* chaps. 6–8; Ro'i, *Soviet Decision Making in Practice,* 22–25; see also Ginat, "Soviet Policy towards the Arab World," 321–35.

34. SACMEC, Cunningham's Papers, box 4, file 3, CO to Gater, 21 November 1945; PRO, FO371/52505/E537, Cunningham to CO, no. 1824, 23 December 1945; PRO, FO371/51128/WR3685, Troutbeck, FO, to Gottlieb, Control Commission for Germany and Austria, 31 December 1945; PRO, WO169/19758, Defence Security Office—Palestine & Transjordan, monthly summary no. 3, December 1945; CZA, report on the activities of the Anglo-American Committee, Vienna, 21 February 1946.

35. Crossman, *Palestine Mission,* 79; LPA, 24/46, vol. B, minutes of meeting of the Zionist Labour Party's Secretariat, Chaim Hoffman, 24 July 1946; ibid., minutes of meeting of the Zionist Labour Party's Secretariat, Dobkin, 29 April 1946; CZA, minutes of meeting of the Jewish Agency Executive, Ben Gurion, 24 February 1946.

36. Crossman, *Palestine Mission,* 75; HP, Chaim Guri Collection, General Testimonies, no. 90, interview with Beeley, July 1978.

37. *Report of the Anglo-American Committee,* 14, paragraph 15.

38. PRO, WO32/10260, extract from the minutes of the 14th (46) meeting of the Defence Committee, 24 April 1946.

39. PRO, FO371/52516/E3663, Grafftey-Smith to FO, no. 159, 23 April 1946; PRO, FO371/52519/E3867, Grafftey-Smith to FO, no. 163, 29 April 1946.

40. PRO, FO371/52516/E3756, Bagdad to FO, no. 331, 25 April 1946.

41. PRO, FO800/446, discussion between Bevin and Byrnes, 26 April 1946; PRO, FO371/52517/E3786, Paris to FO, no. 7, 27 April 1946; *FRUS,* 1946, 7:587–88, memorandum by Freeman H. Matthews, director of the Office of European Affairs, 27 April 1946.

42. Burridge, *Clement Attlee,* 259–61; Bullock, *Ernest Bevin,* 234; see also Introduction.

43. PRO, CAB129/9, report of Committee of Officials, C.P.(46) 173, 27 April 1946.

44. PRO, CAB128/5, Cabinet meeting, C.M. 38 (46), 29 April 1946; PRO, FO371/52520/E4016, meeting of prime ministers, P.M.M. (46) 8th meeting, 30 April 1946; about the high commissioner in Palestine's assumption of the reactions in Palestine to the publication of the Anglo-American Committee's report, see PRO, AIR20/4963, Cunningham to CO, no. 666, 29 April 1946.

45. *FRUS,* 1946, 7:588–89, Acheson to Byrnes, 30 April 1946; *Public Papers of Truman, 1946,* no. 92.

46. PRO, FO371/52519/E3921, Paris to FO, no. 26, 30 April 1946; PRO, FO371/52520/E3983, FO to Paris, no. 41, 1 May 1946; PRO, CAB128/5, Cabinet meeting, 1 May 1946.

47. Michael J. Cohen, *Palestine and the Great Powers,* 119–20, 192–93; Nachmani, *Great Power Discord,* 205–10; Khalidi, "Arab Perspective," 110–12. On the Arab Higher Committee's reaction, see PRO, PREM8/627, memorandum by the secretary of state for the colonies, C.P.(46) 220, 6 June 1946.

48. PRO, CO537/1736, Halifax to FO, no. 2858, 4 May 1946.

49. PRO, FO371/52521/E4089, Halifax to FO, no. 2824, 3 May 1946; PRO, FO371/52520/E4055, Halifax to FO, no. 2829, 3 May 1946; PRO, FO371/52524/E4617, Balfour to FO, no. 374, 18 May 1946; *P.M.* was a New York intellectual-progressive tabloid in the 1940s. About Stone's stand, see his book, Stone, *Underground to Palestine.*

50. PRO, FO371/52520, Halifax to FO, no. 2827, 3 May 1946.

51. *FRUS,* 1946, 7:591–92, Hildring to Acheson, 3 May 1946; Ganin, *Truman, American Jewry and Israel,* 66; Michael J. Cohen, *Palestine and the Great Powers,* 114–15.

52. *FRUS,* 1946, 7:598–99, Merriam to Acheson, 8 May 1946.

53. Louis, *British Empire,* 424; TL, Oral History Interview with Loy W. Henderson.

54. PRO, FO371/52523/E4345, FO to Washington, no. 4452, 9 May 1946; PRO, CAB127/270, Attlee to Truman, 9 May 1946, and Truman to Attlee, 17 May 1946; PRO, CAB128/5, Cabinet meeting, 20 May 1946.

55. PRO, CAB120/659, Truman to Attlee, 5 June 1946. About the Zionist pressure, see PRO, FO371/52527/E5226, Inverchapel to FO, no. 3803, 7 June 1946; PRO, FO800/485, FO to Washington, 10 June 1946; PRO, FO371/52528/E5352, Inverchapel to FO, no. 3888, 12 June 1946; PRO, CAB127/270, Truman to Attlee, 14 June 1946; PRO, FO371/52530/E5627, Bevin to Attlee, 14 June 1946; PRO, FO800/485, FO to Washington, no. 5879, 15 June 1946; TL, PSF, Subject File, Foreign Affairs, Palestine, file Palestine 1945–47, Wagner to Truman, 20 June 1946; TL, WHOF: OF 204 miscellaneous (June 1946), Emanuel Celler to Matthew J. Connelly, secretary to the president, 25 June 1946; NACP, RG 107, Secretary of War (Patterson), Safe File, 27 September 1945–24 July 1946, file Palestine Committee, Executive Order: Establishing a Cabinet Committee on Palestine and Related Problems, 11 June 1946.

56. PRO, FO371/52529/E5546, FO to Washington, no. 5827, 14 June 1946; PRO, FO800/485, Inverchapel to FO, no. 3900, 13 June 1946; see also the interview with Beeley, July 1978.

57. *Public Papers of Truman, 1945,* no. 225; TL, WHOF: OF 127, acting commissioner of immigration and naturalization to Truman, 7 August 1946.

58. Dinnerstein, *America and the Survivors,* 114–15.

59. PRO, FO371/52569/E5675, "Current Zionist Activities," 14 June 1946; PRO, FO371/52530, FO to Washington, no. 6076, 20 June 1946.

60. PRO, FO371/52569/E5546, Inverchapel to FO, no. 3947, 14 June 1946.

61. Bullock, *Ernest Bevin,* 333.

62. *Public Papers of Truman, 1945,* no. 136, paragraph 14, press conference, 14 June 1946.

63. PRO, FO800/485, Inverchapel to FO, no. 3900, 13 June 1946.

64. PRO, CAB128/6, Cabinet meeting, C.M. 66 (46), 8 July 1946.

65. PRO, FO371/52529/E5446, FO to Washington, no. 6033, 19 June 1946.

66. PRO, CAB129/10, memorandum by the secretary of state for the colonies, C.P.(46)

238, 19 June 1946; PRO, FO371/52530/E5671, Paris to FO, no. 228, 20 June 1946; PRO, CAB128/5, Cabinet meeting, 20 June 1946; Niv, *The Irgun Zvai Leumi,* 267–73; Slutsky, *History of the Hagana,* 3:880–87.

67. PRO, FO371/52533/E6062, combined study of the implications of the report of the AAC, 27 June 1946; see also PRO, FO371/52530/E5640, record of Brook-Harriman 1st meeting, 17 June 1946; PRO, FO371/52531/E6767, record of Brook-Harriman 2nd meeting, 18 June 1946; PRO, FO945/383, FO to Paris, no. 324, 18 June 1946.

68. PRO, CAB127/270, Attlee to Truman, no. T.53, 25 June 1946, and no. T.375/46, 4 July 1946.

69. Michael J. Cohen, *Palestine and the Great Powers,* 84–90.

70. PRO, CAB128/6, Cabinet meeting, 11 July 1946; PRO, CAB133/83, Combined Study of the Anglo-American Committee, Recommendation 1: Jewish Refugees in Europe, note by the British delegation, P. 27, 11 July 1946; PRO, FO371/52537/E6475, memorandum by the secretary of state for the colonies, C.P. (46) 258, 8 July 1946; PRO, WO32/10260, Army Secretariat, brief for the secretary of state, 11 July 1946.

71. PRO, CAB133/730, Combined Study of Report of Anglo-American Committee, 7th meeting, 13 July 1946.

72. PRO, CAB129/12, Statement of Policy, 26 July 1947; see also PRO, CAB133/83, report of subcommittee on recommendation 1, P. 33, 23 July 1946; PRO, FO371/52546/E7974, record of Brook-Harriman 11th meeting, 23 July 1946.

73. PRO, CAB128/6, Cabinet meeting, 25 July 1946; see also PRO, FO371/52550/E7588, Inverchapel to FO, no. 4964, 5 August 1946; PRO, FO371/52544, FO to Washington, no. 7339, 25 July 1946; PRO, FO800/485, memorandum for the prime minister, 26 July 1946.

74. *FRUS,* 1946, 7:670–71, record of teletype conference between Washington and London, 26 July 1946, and 648–49, Byrnes to Harriman, 22 July 1946; PRO, FO371/52545/E7231, FO to Washington, no. 7403, 27 July 1946.

75. PRO, CAB128/6, Cabinet meeting, 29 July 1946.

76. *Hansard, Commons,* vol. 426, cols. 957ff.

77. Truman, *Years of Trial and Error,* 180; Michael J. Cohen, *Palestine and the Great Powers,* 128–31; Ganin, *Truman, American Jewry and Israel,* 79–83; Louis, *British Empire,* 436–38; Donovan, *Conflict and Crisis,* 319–20; *Public Papers of Truman, 1946,* no. 186, paragraph 3, note 1, press conference, 1 August 1946.

78. TL, reel 23, Truman's Office Files, 1945–53, Part 3: Subject File, Truman to Attlee, 9 August 1946.

79. PRO, CAB120/659, Truman to Attlee, no. T408/46, 13 August 1946; see also PRO, CAB127/280, Paris to FO, no. 487, 13 August 1946; Ganin, "Partition Plan," 227–62.

80. TL, WHOF: OF 204, Truman's announcement, 16 August 1946.

81. PRO, FO371/52546/E7325, Inverchapel to FO, no. 4862, 31 July 1946; see also LSE, Hugh Dalton Diary, vol. 34, 1 August 1946. On the Jewish lobby, see Benson, *Harry S. Truman,* chap. 7.

82. PRO, CO537/1767, Inverchapel to FO, no. 585, 28 August 1946.

83. Dinnerstein, *America and the Survivors,* 115.

84. Quoted in Hathaway, *Ambiguous Partnership,* 282; TL, PSF, Subject File Foreign Affairs, Palestine, file Palestine-Jewish Immigrants, memorandum for President Truman

from James G. MacDonald, 25 July 1946; TL, reel 1, Map Room, 1945–56, Dean Acheson to the embassy in London, no. 5973, 12 August 1946; Jones, *Failure in Palestine,* 134–43.

85. About the London conference, see chap. 3.

86. PRO, FO800/486, FO to Washington, no. 9551, 4 October 1946; Ganin, *Truman, American Jewry and Israel,* 103–7; Michael J. Cohen, *Truman and Israel,* 137–46; Ovendale, *Britain, the United States,* chap. 5; Louis, *British Empire,* 440–43; Hathaway, *Ambiguous Partnership,* 283–85.

87. PRO, CO537/1737, Inverchapel to FO, no. 585, 28 August 1946; PRO, FO945/388, Inverchapel to FO, no. 5506, 5 September 1946.

88. PRO, FO800/486, FO to Washington, no. 9561, 4 October 1946; about the Bevin and Attlee consultations, see PRO, FO371/52560/E10162, FO to Paris, no. 1749, 4 October 1946; PRO, FO371/52560/E9960, Paris to FO, no. 863, 4 October 1946; PRO, FO371/52560/E9999, Paris to FO, no. 867, 4 October 1946.

89. *Public Papers of Truman, 1946,* no. 227; PRO, FO371/52560/E10163, FO to Paris, no. 1761, 4 October 1946.

90. PRO, CAB120/659, Attlee to Truman, no. T460/46, 4 October 1946; Harris, *Attlee,* 395–96.

91. PRO, CAB120/659, Truman to Attlee, no. T468/46, 10 October 1946.

92. PRO, FO800/480, Attlee to Truman, 10 October 1946; see also Williams, *A Prime Minister Remembers,* 181–82.

93. NACP, RG 59, GRDS, Office of Near Eastern Affairs, Top Secret, Questions of Position on Palestine for General Assembly of U.N., Henderson to Acheson, 10 October 1946; Michael J. Cohen, "Truman and Palestine," 6–9.

94. PRO, FO371/52560/E9938, Inverchapel to FO, no. 5901, 3 October 1946.

95. Ibid., Inverchapel to FO, no. 5905, 4 October 1946.

96. Michael J. Cohen, *Palestine and the Great Powers,* 163–65; Ganin, *Truman, American Jewry and Israel,* 105.

97. Truman, *Years of Trial and Hope,* 182.

98. Hathaway, *Ambiguous Partnership,* 283; Donovan, *Conflict and Crisis,* 319–22.

99. PRO, FO371/52561/E10358, Inverchapel to FO, no. 2442, 12 October 1946.

100. PRO, FO371/52571/E11651, Inverchapel to Bevin, no. 2775, 22 November 1946; Snetsinger, *Truman, the Jewish Vote,* 44.

101. PRO, FO371/52651/E9670, minute by Rundall, 6 December 1946.

102. PRO, FO800/486, minute by Sargent, 23 November 1946.

103. PRO, FO371/57773/WR3133, minute by Rendel, 7 December 1946; see also PRO, FO371/61748/E1251, Dominion Office to Dominions Governments, no. 119, 10 February 1947.

104. PRO, FO371/52571/E11651, Inverchapel to Bevin, no. 2775, 22 November 1946; PRO, CAB128/6, Cabinet meeting, 25 October 1946.

105. PRO, CAB127/281, Bevin to Attlee, 26 November 1946, and New York to FO, no. 1981, 26 November 1946; PRO, CO537/2331, FO to Washington, no. 402, 13 January 1947.

106. Dinnerstein, *America and the Survivors,* chaps. 5–9; Genizi, *America's Fair Share,* chap. 5.

107. See chap. 3.

108. *Hansard, Commons,* vol. 433, col. 1908; Williams, *Ernest Bevin,* 259–60; see also Gavriel Cohen, "British Policy," 89–91; Gorni, *British Labour Movement,* 214–18.

109. PRO, FO371/61769/E1832, FO to Washington, no. 1851, 26 February 1947.

110. *FRUS,* 1947, 5:1058–59, Gellman to Marshall, 26 February 1947.

111. TL, WHOF: OF 204, statement issued by the White House, 26 February 1947; Snetsinger, *Truman, the Jewish Vote,* 48.

112. Truman, *Years of Trial and Hope,* 182.

113. Bullock, *Ernest Bevin,* 368–70.

114. Truman, *Years of Trial and Hope,* 125.

115. See Acheson, *Present at the Creation,* 169; Louis, *British Empire,* 424.

116. PRO, FO371/66673/WR3958, memorandum for the secretary of state on the refugee problem, 8 October 1947; see also TL, WHOF: OF 127, President's message to the Congress of the United States, 7 July 1947; NACP, RG 107, ASW, FSCC of Petersen, December 1945–August 1947, statement by Rabbi Bernstein before the House Subcommittee on Immigration and Naturalization, 20 June 1947.

117. *The DP Story,* 12–16; Dinnerstein, *America and the Survivors,* 132–35.

118. Hartmann, *Truman and the 80th Congress,* 175–79; *The DP Story,* 17–41; Dinnerstein, *America and the Survivors,* 137–271; Snetsinger, *Truman, the Jewish Vote,* 133–39.

119. JA, box 6-A, file C-45.069, report of Rabbi Bernstein, 20 October 1947; Bauer, *Flight and Rescue,* 319. According to Dinnerstein, approximately two-thirds of the forty-one thousand DPs who arrived in the United States under the Truman directive were Jews. Dinnerstein, *America and the Survivors,* 263; see also Genizi, *America's Fair Share,* 205.

120. Ganin, *Truman, American Jewry and Israel,* chaps. 9, 11; Snetsinger, *Truman, the Jewish Vote,* 72, 78–81, 203; Hathaway, *Ambiguous Partnership,* 238–43; McCullough, *Truman,* 595–604.

121. See Parts III and IV.

CHAPTER SIX

1. HIA, Fait Collection, box 1, file 4, McNarney to Office of Military Government (Western District), 13 October 1945.

2. BGA, Ben Gurion Diary, 20 October 1945; LPA, 26/45, minutes of the Political Department, 22 November 1945, Ben Gurion; Gelber, *Standard Bearers,* 490–99.

3. BGA, Correspondence Division, Hoffman (Munich) to Dobkin, 25 December 1945; HA, 14/158, Erich (Frank) to Merkaz Lagolah (Center for the Diaspora), 3 January 1946; about the Merkaz Lagolah, see Bauer, *Out of the Ashes,* 25; HA, 14/77a, Avriel from Prague, 11 January 1946; HA, 14/502, "Ernest" (Frank) to Surkiss, 20 January 1946.

4. NACP, RG 84, Foreign Service Post U.S. Political Advisor, Berlin, Top Secret, Correspondence of the Political Advisor, Robert Murphy, T.S. 840.1 Jews, USFET to OMGUS, no. S-32479, 26 November 1945.

5. YIVO, Schwartz Papers, file 9/63, Eli Rock to Judge Rifkind, 8 November 1945, and memorandum for Judge Rifkind, 13 December 1945; Keynan, *Holocaust Survivors,* 53–56; Rosenfield, "Central Europe," 305–6.

6. *FRUS,* 1945, 2:1215–18, Patterson to Acheson, 19 December 1945.

7. PRO, FO1005/835, Allied Control Authority, Directorate of Prisoners of War and

Displaced Persons, note by the secretariat on "Treatment of Jewish Refugees," 7 December 1945; see also PRO, FO371/57685/WR125, Strang to FO, no. 61, 12 January 1946. About Jewish DPs in Berlin, see Königseder, *Flucht nach Berlin*.

8. *FRUS*, 1945, 2:1215–18, Patterson to Acheson, 19 December 1945; NACP, RG 59, 800.4016 DP/12-45-800.4016, DP/12-3145, Murphy to secretary of state, 28 December 1945. About the decisions made at Potsdam regarding Germans who had been Polish, Hungarian, or Czechoslovakian citizens, see *Public Papers of Truman, 1945,* no. 91, pp. 194–95.

9. NACP, RG 59, GRDS, Records of the Office of Eastern European Affairs, 1941–53, Records of the Polish Desk Officer, 1941–52, Poland Alph-Numeric File, 2210 Jewish Matters, memorandum on the "Question of unauthorized arrivals of Polish Jews in Berlin and in the U.S. zone in Bavaria," 20 December 1945; see also Donovan, *Conflict and Crisis,* 267–68, 315.

10. NACP, RG 59, GRDS, Records of the Office of Eastern European Affairs, 1941–53, Records of the Polish Desk Officer, 1941–52, Poland Alph-Numeric File, 2210 Jewish Matters, memorandum by Dubrow on "Question of unauthorized arrivals of Polish Jews in Berlin and in the U.S. zone in Bavaria," 20 December 1945.

11. NACP, RG 59, GRDS, Records of the Office of Eastern European Affairs, 1941–53, Records of the Polish Desk Officer, 1941–52, Poland Alph-Numeric File, 2210 Jewish Matters, Byrnes to Kenneth C. Royall, acting secretary of war, 7 January 1946.

12. NACP, RG 107, ASW, FSCC of Petersen, December 1945–August 1947, ASW383.7, Refugees and DPs, WARCOS to CG USFET, no. 93804, 19 January 1946.

13. PRO, FO371/57686/WR267, FO to Washington, no. 1110, 2 February 1946.

14. PRO, FO945/655, Halifax to FO, no. 819, 6 February 1946; NACP, RG 59, General Records of the Department of State, Records of the Office of Eastern European Affairs, 1941–53, Records of the Polish Desk Officer, 1941–52, Poland Alph-Numeric File, 2210 Jewish Matters, memorandum of conversation between A. H. Tandy and C. Burke Elbrick, 5 February 1946.

15. PRO, FO371/57687/WR541, Halifax to FO, no. 1163, 21 February 1946; Bauer, *Out of the Ashes,* 91–92.

16. PRO, FO943/485, McCreery to Street, War Department, 28 February 1946; Bauer, *Flight and Rescue,* 82.

17. Crum, *Behind the Silken Curtain,* 138; Crossman, *Palestine Mission,* 82–86; YIVO, Schwartz Papers, file 11/90, memorandum presented by Brigadier General S. R. Mickelsen to the Anglo-American Committee, February 1946; YIVO, Schwartz Papers, file 9/64, Dr. Zalman Grinberg to Morgan, 26 March 1946; *Report of the Anglo-American Committee,* 48–49, paragraphs 9–12.

18. NACP, RG 165, War Department, General and Special Staff, ABC Decimal File, 1942–48, memorandum for the President "Policy as to Future Entry of Jewish Refugees into U.S. Zones of Germany and Austria," 3 May 1946.

19. NACP, RG 107, ASW, FSCC of Petersen, December 1945–August 1947, ASW383.7, Refugees and DPs, memorandum for the president, 2 May 1946, Patterson to Acheson, 27 April 1946, and McNarney to Eisenhower, 1 May 1946.

20. See chaps. 1 and 5.

21. *FRUS,* 1946, 5:588–89, Acheson to Byrnes, 30 April 1946.

22. NACP, RG 165, War Department, General and Special Staff, ABC Decimal File, 1942–48, Hildring to Petersen, 8 May 1946; NACP, RG 107, ASW, FSCC of Petersen, December 1945–August 1947, ASW383.7, Refugees and DPs, Petersen to McNarney, Clark, and Clay, 8 May 1946.

23. NACP, RG 107, ASW, FSCC of Petersen, December 1945–August 1947, ASW 383.7, Refugees and DPs, McNarney to War Office, no. 6224, 23 June 1946, teletype conference, 27 June 1946, and McNarney to Eisenhower, no. 6553, 28 June 1946.

24. NACP, RG 165, War Department, General and Special Staff, ABC Decimal File, 383.6 TS (Case 7 only), memorandum by Colonel Charles B. Westover "Closing Borders of U.S. Zones of Germany and Austria," 2 July 1946, and note for record of a meeting on 5 July 1946 of the secretaries of war, state, and navy "Policy as to Future Entry of Jewish Refugees into US Zones of Germany and Austria," 12 July 1946.

25. *FRUS,* 1946, 5:175, Lane to State Department, 25 July 1946.

26. NACP, RG 107, ASW, FSCC of Petersen, December 1945–August 1947, ASW383.7, Refugees and DPs, Clark to Petersen, no. 1178, 14 July 1946, Vienna to War Department, no. 1217, 15 July 1946, and McNarney to War Department, no. 7442, 16 July 1946. Like Berlin, Vienna, too, was divided among the four occupation powers.

27. TL, PSF, Subject File Foreign Affairs Palestine, file Palestine-Jewish Immigrants, Byrnes to Truman, 26 July 1946; NACP, RG 165, War Department, General and Special Staff, ABC Decimal File, 383.6 TS (Case 7 only), Patterson to McNarney, 23 July 1946, and memorandum by Major General Lauris Norstad, 23 July 1946.

28. YIVO, Schwartz Papers, file 13/107, Warburg to Hildring, 23 August 1946; see also Kochavi, "British Response to the Involvement of the American Jewish Joint Distribution Committee," 223–34; Bauer, *Out of the Ashes,* 256–60.

29. PRO, FO371/57694/WR2215, *Times,* 10 August 1946; *New York Times,* 24 August 1946.

30. HIA, Fait Collection, box 2, file 2, Bernstein to McNarney, 20 August 1946; see also *New York Times,* 23 August 1946.

31. NACP, RG 107, ASW, FSCC of Petersen, December 1945–August 1947, ASW383.7, Refugees and DPs, Byrnes to Truman, 13 August 1946; TL, PSF, file Palestine-Jewish Immigration, John W. McCormack, Majority Leader, House of Representatives, to Truman, 22 July 1946; TL, PSF, Subject File Foreign Affairs Palestine, file Palestine-Jewish Immigration, Truman to McCormack, 24 July 1946; Dinnerstein, *America and the Survivors,* 105–13; Bauer, *Flight and Rescue,* 247–50; Genizi, *Adviser on Jewish Affairs,* 61–63.

32. NACP, RG 107, ASW, FSCC of Petersen, December 1945–August 1947, ASW383.7, Refugees and DPs, McNarney to War Department, no. 2003, 15 August 1946, and War Department to OMGUS, Berlin, no. 97404, 14 August 1946; Keynan, *Holocaust Survivors,* 60–64.

33. *FRUS,* 1946, 5:178, Acheson to Lane, 12 August 1946, and 185–86, Erhardt to secretary of state, 3 September 1946.

34. Ibid., 179–80, Acheson to Key, 14 August 1946, and 175–76, Erhardt to secretary of state, 3 August 1946; NACP, RG 107, ASW, FSCC of Petersen, December 1945–August 1947, ASW383.7, Refugees and DPs, Key to secretary of state, no. 3555, 20 August 1946.

35. PRO, FO371/57694/WR2205, minute by Henderson, 16 August 1946.

36. *FRUS,* 1946, 5:183, Key to secretary of state, 28 August 1946; see also chap. 10.

37. PRO, FO371/57696/WR3023, Cadogan to FO, no. 1258, 19 October 1946; NACP, RG 107, ASW, FSCC of Petersen, December 1945–August 1947, ASW383.7, Refugees and DPs, memorandum for secretary of war, 11 October 1946; Kochavi, "Anglo-American Discord," 545–46.

38. PRO, FO371/57696/WR3178, FO to Rome, no. 1820, 8 November 1946; PRO, FO371/57696/WR3170, British embassy, Rome, to FO, 22 October 1946; see also Genizi, *Adviser on Jewish Affairs*, 67–68.

39. HIA, Fait Collection, box 1, file 14, AGWAR to USFET, no. 87609, 13 December 1946.

40. PRO, CAB127/280, FO to Washington, no. 9307, 25 September 1946.

41. PRO, FO371/57694, Inverchapel to FO, no. 5136, 14 August 1946.

42. PRO, FO371/57696/WR3178, Cadogan to FO, no. 39, 27 September 1946; see also HIA, Fait Collection, box 2, file 3, statement by McNarney, 8 October 1946.

43. PRO, FO943/543, Allied Commission for Germany and Austria to Control Commission for Germany and Austria, no. 450, 19 August 1946; PRO, FO371/52629, minute by Beith, 21 August 1946; PRO, FO371/52631, British consulate general, Marseilles to foreign secretary, no. 52, 28 August 1946.

44. PRO, FO371/57698/WR3689, Rendel (New York) to FO, no. 131, 28 August 1946; PRO, FO371/57698/WR3413, Cooper to FO, no. 476, 14 November 1946; see also chaps. 10 and 11.

45. HIA, Fait Collection, box 2, file 3, the commander in chief's press conference, 16 April 1947, and Headquarters, European Command, Public Relations Division, announcement to be released at conclusion of Clay's press conference, 16 April 1947, and box 1, file 14, Headquarters, European Command, to UNRRA, U.S. Zone, Headquarters, 3 May 1947.

46. Ibid., Civil Affairs Division to USFA, no. 97235, 1 May 1947; NACP, RG 107, ASW, FSCC of Petersen, December 1945–August 1947, 383.7 Books 2&3, Hildring to Petersen, 20 June 1947, and War Department to Vienna, no. 80788, 24 June 1947.

47. Ibid., Keys to War Department, no. 7464, 27 June 1947; Genizi, *Adviser on Jewish Affairs*, annex 5.

48. NACP, RG 107, ASW, FSCC of Petersen, December 1945–August 1947, 383.7 Book 2&3, Patterson to Petersen, 30 June 1947, and Petersen to Hildring, 15 July 1947.

49. About the escape from Rumania, see chap. 9.

50. JA, box 25-A, file 1169.2, Joel Fischer to Arthur Altmeyer, 18 July 1947; Rhodes House, Oxford, Arthur Creech Jones Papers, United Nations, Official Records of the Second Session of the General Assembly, Supplement No. 11, United Nations Special Committee on Palestine, Report to the General Assembly, vol. 2, Lake Success (New York, 1947), annex 18; HP, General Testimonies, no. 188, Leo W. Schwartz; YIVO, Schwartz Papers 71/10, Judge Louis E. Levinthal, adviser on Jewish Affairs, to the commander in chief, European Command, 13 August 1947; YIVO, Schwartz Papers 71/10, Judge Louis E. Levinthal to Meir Grossman, American Jewish Conference, 19 August 1947; YIVO, Schwartz Papers 69/10, report of Rabbi Bernstein to the Five Cooperating Organizations, May 1946 to August 1947; Genizi, *Adviser on Jewish Affairs*, 63–65, 87–90; Yahil, "Activities of the Palestine Jewry's Mission," 154–55.

51. PRO, FO371/66668/WR2929, Mack to FO, no. 736, 9 August 1947; see also NACP,

RG 165 (General and Special Staff), Civil Affairs Division, IRO, Country file of Colonel D. H. Frost, Mass Influx of Hungarian and Rumanian Jews into Austria, Bernstein to commander in chief European Theater, 5 August 1947, and Mass Influx of Hungarian and Rumanian Jews into Austria, memorandum for the secretary of war, 29 August 1947.

52. PRO, FO371/66669, Mack to FO, no. 105, 18 August 1946.

53. NACP, RG 59, 800.4016 DP/9-1247, Vienna to State Department, no. 853, 12 September 1947.

54. PRO, FO371/81827/E8570, George L. Warren to D. D. Maclean, 4 September 1947; PRO, FO371/61807/E3979, Balfour to Acheson, 26 May 1947; PRO, FO945/494, FO to Washington, no. 5068, 21 May 1947; PRO, FO945/494, FO to British embassy, Washington, 7 August 1947.

55. PRO, FO371/61811/E5176, memorandum of the Italian Foreign Ministry, 10 April 1947.

56. PRO, FO371/66671/WR3177, Mack to FO, no. 872, 18 September 1947.

57. PRO, FO371/52565/E1424, memorandum of conversation between Bevin and Silver, 14 November 1946; PRO, FO371/52511, Higham to Beith, 28 November 1946; PRO, FO371/61806/E3659, minute Beith, 28 April 1947.

58. PRO, CO537/2331, FO to Washington, no. 35, 1 January 1947; PRO, FO371/61799/E207, Inverchapel to FO, no. 43, 4 January 1947.

59. PRO, CAB104/275, Inverchapel to FO, no. 2004, 3 April 1947.

60. NACP, RG 59, GRDS, Office of Near Eastern Affairs, Top Secret, Palestine, 5 January 1946–29 June 1946, Loy Henderson to Balfour, 27 December 1946.

61. Schaary, *Cyprus Detention Camps,* 80–83.

62. PRO, FO115/4307, memorandum of the British embassy, Washington, "Illegal Immigration into Palestine," 18 March 1947.

63. PRO, CAB104/275, Inverchapel to FO, no. 1802, 24 March 1947; PRO, FO371/61805/E3377, Inverchapel to FO, no. 2397, 22 April 1947; NACP, RG 59, GRDS, Office of Near Eastern Affairs, Palestine, Top Secret, folder 1947, Acheson to Villard, NEA, 1 May 1947.

64. PRO, FO371/61756/E5489, Inverchapel to FO, no. 1466, 16 June 1947.

65. TL, WHOF: OF 204, statement by the president, 5 June 1947; PRO, FO371/61811/E5001, minutes of a meeting of the Cabinet Committee on Illegal Immigration, 3rd meeting, 9 June 1947.

66. PRO, FO371/61811/E5001, Bevin to Marshall, 27 June 1947.

67. PRO, FO371/61821/E7400, Marshall to Bevin, 7 August 1947; see also PRO, FO371/61757/E6906, British embassy, Washington, to State Department, 22 July 1947.

68. See chap. 11.

69. *FRUS,* 1947, 5:1139–40, Lovett to American embassy, London, 27 August 1947; PRO, FO371/61824/E7938, Inverchapel to FO, no. 4720, 27 August 1947, and FO to Washington, no. 48845, 29 August 1947; see also PRO, FO371/61824/E8002, Wise to Inverchapel, 21 August 1947; PRO, FO371/61822/E7490, Balfour to FO, no. 4471, 14 August 1947; PRO, FO371/61822/E7742, Balfour to FO, no. 4608, 21 August 1947; Halamish, "The United States' Position in the 'Exodus' Affair," 209–25; Eilat, *Struggle for Statehood,* 2:214–15, 218.

70. PRO, FO371/61822/E7490, FO to Washington, no. 8281, 16 August 1947; PRO,

FO371/61822/E7742, FO to Washington, no. 8575, 22 August 1947; PRO, FO371/61822/E8049, minute by Makins, 28 August 1947.

71. PRO, FO371/61828/E8804, British embassy, Washington, to Eastern Department, FO, 16 September 1947.

72. PRO, FO115/4334, Inverchapel to Marshall, 18 October 1947; PRO, FO371/61851/E10257, Inverchapel to FO, no. 6123, 1 November 1947; *FRUS, 1947,* 5:1196–98, memorandum of conversation by Henderson, 22 October 1947; see also Krammer, *Forgotten Friendship,* 44–46.

73. PRO, FO371/61854/E11994, Holman to FO, no. 1526, 17 December 1947.

74. *FRUS, 1947,* 5:1247–48, Marshall to Bevin, 7 November 1947; Hadari and Tsahor, *Voyage to Freedom,* 62–66.

75. PRO, FO115/4334, Marshall to Inverchapel, 10 November 1947.

76. Ibid., Bromely to Beeley, 12 November 1947; PRO, FO371/61852/E10743, Inverchapel to FO, no. 6542, 15 November 1947; PRO, FO371/61853/E1197, British embassy, Washington, to Eastern Department, FO, 20 November 1947; see also PRO, FO371/61853/E10980, Holman to FO, no. 1381, 20 November 1947, and Holman to FO, no. 1342, 24 November 1947.

77. PRO, FO800/487, memorandum of conversation between Bevin and Marshall, 4 December 1947; *FRUS, 1947,* 5:1300–1302, Marshall to Lovett, 6 December 1947.

78. *FRUS, 1947,* 5:1302–4, memorandum of conversation by Henderson, 8 December 1947; *FRUS, 1947,* 5:1311–12, memorandum of conversation by Armour, assistant secretary of state for political affairs, 12 December 1947.

79. PRO, FO371/61833/E12231, Inverchapel to FO, no. 7167, 23 December 1947.

80. See chap. 3.

81. PRO, ADM1/20793, FO to Washington, no. 13356, 27 December 1947.

82. LPA, 24/47, minutes of the Labour Party Secretariat, 9 December 1947; LA, minutes of the Executive Committee of the Histadrut, 30 December 1947–1 January 1948, Shertok; Hadari and Tsahor, *Voyage to Freedom,* chap. 5; Tsachor, "Ben-Gurion and the 'Ha'apala,'" 438–42.

83. Ganin, *Truman, American Jewry and Israel,* 147–48; Michael J. Cohen, *Palestine and the Great Powers,* 345–46.

CHAPTER SEVEN

1. Since we are dealing with illegal immigration, it is difficult to estimate the number of Jews who left Poland. Although there are few differences among the various sources regarding the number of Jews who left Poland through the organized *Brichah*—120,000—the statistical data on the number of Jews who did not leave through the organization differ greatly. Yohanan Cohen estimates that, in all, between approximately 139,000 and 142,000 Jews left Poland between the end of 1944 and February 1947, while Engel's figures are much higher, between 161,000 and 193,000. Cohen, *Operation "Briha,"* 419–22, 468, 471; Engel, *Between Liberation and Flight,* 150–51, 154–55 n. 7, 244 n. 24.

2. Coutouvidis and Reynolds, *Poland,* chaps. 3–7; Prażmowska, *Britain and Poland,* chaps. 4–7; Garliński, *Poland in the Second World War,* chaps. 9, 21, 23–24; Rothwell, *Britain and the Cold War,* 151–80; Kitchen, *British Foreign Policy,* chap. 10; Ross, *The Foreign Office and the Kremlin,* chap. 2; Crister and Garrett, "Death and Politics," 429–46.

3. Coutouvidis and Reynolds, *Poland,* chaps. 8–10; Lotarski, "Communist Takeover in Poland," 339–67; Lundestad, *American Non-Policy,* 205–24; Bullock, *Ernest Bevin,* 17–20, 23–24, 140–42, 274, 346, 384–85; Mikołajczyk, *Rape of Poland.*

4. Checinski, *Poland,* 8–9; Gutman, *Jews in Poland,* 28–29; Bauer, *Flight and Rescue,* 114–15; Kahane, *After the Deluge,* 59.

5. Engel, *Between Liberation and Flight,* 39–42; Gutman, *Jews in Poland,* 11–12.

6. GFHA, box "Italy 1946–1949," a letter from Chaim, 31 May 1945; WA, Leo Cohen to Weizmann, July 1945; Gutman, *Jews in Poland,* 12; Dobroszycki, *Survivors of the Holocaust in Poland,* chaps. 1 and 6; Weinryb, "Poland," 241.

7. PRO, FO371/51117/WR1537, Jane E. Leverson to Jewish Committee for Relief Abroad, 6 May 1947. On a poll that was conducted among the survivors of Dachau in May 1945, see Gelber, *Standard Bearers,* 364.

8. PRO, FO371/57695/WR2508, extract from a memorandum submitted by the director of the IGCR to the Joint Anglo-American Commission on Palestine, 23 January 1946.

9. LPA, 25/45, minutes of the Labour Party Political Department, 21 March 1945, Avriel; LA, minutes of the sixth convention of the Histadrut, 28 January–2 February 1945, Dobkin; HA, 14/160a, report of the Jewish Agency on the situation of the Jews in liberated Poland, 23 March 1945.

10. LA, minutes of the meeting of the Executive Committee of the Histadrut, 19 August 1945, Kovner, and Dobkin's report on the pogrom in Radom, 5 September 1945; see also LPA, 24/46, minutes of Mapai (Eretz Israel workers party; the dominant party in the Yishuv) Secretariat, 27 August 1945, Lubianker; HA, 14/158, Duvdevani to Meirov, 13 September 1945; GFHA, box "Italy 1946–1949," a letter from Duvdevani (Italy), 20 October 1945; Engel, *Between Liberation and Flight,* 47–53.

11. NACP, RG 226, Duker/Dwork Papers, Entry 191, Palestine, Jewish-Arab Activity, memorandum by the Research and Analysis Branch of the OSS "Situation of Jews in Poland," 26 May 1946.

12. *FRUS,* 1945, 2:1212–14, Emerson to Johnson, the third secretary of embassy in the United Kingdom, 13 December 1945, and 1211, Gallman to the secretary of state, 28 February 1946; PRO, FO371/57686/WR313, Warsaw to FO, no. 53, 9 January 1946.

13. CZA, S-25/5210, discussion at the Emissaries Department, Jewish Agency, 12 February 1947, Yohanan Cohen; LA, minutes of the meeting of the Executive Committee of the Histadrut, 23 May 1946, Moshe Ishai; HA, Dekel Collection, file Poland, report of Cohen on the *Brichah,* 3 April 1947; HP, General Testimonies, Chaim Guri Collection, no. 9, Zvi Netzer testimony; Weinryb, "Poland," 247–49. About the co-option of the Jews in the Polish administration, see Gutman, *Jews in Poland,* 28–31; Bauer, *Flight and Rescue,* 114–15; Nussbaum, *Story of an Illusion,* 187–91; Kahane, *After the Deluge,* 31–32. About anti-Semitism in Poland before the war, see Meltzer, *Political Strife in a Blind Alley;* Gutman, "Polish Antisemitism between the Wars," 97–108; Polonsky, "Failed Pogrom," 109–25. See also Gutman, "Polish and Jewish Historiography," 177–89.

14. PRO, FO688/31, File no. 48, Cavendish-Bentinck to Charles W. Baxter, 17 September 1945.

15. See, for example, Breitman, *Official Secrets,* 9, 119–20, 230–31; Wasserstein, *Brit-*

ain and the Jews of Europe, 241; see also PRO, FO371/57686/E53, Warsaw to FO, no. 53, 9 January 1946.

16. PRO, FO943/699, Control Commission for Germany to War Office, no. 224, 8 December 1945; PRO, CAB134/595, Strang to FO, no. 44, 15 December 1945.

17. PRO, FO371/51129/WR3735, Shuckburgh to Bevin, no. 252, 8 December 1945.

18. PRO, FO371/57684/WR15, Cavendish-Bentinck to Bevin, 18 December 1945; PRO, FO371/51127/WR3418, Cavendish-Bentinck to FO, no. 956, 19 November 1945; PRO, FO688/31, File no. 48, Hilary Young, Political Division, Control Commission for Germany, to Robin M. A. Hankey, chargé d'affaires at Warsaw, 5 December 1945, Hankey to Baxter, 8 December 1945, and Hankey to Young, 18 December 1945.

19. PRO, FO945/655, Halifax to FO, no. 15, 2 January 1946; *New York Times,* 3 January 1945; Bauer, *Flight and Rescue,* 194–98.

20. WA, a circular of the World Jewish Congress signed by Barou and Easterman, 3 January 1946; HIA, Fait Collection, box 2, file 2, Jacob L. Trobe, director of the JDC in Germany, to Morgan, 4 January 1946, and message to the press, 4 January 1946.

21. PRO, FO371/57684/WR65, FO to Washington, no. 114, 4 January 1946.

22. PRO, CAB128/5, Cabinet meeting, 8 January 1946; PRO, WO275/63, Fortnightly Intelligence Newsletter for the period 5–18 January 1946.

23. Kochavi, "Anglo-American Discord," 534–35. About Morgan's interpretations of the events, see Khalidi, *From Haven to Conquest,* chap. 54.

24. PRO, FO371/57684/WR65, FO to Warsaw, no. 50, 6 January 1946, and FO to Warsaw, no. 27, 4 January 1946.

25. PRO, FO371/57686/WR213, Warsaw to FO, nos. 53, 54, 55, 9 January 1946; see also an article published in the *Jewish Chronicle* on 18 January 1946. On the agreement between the British and the Poles on transferring Polish citizens of German nationality, see Oppen, *Documents on Germany,* 107–10.

26. PRO, FO371/57684/WR111, Cavendish-Bentinck to FO, no. 70, 10 January 1946.

27. PRO, FO688/34, memorandum by Banks, 8 January 1946, and minutes of the British embassy, Warsaw, 9, 10 January 1946.

28. PRO, FO371/57686/WR213, Warsaw to FO, no. 55, 9 January 1946. At the end of January 1946, both Britain and the United States condemned the political murders in Poland. See Lundestad, *American Non-Policy,* 209.

29. PRO, FO688/34, minute by Banks, 28 January 1946.

30. A report from Italy spoke of 670. Yizhak Steiner, a Brichah emissary in Czechoslovakia, told of eight hundred killed, and Abba Kovner claimed in August 1945 that since the liberation more than twelve hundred Jews had been slain. HA, 14/81, a letter from Duvdevani (Italy), 8 July 1945; HA, 14/176a, Steiner to "Artzi" (code name for the institute for organizing illegal immigration into Palestine), 6 May 1946; Bauer, *Flight and Rescue,* 115; Gutman, *Jews in Poland,* 33; Checinski, *Poland,* 17; Weinryb, "Poland," 252; Ishai, *In the Shadow of the Holocaust,* 55–56.

31. PRO, FO371/57684, WR75, record of a meeting held at the Refugee Department, FO, on 7 January 1946 regarding Jewish migration from Poland into Germany, Czechoslovakia, Austria, and Italy; PRO, FO945/655, memorandum by Rendel "Treatment of New Jewish Refugees in British Zone in Germany," 9 January 1946.

32. PRO, FO371/57684/WR88, memorandum by Henderson, 11 January 1946; see also PRO, FO371/57689/WR88, minute, 9 January 1946.

33. PRO, CAB134/595, Cabinet Overseas Reconstruction Committee, O.R.C. (46) 2nd meeting, 25 January 1946.

34. PRO, FO1005/838, Allied Control Authority, Directorate of Prisoners of War and DPs, note by the secretariat "Treatment of Jewish Refugees," 7 December 1945.

35. PRO, FO945/655, Acarbit Vienna to Troopers (War Office), no. 7758, 18 October 1945.

36. See chap. 1.

37. PRO, FO371/57684/WR103, Cavendish-Bentinck to FO, no. 56, 9 January 1946.

38. PRO, FO945/655, report of the British Intelligence in Austria, no. 564, 19 January 1946.

39. PRO, FO945/655, Halifax to FO, no. 819, 6 February 1946; PRO, FO371/52627/E7855, Halifax to FO, no. 1163, 21 February 1946.

40. PRO, FO181/1009/7, Bevin to British representatives in Arab countries, no. 279, 18 October 1945, and minute, 15 November 1945.

41. PRO, FO371/57687/WR54, FO to Warsaw, nos. 242, 243, 2 February 1946; PRO, FO371/57686/WR267, minute by Rendel, 30 January 1946.

42. Ibid., FO to Washington, no. 1110, 2 February 1946; PRO, FO371/52627/E7855, Halifax to FO, no. 1163, 21 February 1946.

43. PRO, FO945/655, Cavendish-Bentinck to FO, no. 237, 7 February 1946. Ishai claims that Olszewski was a Jew who hid this fact. Ishai, *In the Shadow of the Holocaust,* 184. On the process of issuing passports and exit visas, see PRO, FO371/52627/E7855, Warsaw to FO, no. 1254, 11 August 1946.

44. PRO, FO371/57688/WR736, Cavendish-Bentinck to Christopher Warner, head of the Northern Department, FO, 20 February 1946.

45. NACP, RG 43, Records of U.S. Participation in International Conferences, Commissions and Expositions, Records of Anglo-American Committee of Inquiry Re Palestine, 1944–46, conversation with Prime Minister Osóbka-Morawski, 1 February 1946.

46. Ibid., AACI Reports, Liaison Office, conversation with Foreign Minister Rzymowski, 8 February 1946.

47. PRO, FO688/34, minute by Hankey, 9 February 1946.

48. PRO, FO371/57688/WR736, Cavendish-Bentinck to Warner, 20 February 1946.

49. PRO, FO688/34, minute by Russell, 16 February 1946.

50. CZA, S-25/5262, report of Ishai, 10 February 1946. About Dr. Sommerstein, see Engel, *Between Liberation and Flight,* 53–54.

51. NACP, RG 43, Records of U.S. Participation in International Conferences, Commissions and Expositions, Records of Anglo-American Committee of Inquiry Re Palestine, 1944–46, AACI Reports, Liaison Office, conference with representatives of the Jewish Central Committee, 9 February 1946. About the committee, see Gutman, *Jews in Poland,* 80–86.

52. NACP, RG 43, Records of U.S. Participation in International Conferences, Commissions and Expositions, Records of Anglo-American Committee of Inquiry Re Palestine, 1944–46, AACI Reports, Liaison Office, conversations with Mons. Zdzanek, secretary to the bishop of Lodz, 10 February 1946.

53. *Report of the Anglo-American Committee,* 52, paragraph 25; Crossman, *Palestine Mission,* 82–86.

54. HA, Oral testimony, Isser Ben-Zvi, no. 1396; HA, Dekel Collection, file Poland, report of Yohanan Cohen on the *Brichah,* 3 April 1947; HP, General Testimonies, Chaim Guri Collection, no. 9, Zvi Netzer testimony; Bauer, *Flight and Rescue,* 28–34; Cohen, *Operation "Briha,"* chaps. 7, 10. About the meeting between the Jews who had left Poland and the emissaries from Poland, see Shapira, *Visions in Conflict,* 325–54; Keynan, *Holocaust Survivors,* chap. 4.

55. HA, 14/397, telegrams sent by Moshe Averbuch (Agami), 19 March, 9 April, 21, 30 May, 24 June 1945; Engel, *Between Liberation and Flight,* 69–70.

56. See chaps. 3 and 9.

57. LA, minutes of the meeting of the Histadrut Central Committee, 19 August 1945; LA, minutes of the meeting of the Executive Committee of the Histadrut, 12 February 1947, Isser Ben-Zvi.

58. Engel, *Between Liberation and Flight,* 64.

59. CZA, 42/1, minutes of the meeting of the Zionist Executive Committee, 21 November 1945, Ben-Gurion.

60. HA, 14/405, report on meeting of emissaries at Prague, 27 January 1946; HA, 14/176a, Steiner to "Artzi," 11 January 1946; HA, 14/502, Ben-Zvi to Surkiss, 9, 30 December 1945; HA, Dekel Collection, file III, report on Brichah activities, Bratislava, 23 March 1946; CZA, minutes of the meeting of the Zionist Executive Committee, 30 April 1946, Dobkin, and 9 June 1946, Zvia Lubetkin; CZA, S-25/5210, discussion at the Emissaries Department, 18 February 1947, Yohanan Cohen.

61. HA, Oral testimonies, no. 3796, Isser Ben-Zvi; Engel, *Between Liberation and Flight,* 106–9.

62. PRO, FO371/57687/WR396, Steel to Warsaw, no. 31, 9 February 1946; PRO, FO371/57687/WR403, JTA, 5 February 1946.

63. The highest estimate was given by Zvi Netzer in his testimony; see HA, Dekel Collection; see also ibid., report of Yohanan Cohen, 3 April 1947; Bauer, *Flight and Rescue,* 126; Cohen, *Operation "Briha,"* annex 10.

64. LA, minutes of the meeting of the Executive Committee of the Histadrut, 12 February 1947, Isser Ben-Zvi; Engel, *Between Liberation and Flight,* 42–44, 121–24; Bauer, *Flight and Rescue,* 125; Gutman, *Jews in Poland,* 20–26; Weinryb, "Poland," 241; Litvak, *Polish-Jewish Refugees,* 331–59. About the repatriation agreement between the Soviet Union and Poland, see Schechtman, *Postwar Population Transfers in Europe,* 155–77.

65. Engel, *Between Liberation and Flight,* 128.

66. Ro'i, *Soviet Decision Making in Practice,* 29.

67. LA, minutes of the meeting of the Executive Committee of the Histadrut, 12 February 1947, Isser Ben-Zvi; HA, Dekel Collection, report of Yohanan Cohen, 3 April 1947.

68. Bauer, *Flight and Rescue,* 205–12, 219–23; Gutman, *Jews in Poland,* 34–41; Checinski, *Poland,* 21–32; Cohen, *Operation "Briha,"* chap. 12; Kahane, *After the Deluge,* 62–67.

69. Kahane, *After the Deluge,* 76; HP, box 44, file 9, Yitzhak Zuckermann to Zvia Lubetkin, 9 August 1946.

70. Checinski, *Poland,* 21–32; Gutman, *Jews in Poland,* 39–41; Bauer, *Flight and Rescue,* 209–10.

71. About other cases of blood libel, see Kahane, *After the Deluge,* 59; HP, General Testimonies, Guri Collection, no. 207, Kahane testimony.

72. HP, box 44, file 9, Yitzhak Zuckermann to Zvia Lubetkin, 9 August 1946; HA, Dekel Collection, report on the *Brichah* by Yohanan Cohen, 3 April 1947; LA, minutes of the meeting of the Executive Committee of the Histadrut, 12 February 1947, Isser Ben-Zvi; Bauer, *Flight and Rescue,* 221–24; Engel, *Between Liberation and Flight,* 134–36. Rabbi Kahane does not think that the Kielce pogrom caused the Polish authorities to permit Jews to leave Poland; see his testimony, HP, General Testimonies, no. 207.

73. HA, Dekel Collection, The *Brichah* Book, file, "Poland-Russia IV," Isser Ben-Zvi to "Mossad" (the Haganah branch in charge of illegal immigration into Palestine), 7 August 1946; LPA, 26/46, minutes of the meeting of the Political Department of Mapai, 26 August 1946, Dobkin; Bauer, *Flight and Rescue,* 211–12; Cohen, *Operation "Briha,"* annex 10.

74. Yahil, "Activities of the Palestine Jewry's Mission," 36–37; HP, Bernstein testimony.

75. PRO, FO371/57697/WR2921, memorandum by Rabbi Bernstein to General Mc-Narney, 2 August 1946; Bauer, *Flight and Rescue,* 241–46. About the Jews in Silesia, see Gutman, *Jews in Poland,* 24–26; Engel, *Between Liberation and Flight,* 112–15.

76. PRO, FO371/57697/WR2921, minute by Rendel, 5 September 1946.

77. PRO, FO371/52627/E7723, Shuckburgh to FO, no. 904, 7 August 1946; PRO, FO371/52629/E8141, Shuckburgh to FO, no. 947, 15 August 1946; PRO, FO371/57694/WR2287, Cavendish-Bentinck to FO, no. 1312, 25 August 1946.

78. *FRUS,* 1946, 5:174, Lane to the secretary of state, 25 July 1946, 175–76, 185–87, Erhardt to the secretary of state, 3 August 1946, 3 September 1946, and 178, Acheson, the acting secretary of state, to Lane, 12 August 1946.

79. PRO, FO371/57694/WR2206, Cabot Coville, American embassy in London, to Baxter, 15 August 1946; *FRUS,* 1946, 5:179, Acheson to Key, chargé d'affaires at Rome, 14 August 1946.

80. PRO, FO371/57693/WR2067, memorandum by C. J. Edmons, FO, 27 August 1946; PRO, FO371/52629/E8141, minute by Beith, 21 August 1946, and minute by Edmonds, 22 August 1946; PRO, FO371/57693/WR2156, report on illegal immigration to Palestine, annex C, August 1946; PRO, FO945/372, Baxter to Nichols, no. 568, 19 August 1946.

81. PRO, FO371/52630/E8422, Russell to Baxter, 21 August 1946; PRO, FO371/52627/E78755, Russell to FO, no. 1254, 11 August 1946; PRO, FO371/57698/WR2662, memorandum by Warner, 3 September 1946.

82. PRO, FO371/57694/WR2287, Cavendish-Bentinck to FO, no. 1312, 25 August 1946.

83. PRO, FO371/57769/WR2494, note of La Guardia's interview with the prime minister, 5 September 1946; PRO, PREM8/384, memorandum by Sargent for the prime minister, 4 September 1946. Officials at the embassy thought that the plan to resettle Jews in Silesia would fail. PRO, FO371/57698/WR2662, minute by Warner, 3 September 1946.

84. PRO, FO371/56534/N10434, memorandum by Hankey and Hancok, 9 August 1946; PRO, FO371/56534/N11739, Cavendish-Bentinck to FO, no. 270, 11 September 1946; PRO, CAB127/280, FO to Washington, no. 9307, 25 September 1946; see also *FRUS,* 1946, 5:186–87, Lane to the secretary of state, 3 September 1946.

85. PRO, FO371/56534/N11440, Cavendish-Bentinck to British consulate in Katowice, no. 39, 31 August 1946; PRO, FO688/34, British consulate, Katowice, to Cavendish-Bentinck, no. 1, 6 September 1946, and memorandum by Banks, 10 September 1946.

86. Bauer, *Flight and Rescue,* 222.

87. PRO, FO371/56534/N10434, FO to Warsaw, no. 1449, 27 August 1946.

88. PRO, FO371/52630/E8339, Cavendish-Bentinck to FO, no. 1291, 21 August 1946; PRO, FO371/52629/E8141, minute by Beith, 21 August 1946.

89. PRO, FO371/56534/N11209, Cavendish-Bentinck to FO, no. 1344, 31 August 1946; PRO, FO371/56534/N11440, Cavendish-Bentinck to Hankey, 1 September 1946.

90. Lundestad, *American Non-Policy,* 214; Coutouvidis and Reynolds, *Poland,* 251–55.

91. PRO, FO371/57694/WR2335, Cavendish-Bentinck to FO, no. 1332, 29 August 1946, and Cavendish-Bentinck to Hankey, 28 August 1946; see also Coutouvidis and Reynolds, *Poland,* 223–28, 267–70.

92. PRO, FO371/57694/WR2280, Charles to FO, no. 86a, 22 August 1946.

93. PRO, FO371/57695/WR2563, Osborne to Bevin, no. 200, 12 September 1946. About the Polish bishops' attitude toward the Jews, see Gutman, *Jews in Poland,* 36–38, annex 9; Kahane, *After the Deluge,* 58–72; Kochavi, "Catholic Church," 116–28; Wasserstein, *Vanishing Diaspora,* 24–25.

94. PRO, FO688/34, Cavendish-Bentinck to Olszewski, no. 309, 11 September 1946.

95. PRO, FO371/57778/WR953, Political Division, Allied Commission for Austria, to German Department, FO, 17 December 1946; Cohen, *Operation "Briha,"* annex 10.

96. HA, 14/73, report of Mordechai Surkiss, 3 April 1947; HP, General Testimonies, Chaim Guri Collection, no. 9, Zvi Netzer testimony.

97. PRO, FO371/61810/E4910, British embassy, Warsaw, to Bevin, no. 205, 3 June 1947; see also CZA, S-6/1169, report of Haim Barlas on his tour in Europe, 20 October 1947; Litvak, "JDC's Contribution," 334–88.

98. PRO, FO371/61759/E11582, Russell to Hankey, 2 December 1947.

99. LA, minutes of the Executive Committee of the Histadrut, 4 February 1948.

CHAPTER EIGHT

1. Max, *The United States, Great Britain, and the Sovietization of Hungary;* Lundestad, *American Non-Policy,* 115–48; Ignotus, "The First Two Communist Takeovers of Hungary," 385–98; Kertesz, *Between Russia and the West,* chap. 2; Lahav, "The Hungarian Communist Party's Path to Power," chaps. 8, 9, 15, 19; Nagy, *The Struggle behind the Iron Curtain,* 57–461.

2. Lundestad, *American Non-Policy,* 149–82; Korbel, *Communist Subversion of Czechoslovakia,* 94–242; Taborsky, *President Edward Beneš,* chaps. 8–9; Rothwell, *Britain and the Cold War,* 367–74; Meyer, "Czechoslovakia," 69–72.

3. LPA, 23/46, minutes of Mapai Center, 29 April 1946; JA, box 14-B, file no. C-36.041, report of Jacobson, director of the JDC in Czechoslovakia, July–November 1946; PRO, FO371/57685/WR178, memorandum by Henderson "Refugee Problems in Czechoslovakia," 18 January 1946, and D. Mackillop, FO, to P. B. B. Nichols, Prague, 5 February 1946; PRO, FO371/52511/E1760, memorandum submitted by the council of Jewish communities in Bohemia, Moravia, and Silesia to the AAC, 10 February 1946; Meyer,

"Czechoslovakia," 70, 78–82; Crum, *Behind the Silken Curtain,* 116–17; Korbel, *Communist Subversion of Czechoslovakia,* 125, 138, 161; Jelinek, "Jews of Czechoslovakia," 155, 157, 163.

4. BGA, Chronological Documentation Division, Epstein to members of the Executive Agency of the Jewish Agency, 18 February 1946; LA, minutes, Central Committee of the Histadrut, 22 August 1945, Abba Kovner; HA, 14/160a, Steiner to "Artzi," 6 September 1946; Dekel, *On the Routes of the Brichah,* 75–76.

5. Crum, *Behind the Silken Curtain,* 116–17; see also PRO, FO371/52511/E1760, Schuckburgh to Bevin, no. 74, 18 February 1946.

6. PRO, FO371/57685/WR178, minute by Henderson, 18 January 1946; PRO, FO371/57689/WR838, memorandum by Henderson "Ruthenian Jews and the Cession of Ruthenia by Czechoslovakia to the Soviet Union," 11 March 1946; PRO, FO371/57688/WR712, Prague to FO, nos. 269, 270, 11 March 1946; PRO, FO371/57688/WR766, Prague to FO, no. 33, 15 March 1946; CZA, vol. 42/2, minutes of the executive of the Jewish Agency, 30 April 1946; Rothkirchen, "Deep Rooted Yet Alien," 147–82; Jelinek, "Jews of Czechoslovakia," 161–62; Jelinek, "The Vatican," 221–55.

7. *Report of the Anglo-American Committee,* 52–53, paragraph 28; see also HA, 14/160a, circular no. B of Merkaz Lagolah, 7 August 1945. About the Czechs' treatment of the Jews until the conclusion of the war, see Rothkirchen, "Czech Attitudes towards the Jews," 287–320; Meyer, "Czechoslovakia," 82–92; Bela Vago, *Shadow of the Swastika,* 113–73; Jelinek, "Jews of Czechoslovakia," 154–64.

8. Ben-Gurion estimated the number of Slovakian Jews at twenty-five thousand. BGA, Ben Gurion Diary, 20 January 1946; see also LPA, 23/46, minutes of Mapai Center, 29 April 1946, Dobkin; Meyer, "Czechoslovakia," 66; Bauer, *Out of the Ashes,* 104.

9. PRO, FO371/52511/E1760, memorandum submitted by the council of Jewish communities in Bohemia, Moravia, and Silesia to the AAC, 10 February 1946. About Slovakian Jewry during the war, see Yahil, *The Holocaust,* 352–55, 401–3, 523–25, 612–14.

10. *Report of the Anglo-American Committee,* 53, paragraph 32; see also HA, minutes of the Central Committee of the Histadrut, 22 August 1946; HA, 14/176a, Steiner to "Artzi," 6 September 1946; BGA, Ben Gurion Diary, 31 January 1946; Meyer, "Czechoslovakia," 105–7.

11. PRO, FO371/51129/WR3735, Schuckburgh to Bevin, no. 252, 8 December 1945; *FRUS,* 1945, 2:1212–14, Emerson to Johnson, third secretary of U.S. embassy in the United Kingdom, 13 December 1945.

12. CZA, S-6/4683, Yitzhak (Steiner), from Prague, 4 October 1945; HA, 14/158, Yehiel Duvdevani to "Artzi," 13 September 1945; HA, 14/160, minutes of the meeting of the emissaries at Bratislava, 20 October 1945; HA, 14/405, report on the Brichah activities, January 1946; HA, 14/77a, Steiner to "Artzi," 11 January 1946, and Avriel from Prague, 11 January 1946; HP, General Testimonies, no. 218, Aharon Ofri, and no. 211, Steiner.

13. Bauer, *Flight and Rescue,* 183–84.

14. LA, minutes of the executive committee of the Histadrut, 24 July 1946; HA, 14/77a, Dr. Mertz, 9 September 1946.

15. HA, Dekel Collection, The *Brichah* Book, file Poland-Russia, Isser Ben-Zvi to "Mossad," 7 August 1946.

16. HA, Dekel Collection, Private file; HA, *Brichah* Files, "Italy-Brigade," report of Surkiss; HP, General Testimonies, no. 208, Surkiss; Bauer, *Flight and Rescue,* 219.

17. LPA, 24/46, vol. B, minutes of Mapai Center, 27 August 1946, Lubianker; HA, 14/77a, Dr. Mertz, 9 September 1946; HA, Oral testimonies, Gafni, Oferi, Steiner, and Surkiss.

18. Dekel, *On the Routes of the Brichah,* 84–85.

19. On the negotiations over the loan, see Lundestad, *American Non-Policy,* 158–80; Korbel, *Communist Subversion of Czechoslovakia,* 179; Hirschmann, *The Embers Still Burn,* chap. 15; Rothwell, *Britain and the Cold War,* 372. Czechoslovakia received essential aid from UNRRA. The Americans financed three-quarters of UNRRA's budget. Woodbridge, *UNRRA,* 2:183–99.

20. PRO, FO371/52627/E7723, Schuckburgh to FO, no. 904, 7 August 1946.

21. *FRUS,* 1946, 5:174, Lane to secretary of state, 25 July 1946, and 175–76, Erhardt to secretary of state, 3 August 1946.

22. PRO, FO371/57693/WR2156, report on illegal immigration to Palestine, August 1946.

23. PRO, FO945/372, Baxter to Nichols, no. 568, 19 August 1946.

24. PRO, FO371/52629/E8141, Schuckburgh to FO, no. 947, 15 August 1946; see also *FRUS,* 1946, 5:185–86, Erhardt to secretary of state, 3 September 1946; Dekel, *On the Routes of the Brichah,* 82–83.

25. PRO, FO371/52629/E8079, Schuckburgh to FO, no. 946, 15 August 1946. About Ripka, see Korbel, *Communist Subversion of Czechoslovakia,* 126–27, 129, 148.

26. PRO, FO371/52629/E8141, minute by Beith, 21 August 1946.

27. PRO, FO371/52629/E8141, FO to Prague, no. 1030, 30 August 1946, and minute by Edmonds, 22 August 1946.

28. PRO, FO371/52631/E8705, Schuckburgh to FO, no. 1036, 2 September 1946.

29. PRO, FO371/52636/E8910, Schuckburgh to FO, no. 1055, 6 September 1946.

30. PRO, FO371/52632/E8947, Schuckburgh to Fierlinger, no. 253, 2 September 1946.

31. PRO, FO371/52632/E9156, Schuckburgh to FO, no. 1095, 14 September 1946.

32. PRO, FO371/52636/E8910, Schuckburgh to FO, no. 1055, 6 September 1946; PRO, FO371/52632/E9156, Schuckburgh to FO, no. 1095, 14 September 1946.

33. JA, box 14-B, file no. C-36.041, Jacobson's report, July–November 1946.

34. HIA, Fait Collection, box 1, file 14, Clay to Director of Civil Affairs, 4 April 1947; NACP, RG 59, 800.4016 DP/4-947, Berlin to the secretary of state, no. 837, 9 April 1947.

35. Dekel, *On the Routes of the Brichah,* 83–84.

36. Krammer, *Forgotten Friendship,* chaps. 3–5; Jelinek, "Jews of Czechoslovakia," 159–60; Ro'i, *Soviet Decision Making in Practice,* 84.

37. Katzburg, "Between Liberation and Revolution," 117; Duschinsky, "Hungary," 396. On the Holocaust in Hungary, see Braham, *Politics of Genocide;* Braham and Katzburg, *History of the Holocaust,* part 2.

38. LPA, 25/45, Section 2, minutes of the political department of Mapai, 21 March 1945, 29 April 1945; LA, minutes of the executive committee of the Histadrut, 21 March 1945; Asher Cohen, *Halutz Resistance in Hungary,* chap. 6.

39. HA, 14/397, Averbuch to "Meir," 30 May 1945, 24 June 1945; HA, 14/176a, Rosen

to "Artzi," 11 August 1945; HA, 14/70, Rosen, 26 January 1947; HA, Oral Testimonies, no. 3793, Artur Ben-Natan; HA, Dekel Collection, file Poland, Chaim Rosenthal testimony; Bauer, *Flight and Rescue,* 103–4, 294–95; Talmi, "Fleeing from Hungary," 239, 246.

40. GFHA, box "The Jewish Agency 1944–1947," minutes of emissaries department, 18 February 1947; HA, 14/405, report on the *Brichah,* January 1946; Dekel, *On the Routes of the Brichah,* 224; Talmi, "Fleeing from Hungary," 239.

41. HA, Dekel Collection, file III, Frank to Merkaz Lagolah, 3 January 1946; HA, 14/176a, Steiner to "Artzi," 11 January 1946; BGA, Ben Gurion Diary, 20 January 1946; HA, Oral testimonies, no. 3793, Ben-Natan; HA, 14/70, Rosen, 26 January 1947; Dekel, *On the Routes of the Brichah,* 255; Talmi, "Fleeing from Hungary," 242, 246.

42. PRO, FO371/51118/WR18477, Mason to Gascoigne, 20 June 1945.

43. PRO, FO371/51120/WR2156, Gascoigne to Mason, 30 June 1945; PRO, FO371/51121/WR2403, Gascoigne to FO, no. 215, 30 July 1945; PRO, FO371/51128/WR3555, Gascoigne to Bevin, no. 447, 6 November 1945; PRO, CO537/1704, Gascoigne to FO, no. 56, 31 January 1946. About the condition of Hungarian Jewry, see Bauer, *Out of the Ashes,* 133–48.

44. PRO, FO371/51129/WR3756, British political mission in Hungary to FO, no. 517, 30 November 1945; see also Duschinsky, "Hungary," 411. About anti-Semitism in Hungary between the world wars, see Braham and Katzburg, *History of the Holocaust,* part 1; Katzburg, "Jewish Question in Hungary," 113–24; Asher Cohen, "Attitude of the Intelligentsia in Hungary," 57–74; Bela Vago, "Communist Pragmatism," 105–15, 119–26.

45. PRO, FO371/52512/E2029, Carse to FO, no. 219, 5 March 1946; see also Duschinsky, "Hungary," 405.

46. PRO, FO371/52568/E2402, Carse to FO, no. 266, 14 March 1946. Crossman estimated that 90 percent of Hungarian Jews would leave the country. LA, minutes of the Executive Committee of the Histadrut, 27 March 1946.

47. PRO, CO537/1704, Gascoigne to Bevin, no. 196, 3 April 1946.

48. See, for example, Kushner, *Persistence of Prejudice,* 119–22; see also chap. 9.

49. PRO, FO945/655, Acarbit Vienna to Troopers (War Office), no. 7758, 18 October 1945, and Acarbit Vienna to WO, no. 9238, 25 November 1945.

50. PRO, WO170/7655, weekly security intelligence report no. 25, period covering 21 December 1945–3 January 1946; PRO, FO945/655, report of the intelligence organization, Allied Commission for Austria, "The Unauthorised Movement and Clandestine Activity of Jewish DPs in Austria," 19 January 1946.

51. PRO, FO945/655, report on illegal Jewish immigration, March 1946.

52. *Report of the Anglo-American Committee,* 48, paragraph 9 and pp. 54–55, paragraphs 36–39.

53. PRO, WO178/78, note of Edgecumb on Allied Control Commission meeting, 21 May 1946; see also PRO, FO371/57690, report of the intelligence organization, Allied Commission for Austria, "The Unauthorised Movement and Clandestine Activity of Jewish DPs in Austria," 8 April 1946; PRO, FO943/485, Acarbit Vienna to WO, no. 293, 8 April 1946; PRO, FO945/590, WO to Acarbit Vienna, no. 234, 11 May 1946.

54. PRO, FO371/52629/E8292, British military mission in Hungary to British commission, Austria, 15 August 1946.

55. HA, 14/79b, Talmi, 26 January 1947; Talmi, "Fleeing from Hungary," 249-50. About Pálfi-Oesterreicher, see Nagy, *Struggle behind the Iron Curtain,* 255, 281, 311–19.

56. PRO, FO371/52630/E8405, Helm to FO, no. 58, 17 August 1946; PRO, FO371/52629/E8092, Helm to FO, no. 905, 17 August 1946; see also Nagy, *Struggle behind the Iron Curtain,* 194.

57. PRO, FO371/58966, notes of Allied Control Commission meeting on 30 August 1946.

58. Kertesz, *Between Russia and the West,* chaps. 8-10; Max, *The United States, Great Britain, and the Sovietization of Hungary,* 88–89; see also *Paris Peace Conference,* 1014–1214.

59. PRO, FO371/52629/E8091, Helm to FO, no. 903, 16 August 1946; PRO, FO371/52630/E8370, memorandum presented to the Hungarian foreign minister, no. 102, 15 August 1946. About Nagy's attitude toward the Jews, see Reuvani, "Antisemitism in Hungary," 182, 189, 195.

60. PRO, CAB104/275, Helm to the FO, no. 876, 8 August 1946.

61. PRO, FO371/58653/R11956, FO to Budapest, no. 798, 16 August 1946; see also PRO, FO371/52627/E7704, Cabinet meeting, C.M.(46)77th conclusions, 7 August 1946.

62. PRO, FO371/52627/E7704, minute by M. S. Williams, 12 August 1946.

63. PRO, FO371/58653, Helm to FO, no. 919, 20 August 1946.

64. HA, 14/79b, Talmi, 26 January 1947.

65. LA, minutes of the Executive Committee of the Histadrut, 29 August 1946, Lubianker; HA, 14/73, meeting on *Brichah* issues, Vienna, 3 April 1947; Duschinsky, "Hungary," 418-31; Lahav, "The Hungarian Communist Party's Path to Power," 287-97; Reuvani, "Antisemitism in Hungary," 188-97; Katzburg, "Between Liberation and Revolution," 123-26; Dekel, *On the Routes of the Brichah,* 224-25; see also Nagy's interpretation of the pogroms, Nagy, *Struggle behind the Iron Curtain,* 245-49. About the situation of Hungarian Jews in 1947, see CZA, S-6/1169, report of Chaim Barlas, 20 October 1947.

66. See next chapter.

67. PRO, FO371/61826/E8324, British political mission, Hungary, to Bevin, no. 257, 4 September 1947.

CHAPTER NINE

1. Saiu, *The Great Powers and Roumania;* Rothwell, *Britain and the Cold War,* 374-82; Bullock, *Ernest Bevin,* 17-20, 133-35, 211-12, 345-46; Lundestad, *American Non-Policy,* 225-56; Quinlan, *Clash over Rumania,* 133-38, 152-54; Fischer-Galati, "Communist Takeover of Roumania," 310-20; Fischer-Galati, *New Rumania,* 1-35; Ionescu, *Communism in Rumania,* 71-143.

2. Ofer, *Escaping the Holocaust,* chap. 13, pp. 294-305; Steinberg, "International Aspects of the Jewish Immigration from and through Rumania," 589-94.

3. PRO, FO371/51121/WR2499, Le Rougtel to Bevin, no. 250, 2 August 1945; see also PRO, FO371/51095/WR1989, Office of the British political representative, Bucharest, to Anthony Eden, no. 176, 16 June 1945. On Rumanian Jews following World War II, see Ancel, "Rumanian Jewry"; Bela Vago, "Communist Pragmatism toward Jewish Assimilation," 105-26; Raphael Vago, "Jews of Rumania," 133-52.

4. PRO, FO770/85, Quarterly Report on Jews, 5 November 1945.

5. Ibid., Major Porter to the commissioner, 20 November 1945, Dr. Alexander Shafran to the British mission, Bucharest, 18 November 1945, and A. L. Zissu, Jewish leader, to the representative of Great Britain, Bucharest, 23 December 1945; Cuperman, *In the Grip of Communism.*

6. PRO, FO371/51116/WR1285, a letter to Mason, 2 May 1945; PRO, CAB119/148, memorandum on Palestine policy, 11 June 1945.

7. HA, file "Brichah," report on a meeting of Brichah emissaries, 19 March 1946. About the Soviets' stand on emigration of Jews from Rumania, see HA, 14/64, from David Zimend, Zionist emissary, 19 August 1945.

8. PRO, ADM116/5561, Holman to FO, no. 422, 4 April 1946, and FO to Bucharest, no. 317, 5 April 1946.

9. PRO, FO 371/52515, E3375, Holman to FO, no. 500, 13 April 1946.

10. HA, 14/68, "Agami" (Moshe Averbuch) to "Artzi," 11, 21 April 1946, 5 May 1946; Steinberg, "International Aspects of the Jewish Immigration from and through Rumania," 702–7.

11. PRO, ADM116/5561, Holman to FO, no. 576, 4 May 1946.

12. Ibid., Holman to FO, no. 774, 11 June 1946, and Holman to FO, no. 749, 12 June 1946; PRO, FO371/59178/R11692, Holman to FO, no. 876, 17 July 1946.

13. PRO, FO371/52522/E4266, Holman to FO, no. 589, 8 May 1946; PRO, FO181/1019, Cunningham to Hull, 30 May 1946; PRO, FO371/59178/R11692, memorandum by Kendall, 18 July 1946.

14. Ro'i, *Soviet Decision Making in Practice,* 22–25.

15. PRO, FO371/52526/E4514, Chiefs of Staff Committee, note by the War Office, Annex II, C.O.S. (46) 148 (o), 23 May 1946.

16. PRO, ADM116/5561, FO to Moscow, no. 1831, 9 June 1946.

17. PRO, FO371/52528/E5403, Peterson to FO, no. 2064, 12 June 1946.

18. PRO, WO178/71, minutes of 27th meeting of Allied Control Commission, Rumania, 20 June 1946.

19. PRO, FO371/52531/E5839, Holman to FO, no. 820, 2 July 1946; PRO, FO371/52534/E6170, Holman to FO, no. 794, 24 June 1946.

20. PRO, CAB128/6, Cabinet meeting, 11 July 1946.

21. PRO, FO371/52538/E6563, Holman to FO, no. 854, 12 July 1946; PRO, FO371/52544/E7150, Holman to FO, no. 901, 25 July 1946.

22. PRO, FO371/52544/E7162, Holman to FO, no. 904, 26 July 1946; PRO, FO371/52549/E7515, Aide Memoire to Ministry of Foreign Affairs, Bucharest, 27 July 1946.

23. PRO, FO371/52629/E8089, Holman to Bevin, no. 184, 8 August 1946; see also Safran, *Resisting the Storm,* 180, 188.

24. PRO, FO371/59178/R11692, memorandum by Kendall, 18 July 1946.

25. Ibid.; Sylvain, "Rumania," part 5; Ancel, "She'erit Hapletah in Romania," 153–55, 164–67.

26. PRO, FO371/52545/E6527, San Jose to FO, no. 55, 28 July 1946; PRO, FO371/52549/E7554, Holman to Brabetianu, secretary general of the Rumanian Ministry of Foreign Affairs, 31 July 1946; PRO, WO178/81, notes on a meeting between Brigadier Greer and

Colonel Molohovski, 30 July 1946; PRO, FO371/52548/E7423, Holman to FO, no. 925, 31 July 1946.

27. See chap. 3.

28. PRO, FO371/52549/E7555, Peterson to V. G. Dekanozov, Ministry of Foreign Affairs, Moscow, 31 July 1946; PRO, FO371/52628/E8043, Peterson to FO, no. 2668, 14 August 1946.

29. PRO, FO371/52627/E7754, Holman to FO, no. 956, 8 August 1946; PRO, FO371/52629/E8078, Holman to FO, no. 985, 15 August 1946.

30. Max, *The United States, Great Britain, and the Sovietization of Hungary,* 81–83; Saiu, *The Great Powers and Roumania,* 195; see also *Paris Peace Conference,* 649–833.

31. PRO, FO371/52630/E8381, Paris to FO, no. 570, 22 August 1946, and Paris to FO, no. 596, 28 August 1946; PRO, FO371/52630/E8533, FO to Adis Ababa, no. 259, 29 August 1946.

32. PRO, FO371/52632/E9006, Roberts to Dekanozov, 31 August 1946; PRO, FO371/52632/E8923, Roberts to FO, no. 2911, 6 September 1946, and Roberts to FO, no. 2927, 7 September 1946.

33. PRO, FO371/52636/E11047, Trunkhanovski to Roger Allen, British first secretary at the embassy in Moscow, 25 October 1946; PRO, FO371/52632/E8923, minute by Beith, 10 September 1946.

34. Bullock, *Ernest Bevin,* 42–43, 129, 139, 307–8, 346; Rothwell, *Britain and the Cold War,* 388–95; Shoup, "Yugoslav Revolution," 244–72; Shelah, *Yugoslav Connection,* 158–60; *Making the Peace Treaties,* 23, 27, 34, 38–41; *Paris Peace Conference,* 1347–1442.

35. Bauer, *Flight and Rescue,* 40–41, 99, 101–2, 155–56; Gelber, *Standard Bearers,* 440, 454, 534, 545, 547, 567; Dekel, *On the Routes of the Brichah,* 245.

36. PRO, FO945/655, report of British Intelligence in Austria, no. 564, 19 January 1946.

37. Ibid., report on illegal Jewish immigration, March 1946.

38. PRO, ADM116/5561, Broad to FO, 341, 6 April 1946.

39. Ibid., Broad to FO, 346, 16 April 1946.

40. PRO, WO204/11135, A.F.H.Q. to A.G.W.A.R., no. 1130, 20 April 1946; PRO, FO371/52517/E3798, Broad to FO, no. 384, 26 April 1946; PRO, FO371/52524/E4581, Broad to FO, no. 433, 18 May 1946; Shelah, *Yugoslav Connection,* 160–65.

41. PRO, FO945/655, FO to Belgrade, no. 869, 4 June 1946.

42. Ibid., Clutton to FO, no. 970, 28 June 1946; PRO, FO371/52534/E6160, Clutton to FO, no. 971, 28 June 1946.

43. PRO, FO371/52548/E7436, FO to Belgrade, no. 1193, 1 August 1946, and memorandum on illegal immigration to Palestine, 31 July 1946.

44. PRO, FO371/52528/E7926, Clutton to FO, no. 1178, 10 August 1946; see also PRO, FO371/52568/E7961, Military attaché Belgrade to BMM Rumania, no. 356A, 8 August 1946.

45. PRO, FO371/62628/E7926, Clutton to FO, no. 1178, 10 August 1946.

46. About the Holocaust in Yugoslavia, see Shelah, *History of the Holocaust;* Yahil, *The Holocaust,* 349–52, 429–31.

47. LA, minutes of the meeting of the Executive Committee of the Histadrut, 30 Janu-

ary 1946, Duvdevani; WA, Leo Cohen to Weizmann, July 1945; Gelber, *Standard Bearers,* 282, 400–401, 418, 462–63; Levinger, "Yugoslavian Jewry," 216–47.

48. *Report of the Anglo-American Committee,* 55, paragraph 41. Commission members did not visit Yugoslavia.

49. PRO, FO371/52627/E7862, Cabinet meeting, 1 August 1946; PRO, FO371/57693/WR2156, report on illegal immigration to Palestine, August 1946.

50. PRO, FO371/52630/E8462, British embassy, Belgrade, to Yugoslav Ministry for Foreign Affairs, no. 646, 20 August 1946.

51. PRO, FO371/52536, Yugoslav Ministry for Foreign Affairs to British embassy, Belgrade, no. 9935, 4 October 1946.

52. PRO, FO371/52636/E10849, Peake to FO, no. 1484, 1 November 1946.

53. PRO, FO371/52636, Higham to Beith, 31 October 1946.

54. About bringing the *Agia Anastasia* to Rumania, see HP, General Testimonies, no. 56, Shaike Dan (Yeshayahu Trachtenberg); HA, 14/397, "Agami" to "Artzi," 10 October 1946; Shelah, *Yugoslav Connection,* 174–78; Hadari, *Second Exodus,* 105–7; Schaary, *Cyprus Detention Camps,* 88–91.

55. PRO, FO371/52571/E11377, Peake to FO, no. 1532, 16 November 1946.

56. Schaary, *Cyprus Detention Camps,* 91–93.

57. PRO, ADM1/20776, Peake to FO, no. 1627, 14 December 1946; about UNRRA's aid to Yugoslavia, see Woodbridge, *UNRRA,* 2:138–70.

58. PRO, CO537/2391, FO to Athens, no. 2561, 21 December 1946.

59. PRO, FO371/61838/E540, Clutton to Tito, 31 December 1946; PRO, CO537/2391, Clutton to FO, no. 21, 4 January 1947.

60. PRO, FO371/61839/E2592, Peake to FO, no. 367, 21 March 1947.

61. PRO, FO371/61826/E8324, British political mission, Hungary, to Bevin, no. 257, 4 September 1947.

62. LPA, 23/47, minutes of Mapai's Center, 24 June 1947, Avriel; HA, Brichah Files, III, minutes of meeting of Brichah emissaries, Basel, 12 December 1946; HA, 14/89, from "Neter" (Paris), 23 June 1946, and from Hadari, 20 July 1947; HP, General Testimonies, no. 56, Shaike Dan; Ettinger, *Blind Jump,* 224; Shelah, *Yugoslav Connection,* 191–94; Rothwell, *Britain and the Cold War,* 394–95.

63. BGA, Meetings Division, memorandum by Epstein, no. 30, 25 June 1947.

64. Ro'i, *From Encroachment to Involvement,* 37–41; for analysis of Gromyko's speech, see Pinkus, "Soviet Policy towards the Jews of the USSR and the Yishuv," 20–21, appendix 4; Ginat, *The Soviet Union and Egypt,* 77–84.

65. HA, 14/70, "Moris" (Constantsa) to "Arnon" (Palestine), no. 15, 20 February 1947, and "Rimon" (Rico Lipski), 10 April 1947, and "Rimon" to "Artzi," 5 May 1947; HA, 14/73, Surkiss, 3 April 1947; LPA, 23/47, minutes of meeting of Mapai's Center, 24 June 1947; HA, 14/107, Hadari, 20 July 1947.

66. BGA, Correspondence Division, a letter from Bucharest to Mapai's Secretariat, 4 February 1947; Ancel, "Rumanian Jewry," 271–77; Bauer, *Out of the Ashes,* 151–52.

67. HA, 14/70, "Rimon," Bucharest, to "Artzi," 10 April 1947; HA, 14/68, Surkiss to Dekel, 8 April 1947; Ancel, "She'erit Hapletah in Rumania," 16–61; Dekel, *On the Routes of the Brichah,* 198; Gefen, *Barriers' Breakers,* 213–14.

68. HA, 14/70, "Rimon" to "Artzi," 5 May 1947; HA, Dekel Collection, file III, Yitzak Ben-Ephraim, 21 February 1947; LPA, 23/47, minutes of Mapai's Center, 21 February 1947, Avriel; HP, General Testimonies, no. 86a, Moshe Agami; Cuperman, *In the Grip of Communism,* 223–27, 234–38; Sylvain, "Rumania," 531.

69. PRO, FO371/61806/E3584, Holman to FO, no. 442, 29 April 1947; PRO, FO371/61807/E4552, Holman to FO, no. 497, 15 May 1947, and British embassy, Bucharest, to FO, 20 May 1947; PRO, FO371/61813/E5513, British embassy, Bucharest, to FO, 11 June 1947; Bauer, *Out of the Ashes,* 233.

70. HA, 14/89, from "Neter" (Paris), 23 June 1946; JTA reported that 150,000 Jews were registered for immigration to Palestine; PRO, CO537/2341, M. Benvenisti and E. Rappaport to Emil Sandstrom, 29 July 1947. See also Sylvain, "Rumania," 530.

71. CZA, S-6/1169, report of Barlas (May–September 1947); Bauer, *Flight and Rescue,* 298–300; Chaim Yahil, "Activities of the Palestine Jewry's Mission," 153–56.

72. JA, box 13-C, file no. C-31.002, Manuel Siegel, the joint representative in Bulgaria, to M. Beckelman, Paris, 30 May 1947; Meyer, "Bulgaria," 616–21; Ettinger, *Blind Jump,* 207.

73. PRO, FO371/61847/E7521, FO to Bucharest, no. 817, 18 August 1947, and FO to Sofia, no. 1072, 18 August 1947; PRO, FO371/61850/E9832, note verbale for the Bulgarian Ministry of Foreign Affairs, no. 159, 20 August 1947; PRO, FO371/61847/E7778, note verbale for the Rumanian Ministry of Foreign Affairs, no. 99, 19 August 1947; PRO, FO371/61848/E8085, note verbale for the Rumanian Ministry of Foreign Affairs, no. 104, 22 August 1947.

74. PRO, FO371/61847/E7771, Holman to FO, no. 875, 22 August 1947.

75. PRO, FO371/61848/E8379, Greer to Susiakov, 25 August 1947; PRO, FO371/61824/E7929, Roberts to FO, no. 1907, 26 August 1947; PRO, FO371/61824/E7931, Roberts to FO, nos. 1920, 1926, 27 August 1947.

76. PRO, FO371/61828/E8831, note verbale for the Rumanian Ministry of Foreign Affairs, 17 September 1947; PRO, FO371/61827/E8633, Holman to FO, no. 973, 17 September 1947.

77. PRO, FO371/61848/E8129, Sterndale-Bennet to FO, no. 1109, 2 September 1947.

78. PRO, FO371/61828/E8867, Sterndale-Bennet to FO, no. 1216, 24 September 1947.

79. PRO, FO371/61828/E9333, note verbale for the British Legation, Bucharest, 26 September 1947.

80. PRO, ADM1/20793, FO to Bucharest, no. 1012, and Sofia, no. 1322, 30 September 1947; PRO, FO371/61830/E9070, Sterndale-Bennet to FO, no. 1237, 30 September 1947; PRO, FO371/61830/E9416, note verbale for Rumanian Foreign Ministry, no. 118, 1 October 1947; Hadari and Tsahor, *Voyage to Freedom,* 30–38.

81. PRO, FO371/61850/E9832, record of interview with the Bulgarian foreign minister, 2 October 1947; PRO, FO371/61849/E9158, Sterndale-Bennet to FO, no. 1244, 2 October 1947.

82. Lundestad, *American Non-Policy,* 257–84; Oren, *Revolution Administered,* chap. 4; Bell, *Bulgarian Communist Party,* chap. 5; Rothwell, *Britain and the Cold War,* 382–88; Bullock, *Ernest Bevin,* 10–20, 129–31, 134–35, 211, 345–46; Oren, "Revolution Administered," 321–38; Ethridge and Black, "Negotiations on the Balkans," 186–93.

83. Ettinger, *Blind Jump,* 217.

84. PRO, WO275/60, summary intelligence report for the period 30 September–11 October 1947.

85. PRO, ADM1/20793, FO to Bucharest, no. 1019, and Sofia, no. 1329, 1 October 1947; PRO, FO371/61826/E9149, Holman to FO, no. 1055, 2 October 1947; PRO, FO371/61829/E9220, Sterndale-Bennet to FO, no. 1247, 3 October 1947; PRO, FO371/61830/E9256, Holman to FO, no. 1063, 3 October 1947.

86. PRO, FO371/61829/E9149, Bucharest to FO, no. 1067, 3 October 1947; PRO, ADM1/20793, Holman to FO, no. 1072, 4 October 1947.

87. PRO, FO371/61831/E10084, note verbale to Bulgarian Foreign Ministry, 15 October 1947; PRO, FO371/61831/E10080, note verbale to Rumanian Foreign Ministry, 17 October 1947.

88. PRO, FO371/61850/E948, Holman to FO, no. 1137, 11 October 1947.

89. PRO, FO371/61831/E10584, report on the situation of the Jews in Rumania, 3 November 1947.

90. Ibid.

91. PRO, FO371/61833/E11968, Kendall to FO, 9 December 1947; PRO, ADM1/20793, Holman to FO, no. 1052, 12 December 1947.

92. HA, 14/110, Dekel to "Arnon," 14 December 1947.

93. Sylvain, "Rumania," 531.

94. PRO, FO371/61854/E11724, FO to Washington, no. 12905, 12 December 1947.

95. PRO, FO371/61854/E12140, Sarrel to FO, no. 1546, 22 December 1947; PRO, FO371/61855/E12225, Sarrel to FO, no. 1545, 23 December 1947.

96. PRO, FO371/61855/E12403, memorandum by Cable "Communist Policy towards Jewish Illegal Immigration," 23 December 1947.

97. PRO, FO371/61855/E1225, Sarrel to FO, no. 1559, 25 December 1947.

98. PRO, FO371/68513/E88, Sterndale-Bennet to Kolarov, 24 December 1947; PRO, FO371/68513/E418, Sterndale-Bennet to Kolarov, 27 December 1947.

99. Ettinger, *Blind Jump,* 238.

100. Hadari and Tsahor, *Voyage to Freedom,* 163–77.

101. PRO, FO371/68515/E908, British embassy, Bucharest, to FO, 14 January 1948.

102. HA, 14/72, Hadari to "Arnon," 14 January 1948.

103. PRO, ADM1/20793, Sterndale-Bennet to FO, no. 1602, 29 December 1947.

104. In fact, 420 youngsters sailed from Bulgaria on board the *Pans;* HP, no. 56/2, Shaike Dan's testimony; BGA, Shaike Dan's testimony; Ettinger, *Blind Jump,* chap. 9; Hadari and Tsahor, *Voyage to Freedom,* 115–16.

105. PRO, FO371/68516/E2086, Sterndale-Bennet to FO, no. 59, 13 January 1948.

106. Ibid., Sterndale-Bennet to Kolarov, 31 January 1948; PRO, FO371/68517/E2754, record of interview between Sterndale-Bennet and the Bulgarian foreign minister, 19 February 1948; PRO, FO371/68517/E2521, Sterndale-Bennet to FO, no. 232, 20 February 1948; PRO, FO371/68518/E3031, Sterndale-Bennet to FO, no. 263, 2 March 1948; PRO, FO371/69518/E3117, Sterndale-Bennet to FO, no. 270, 4 March 1948; Shelah, *Yugoslav Connection,* 196–97.

107. Rothwell, *Britain and the Cold War,* 388.

108. BGA, Shaike Dan's testimony; Ettinger, *Blind Jump,* 207, 213–16, 242–43, 248; Tamir, *Bulgaria and Her Jews,* 227–28.

109. PRO, FO371/52560/E10080, British embassy, Prague, to Baxter, 1 October 1946; PRO, FO371/52629/E8141, minute by Beith, 21 August 1946; PRO, CAB127/280, FO to Washington, no. 9307, 25 September 1946.

110. Ro'i, *Soviet Decision Making in Practice,* 22–29; Pinkus, "Soviet Policy towards the Jews of the USSR and the Yishuv," 18–25; Bauer, *Flight and Rescue,* 148, 223.

111. PRO, FO945/372, minutes of the 56th meeting of the Executive Committee, Allied Control Commission for Austria, 29 September 1946; PRO, FO1007/150, minutes of the 37th meeting of the Directorate, Allied Commission for Austria, 10 September 1946.

CHAPTER TEN

1. Wheeler-Bennett and Nicholls, *Semblance of Peace,* 65–78, 328–32, 421–23, 434–36, 442–50, 657–709; Woodward, *British Foreign Policy,* 2:501–45, and 5:467–82; Bullock, *Ernest Bevin,* 129–30, 261–64, 281–82, 318–19; Divine, *Foreign Policy,* 144–45; Nolfo, "Shaping of Italian Foreign Policy," 485–500; U.S. Department of State, *United States and Italy; Paris Peace Conference,* 71–648.

2. Lipgens, *History of European Integration,* 1:248–49, 252–58, 500–504; Bullock, *Ernest Bevin,* 488–89, 543–46; Mammarella, *Italy after Fascism,* part 2, chaps. 4–5, 7–8.

3. Mammarella, *Italy after Fascism,* part 2, chap. 3; Lipgens, *History of European Integration,* 249–50.

4. Bullock, *Ernest Bevin,* 48–89.

5. HA, 14/397, "Agami" to "Meir" (Turkey), 24 June 1945, 19 July 1945; HA, 14/81a, Duvdevani to "Artzi," 28 July, 3 August 1945; CZA, S-25/5243, Duvdevani to Moshe and Dobkin, 20 July 1945; Gelber, *Standard Bearers,* passim; Bauer, *Flight and Rescue,* 40–42, 63–64, 97–99; Weitz, "First Contacts between the Soldiers of the Jewish Brigade," 227–46.

6. HA, 14/159, Duvdevani to Meirov, no. 17, 10 September 1945; HA, 14/52, "Agami" to Mulia Ben-Hayim, 6 September 1945; HA, 14/397, "Agami" to "Meir" (Turkey), 27 September 1945; Bauer, *Flight and Rescue,* 106, 166–68; Gefen, *Barriers' Breakers,* 63–68.

7. PRO, FO945/655, Broad to FO, no. 2149, 30 December 1945; PRO, FO371/51129/WR3804, Vienna to FO, no. 52, 12 December 1945; PRO, FO371/57684/WR75, memorandum for Rendel, 5 January 1946; PRO, WO220/376, Headquarters Allied Commission, Displaced Persons and Repatriation Sub Commission, "Progress Report for the month of August 1945," 9 September 1945.

8. HA, 14/17a, report no. 3 of the C.I.D. on illegal Jewish immigration to Palestine, 15 October 1945; PRO, FO945/599, Acarbit Vienna to War Office, 25 November 1945.

9. PRO, FO945/655, Charles to FO, no. 42, 10 January 1946.

10. PRO, FO371/51124/WR2991, Broad to Rome, no. 659, 6 October 1945.

11. PRO, CAB119/148, note of a meeting held at the Colonial Office, 12 October 1945, and G.H.Q. Middle East to Cabinet Offices, 26 November 1945; PRO, FO371/45384, CO to Palestine, no. 1767, 10 November 1945; Gelber, *Standard Bearers,* 595–96.

12. PRO, CAB134/595, Cabinet Overseas Reconstruction Committee, O.R.C. (46) 2nd meeting, 25 January 1945.

13. PRO, FO371/52507/E776, Baxter to Trafford Smith, 30 January 1946.

14. PRO, FO371/52508/E1056, Charles to FO, no. 180, 4 February 1946.

15. PRO, FO371/57686/WR267, FO to Washington, no. 1110, 2 February 1946.

16. PRO, FO945/655, Broad to FO, no. 340, 5 April 1946; see also Gelber, *Standard Bearers*, 650–60; Avriel, *Open the Gates*, chap. 20; HA, Oral Testimonies, file no. 12, Yehuda Arazi.

17. PRO, FO945/655, Charles to FO, no. 510, 5 April 1946.

18. PRO, ADM116/5561, Rome to FO, no. 538, 11 April 1946, and Charles to FO, no. 539, 11 April 1946; PRO, FO800/485, Charles to FO, no. 545, 11 June 1946.

19. PRO, PREM8/298, Hall to Attlee, 15 April 1946; PRO, FO371/52516/E3571, memorandum for the secretary of state, 17 April 1946; PRO, FO371/52515/E3428, Trafford Smith to the Jewish Agency, 13 April 1946.

20. PRO, FO371/52515/E3539, Charles to FO, no. 584, 18 April 1946.

21. PRO, FO371/52519/E3914, Charles to FO, no. 638, 30 April 1946; PRO, ADM116/5561, Charles to FO, no. 643, 1 May 1946.

22. PRO, FO371/52527/E4242, B. Migone, Italian chargé d'affaires, to F. R. Hoyer Miller, FO, 6 May 1946.

23. PRO, FO371/52519/E3898, draft note on the Jews at La Spezia for the Foreign Secretary, 23 April 1946; PRO, WO169/23022, fortnightly intelligence letter no. 13, issued by HQ British Troops in Palestine and Transjordan for period 15–28 April 1946; PRO, ADM116/5561, Charles to FO, no. 610, 25 April 1946, Cunningham to CO, no. 700, 28 April 1946, Broad to FO, no. 387, 26 April 1946, and Broad to FO, no. 643, 1 May 1946.

24. PRO, FO371/57690/WR1054, report of the Intelligence Organization, Allied Commission for Austria, on the unauthorized movement and clandestine activity of Jewish DPs in Austria, 8 April 1946; PRO, FO945/655, report on illegal immigration to Palestine, March 1946; PRO, FO371/57690/WR1168, Trafford Smith to Maunsel, 4 April 1946; PRO, FO371/57689/WR932, Broad to FO, no. 332, 2 April 1946, and War Office to Acarbit Vienna, 3 May 1946; CZA, S-6/3745, report of Nachon, 20 June 1946; Gefen, *Barriers' Breakers*, 96–98.

25. See, for example, PRO, WO204/113, no. 794, 8 June 1946; PRO, FO371/52630/E8402, Charles to FO, no. 1321, 23 August 1946; PRO, FO371/57695/WR2386, Malcolm to FO, no. 1368, 3 September 1946.

26. PRO, WO204/11135, report on frontier control (Resia pass), 3 July 1946.

27. PRO, WO204/113, Major G. Hartmann, emigration and advisory officer, HQ Allied Commission, 8 June 1946; PRO, FO371/52630/E8402, Charles to FO, no. 1321, 23 August 1946; PRO, FO371/57695/WR2386, Malcolm to FO, no. 1368, 3 September 1946; PRO, FO371/52632/E9055, Malcolm to FO, no. 1403, 10 September 1946.

28. PRO, WO204/11135, Italian Ministry of Interior to Public Safety, 10 August 1946, and Colonel Bye to Italian Ministry of Interior, no. 394, 23 May 1946; PRO, FO371/52629/E8212, Charles to Vienna, no. 241, 19 August 1946; PRO, FO371/57698, note verbale by Italian Foreign Ministry, 7 October 1946; PRO, FO371/57698/WR3512, Malcolm to Attlee, no. 551, 12 November 1946.

29. PRO, FO371/577703/WR777, British embassy, Rome, to Bevin, 1 March 1946; PRO, PREM8/627, report prepared for the prime minister by the Refugee Department, FO,

7 December 1946; PRO, CAB133/831, report of Fact-Finding Sub-Committee on Jewish Displaced Persons Problem in Germany, Austria, and Italy, 21 June 1946.

30. PRO, FO371/52549/E7436, Charles to FO, no. 1214, 3 August 1946; PRO, FO371/52549/E7532, Charles to FO, no. 1212, 3 August 1946; PRO, FO371/52548/E7436, FO to Rome, no. 1295, 1 August 1946.

31. See De Gasperi's speech at the Peace Conference at Paris, Wheeler-Bennett and Nicholls, *Semblance of Peace,* 434–35.

32. PRO, FO371/52547/E7339, Cabinet meeting, 30 July 1946; PRO, FO371/52548/E7436, Charles to FO, no. 1207, 3 August 1946.

33. PRO, FO371/52548/E7499, minute, 7 August 1946; see, for example, Byrnes's speech after the first session of the CFM. *United States and Italy,* document no. 101.

34. PRO, FO371/57695/WR2486, Charles to secretary general of the Italian Foreign Ministry, 19 August 1946.

35. PRO, FO371/57693/WR2177, FO to Geneva, no. 43, 14 August 1946; Kochavi, "British Response to the Involvement of the American Jewish Joint Distribution Committee," 226–32.

36. According to statistical data given by the Italian government in April 1947, UNRRA assisted 24,000 Jewish DPs. PRO, FO371/61804/E2906, Charles to FO, no. 757, 3 April 1947. According to UNRRA's statistical data from the end of July 1947, of the 21,981 DPs in Italy who received assistance from the organization, 19,768 were Jews. PRO, FO371/66694/WR3075, secretary general of UNRRA to Allied Commission, 30 July 1947.

37. PRO, FO371/66691/WR364, draft minute of the 34th meeting of UNRRA's Committee of Council for Europe, 12 December 1946.

38. About UNRRA's aid to Italy, see Woodbridge, *UNRRA,* 2:257–94; *United States and Italy,* documents 71–89.

39. PRO, FO800/486, Bevin to Byrnes, 9 November 1946. About the Irgun attack on the British embassy, see Tavin, *Second Front,* 63–76.

40. PRO, FO371/67796/Z864, Charles to Bevin, no. 12, 14 January 1947.

41. PRO, FO371/67796, memorandum, 10 January 1947.

42. PRO, FO371/67796, Italian Ministry of Foreign Affairs to Charles, 22 January 1947; PRO, WO204/11135, memorandum for the Allied Commission, 10 January 1947, and Brigadier M. Carr, executive commissioner, to Allied Force Headquarters, 21 January 1947.

43. PRO, FO371/61804/E2716, Charles to FO, no. 713, 27 March 1947.

44. Ibid., Charles to FO, no. 714, 27 March 1947.

45. PRO, FO371/67796/Z1755, Charles to Bevin, no. 54, 6 February 1947; PRO, FO945/494, Charles to FO, no. 824, 12 April 1947; see also Kochavi, "Anglo-American Discord," 529–51.

46. PRO, ADM1/20779, Charles to Sforza, 1 April 1947.

47. PRO, FO371/66733, Refugee Department, FO, to British embassy, Rome, 12 March 1947.

48. PRO, FO371/61804/E2906, Charles to FO, no. 756, 3 April 1947; PRO, FO371/61811/E5176, memorandum by the Italian Foreign Ministry, 10 April 1947.

49. PRO, FO371/61804/E2905, Charles to FO, no. 757, 3 April 1947; PRO, FO371/61813/

E5596, extract from report of a conversation between P. M. Lee, British embassy, Rome, and Dr. Migliore, 8 May 1947.

50. PRO, CAB104/276, Charles to FO, no. 1045, 7 May 1945; PRO, FO371/66747/WR2131, Aide Memoire, 3 May 1947; PRO, FO371/61805/E3538, Eastern Department, FO, to British embassy, Rome, 5 May 1947; PRO, FO371/61842/E4166, Charles to FO, no. 1117, 16 May 1947.

51. PRO, FO371/61840/E3007, FO to Rome, no. 945, 2 May 1947; PRO, FO371/61841/E3792, Charles to FO, no. 1037, 6 May 1947; PRO, FO371/61813/E5596, extract from report of a conversation between P. M. Lee, British embassy, Rome, and Dr. Migliore, 8 May 1947; PRO, FO371/61841/E3895, Charles to FO, no. 1059, 9 May 1947; PRO, FO371/61841/E3932, Charles to FO, no. 1062, 9 May 1947.

52. PRO, FO371/61842/E4220, Charles to the Italian Foreign Ministry, 11 May 1947; PRO, FO945/467, minutes of the Cabinet Committee on Illegal Immigration, 2nd meeting, 13 May 1947.

53. PRO, FO371/61810/E4911, Sargent to Bevin, 29 May 1947; Sereni, *Ships without Flags*, 132–34; HP, Oral Testimonies, Yosi Hamburger (Harel), no. 4272.

54. PRO, FO371/61811, Charles to FO, no. 1295, 13 June 1947.

55. PRO, FO371/61845/E4179, Charles to FO, no. 1128, 18 May 1947; PRO, FO371/61841/E3499, Charles to FO, no. 946, 24 April 1947.

56. PRO, FO371/61842/E4180, Charles to FO, no. 1129, 18 May 1947.

57. PRO, FO371/61844/E5222, Charles to the Italian Foreign Ministry, 6 June 1947.

58. See chap. 3.

59. PRO, CAB104/276, Charles to FO, no. 1045, 7 May 1947; PRO, FO371/61841/E3950, Charles to FO, no. 1082, 12 May 1947; PRO, FO371/61809/E4088, Charles to FO, no. 1210, 30 May 1947.

60. PRO, FO371/61811/E5001, Bevin to Sforza, 27 June 1947; PRO, FO371/61842/E4177, Charles to FO, no. 1115, 16 May 1947.

61. PRO, FO371/61811/E5175, Bevin to Sforza, 3 June 1947.

62. PRO, CAB104/276, Charles to FO, no. 1045, 7 May 1947; PRO, FO371/61813/E5596, British embassy, Rome, to Eastern Department, FO, 20 June 1947.

63. PRO, FO371/61812/E5405, Charles to FO, no. 1346, 26 June 1947; PRO, FO371/61814/E5623, Charles to FO, no. 1386, 26 June 1947; PRO, FO371/61818/E6604, Fransoni to Charles, 9 July 1947; PRO, FO371/61814/E6075, Charles to FO, no. 1450, 5 July 1947; PRO, FO371/61815/E6197, Charles to FO, no. 1505, 12 July 1947.

64. PRO, FO371/61816/E6476, Mack to FO, no. 666, 18 July 1947.

65. PRO, FO371/61821/E7310, Charles to Bevin, no. 337, 4 August 1947; PRO, FO371/61823/E7835, memorandum of the British embassy, Rome, 14 August 1947; PRO, FO371/61817/E6589, Zopi to Ward, British embassy, 18 July 1947, and Ward to Zopi, 9 August 1947; PRO, FO371/61819/E6837, Mack to FO, no. 684, 27 July 1947; PRO, FO371/61822/E7533, Zopi to Ward, 5 August 1947.

66. HA, 14/106, from "Neter" (Paris), 18 May 1947, 23 June 1947; LPA, 23/47, minutes of meeting of Mapai's Center, 23 June 1947, Avriel; HA, 14/107, from Hadari, 20 July 1947; Sereni, *Ships without Flags*, 132–40.

67. PRO, FO371/61854, report of expert, August 1947.

68. PRO, FO371/92850/E8900, minute by Cable, 23 October 1947; PRO, ADM1/20793, Cunningham to CO, no. 1984, 1 October 1947.

69. Ibid., Ward to FO, no. 1865, 29 September 1947; PRO, FO371/61850/E9629, memorandum for the Italian Government, 8 October 1947. At the beginning of October, Britain expressed its disappointment over the Italian decision to allow the *Pan Crescent* to sail. On 30 August the British had sabotaged the boat, but it was repaired and on 25 September the Italians notified the British that they could not prevent the ship from sailing without passengers. PRO, ADM1/20793, Ward to FO, no. 1865, 20 September 1947; PRO, FO371/61850/E9629, Aide Memoire to the Italian Government, 8 October 1947; Sereni, *Ships without Flags*, 135–38; Hadari and Tsahor, *Voyage to Freedom*, 31–38.

70. PRO, FO371/61850/E9432, Ward to FO, no. 1941, 8 October 1947.

71. PRO, FO371/61850/E9800, minute by Cable, 23 October 1947.

72. PRO, FO371/66671/WR3177, Mack to FO, no. 872, 18 September 1947.

73. PRO, FO371/61854/E11716, report on infiltration across the border, December 1947.

74. HA, 14/109, Hadari to "Arnon," 3 November 1947.

75. JA, box 9-A, File no. C-54.003, Trobe to the JDC, Paris, 18 November 1947, the Joint, Rome, to the Joint, Paris, 7 November 1947, and Trobe to the Joint, Paris, 21 October 1947.

76. PRO, FO371/61853/E11278, Mallet to FO, no. 2218, 28 November 1947.

77. PRO, FO371/61854/E11642, note verbale to the Italian Foreign Ministry, no. 723, 3 December 1947; JA, box 9-A, File no. C-54.003, no. 723, 3 December 1947.

78. PRO, FO371/68517/E2638, translation of note verbale from Ministry of Foreign Affairs, 19 January 1948; PRO, FO371/68514/E808, note verbale, no. 22, 13 January 1948; PRO, CAB104/279, minute, 14 January 1948, and Mallet to Fransoni, 31 December 1947.

79. PRO, FO371/68517/E2638, translation of a letter from the secretary general of the Italian Ministry of Foreign Affairs, 19 January 1948.

80. PRO, CAB104/279, Mallet to FO, no. 11, 21 January 1948.

81. HP, General Testimonies, no. 296, Sereni testimony.

82. PRO, FO371/68517/E2638, Mallet to Fransoni, 17 February 1948.

83. HA, no. 4688, testimony Arieh Oron (Stern); HP, General Testimonies, no. 91, Adda Sereni; HA, Personal File, Dekel, "My Way to the *Brichah*"; Gefen, *Barriers' Breakers,* 56. The British embassy in Italy attributed the help given by the Italian police to the infiltration of the Jews to bribery given to the latter. PRO, CAB104/279, British embassy, Rome, to Eastern Department, FO, 11 December 1947.

CHAPTER ELEVEN

1. Young, *Britain, France,* 1–95; Young, *France, the Cold War and the Western Alliance,* 1–197; Bullock, *Ernest Bevin,* 44, 144–50, 249–50, 270–71, 279–80, 316–18, 327, 357–59, 374, 378, 405–8, 419–27, 486–89; Rothwell, *Britain and the Cold War,* 227, 236–38, 298–99, 305, 314–18, 413–25, 443–56; Lipgens, *History of European Integration,* 201–30; Wall, *The United States and the Making of Postwar France,* 11–95; Wheeler-Bennett and Nicholls, *Semblance of Peace,* 274–78, 282–83, 572–75, document 7; Young, "Duff Cooper and the British Embassy," 98–120; Greenwood, "Ernest Bevin, France, and 'Western Union,'"

319–38; Zeeman, "Britain and the Cold War," 343–67; Charmley, "Duff Cooper and Western European Union," 53–64; Milward, *Reconstruction of Western Europe*, chap. 4; Bidault, *Resistance*, 96–103; Cooper, *Old Men Forget*, 364, 369, 372–73.

2. PRO, FO371/52630/E8403, Cooper to FO, no. 379, 24 August 1946; see also PRO, FO371/52629/E8090, FO to Paris, no. 742, 17 August 1946, and Cooper to FO, no. 418, 18 August 1946.

3. HA, 14/103, Lulu, 6 November 1946; Gefen, *Barriers' Breakers*, 160–61.

4. PRO, FO371/52630/E8511, French Foreign Ministry to British embassy, Paris, 23 August 1946; PRO, FO371/52630/E8404, Cooper to FO, no. 380, 24 August 1946; see also HA, 14/103, Moshe Karmil to "Artzi," no. 66, 16 November 1946.

5. PRO, FO371/57693/WR2067, Emerson to Edmonds, 30 July 1946, and minute by Edmonds, 27 August 1946; PRO, FO371/57694/WR2203, Emerson to Edmonds, 26 August 1946; PRO, FO371/57695, minute by McNeil, 12 August 1946.

6. PRO, FO943/543, Allied Commission for Austria to Control Office for Germany and Austria, no. 450, 19 August 1946; see also chap. 10.

7. PRO, FO371/51129/WR3804, Vienna to FO, no. 52, 12 December 1945; PRO, FO945/655, Broad to FO, no. 2149, 30 December 1945.

8. PRO, FO371/57685/WR163, Mack to FO, no. 64, 16 January 1946.

9. PRO, T220/143, Allied Commission for Austria to Control Office for Germany and Austria, no. 475, 12 September 1946; PRO, FO1005/838, minutes of meeting of the Directorate of Prisoners of War and Displaced Persons, 10 September 1946; see also Gefen, *Barriers' Breakers*, 64–76, 96–98.

10. PRO, FO371/57698, translation of note verbale from the Italian Ministry of Foreign Affairs, 7 October 1946; PRO, FO371/52632/E9055, Rome to FO, no. 1403, 10 September 1946.

11. PRO, FO371/52631/E8841, British consulate general, Marseilles, to Bevin, 28 August 1946.

12. PRO, FO371/57697/WR3183, Cooper to FO, no. 573, 31 October 1946; PRO, FO371/52636/E11025, minute by Beith, 4 November 1946; PRO, FO371/57698/WR3413, Cooper to FO, no. 476, 14 November 1946, and Refugee Department, FO to British embassy, Paris, 23 November 1946; Gefen, *Barriers' Breakers*, 160–61.

13. PRO, FO371/55215/E3410, Cunningham to CO, no. 587, 11 April 1946; PRO, ADM116/5561, FO to Cooper, no. 913, 3 May 1946; PRO, FO371/52523/E4397, copy of aide memoire to the French Ministry for Foreign Affairs, 10 May 1946; PRO, FO371/52529/E5437, report of Criminal Investigation Department, Palestine Police, Jerusalem, 10 May 1946. About the headquarters in Paris, see Gelber, *Standard Bearers*, 620–25, 640–42; Hadari, *Second Exodus*, 142–45.

14. PRO, FO371/52545/E7206, Ashley Clarke, minister at the British embassy in Paris, to FO, no. 315, 26 July 1946; PRO, FO371/52549/E7556, Cooper to Bevin, no. 678, 30 July 1946; PRO, CAB128/6, Cabinet meeting, C.M.(46)76, 1 August 1946.

15. On the relations between the two countries at the time, see Young, *Britain, France and the Unity of Europe*, 31–33; Bullock, *Ernest Bevin*, 279–80, 316.

16. PRO, FO371/52636/E11074, British consulate general, Marseilles, to Bevin, no. 67, 6 November 1946.

17. PRO, FO371/52638, L. J. Rolfe, protective officer, UNRRA, to chief protective officer, 9 November 1946.

18. PRO, FO371/52637/E11118, G. E. Millard, British embassy in Paris, to Beith, 8 November 1946.

19. Poznanski, "World War II Heritage," 144–66.

20. PRO, FO371/52637/E11308, Clarke to Bidault, no. 1087, 16 November 1946; PRO, FO371/52637/E11538, British embassy, Paris, to the French Ministry of Foreign Affairs, 29 November 1946; PRO, FO371/61799/E189, British embassy, Paris, to Eastern Department, FO, 31 December 1946.

21. PRO, FO371/61800/E744, Cooper to FO, no. 67, 21 January 1947; PRO, FO371/61838/E1024, Cooper to FO, no. 105, 31 January 1947; Eliav, *Voyage of the Ulua*.

22. PRO, FO371/52637, Paris to FO, no. 616, 22 November 1946.

23. PRO, FO371/52638/E11577, British embassy, Paris, to Eastern Department, FO, 23 November 1946.

24. PRO, FO371/61750/E259, Cooper to the French Ministry of Foreign Affairs, 7 January 1947; PRO, FO371/61750/E431, Cooper to FO, no. 16, 11 January 1947. About the French Jewish community, see Weinberg, "Reconstruction of the French Jewish Community after World War II," 168–86.

25. PRO, FO371/61750/E597, Clarke to FO, no. 25, 15 January 1947.

26. PRO, FO371/61750/E848, Clarke to Beith, 18 January 1947; PRO, FO371/61804/E2894, Cooper to FO, no. 261, 3 April 1947; PRO, FO371/61804/E2888, Paris to FO, no. 267, 4 April 1947, and FO to Moscow, no. 599, 5 April 1947; PRO, FO371/61804/E2913, Bevin to Bidault, 7 April 1947, and Bidault to Bevin, 8 April 1947.

27. HP, General Testimonies, no. 294; Hadari, *Second Exodus,* 145–50.

28. PRO, WO32/10260, extract from the minutes of the 7th (47) meeting of the Defence Committee, 12 March 1947; PRO, FO371/61801/E1616, Higham, CO, to Beith, 14 February 1947, and minute by Beith, 14 February 1947; PRO, FO371/61839/E2141, Higham to FO, 6 March 1947.

29. PRO, CO537/2334, CO to the officer administering the government of Palestine, 3 March 1947.

30. PRO, FO800/487, McNeil to Eastern Department, 12 March 1947.

31. PRO, FO371/61803/E2667, Cooper to Bidault, 21 March 1947; PRO, FO371/61804/E2894, FO to Paris, no. 435, 15 March 1947.

32. PRO, FO371/61804/E2894, Cooper to FO, no. 261, 3 April 1947; PRO, FO371/61804/E2888, Paris to FO, no. 267, 4 April 1947, and FO to Moscow, no. 599, 5 April 1947; PRO, FO371/61804/E2913, Bevin to Bidault, 7 April 1947.

33. PRO, FO371/61804/E2888, Paris to FO, no. 267, 4 April 1947; PRO, WO32/10260, extract from the minutes of the 14th meeting of the Defence Committee, 16 April 1947; PRO, FO371/61805/E3424, Creech Jones to McNeil, 21 April 1947; PRO, ADM116/5648, minutes of a meeting of the Cabinet Committee on Illegal Immigration, 2 May 1947.

34. PRO, FO371/61805/E3561, T. J. Teitgen, Quai d'Orsay, to Cooper, 24 April 1947; PRO, CAB104/276, Cooper to FO, no. 321, 24 April 1947.

35. PRO, FO371/61805/E3481, Cooper to FO, no. 324, 25 April 1947; PRO, FO800/487, McNeil to Attlee, 30 April 1947; PRO, FO371/61805/E2894, Cooper to FO, no. 321,

25 April 1947; PRO, FO371/61808/E4402, memorandum by Beith, 28 May 1947; PRO, FO371/61804/E2894, Cooper to FO, no. 327, 25 April 1947.

36. PRO, FO371/61804/E2894, Cooper to FO, no. 327, 25 April 1947.

37. PRO, FO371/66667/WR1621, memoranda, 29–30 April 1947.

38. Ibid., memorandum, 2 May 1947, and FO to Paris, no. 682, 2 May 1947.

39. PRO, FO945/494, Strang to FO, no. 743, 12 May 1947.

40. PRO, FO371/61808/E4402, Cooper to FO, no. 126, 20 May 1947. About the differences between the British Foreign Office and the embassy in Paris about the incentives to be given to the French to encourage them to act against the illegal sailings, see PRO, FO945/468, Cooper to FO, no. 851, 1 September 1947; PRO, FO371/61827/E8570, Beith to C. A. Crossley, British embassy, Paris, 1 October 1947.

41. PRO, FO945/468, minute by Beith, 26 June 1947; PRO, FO945/494, Beith to Crossley, 7 August 1947; PRO, FO371/61808/E4402, minute by Beith, 28 May 1947; PRO, FO371/61807/E3979, minute by Beith, 22 May 1947; PRO, FO371/61808/E4522, FO to Rome, no. 1099, 27 May 1947.

42. About the *Exodus* affair, see Halamish, *Exodus Affair;* Bethell, *Palestine Triangle,* 316–36, 340–43; Zertal, *From Catastrophe to Power,* chap. 2; Hadari, *Second Exodus,* chap. 15; Derogy, *La Loi du retour;* Depreux, *Souvenirs d'un militant,* 295–306; see also chap. 3.

43. PRO, FO371/61842/E4280, FO to British embassy in Paris, no. 464, 13 June 1947; PRO, FO371/61811/E5142, Charles to FO, no. 1295, 13 June 1947, and FO to Paris, no. 1067, 14 June 1947; PRO, FO371/61812/E5187, Cooper to FO, no. 540, 16 June 1947; PRO, FO371/61812/E5239, Marseilles to Paris, no. 63, 16 June 1947; PRO, FO371/61811/E5001, Bevin to Bidault, 27 June 1947.

44. PRO, FO371/61815/E6272, Bevin to Bidault, 12 July 1947; PRO, FO371/61815/E6218, Cooper to FO, no. 682, 12 July 1947; PRO, FO371/61816/E6313, FO to Paris, no. 1535, 14 July 1947.

45. Ibid., Cooper to FO, no. 686, 13 July 1947.

46. Ibid., memorandum by J. E. Cable, 16 July 1947.

47. PRO, FO371/61816/E6358, memorandum for the secretary of state, 17 July 1947, and Cooper to FO, no. 695, 16 July 1947.

48. PRO, FO371/61816/E6448, Cooper to FO, no. 713, 18 July 1947.

49. PRO, FO371/61816/E6374, Cooper to FO, no. 699, 17 July 1947.

50. PRO, FO371/61816/E6358, FO to Paris, no. 1622, 19 July 1947; PRO, FO371/61816/E6360, CO to Cunningham, no. 1585, 19 July 1947.

51. PRO, FO371/61816/E6448, Cooper to FO, no. 725, 21 July 1947.

52. PRO, FO371/61818/E6711, Cooper to Marseilles, no. 71, 22 July 1947; PRO, FO371/61817/E6583, Cooper to FO, no. 729, 22 July 1947.

53. PRO, FO371/61818/E6698, Cooper to FO, no. 743, 24 July 1947; PRO, FO371/61818/E6733, Cooper to FO, no. 750, 25 July 1947; PRO, FO371/61818/E7135, FO to Paris, no. 1709, 26 July 1947.

54. PRO, FO371/61818/E6643, Cooper to FO, no. 734, 23 July 1947.

55. See, for example, PRO, FO371/61820/E6993, "The Drama of the 'Exodus,'" by Leon Blum, translated from *Le Populaire,* 1 August 1947; Young, *Britain, France and the Unity of Europe,* chap. 5.

56. PRO, FO371/61818/E6643, Cooper to FO, no. 743, 24 July 1947.

57. PRO, FO371/61818/E6698, FO to Paris, no. 1701, 25 July 1947, and memorandum by Cable, 25 July 1947.

58. PRO, FO371/61820/E714, Cooper to FO, no. 754, 26 July 1947; PRO, FO371/61819/E6761, Cooper to FO, no. 755, 26 July 1947; PRO, FO371/61819/E6760, FO to Marseilles, 27 July 1947.

59. PRO, FO371/61846/E6840, Marseilles to FO, no. 107, 29 July 1947; PRO, FO371/61819/E6862, Marseilles to FO, no. 109, 29 July 1947.

60. PRO, FO371/61819/E6860, Cooper to FO, no. 764, 29 July 1947; PRO, FO371/61819/E6867, Cooper to FO, no. 769, 30 July 1947; PRO, FO371/61819/E6871, Cooper to FO, no. 770, 30 July 1947; PRO, FO371/61819/E6862, no. 1741, 30 July 1947; PRO, FO371/61821/E7345, memorandum by J. E. Coulson, 1 August 1947.

61. PRO, CAB128/10, Cabinet meeting, C.M.66(47), 31 July 1947; PRO, FO371/61810/E7114, memorandum for the secretary of state, 30 July 1947.

62. PRO, FO371/61821/E7339, Cooper to FO, no. 808, 11 August 1947.

63. Ibid., minutes of meeting of the Official Committee on Jewish Illegal Immigration, 14 August 1947; PRO, FO371/61822/E7617, Creech Jones to Bevin, 14 August 1947; PRO, FO371/61822/E7488, FO to Berlin, no. 2385, 16 August 1947.

64. PRO, FO371/61822/E7744, "Latest from Paris," 21 August 1947, and Marseilles to Paris, 21 August 1947.

65. PRO, FO371/61823/E7766, Cooper to FO, no. 883, 22 August 1947. The Jewish Agency refused a British proposal to convince the *ma'apilim* to disembark in Cyprus. CZA, S-25/26381, Berl Locker to Trafford Smith, 21 August 1947; see also minutes of their conversation, CZA, S-25/2630, 21 August 1947.

66. Slutsky, *History of the Hagana,* 3:925–29.

67. PRO, FO371/61824/E8050, memorandum by Beeley "'President's Warfield's' Passengers," 30 August 1947, and memorandum for the secretary of state, 30 August 1947; PRO, FO371/61824, FO to Paris, no. 1960, 31 August 1947; PRO, FO371/61824/E8051, Cooper to FO, no. 847, 1 September 1947, and FO to Paris, no. 1967, 2 September 1947; PRO, FO371/61825/E8131, Cooper to FO, no. 854, 2 September 1947; PRO, FO371/61825/E8170, Clarke to FO, no. 863, 4 September 1947.

68. PRO, FO371/61824/E8035, Cooper to FO, no. 843, 30 August 1947, and FO to Paris, no. 2005, 6 September 1947; PRO, FO1014/639, FO to Lubbecke, 8 September 1947; Derogy, *La Loi du retour,* 241–42.

69. PRO, FO371/61825/E8270, Cooper to FO, no. 874, 7 September 1947.

70. PRO, FO371/61825/E6277, Bevin to Bidault, no. 874, 12 July 1947; PRO, FO371/61846/E6739, Clarke to Bousquet, 22 July 1947; PRO, FO371/61818/E6697, Bordeaux to FO, no. 44, 24 July 1947; PRO, FO371/61847/E7360, British embassy in Paris to the French Ministry of Foreign Affairs, no. 726, 8 August 1947.

71. PRO, FO371/61823/E7751, Cooper to FO, no. 830, 21 August 1947.

72. See chap. 9.

73. PRO, ADM1/20793, FO to Paris, no. 2142, 2 October 1947; PRO, FO371/61849/E9277, British embassy in Paris to the French Ministry of Foreign Affairs, 3 October 1947; PRO, FO371/61850/E9869, British consulate general in Marseilles to Clarke, 10 October 1947.

74. PRO, FO371/61814/E6075, Charles to FO, no. 1450, 5 July 1947; see also chap. 10.

75. PRO, FO371/66671/WR3240, Mack to FO, no. 872, 18 September 1947.

76. PRO, FO371/61854/E11627, minutes of the Allies meeting in Austria, 17 November 1947; PRO, FO945/372, Mack to FO, no. 1084, 21 November 1947.

77. Bauer, *Out of the Ashes,* 238.

78. HA, 14/89, from Paris, 23 June 1947; LPA, 23/47, minutes of meeting of Mapai's Center, 24 June 1947, Avriel; HA, 14/107, from Hadari, 20 July 1947; HP, General Testimonies, no. 294, Hadari.

79. Rioux, *Fourth Republic,* 122–29; Young, *Britain, France and the Unity of Europe,* 70–76; Young, *France, the Cold War and the Western Alliance,* chaps. 7–8; Bullock, *Ernest Bevin,* 486–88.

BIBLIOGRAPHY

ARCHIVES AND MANUSCRIPT COLLECTIONS

Great Britain
London School of Economics–British Library of Economics and Political Science
   Hugh Dalton, Diaries and Papers
Middle East Center, St. Antony's College, Oxford
   Alan Cunningham Papers
Public Record Office, Kew
   Admiralty Records
      ADM 1 Admiralty and Secretariat Papers
      ADM 116 Admiralty and Secretariat Cases
   Air Ministry
      AIR 20 Mediterranean and Middle East Policy
      AIR 23 Overseas Command
   Cabinet Records
      CAB 21 Cabinet Office: Registered Files
      CAB 65 War Cabinet Minutes
      CAB 95 War Cabinet Committees on the Middle East and Africa
      CAB 104 Supplementary Registered Files
      CAB 119 Joint Planning Staff: Files
      CAB 120 Minister of Defence: Secretariat Files
      CAB 128 Cabinet Minutes and Conclusions
      CAB 129 Cabinet Papers
      CAB 133 Commonwealth and International Conferences
      CAB 134 Cabinet Committees: General Series
   Colonial Office
      CO 537 Palestine: Supplementary Original Correspondence
      CO 733 Palestine: Original Correspondence
   Defence
      DEFE 4 Chiefs of Staff Committee: Minutes and Meetings
      DEFE 5 Chiefs of Staff Committee: Memoranda
      DEFE 7 Ministry of Defence: Memoranda
   Foreign Office
      FO 115 Embassy and Consular Archives: United States of America
         Correspondence
      FO 141 Embassy and Consular Archives: Egypt Correspondence
      FO 181 Embassy and Consular Archives: Russia Correspondence

FO 226 Embassy and Consular Archives Turkey: Beirut Correspondence
FO 371 Foreign Office: General Correspondence, Political
FO 688 Embassy and Consular Archives: Poland Correspondence
FO 770 Embassy and Consular Archives: Romania Correspondence
FO 800 Private Collections: Ministers and Officials, Various
FO 938 Control Office: Private Office Papers
FO 943 Control Office: Economic
FO 945 Control Office: General Department
FO 1005 Control Commission for Germany (British Element): Records Library
FO 1007 Allied Commission for Austria
FO 1014 Control Commission for Germany (British Element): Hansestadt
Hamburg
FO 1032 Control Commission for Germany (British Element): Planning
Sections and Headquarters Secretariat
FO 1049 Control Commission for Germany (British Element): Political
Division
FO 1052 Control Commission for Germany (British Element): Prisoners of War
and Displaced Persons Division
Prime Minister Private Office
PREM 8 Correspondence and Papers
Treasury Office
T 220 Imperial and Foreign Division: Files
War Office
WO 32 Registered Files: General Series
WO 169 War Diaries: Middle East Forces
WO 170 War Diaries: Central Mediterranean Forces
WO 178 War Diaries: Military Missions
WO 204 Military Headquarters Papers, Allied Force Headquarters
WO 216 Chief of the (Imperial) General Staff
WO 220 Directorate of Civil Affairs
WO 275 Sixth Airborne Division
Rhodes House, Oxford
Arthur Creech Jones Papers

United States
Hoover Institution Archives, Stanford, California
Margaret Eleanor Fait Collection
National Archives, College Park, Maryland
RG 43, Records of the Anglo-American Committee of Inquiry Re Palestine
RG 59 General Records of the Department of State
Decimal Files
Lot Files:
Records of the Office of the Eastern European Affairs, Polish Desk Officer
Records of the Office of the Near Eastern Affairs
Records of the Western European Affairs

Records Relating to Intergovernmental Committee on Refugees
RG 84 Office of U.S. Political Advisor, Berlin
RG 107 Assistant Secretary of War, Howard C. Peterson
RG 107 Secretary of War, Robert Patterson
RG 165 Records of the Civil Affairs Division, International Refugee Organization
RG 165 Records of the General and Special Staff
RG 200 Duker/Dwork Papers, OSS R&A Jewish Desk
RG 226 Duker/Dwork Papers, Palestine, Jewish-Arab Activity
RG 338 Records of U.S. Army Command, Secretary, General Staff
RG 338 Records of U.S. Army Command, European Theatre of Operation,
    Historical Division
Franklin D. Roosevelt Library, Hyde Park, New York
    War Refugee Board, 1944–45
Harry S. Truman Library, Independence, Missouri
    Oral History Collection
    President's Secretary's Files
    White House Official Files
YIVO Institute for Jewish Studies, New York
    Leo S. Schwartz Papers

Israel
Archive of the American Joint Distribution Committee, Jerusalem
    6-A Reports of Rabbi Philip Bernstein, Germany, U.S. Zone
    7-A Reports, Germany, British Zone, 1946–51
    9-A Articles Concerning Clandestine Entry of Jews into Italy
    14-B Emigration, Bratislava
Archive of the History of the Haganah, Tel Aviv
    Dekel Collection
    Files of *Aliyah Bet* ("class B immigration") 14
    Chaim Guri Collection
    Oral Testimonies
Ben Gurion Archives, Sde Boker
    Ben Gurion Diary
    Chronological Documentation Division
    Correspondence Division
Central Zionist Archives, Jerusalem
    Minutes of the Meeting of the Executive of the Jewish Agency
    S-6 Files of the Immigration Department
    S-25 Files of the Political Department
    Z-4 Files of the Office of the Zionist Organization in London
Ghetto Fighters House Archive, Beit Lohamei Haghetaot
    Italy, 1946–49
    The Jewish Agency, 1944–47
Information Center of the Ha'apala Project, University of Tel Aviv
    Oral Documentation Center of the Institute for Contemporary Jewry

Labour Movement (Histadrut) Archives, Tel Aviv
    Minutes of the Central Committee of the Histadrut
    Minutes of the Executive Committee of the Histadrut
    Minutes of the Sixth Convention of the Histadrut
Labour Party Archives, Beit Berl, Kfar-Saba
    Unit 23, Minutes of the Labour Party Center
    Unit 24, Minutes of the Labour Party Secretariat
    Unit 25, Minutes of the Labour Party Bureau
    Unit 26, Minutes of the Political Committee
Weizmann Archives, Rehovot
    Papers and Letters of Chaim Weizmann
Yad Vashem Archives, Jerusalem
    0-70, Minutes of the Central Jewish Committee Meetings in Bergen-Belsen
    Bergen-Belsen Archive on the Name of Josef Rosensaft

PUBLISHED PRIMARY SOURCES

Blumenson, Martin. *The Patton Papers, 1945–1949.* 2 vols. Boston, 1974.
Chandler, Alfred D., Jr., and Louis Galambos. *The Papers of Dwight David Eisenhower.* Vol. 6. Baltimore, 1978.
The DP Story: The Final Report of the United States Displaced Persons Commission. 22 vols. Washington, D.C., 1952.
Friedlander, Henry, and Sybil Milton. *Archives of the Holocaust: An International Collection of Selected Documents.* Vol. 10, part 2. New York, 1995.
Khalidi, Walid. *From Haven to Conquest: Readings in Zionism and the Palestine Problem until 1948.* Beirut, 1971.
Oppen, Beate Ruhm von. *Documents on Germany under Occupation, 1945–1954.* London, 1955.
Paris Peace Conference, 1946: Selected Documents. Washington, D.C., n.d.
Public Papers of the Presidents of the United States, Harry S. Truman, 1945 and 1946. 2 vols. Washington, D.C., 1961–62.
Report of the Anglo-American Committee of Enquiry Regarding the Problems of European Jewry and Palestine, Lausanne, 20th April 1946. London, Cmd. 6808.
Ro'i, Yaacov. *From Encroachment to Involvement: A Documentary Study of Soviet Policy in the Middle East, 1945–1973.* New York, 1974.
U.S. Department of State. *Foreign Relations of the United States: Diplomatic Papers.* Washington, D.C., 1967–72. 1945, Vols. 2, 7; 1946, Vol. 5; 1947, Vol. 2.
———. *Making the Peace Treaties, 1941–1947.* Washington, D.C., 1947.
———. *United States and Italy, 1936–1946, Documentary Record.* Washington, D.C., 1946.
Whom We Shall Welcome: Report of the President's Commission on Immigration and Naturalization. Washington, D.C., 1953.
Woodward, Llewellyn. *British Foreign Policy in the Second World War.* Vols. 2, 5. London, 1971–76.

DIARIES AND MEMOIRS

Acheson, Dean. *Present at the Creation: My Years at the State Department.* London, 1976.

Avriel, Ehud. *Open the Gates: A Personal Story of "Illegal" Immigration to Israel.* New York, 1975.

Bentwich, Norman. *They Found Refuge: An Account of British Jewry Victims of Nazi Persecution.* London, 1956.

Bidault, Georges. *Resistance.* London, 1965.

Clay, Lucius D. *Decision in Germany.* Melbourne, 1950.

Cohen, Yohanan. *Operation "Briha": Poland, 1945–1946.* Tel Aviv, 1995. (Hebrew).

Cooper, Duff. *Old Men Forget.* London, 1957.

Crossman, Richard. *Palestine Mission: A Personal Record.* New York, 1947.

Crum, Bartley C. *Behind the Silken Curtain: A Personal Account of Anglo-American Diplomacy in Palestine and the Middle East.* New York, 1947.

Dekel, Ephraim. *On the Routes of the Brichah.* Tel Aviv, 1958. (Hebrew).

Depreux, Edouard. *Souvenirs d'un militant.* Paris, 1972.

Easterman, A. L. "Liberated—But Not Freemen." In *Belsen.* Tel Aviv, 1958. (Hebrew).

Eilat, Eliahu. *The Struggle for Statehood: Washington, 1945–1948.* 2 vols. Tel Aviv, 1982. (Hebrew).

Eliav, (Lova) Arie. *The Voyage of the Ulua.* New York, 1970.

Ettinger, Amos. *Blind Jump: The Story of Yeshayahu (Shaike) Dan.* Tel Aviv, 1986. (Hebrew).

Gefen, Abba. *Barriers' Breakers.* Tel Aviv, 1961. (Hebrew).

Heymont, Irving. *Among the Survivors of the Holocaust, 1945: The Landsberg DP Camp, Letters of Major Irving Heymont, United States Army.* Cincinnati, 1982.

Hirschmann, Ira A. *The Embers Still Burn.* New York, 1949.

Ishai, Moshe. *In the Shadow of the Holocaust: Memoirs of a Mission to Poland, 1945–1946.* Tel Aviv, 1973. (Hebrew).

Kahane, David. *After the Deluge.* Jerusalem, 1981. (Hebrew).

Mikołlajczyk, Stanisław. *The Rape of Poland: Pattern of Soviet Aggression.* Westport, Conn., 1948.

Montgomery, Bernard Law. *The Memoirs of Field-Marshal the Viscount Montgomery of Alamein.* London, 1958.

Nadich, Judah. *Eisenhower and the Jews.* New York, 1953.

Nagy, Ferenc. *The Struggle behind the Iron Curtain.* New York, 1948.

Rendel, George. *The Sword and the Olive.* London, 1957.

Rosensaft, Josef. "Our Belsen." In *Belsen.* Tel Aviv, 1958. (Hebrew).

Safran, Alexandre. *Resisting the Storm: Romania, 1940–1947—Memoirs.* Jerusalem, 1987. (Hebrew).

Schwartz, Leo W. *The Redeemers: A Saga of the Years 1945–52.* New York, 1953.

Sereni, Ada. *Ships without Flags.* Tel Aviv, 1975. (Hebrew).

Stone, Isidor F. *Underground to Palestine.* New York, 1978.

Talmi, Yehuda. "Fleeing from Hungary." *Massua: A Yearbook on the Holocaust and Heroism* 5 (April 1977): 229–54. (Hebrew).

Truman, Harry S. *Years of Trial and Hope.* 2 vols. New York, 1956.

Williams, Francis. *A Prime Minister Remembers: The War and Post-War Memoirs of The Rt. Hon. Earl Attlee.* London, 1961.

Yahil, Chaim. "The Activities of the Palestine Jewry's Mission to the Survivors of the Holocaust, 1945–1949." *Yalkut Moreshet* 30 (November 1980): 7–40. (Hebrew).

———. "The Activities of the Palestine Jewry's Mission to the Survivors of the Holocaust, 1945–1949 (B)." *Yalkut Moreshet* 31 (April 1981): 133–76. (Hebrew).

SECONDARY SOURCES

Abzug, Robert H. *Inside the Vicious Heart: Americans and the Liberation of Nazi Concentration Camps.* New York, 1985.

Ancel, Jean. "The Rumanian Jewry, 23.8.1944–30.12.1947." Ph.D. diss., Hebrew University, Jerusalem, 1979. (Hebrew).

———. "She'erit Hapletah in Romania during the Transition Period to a Communist Regime, August 1944–December 1947." In *She'erit Hapletah, 1944–1948: Rehabilitation and Political Struggle,* edited by Yisrael Gutman and Avital Saf, 143–67. Jerusalem, 1985. (Hebrew).

Avizohar, Meir. "Ben-Gurion's Visit to the D.P. Camps and His National Outlook in the Aftermath of World War II." In *Eastern European Jewry, From Holocaust to Redemption, 1944–1948,* edited by Benjamin Pinkus, 253–70. Sde Boker, 1987. (Hebrew).

Backer, John H. *Priming the German Economy: American Occupational Policies, 1945–1948.* Durham, 1971.

Balabkins, Nicholas. *Germany under Direct Controls: Economic Aspects of Industrial Disarmament, 1945–1948.* New Brunswick, 1964.

Balfour, Michael. *West Germany: A Contemporary History.* London, 1982.

Bauer, Yehuda. *American Jewry and the Holocaust: The American Jewish Joint Distribution Committee, 1939–1945.* Detroit, 1981.

———. *Flight and Rescue: Brichah.* New York, 1970.

———. *Jews for Sale? Nazi-Jewish Negotiations, 1933–1945.* New Haven, 1994.

———. *Out of the Ashes: The Impact of American Jews on Post-Holocaust European Jewry.* Oxford, 1989.

Bell, John D. *The Bulgarian Communist Party from Blagoev to Zhivkov.* Stanford, 1986.

Bennett, Marion T. *American Immigration Policies.* Washington, D.C., 1963.

Benson, Michael T. *Harry S. Truman and the Founding of Israel.* Westport, Conn., 1997.

Bethell, Nicholas. *The Last Secret: The Delivery to Stalin of over Two Million Russians by Britain and the United States.* New York, 1974.

———. *The Palestine Triangle: The Struggle between the British, the Jews and the Arabs, 1945–1948.* London, 1979.

Bogner, Nahum. *The Deportation Island: Jewish Illegal Immigrant Camps on Cyprus, 1946–1948.* Tel Aviv, 1991. (Hebrew).

Bolchover, Richard. *British Jewry and the Holocaust.* Cambridge, Eng., 1993.

Braham, Randolph L. *The Politics of Genocide: The Holocaust in Hungary.* New York, 1981.

Braham, Randolph L., and Nathaniel Katzburg. *History of the Holocaust: Hungary.* Jerusalem, 1992. (Hebrew).

Breitman, Richard. *Official Secrets: What the Nazis Planned, What the British and Americans Knew.* New York, 1998.

Breitman, Richard, and Alan M. Kraut. *American Refugee Policy and European Jewry, 1933–1945.* Bloomington, 1987.

Brenchley, Frank. *Britain and the Middle East: An Economic History, 1945–87.* London, 1989.

Brenner, Michael. *After the Holocaust: Rebuilding Jewish Lives in Postwar Germany.* Princeton, N.J., 1997.

―――. "East European and German Jews in Postwar Germany, 1945–50." In *Jews, Germans, Memory: Reconstructions of Jewish Life in Germany,* edited by Y. Michal Bodemann, 49–63. Ann Arbor, 1996.

Bridgman, Jon. *The End of the Holocaust: The Liberation of the Camps.* London, 1990.

Bullock, Alan. *Ernest Bevin, Foreign Secretary, 1945–1951.* New York, 1983.

Bungert, Heike. "A New Perspective on French-American Relations during the Occupation of Germany, 1945–1948: Behind-the-Scenes Diplomatic Bargaining and the Zonal Merger." *Diplomatic History* 18 (Summer 1994): 333–52.

Burridge, Trevor. *Clement Attlee: A Political Biography.* London, 1985.

Carden, Robert W. "Before Bizonia: Britain's Economic Dilemma in Germany, 1945–1946." *Journal of Contemporary History* 14 (1979): 535–55.

Cesarani, David. "Great Britain." In *The World Reacts to the Holocaust,* edited by David S. Wyman. Baltimore, 1996.

Charmley, John. "Duff Cooper and Western European Union, 1944–1947." *Review of International Studies* 11 (1985): 53–64.

Charters, David A. *The British Army and Jewish Insurgency in Palestine, 1945–47.* London, 1989.

Checinski, Michael. *Poland: Communism—Nationalism—Antisemitism.* New York, 1982.

Childs, David. *Britain since 1945: A Political History.* London, 1979.

Cohen, Asher. "The Attitude of the Intelligentsia in Hungary toward Jewish Assimilation between the Two World Wars." In *Jewish Assimilation in Modern Times,* edited by Bela Vago, 57–74. Boulder, Colo., 1981.

―――. *The Halutz Resistance in Hungary, 1942–1944.* Boulder, Colo., 1986.

Cohen, Gavriel. "British Policy on the Eve of the War of Independence." In *They That Dream,* edited by Yehuda Wallach, 13–166. Givatayim, 1985. (Hebrew).

Cohen, Michael J. *Churchill and the Jews.* London, 1985.

―――. *Palestine: Retreat from the Mandate, the Making of British Policy, 1936–1945.* New York, 1978.

―――. *Palestine and the Great Powers.* Princeton, 1982.

―――. *Truman and Israel.* Berkeley, 1990.

―――. "Truman and Palestine, 1945–1948: Revisionism, Politics and Diplomacy." *Modern Judaism* 2 (1982): 1–22.

Cohen, Stuart A. "Imperial Policing against Illegal Immigration: The Royal Navy and

Palestine, 1945–1948." *Journal of Imperial and Commonwealth History* 22 (May 1994): 275–93.

Coutouvidis, John, and Jamie Reynolds. *Poland, 1939–1947.* Leicester, 1986.

Crister, S. Garrett, and Stephen A. Garrett. "Death and Politics: The Katyn Forest Massacre and American Foreign Policy." *East European Quarterly* 20 (Winter 1986): 429–46.

Cromwell, William C. "The Marshall Plan, Britain and the Cold War." *Review of International Studies* 8 (1982): 233–49.

Cronin, Audrey Kurth. *Great Powers Politics and the Struggle over Austria, 1945–1955.* Ithaca, N.Y., 1986.

Cuperman, Jafa. *In the Grip of Communism: The Zionist Federation in Rumania, 1944–1949.* Tel Aviv, 1995. (Hebrew).

Deighton, Anne. *The Impossible Peace: Britain, the Division of Germany and the Origins of the Cold War.* Oxford, 1990.

Derogy, Jacques. *La Loi du retour.* Paris, 1970.

Dinnerstein, Leonard. *America and the Survivors of the Holocaust.* New York, 1982.

———. *Antisemitism in America.* New York, 1994.

———. *Uneasy at Home: Antisemitism and the American Jewish Experience.* New York, 1987.

Divine, Robert A. *Foreign Policy and U.S. Presidential Elections, 1940–1948.* New York, 1974.

Dobroszycki, Lucjan. *Survivors of the Holocaust in Poland: A Portrait Based on Jewish Community Records, 1944–1947.* New York, 1994.

Dobson, Alan P. *U.S. Wartime Aid to Britain, 1940–1946.* London, 1986.

Donovan, Robert J. *Conflict and Crisis: The Presidency of Harry S. Truman, 1945–1948.* New York, 1977.

Duschinsky, Eugene. "Hungary." In *The Jews in the Soviet Satellites,* edited by Peter Meyer, Bernard D. Weinryb, Eugene Duschinsky, and Nicolas Sylvain, Part 4. Westport, Conn., 1953.

Eatwell, Roger. *The 1945–1951 Labour Governments.* London, 1979.

Edmonds, Robin. *Setting the Mould: The United States and Britain, 1945–1950.* Oxford, 1986.

Edward, Peterson N. *The American Occupation of Germany.* Detroit, 1977.

Elliott, Mark R. *Pawns of Yalta: Soviet Refugees and America's Role in Their Repatriation.* Urbana, 1982.

Engel, David. *Between Liberation and Flight: Holocaust Survivors in Poland and the Struggle for Leadership, 1944–1946.* Tel Aviv, 1996. (Hebrew).

Ethridge, Mark, and C. E. Black. "Negotiating on the Balkans, 1945–1947." In *Negotiating with the Russians,* edited by Raymond Dennett and Joseph E. Johnson, 171–206. Boston, 1951.

Feingold, Henry L. *The Politics of Rescue: The Roosevelt Administration and the Holocaust, 1938–1945.* New Brunswick, 1970.

———. *A Time for Searching: Entering the Mainstream, 1920–1945.* Baltimore, 1992.

Fischer-Galati, Stephen. "The Communist Takeover of Roumania: A Function of

Soviet Power." In *The Anatomy of Communist Takeovers*, edited by Thomas T. Hammond, 310–20. New Haven, 1975.

———. *The New Rumania: From People's Democracy to Socialist Republic*. Cambridge, Mass., 1967.

Freundlish, Yehoshua. "The Hearings and Recommendations of UNSCOP in Palestine." *Zionism: Studies in the History of the Zionist Movement and of the Jewish Community in Palestine* 13 (1988): 27–51. (Hebrew).

Gaddis, John Lewis. *The Long Peace: Inquiries into the History of the Cold War*. New York, 1987.

Ganin, Zvi. "The Partition Plan and Dr. Nahum Goldman's Mission to Washington in the Summer of 1946." *Zionism: Studies in the History of the Zionist Movement and of the Jewish Community in Palestine* 5 (1978): 227–62. (Hebrew).

———. *Truman, American Jewry and Israel*. New York, 1979.

Garliński, Józef. *Poland in the Second World War*. Basingstoke, Hampshire, 1985.

Gelber, Yoav. *The Standard Bearers*. Jerusalem, 1983. (Hebrew).

Genizi, Haim. *The Adviser on Jewish Affairs to the American Army and the Displaced Persons, 1945–1949*. Tel Aviv, 1987. (Hebrew).

———. *America's Fair Share: The Admission and Resettlement of Displaced Persons, 1945–1952*. Detroit, 1993.

———. "Philip S. Berenstein: Adviser on Jewish Affairs, May 1946–August 1947." *Simon Wiesenthal Center Annual* 3 (1986): 139–76.

Gilbert, Martin. *Auschwitz and the Allies: How the Allies Responded to the News of Hitler's Final Solution*. London, 1981.

Gimbel, John. *The American Occupation of Germany*. Stanford, 1968.

Ginat, Rami. "Soviet Policy towards the Arab World, 1945–1948." *Middle Eastern Studies* 32 (October 1996): 321–35.

———. *The Soviet Union and Egypt, 1945–1955*. London, 1993.

Gomaa, Ahmed Mahmoud H. *The Foundation of the League of the Arab States*. London, 1977.

Gorni, Joseph. *The British Labour Movement and Zionism, 1917–1948*. London, 1983.

Greenwood, Sean. "Ernest Bevin, France, and 'Western Union': August 1945–February 1946." *European History Quarterly* 14 (1984): 319–38.

Grobman, Alex. *Rekindling the Flame: American Jewish Chaplains and the Survivors of European Jewry, 1944–1948*. Detroit, 1993.

Gutman, Yisrael. *The Jews in Poland after World War II*. Jerusalem, 1985. (Hebrew).

———. "Polish and Jewish Historiography on the Question of Polish-Jewish Relations during World War II." In *The Jews in Poland*, edited by Chimen Abramsky, Maciej Jachimczyk, and Antony Polonsky. Oxford, 1987.

———. "Polish Antisemitism between the Wars: An Overview." In *The Jews of Poland between Two World Wars*, edited by Yisrael Gutman, Ezra Mendelson, Jehuda Reinharz, and Chone Shmeruk, 97–108. Hanover, 1989.

Hadari, Ze'ev Venia. *Second Exodus: The Full Story of Jewish Illegal Immigration to Palestine, 1945–1948*. London, 1991.

Hadari, Ze'ev Venia, and Ze'ev Tsahor. *Voyage to Freedom: An Episode in the Illegal Immigration to Palestine*. London, 1985.

Halamish, Aviva. *The Exodus Affair: Holocaust Survivors and the Struggle for Palestine.* New York, 1998.

———. "The United States' Position in the 'Exodus' Affair." *Yahadut Zémanenu (Contemporary Jewry): A Research Annual* 3 (1986): 209–25. (Hebrew).

Hamby, Alonzo L. *Man of the People: A Life of Harry S. Truman.* New York, 1995.

Harbutt, Fraser J. *The Iron Curtain: Churchill, America, and the Origins of the Cold War.* New York, 1986.

Harris, Kenneth. *Attlee.* London, 1982.

Hartmann, Susan M. *Truman and the 80th Congress.* New York, 1971.

Hathaway, Robert M. *Ambiguous Partnership: Britain and America, 1944–1947.* New York, 1981.

Heller, Joseph. *The Stern Gang: Ideology, Politics and Terror, 1940–1949.* London, 1995.

Hogan, Michael J. *The Marshall Plan: America, Britain, and the Reconstruction of Western Europe, 1947–1952.* Cambridge, Mass., 1987.

Holborn, Louise W. *The World's Refugees: Everyone's Concern.* Washington, D.C., 1960.

Hyam, Ronald, ed. *The Labour Government and the End of the Empire, 1945–1951.* London, 1992.

Ignotus, Paul. "The First Two Communist Takeovers of Hungary, 1919–1948." In *The Anatomy of Communist Takeovers,* edited by Thomas T. Hammond, 385–98. New Haven, 1975.

Ilan, Amitzur. *America, Britain and Palestine.* Jerusalem, 1979. (Hebrew).

Ionescu, Ghita. *Communism in Rumania, 1944–1962.* London, 1964.

Jacobmeyer, Wolfgang. *Vom Zwangsarbeiter zum Heimatlosen Ausländer. Die Displaced Persons in Westdeutschland, 1945–1951.* Göttingen, 1985.

Jasse, Richard L. "Great Britain and Palestine towards the United Nations, 1947." *Middle Eastern Studies* 30 (July 1994): 558–78.

Jelinek, Yeshajahu. "The Jews of Czechoslovakia between the Joy of Liberation and the Bitterness of the Day, 1944–1948." In *Eastern-European Jewry, From Holocaust to Redemption, 1944–1948,* edited by Benjamin Pinkus, 153–73. Sde Boqer, 1987. (Hebrew).

———. "The Vatican, the Catholic Church, the Catholics and the Persecution of the Jews during World War II: The Case of Slovakia." In *Jews and Non-Jews in Eastern Europe, 1918–1945,* edited by Bela Vago and George L. Mosse, 221–55. New York, 1974.

Jones, Martin D. *Failure in Palestine: British and United States Policy after the Second World War.* London, 1986.

Kacewicz, George V. *Great Britain and the Polish Government in Exile.* The Hague, 1979.

Katzburg, Nathaniel. "Between Liberation and Revolution: Hungarian Jewry, 1945–1948." In *She'erit Hapletah, 1944–1948: Rehabilitation and Political Struggle,* edited by Yisrael Gutman and Avital Saf, 117–42. Jerusalem, 1990.

———. "The Jewish Question in Hungary during the Inter-War Period—Jewish Attitudes." In *Jews and Non-Jews in Eastern Europe, 1918–1945,* edited by Bela Vago and George L. Mosse, 113–24. New York, 1974.

Kaufman, Menahem. *Non-Zionists in America and the Struggle for Jewish Statehood.* Jerusalem, 1984. (Hebrew).

Kemp, Paul. "The British Army and the Liberation of Bergen-Belsen, April 1945." In *Belsen in History and Memory,* edited by Jo Reilly, David Cesarani, Tony Kushner, and Colin Richmond, 134–48. London, 1997.

Kertesz, Stephen D. *Between Russia and the West: Hungary and the Illusions of Peacemaking, 1945–1947.* Notre Dame, 1984.

Keynan, Irit. *Holocaust Survivors and the Emissaries from Eretz-Israel: Germany, 1945–1948.* Tel Aviv, 1996. (Hebrew).

Khalidi, Walid. "The Arab Perspective." In *The End of the Palestine Mandate,* edited by William Roger Louis and Robert W. Stookey, 104–36. London, 1986.

Kimball, Warren F. *Forged in War: Churchill, Roosevelt and the Second World War.* New York, 1997.

Kitchen, Martin. *British Foreign Policy towards the Soviet Union during the Second World War.* Basingstoke, Hampshire, 1986.

Klieman, Aaron S. *Divide or Rule: Britain, Partition and Palestine, 1936–1939.* Jerusalem, 1983. (Hebrew).

Kochavi, Arieh J. "Anglo-American Discord: Jewish Refugees and United Nations Relief and Rehabilitation Administration Policy, 1945–1947." *Diplomatic History* 14 (Fall 1990): 529–51.

———. "British Response to the Involvement of the American Jewish Joint Distribution Committee in Illegal Jewish Immigration to Palestine." *Immigrants and Minorities* 8 (November 1989): 223–34.

———. "The Catholic Church and Antisemitism in Poland Following World War II as Reflected in British Diplomatic Documents." In *Gal-Ed* 11, edited by Emanuel Meltzer and David Engel, 116–28. Tel Aviv, 1989.

———. *Prelude to Nuremberg: Allied War Crimes Policy and the Question of Punishment.* Chapel Hill, 1998.

Kollat, Israel, Michael J. Cohen, A. Ilan, Gavriel Cohen, and J. Heller. "Discussion: The British Decision to Evacuate Palestine." *Cathedra* 15 (April 1980): 140–93. (Hebrew).

Königseder, Angelika. *Flucht nach Berlin: Jüdische Displaced Persons, 1945–1948.* Berlin, 1998.

Königseder, Angelika, and Juliane Wetzel. *Lebensmut im Wartesaal: Die jüdischen DPs (Displaced Persons) im Nachkriegsdeutschland.* Frankfurt, 1994.

Korbel, Josef. *The Communist Subversion of Czechoslovakia, 1938–1948: The Failure of Coexistence.* Princeton, 1959.

Krammer, Arnold. *The Forgotten Friendship: Israel and the Soviet Bloc, 1947–1953.* Urbana, 1974.

Kuniholm, Bruce R. *The Origins of the Cold War in the Near East: Great Power Conflict and Diplomacy in Iran, Turkey and Greece.* Princeton, 1980.

Kushner, Tony. *The Holocaust and the Liberal Imagination: A Social and Cultural History.* Oxford, 1994.

———. *The Persistence of Prejudice: Antisemitism in British Society during the Second World War.* Manchester, 1989.

Lahav, Jehuda. "The Hungarian Communist Party's Path to Power, 1944–1948." Ph.D. diss., Hebrew University, Jerusalem, 1976. (Hebrew).

Lavski, Hagit. "The Day After: Bergen-Belsen from Concentration Camp to the Centre of the Jewish Survivors in Germany." *German History* 11 (February 1993): 36–59.

———. "Liberated but Not Free—The Nature of the Jewish Organization of Bergen-Belzen." *Zionism: Studies in the History of the Zionist Movement and of the Jewish Community in Palestine* 18 (1994): 9–37.

Levenberg, Haim. *Military Preparations of the Arab Community in Palestine, 1945–1948.* London, 1993.

Levinger, Yosef. "Yugoslavian Jewry: The Pangs of Redemption and Rehabilitation, 1944–1948." *Eastern-European Jewry, From Holocaust to Redemption, 1944–1948,* edited by Benjamin Pinkus, 216–47. Sde Boker, 1987. (Hebrew).

Lipgens, Walter. *A History of European Integration.* Oxford, 1982.

Litvak, Yosef. "The JDC's Contribution on the Rehabilitation of the Jewish Survivors in Poland, 1944–1949." In *Eastern European Jewry, From Holocaust to Redemption, 1944–1948,* edited by Benjamin Pinkus, 334–88. Sde Boker, 1987. (Hebrew).

———. *Polish-Jewish Refugees in the USSR, 1939–1946.* Jerusalem, 1988. (Hebrew).

Lotarski, Susane. "The Communist Takeover in Poland." In *The Anatomy of Communist Takeover,* edited by Thomas T. Hammond, 339–67. New Haven, 1975.

Louis, William Roger. "American Anti-Colonialism and the Dissolution of the British Empire." *International Affairs* 61 (Summer 1985): 395–420.

———. *The British Empire in the Middle East, 1945–1951.* Oxford, 1984.

———. "British Imperialism and the End of Palestine Mandate." In *The End of the Palestine Mandate,* edited by William Roger Louis and Robert W. Stookey, 1–31. London, 1986.

Lundestad, Geir. *The American Non-Policy towards Eastern Europe.* New York, 1975.

Mammarella, Giuseppe. *Italy after Fascism: A Political History, 1943–1963.* Montreal, 1963.

Marrus, Michael R. *The Unwanted: European Refugees in the Twentieth Century.* Oxford, 1985.

Marshall, Barbara. "German Attitudes to British Military Government, 1945–47." *Journal of Contemporary History* 15 (1980): 655–84.

Max, Stanley M. *The United States, Great Britain, and the Sovietization of Hungary, 1945–1948.* New York, 1978.

Mayer, Thomas. "Arab Unity of Action and the Palestine Question, 1945–48." *Middle Eastern Studies* 22 (1986): 331–49.

Mayers, David A. *The Ambassadors and America's Soviet Policy.* New York, 1995.

McCullough, David. *Truman.* New York, 1992.

Meltzer, Emanuel. *Political Strife in a Blind Alley: The Jews in Poland, 1935–1939.* Tel Aviv, 1982. (Hebrew).

Messer, Robert L. *The End of an Alliance: James F. Byrnes, Roosevelt, Truman, and the Origins of the Cold War.* Chapel Hill, 1982.

Meyer, Peter. "Bulgaria." In *The Jews in the Soviet Satellites,* edited by Peter Meyer,

Bernard D. Weinryb, Eugene Duschinsky, and Nicolas Sylvain, Part 6. Westport, Conn., 1953.

————. "Czechoslovakia." In *The Jews in the Soviet Satellites,* edited by Peter Meyer, Bernard D. Weinryb, Eugene Duschinsky, and Nicolas Sylvain, Part 1. Westport, Conn., 1953.

Milward, Alan S. *The Reconstruction of Western Europe, 1945–1951.* London, 1984.

Morgan, Kenneth O. *Labour in Power, 1945–1951.* Oxford, 1984.

Nachmani, Amikam. *Great Power Discord: The Anglo-American Committee of Inquiry into the Problems of European Jewry and Palestine, 1945–1946.* London, 1987.

Naor, Mordechai. *The Ha'apala, 1934–1948.* Tel Aviv, 1978. (Hebrew).

Nevo, Joseph. "The Arabs of Palestine, 1947–1948: Military and Political Activity." *Middle Eastern Studies* 23 (January 1987): 3–38.

Niv, David. *The Irgun Zvai Leumi: Battle for Freedom (1944–1946).* 6 vols. Tel Aviv, 1973. (Hebrew).

Nolfo, Ennio Di. "The Shaping of Italian Foreign Policy during the Foundation of East-West Blocs: Italy between the Superpowers." In *Power in Europe?,* edited by Josef Becker and Franz Knipping, 485–502. Berlin, 1986.

Nussbaum, Kalman. *A Story of an Illusion: The Jews in the Polish People's Army in the USSR.* Tel Aviv, 1984. (Hebrew).

Ofer, Dalia. *Escaping the Holocaust: Illegal Immigration to the Land of Israel, 1939–1944.* New York, 1990.

Oren, Nissan. *Revolution Administered: Agrarianism and Communism in Bulgaria.* Baltimore, 1973.

————. "A Revolution Administered: The Sovietization of Bulgaria." In *The Anatomy of Communist Takeovers,* edited by Thomas T. Hammond, 321–38. New Haven, 1975.

Ovendale, Ritchie. *Britain, the United States, and the End of the Palestine Mandate, 1942–1948.* Woodbridge, Suffolk, 1989.

————. *Britain, the United States, and the Transfer of Power in the Middle East, 1945–1962.* London, 1996.

————. *The English-Speaking Alliance: Britain, the United States, the Dominions and the Cold War, 1945–1951.* London, 1985.

————. "The Palestine Policy of the British Labour Government, 1947: The Decision to Withdraw." *International Affairs* 56 (1980): 73–93.

Pappé, Ilan. *The Making of the Arab-Israeli Conflict, 1947–1951.* London, 1992.

Pelling, Henry. *The Labour Governments, 1945–1951.* London, 1984.

Penkower, Monty Noam. *The Jews Were Expendable: Free World Diplomacy and the Holocaust.* Urbana, 1983.

Penrose, E. F. "Negotiating on Refugees and Displaced Persons, 1946." In *Negotiating with the Russians,* edited by Raymond Dennett and Joseph E. Johnson, 139–68. Boston, 1951.

Pimlott, Ben. *Hugh Dalton.* London, 1985.

Pinkus, Benjamin. "Soviet Policy towards the Jews of the USSR and the Yishuv, 1945–1948." In *Eastern-European Jewry, From the Holocaust to Redemption, 1944–1948,* edited by Benjamin Pinkus, 3–63. Sde Boker, 1987. (Hebrew).

Polonsky, Antony. "A Failed Pogrom: The Demonstrations in Lwow, June 1929." In *The Jews of Poland between Two World Wars*, edited by Yisrael Gutman, Ezra Mendelson, Jehuda Reinharz, and Chone Shmeruk, 109–25. Hanover, 1989.

Porath, Yehoshua. *In Search of Arab Unity, 1930–1945*. London, 1986.

———. *The Palestinian Arab National Movement: From Riots to Rebellion.* London, 1977.

Poznanski, René. "World War II Heritage: Zionism in France, 1944–1947." In *French Jewry, Zionism and the State of Israel,* edited by Benjamin Pinkus and Doris Bensimon, 144–66. Sde Boker, 1992. (Hebrew).

Prażmowska Anita J. *Britain and Poland, 1939–1943: The Betrayed Ally.* Cambridge, Eng., 1995.

Proudfoot, Malcolm J. *European Refugees, 1939–1945.* Evanston, 1956.

Quinlan, Paul D. *Clash over Romania: British and American Policies toward Romania, 1938–1947.* Los Angeles, 1977.

Reilly, Joanne. *Belsen: The Liberation of a Concentration Camp.* London, 1998.

Reuvani, Sary. "Antisemitism in Hungary in the Years 1945–1946." *Yalkut Moreshet* 43–44 (1987): 177–200.

Rioux, Jean-Pierre. *The Fourth Republic, 1944–1958.* Cambridge, Eng., 1987.

Ro'i, Ya'acov. *Soviet Decision Making in Practice: The USSR and Israel, 1947–1954.* New Brunswick, 1980.

Rosenfield, Geraldine. "Central Europe: Germany, DPs." *American Jewish Year Book* 48 (1946–47): 302–5.

Ross, Graham. *The Foreign Office and the Kremlin: British Documents on Anglo-Soviet Relations, 1941–1945.* Cambridge, Mass., 1984.

Rothkirchen, Livia. "Czech Attitudes towards the Jews during the Nazi Regime." *Yad Vashem Studies* 13 (1979): 287–320.

———. "Deep Rooted Yet Alien: Some Aspects of the History of the Jews in Subcarpathian Ruthenia." *Yad Vashem Studies* 12 (1977): 147–79.

Rothwell, Victor. *Britain and the Cold War, 1941–1947.* London, 1982.

Rubin, Barry. *The Arab States and the Palestine Conflict.* Syracuse, 1981.

———. *The Great Powers in the Middle East, 1941–1947: The Road to the Cold War.* London, 1980.

Sachar, Abram L. *The Redemption of the Unwanted: From the Liberation of the Death Camps to the Founding of Israel.* New York, 1983.

Saiu, Liliana. *The Great Powers and Roumania, 1944–1946: A Study of the Early Cold War.* New York, 1992.

Saville, John. *The Politics of Continuity: British Foreign Policy and the Labour Government, 1945–1946.* London, 1993.

Schaary, David. *The Cyprus Detention Camps for Jewish "Illegal" Immigrants to Palestine, 1946–1949.* Jerusalem, 1981. (Hebrew).

Schechtman, Joseph B. *Postwar Population Transfers in Europe, 1945–1955.* Philadelphia, 1962.

———. *The Refugee in the World.* New York, 1963.

Schulze, Rainer. "Growing Discontent: Relations between Native and Refugee

Populations in Rural Districts in Western Germany after the Second World War."
German History 7 (1989): 332–49.

Shapira, Anita. *Visions in Conflict.* Tel Aviv, n.d. (Hebrew).

Shelah, Menachem. *History of the Holocaust: Yugoslavia.* Jerusalem, 1990. (Hebrew).

———. *The Yugoslav Connection: Illegal Immigration of Jewish Refugees to Palestine through Yugoslavia, 1938–1948.* Tel Aviv, 1994. (Hebrew).

Sherman, A. J. *Island Refuge: Britain and Refugees from the Third Reich, 1933–1939.* London, 1973.

Shoup, Paul. "The Yugoslav Revolution: The First of a New Rape." In *The Anatomy of Communist Takeovers,* edited by Thomas T. Hammond, 244–72. New Haven, 1975.

Slutsky, Yehuda. *History of the Hagana: From Resistance to War.* 9 vols. Tel Aviv, 1973. (Hebrew).

Smyser, W. R. *From Yalta to Berlin: The Cold War Struggle over Germany.* Basingstoke, Hampshire, 1999.

Snetsinger, John. *Truman, the Jewish Vote, and the Creation of Israel.* Stanford, 1974.

Steinberg, Arie. "The International Aspects of the Jewish Immigration from and through Romania, 1938–1947." Ph.D. diss., University of Haifa, 1984. (Hebrew).

Stern, Frank. *The Whitewashing of the Yellow Badge: Antisemitism and Philosemitism in Postwar Germany.* Oxford, 1992.

Stevens, Richard P. *American Zionism and U.S. Foreign Policy, 1942–1947.* New York, 1962.

Stoessinger, John G. *The Refugee and the World Community.* Minneapolis, 1956.

Stoler, Mark A. *George C. Marshall: Soldier-Statesman of the American Century.* New York, 1989.

Sylvain, Nicolas. "Rumania." In *The Jews in the Soviet Satellites,* edited by Peter Meyer, Bernard Weinryb, Eugene Duschinsky, and Nicolas Sylvain, Part 4. Westport, Conn., 1953.

Taborsky, Edward. *President Edward Beneš: Between East and West, 1938–1948.* Stanford, 1981.

Tamir, Vicki. *Bulgaria and Her Jews: The History of a Dubious Symbiosis.* New York, 1979.

Tavin, Ely J. *The Second Front: The Irgun Tzvai Leumi in Europe, 1946–1948.* Tel Aviv, 1973. (Hebrew).

Taylor, Peter J. *Britain and the Cold War: 1945 as a Geopolitical Transition.* London, 1990.

Tolstoy, Nicholai. *The Secret Betrayal.* New York, 1977.

Tsachor, Ze'ev. "Ben-Gurion and the 'Ha'apala,' 1934–1948." In *Eastern European Jewry, From Holocaust to Redemption, 1944–1948,* edited by Benjamin Pinkus, 422–47. Sde Boqer, 1987. (Hebrew).

Vago, Bela. "Communist Pragmatism toward Jewish Assimilation in Romania and Hungary." In *Jewish Assimilation in Modern Times,* edited by Bela Vago, 105–26. Boulder, Colo., 1981.

———. *The Shadow of the Swastika: The Rise of Fascism and Anti-Semitism in the Danube Basin, 1936–1939.* London, 1975.

Vago, Raphael. "The Jews of Romania under the Communist Regime, 1944–1948." In

Eastern-European Jewry, From the Holocaust to Redemption, 1944–1948, edited by Benjamin Pinkus, 133–52. Sde Boqer, 1987. (Hebrew).

Vernant, Jacques. *The Refugee in the Post-War World.* Geneva, 1951.

Wall, Irwin M. *The United States and the Making of Postwar France, 1945–1954.* Cambridge, Mass., 1991.

Wasserstein, Bernard. *Britain and the Jews of Europe, 1939–1945.* Oxford, 1979.

———. *Vanishing Diaspora: The Jews in Europe since 1945.* Cambridge, Mass., 1996.

Watt, D. C. "Britain, the United States and the Opening of the Cold War." In *The Foreign Policy of the British Labour Government, 1945–1951,* edited by Ritchie Ovendale, 43–60. Leicester, 1984.

Weinberg, David. "The Reconstruction of the French Jewish Community after World War II." In *She'erit Hapletah, 1944–1948: Rehabilitation and Political Struggle,* edited by Yisrael Gutman and Avital Saf, 168–86. Jerusalem, 1990.

Weinryb, Bernard D. "Poland." In *The Jews in the Soviet Satellites,* edited by Peter Meyer, Bernard D. Weinryb, Eugene Duschinsky, and Nicolas Sylvain, Part 2. Westport, Conn., 1953.

Weitz, Yehiam. "First Contacts between the Soldiers of the Jewish Brigade and the Jewish Survivors." *Yahadut Zémanenu (Contemporary Jewry): A Research Annual* 3 (1986): 227–46. (Hebrew).

Wheeler-Bennett, John, and Anthony Nicholls. *The Semblance of Peace: The Political Settlement after the Second World War.* London, 1972.

Williams, Francis. *Ernest Bevin, Portrait of a Great Englishman.* London, 1952.

Willis, Roy F. *The French in Germany, 1945–1949.* Stanford, 1962.

Woodbridge, George. *UNRRA: The History of the United Nations Relief and Rehabilitation Administration.* 3 vols. New York, 1950.

Wyman, David S. *The Abandonment of the Jews: America and the Holocaust, 1941–1945.* New York, 1984.

Wyman, Mark. *Europe's Displaced Persons, 1945–1951.* Philadelphia, 1989.

Yahil, Leni. *The Holocaust: The Fate of European Jewry, 1932–1945.* New York, 1991.

Young, John W. *Britain, France, and the Unity of Europe, 1945–1951.* Leicester, 1984.

———. "Duff Cooper and the British Embassy, 1945–1947." In *British Officials and British Foreign Policy, 1945–1950,* edited by John Zametica, 98–120. Leicester, 1990.

———. *France, the Cold War and the Western Alliance, 1944–1949: French Foreign Policy and Post-War Europe.* Leicester, 1990.

Zeeman, Bert. "Britain and the Cold War: An Alternative Approach, the Treaty of Dunkirk Example." *European History Quarterly* 16 (1986): 343–67.

Zertal, Idit. *From Catastrophe to Power: Holocaust Survivors and the Emergence of Israel.* Berkeley, 1998.

Ziemke, Earl Z. *The U.S. Army in the Occupation of Germany, 1944–1946.* Washington, D.C., 1975.

Zink, Harold. *American Military Government in Germany.* New York, 1947.

Zweig, Ronald W. *Britain and Palestine during the Second World War.* London, 1986.

Zweiniger-Bargielowska, Ina. "Bread Rationing in Britain, July 1946–July 1947." *20th Century British History* 4 (1993): 57–85.

INDEX

and Bevin, 129–31; and Dubrow, 137; and Jewish infiltrators from Poland, 137–38, 166, 169, 174; and Jewish DPs from Eastern Europe, 142–43, 145–46, 260; JDC, 248; and France, 258; and World War II, 276

Anglo-Egyptian agreement of 1936, 5

Anti-Semitism: and Jewish exodus, xi; of non-Jewish DPs, 37, 42; and German Jews, 57, 58; and U.S. occupation zone in Germany, 93, 95–96, 140; and Palestine, 100; and U.S. Jewish community, 100, 106–7, 126; and Bevin, 106, 114, 164; in United States, 126, 128, 131; in Poland, 159–67, 170, 171–72, 176, 177, 179, 180–81, 182, 229; and Morgan, 163; in Czechoslovakia, 185, 186; in Hungary, 194, 195, 198, 199, 216, 229; in Rumania, 203, 204, 208, 216, 217, 229, 281; in Yugoslavia, 212; and Communism, 229–30

Arab League, 61, 63, 70, 74, 111

Arabs: and British relations, ix, 5–7, 9, 74, 80, 84, 86, 98, 108, 121, 152, 206, 227, 230, 276; and Jewish immigration, ix, 7, 9, 61, 62, 63, 64, 72–77, 83, 84, 105, 108, 109, 110, 111, 122, 129, 242, 276, 284; and White Paper, 7–8; and *Patria* incident, 9; and Jewish illegal immigration to Palestine, 62, 68, 69, 70, 71, 74–75, 84, 150, 152, 242, 283; and King David Hotel, 66; and deportation of Jewish illegal immigrants to Cyprus, 69, 70; and Morrison-Grady Plan, 69, 72; and Zionists, 69–70, 73–74, 109, 111; and U.S. policy, 100, 113; and AAC, 103, 110, 111, 119; and Bevin Plan, 284

Arazi, Yehuda, 241–42

Atlantic, 8, 60

Atlit camp, 63, 66, 69

Attlee, Clement: and Jewish DPs, x, 36, 52, 106, 123, 277; and Middle East, 5, 6, 109; and DPs, 27; and Truman, 36, 98, 99, 111, 112, 119, 121, 122–23, 124; and Jewish illegal immigration to Pales-

tine, 68–69; and British withdrawal from Palestine, 75; and Marshall, 76; and Palestine, 102; and AAC, 108, 110; and Byrnes, 118; and Jewish DPs from Poland, 178; and Italy, 242; and France, 263

Auschwitz, 162

Australia, 6, 30, 194

Austria: and DPs, ix, xi, 13, 22, 27, 29; and Soviet Union, 1; Jewish refugees from, 7; Jewish infiltrators from Poland in, 43, 140; Soviet occupation zone in, 49, 51, 107, 169, 193, 198, 243, 280; Jewish DPs in, 89, 116, 132, 133, 141, 179, 218, 230, 278; U.S. military interests in, 112; French occupation zone in, 139, 140, 145, 239, 243, 245, 251–52, 256, 260, 273; Jewish infiltrators from Rumania in, 144; Jewish DPs from Poland in, 157, 172, 227; and Jewish DPs from Hungary, 197; Jewish DPs from Rumania in, 199, 217, 218, 223; and Zionists, 203; and Yugoslavia, 211, 212; and Italy, 235, 238, 239, 243, 252; Jewish infiltrators in Italy from, 243–49, 251–55, 260, 273, 281; and *Brichah* movement, 276. *See also* British occupation zone in Austria; U.S. occupation zone in Austria

Austria-Hungary, 211

Averbuch, Moshe, 205, 224

Avriel, Ehud, 160, 215

Azzam, Abd Al-Rahman, 61, 70, 74

Balfour, John, 148–49

Balfour Declaration, 59

Balkans: Jews fleeing from, ix; and U.S. policy, 2, 279; and Jewish illegal immigration to Palestine, 60, 67, 149, 157, 201, 202, 211, 218; Muslim DPs from, 73; potential U.S. immigrants from, 114. *See also* Bulgaria; Rumania; Yugoslavia

Balogh, István, 194

Baltic republics, 2, 15, 27, 30, 158

British Cabinet Committee on Palestine, 60–61

British Cabinet Defence Committee, 6, 76, 77, 82, 84, 108, 263–64

British Cabinet Overseas Reconstruction Committee, 26, 45, 55, 57, 166

British Jewish community, xi, 33, 37, 38, 40, 41, 46, 49, 55, 59, 282

British occupation zone in Austria: and Jewish DPs, xi, 144; and Jewish infiltrators from Hungary, 43, 49, 195–96, 198, 228; and Jewish infiltrators from Poland, 43, 51, 137–38, 162, 165, 168, 169, 172, 178, 183, 195; and Soviet Union, 51, 157, 167, 168; and Jewish DPs from Rumania, 183; and Italy, 239, 243, 245, 252; and Zionists, 282

British occupation zone in Germany: and Jewish DPs, xi, 31, 38, 41, 49, 55, 59, 99, 102, 166, 282; and DPs, 14, 15, 20, 25, 27, 28–29, 30, 289 (n. 33); Polish officers in, 18, 20–21; and repatriation efforts, 20–22, 25, 31; ethnic Germans in, 26; and Jewish liaison officer, 33, 34, 35–36, 37, 38, 39, 282; adviser for Jewish affairs, 38, 39, 42, 46, 283; central Jewish committee for Jewish DPs, 38, 41, 55–56, 293 (n. 26); conditions of, 41–43; and Jewish infiltrators from Poland, 43–46, 51, 55, 136, 137–38, 162, 165, 169, 172, 178, 183; and withholding of food rations, 50, 51–52; German Jews separated from Jewish DPs, 56–59; and Jewish illegal immigration to Palestine, 65; and AAC, 103; and U.S. occupation zone in Germany, 135, 139; routes to, 157; and Jewish DPs from Rumania, 183; and Italy, 245; and France, 257, 264–65, 270, 272

British policy: and Zionists, ix, xi, 10, 37, 41, 56, 59, 74, 75, 76, 80, 84, 85, 152; and Yugoslavia, xi, 211–16; and Polish DPs, xi–xii, 25, 27, 31, 42, 50; and Egypt, 5, 6, 9; and Palestine immigration

quotas, 7–8, 9, 36, 38, 40, 49–50, 51, 60–61, 63–64, 74, 76, 78, 83, 91, 98, 99, 111, 121, 122, 123, 124, 131, 166, 242; and *Ha'apala*, 8, 75–76, 86, 235, 276; and forced repatriation, 13, 18, 20, 25, 31, 38, 49; and resettlement options, 29–30, 103; and German Jews, 34, 40, 41, 45, 46, 49, 55–59, 56–59, 81, 282, 283; and AAC, 128–29; and Jewish DPs from Poland, 157, 161–69, 173, 177–79, 180–82; and Soviet Union, 158, 199; and Hungary, 183–84, 193–99; and Czechoslovakia, 188–89, 191–92; and Rumania, 201–11, 216, 218, 219, 220, 223, 224–25, 230; and Italy, 240–41, 244–45

British policy on Jewish DPs: and Palestine problem, ix, x, 10, 36–37, 38, 41, 49–50, 52, 59, 85, 97, 133, 276, 278; and Anglo-American relations, x, xii, 5, 36, 97, 105, 130, 278–80; and denial of Jews as nation, xi, 56, 58, 59, 277; and Middle East policy, xii, 277; and repatriation, 32, 33–34, 35, 38–39, 103; and Jewish liaison officer, 33, 34, 35–36, 37, 38, 39, 46, 282; and separation of Jewish DPs, 33–42, 45, 46, 50, 56, 58, 99, 276–77, 293 (n. 26); Harrison Report's criticism of, 36; and Rosensaft, 40–41; and Jewish infiltrators from Poland, 43–46, 50, 51–55; and withholding of food rations, 50, 51–52, 54; and German Jews, 56–59

British policy on Jewish illegal immigration to Palestine: and diplomatic and operative campaign, x, 61, 66, 86, 229; and Anglo-American relations, x, 65–66, 146–50, 152–53, 241; and *Patria* incident, 8–9; and immigration quotas, 50, 51, 61, 63–64, 66, 74, 76, 77, 78, 79, 82–84, 118; and deportation to Cyprus, 50–51, 62, 64–79, 81–85, 152, 210, 214, 220, 225, 245, 252, 267, 269, 270, 283; debate on, 60–66; and deportation to ports of embarkation, 62, 64–65, 67, 78–81, 85, 250, 254, 267, 269, 270; and Yishuv, 62–63, 64, 65, 67, 70, 72, 74, 77; and Czechoslovakia, 191; and Rumania, 201, 204–5, 209, 210, 218, 223–25, 229, 230, 281; and Yugoslavia, 211–16, 228, 229; and Bulgaria, 219–20, 222–23, 225–26, 230, 281; and Italy, 235, 239–54, 281; and France, 259–75, 281

British policy on Middle East: and economics, ix, 5; and Jewish DP policy, xii, 277; and Arab relations, 5–6, 100; and military presence, 5–7; and Palestine partition, 9–10; and Jewish immigration to Palestine, 61, 74, 102, 105, 108–10, 119; and Jewish illegal immigration to Palestine, 66, 153, 282; and Soviet Union, 280

British policy on Palestine: and Jewish DPs, ix, x, 10, 36–37, 38, 41, 49–50, 52, 59, 85, 97, 133, 276, 278; and Jewish illegal immigration, ix–x, 60–61, 62, 65, 66, 283; and Anglo-American relations, 5, 49, 65, 66, 68, 70, 80, 97, 102–10, 113, 119–33, 173, 280; and Arab relations, 6, 7, 9, 72, 84, 111; and partition plan, 7, 9–10; and Jewish immigration quotas, 7–8, 9, 36, 38, 40, 49–50, 51, 60–61, 63–64, 74, 76, 78, 83, 91, 98, 99, 111, 121, 122, 123, 124, 131, 166, 242; and Jewish infiltration from Poland, 52, 53; and United Nations, 75, 76, 80, 128, 248; and withdrawal, 75, 79–86, 109, 152, 283, 284; and U.S. Jewish community, 100

Broad, Philip, 239

Brodetsky, Selig, 39

Bromley, T. E., 125–27, 128

Brook, Norman, 68, 110, 116, 117, 118

Bruna, 272

Budnaras, Emil, 207–8, 210

Bukovina, 158

Bulgaria: and Jewish exodus, xi; and

Soviet Union, 1, 107, 199, 226; and Jewish illegal immigration to Palestine, 62, 81, 157, 201, 216, 219–26, 230, 273, 279, 281; and Jewish infiltrators from Hungary, 197; and U.S. policy, 201, 220, 226; and Bulgarian Jews, 216, 219, 225, 226

Byrnes, James F.: and CFM, 3–4; and U.S. occupation zone in Germany, 4, 137; and DPs, 21, 23; and AAC, 102–4, 109, 118; and Palestine, 115; and provincial autonomy plan, 120; and U.S. immigration quotas, 128; and Bevin, 129–30; and Jewish illegal immigration to Palestine, 147; and Czechoslovakia, 188; and Italy, 246

Cable, J. E., 225

Campbell, Ronald I., 70

Canada, 30

Carse, W. M., 195

Catholic Church, 23, 31, 139, 159, 175, 180–81, 182

Cavendish-Bentinck, Victor, 161–63, 165, 168, 169–70, 178, 179–80, 181

Central America, 30

Central Europe: situation for Jews in, 7; and Jewish illegal immigration to Palestine, 8, 65, 228–29; potential U.S. immigrants from, 114; Jewish infiltrators from, 140; and Zionists, 216; and Italy, 235, 238, 239; and Soviet Union, 280

Central Jewish Committee, 40, 41, 54, 55, 56, 165–66, 171, 172, 174

Central Union of Jewish Communities in Slovakia, 186

CFM. *See* Council of Foreign Ministers

Charles, Noel, 78, 79, 239, 241, 242, 244–45, 247–49, 250, 252

China, 2

Churchill, Winston S.: and U.S. relations, 2, 3; and White Paper, 8, 98; and *Patria* incident, 9; and Palestine partition,

DPs. *See* Displaced persons; Jewish displaced persons; Polish displaced persons
Dubrow, Elbridge, 136

East Asia, 2
Easterman, A. L., 38
Eastern Europe: and U.S. policy, 2, 3, 134, 279; DPs from, 13, 23, 29, 31; ethnic Germans deported from, 21, 26, 27; Holocaust survivors in, 52; potential U.S. immigrants from, 114; and Soviet Union, 228, 280; and Italy, 235, 238; and Anglo-American relations, 280. *See also* Jewish displaced persons from Eastern Europe
Edelman, Maurice, 79
Eden, Anthony, 9, 158
Edgecumb, O. P., 196, 197
Egypt, 5, 6, 9, 64, 73, 80, 108
Eisenhower, Dwight D., 18, 39, 90–97, 134, 136, 305 (n. 14)
Eliahu Golumb, 65, 242
Emerson, Herbert, 160, 259
Enzio Sereni, 63, 240
Epstein, Eliahu, 185, 216
Eritrea, 5, 237
Ethiopia, 5, 210, 237, 261
Europe: illegal immigration to Palestine from, ix, 50, 65, 70, 77, 157, 188, 213, 214; and U.S. policy, 2–4, 258, 279; and British policy, 10; Jewish DPs resettled in, 117, 119, 141; and French policy, 185; and Germany, 257; and International Conference on Europe Reconstruction, 266; and *Brichah* movement, 276. *See also* Central Europe; Eastern Europe
Evian Conference, 7, 35, 99, 117
Exodus affair, 79, 81, 82, 85, 250, 253, 266–72, 274, 275, 281, 284
Exodus ma'apilim, 148, 149
Export-Import Bank, 188

Farenwald camp, 135
Federal Council of Churches, 23

Fierlinger, Zdeněk, 184
Fiji Islands, 72, 77
Finland, 158
Fitzpatrick, Paul E., 120–21
France: and British relations, x, xi, 133, 257–75, 276, 281–82; and illegal sailings to Palestine, xi, 70, 78–79, 81, 133, 143, 146, 157, 218, 235, 257, 259, 261–75, 281, 282; German occupation zone of, 15, 28–29, 43, 139, 140, 258, 260; Austrian occupation zone of, 139, 140, 145, 239, 243, 245, 251–52, 256, 260, 273; Jewish DPs in, 141, 143, 145, 146, 259–60, 273–74, 275; and Polish Jews, 143, 259–60; and Europe's rebuilding, 185; and Italy, 235, 236, 237, 241; and *Exodus* affair, 266–72, 274, 275, 281
Fransoni, Francesco, 248, 249–50, 254

Gallman, John W., 129
Gascoigne, Alvary D., 193–94, 195, 198
Gater, George, 65–66
Gelber, Lionel, 149
German Jews: as DPs, 33; and British policy, 34, 40, 41, 45, 46, 49, 55–59, 81, 282, 283; separated from Jewish DPs, 56–59
German population: DPs separated from, 14, 22; DPs competing for work with, 20, 25, 26; and U.S. policy, 21; ration allocations to, 24, 33; condition of compared to DPs, 25, 42, 91, 92; and Jewish DPs, 43, 90, 94, 96, 139; and Jewish infiltrators from Poland, 54, 55; and German Jews, 56, 57, 58; and German labor for France, 264–65
Germany: and DPs, ix, xi, xii, 13–31; Jewish DPs in, xii, 31, 37, 89, 91, 93, 116, 132, 133, 179, 230, 278; and Soviet Union, 1; Jewish refugees from, 7; Soviet occupation zone in, 14–15, 43, 51, 107, 135–36, 138, 191, 227; French occupation zone in, 15, 28–29, 43, 139, 140, 258, 260; German Jews' resettlement in, 56–59, 81; deportation of

109, 110, 111, 119, 126; British soldiers killed by, 109; and Brook, 110; and provincial autonomy plan, 119, 120, 278; and Attlee, 122; and Polish Jews' conditions, 166; and Czechoslovakia, 188, 192; and Hungary, 193, 196, 198, 203; and Rumania, 196, 204, 207, 218, 223–24, 225, 230, 281; and Yugloslavia, 215–16; and Bulgaria, 223, 226, 230, 281; and Italy, 238, 239, 244, 246, 252, 253; and France, 262, 264, 274; and Labour Party, 277

Zopi, Vittorio, 253

Zuckermann, Antek, 175, 179